TARGET
DE GAULLE

the <u>true</u> story of
the 31 attempts
on the life of
the French
president

Target
de
Gaulle

Pierre Démaret
and
Christian Plume

TRANSLATED FROM THE FRENCH
BY RICHARD BARRY

THE DIAL PRESS
NEW YORK
1975

Originally published in French as *Objectif de Gaulle*

Copyright © 1973 by Editions Robert Laffont, S.A.
English translation copyright © 1974 by Martin Secker & Warburg Limited

Manufactured in the United States of America

First U.S. printing, 1975

Library of Congress Cataloging in Publication Data

Démaret, Pierre, fl. 1972–
    Target de Gaulle.
    Translation of Objectif de Gaulle.

    1.   Gaulle, Charles de, Pres. France, 1890–1970—Assassination attempts.
    I.   Plume, Christian, joint author.   II.   Title.
DC373.G3D4513   944.083'092'4 [B]   74-20658
ISBN 0-8037-8514-3

CONTENTS

PART II HIGH NOON

PART III DUSK

FOREWORD

This book is the story of a handful of men who, rightly or wrongly, were determined to do the right thing and thought that they were doing it. The law judged and condemned many of them. Some paid for what they did with their lives. All await the judgement of history.

What cannot be denied them is that they were honest, courageous in their ideas and of complete integrity. Most of the time they had no money —not enough to buy a metro ticket, not even enough to eat.

In a country that was frequently hostile or indifferent they were upheld solely by their steadfast faith in the justice, as they thought, of the aim they pursued—to strike down General de Gaulle.

Today, now that passions have cooled, the object of this book has been to establish or re-establish the entire truth, removing the cloak of silence and obscurity under which truth has either been officially hidden or, inevitably, concealed in the interests of expediency.

We have made a detailed investigation lasting two long years. We have discovered and questioned the majority of the protagonists in these events, recording their statements which we have used with their agreement. Thanks to unpublished documents, originating from the police and the judiciary, together with secret documents originating from the OAS, thanks also to the understanding and kindness of everybody concerned—and here we wish to record our gratitude to them all—we have been able to reconstruct in detail all the attempts or planned attempts against Charles de Gaulle. There were thirty-one in all, five well known and twenty-six unknown or concealed—a world record for a head of state.

Where, on occasions, we have not been able to give names, the reader will understand that certain of the actors in this historic drama still prefer to remain anonymous today—for reasons which may be simple or complex.

Finally, we would merely say that, in our view, it was essential for this book to be written since, whatever feelings the story may evoke in the reader, it cannot be denied that the story of these men forms part of the history of France.

Pierre Démaret
Christian Plume

FOREWORD

Note: The background to this book, of course, is the whole sequence of events which has come to be known, both in Algeria and in France, as the Algerian drama. There can be no question of giving a complete account of these events here, but to assist the reader to understand and to refresh his memory, there follows an abridged chronology of events.

CHRONOLOGY

November 1954

Indo-China war ends with opening of Geneva Conference. At the same time violence flares up in Algeria. Moslems demonstrate their hostility to the presence of the French by organising a series of terrorist attacks all over the country during the night of 31 October/1 November.

Early 1955

The Revolutionary Union and Action Committee (CRUA) under Ahmed Ben Bella, Krim Belkacem, Raba Bitat, Mourad Didouche and others, which had organised the revolt of November 1954, becomes the FLN (Front de Libération Nationale—National Liberation Front).

6 February 1956

For the first time the Europeans of Algiers demonstrate their opposition to the Algerian policy of Paris. By a mass demonstration they force Guy Mollet, the Prime Minister, to give way. Robert Lacoste appointed Resident Minister in Algeria, replacing Soustelle.

February 1957

The Battle of Algiers begins. General Massu's parachutists put an end to the FLN terrorism which was drenching the city in blood.

13 May 1958

Taking as a pretext the execution of three young French soldiers held prisoner in Tunisia, the Europeans of Algeria rise and seize power in Algiers in order to save French Algeria. A committee of public safety is set up under the chairmanship of General Massu. Gaullist elements infiltrate it. Raoul Salan at this time Commander-in-Chief in Algeria.

4 June 1958

De Gaulle, who had been summoned to take over the Premiership by

René Coty a few days before, arrives in Algiers. From the balcony of the government building overlooking the Forum, he utters the famous words: 'I have understood you.'

October 1958

Official inauguration of the Fifth Republic. A large majority vote 'Yes' in the referendum, approving the new constitution.

September 1959

De Gaulle makes a speech in which he refers for the first time to self-determination for the Algerian people. Anger begins to mount among the Europeans of Algeria.

24 January 1960

The revolt known as that of the 'Barricades' breaks out following the recall to France of General Massu (the last of the generals of 13 May still serving in Algeria). Entrenched in their camp, the insurgents hold out for a week.

Summer 1960

General Salan, who has retired, dissociates himself from de Gaulle's Algerian policy at a press conference in the Hôtel d'Orsay. Shortly afterwards he moves to Spain.

4 November 1960

In a televised address de Gaulle says: 'I have decided to pursue a new path. This path leads, not to an Algeria governed from France, but to an Algerian Algeria.' This speech sets the cat among the pigeons. In Paris the 'Barricades' trial is under way.

11 December 1960

De Gaulle makes his 'tour of officers' messes' in Algeria in an attempt to convince *his* soldiers. A European revolt directed by the FAF (Front de l'Algérie Française—French Algeria Front) breaks out in Algiers. Europeans and FLN moslems confront each other for first time. 120 dead.

8 January 1961

Referendum on self-determination gives support to de Gaulle.

February 1961

Two ex-presidents of the Algiers Students' Association, Jean-Jacques

Susini and Pierre Lagaillarde, set up the OAS. The chairmanship is offered to General Raoul Salan.

22 April 1961

Algiers wakes up in a state of complete euphoria. Power seized by four generals, Maurice Challe, Edmond Jouhaud, André Zeller and Raoul Salan. This is 'the *putsch*'. It lasts four days.

May 1961

The OAS sets itself up underground in Algeria and carries out its first operations.

Summer to autumn 1961

Contacts between FLN representatives and those of the French government become increasingly frequent. People sense that an agreement is about to be signed. The OAS steps up its campaign of violence.

19 March 1962

Cease-fire agreement signed in Evian by Louis Joxe, representing the French government, and Krim Belkacem, in the name of the 'Provisional Government of the Algerian Republic'.

22 March 1962

The National Assembly in Paris declares an official amnesty applying to members of the FLN and the French security forces. It does not apply to the defenders of French Algeria.

26 March 1962

Following the popular revolt of Bab el-Oued the French army fires on an unarmed Algerian crowd in the Rue d'Isly—100 dead, 200 wounded. General Jouhaud, General Salan's second-in-command in the OAS, arrested in Oran.

7 April 1962

Lieutenant Roger Degueldre, a deserter since December 1960 and leader of the famous 'Delta' commandos, arrested in Algiers.

14 April 1962

General Jouhaud sentenced to death by the High Military Tribunal.

20 April 1962

General Salan, head of the OAS, captured by the security forces together with his ADC, Captain Jean Ferrandi.

10 May 1962

First contacts between the OAS and the FLN.

23 May 1962

General Salan sentenced to life imprisonment by the High Military Tribunal. The Tribunal immediately dissolved by de Gaulle.

7 June 1962

Two members of the 'Delta' commandos, Claude Piegts and Bobby Dovecar, shot in Paris at the Trou d'Enfer.

17 June 1962

Representatives of the OAS and FLN agree to stop the fighting. Increasing exodus of Europeans from Algeria.

1 July 1962

Algeria becomes independent. De Gaulle does not recognise the *de facto* position until 3 July in a televised address. Meanwhile Ben Bella takes over in Algiers.

5 July 1962

Roger Degueldre executed by firing squad at the Fort d'Ivry.

28 November 1962

Jouhaud reprieved. He had spent 299 days in the condemned cell.

5 March 1963

Colonel Bastien-Thiry sentenced to death with two other participants in the Petit-Clamart attempt, Alain Bougrenay de la Tocnaye and Jacques Prévost.

11 March 1963

Colonel Bastien-Thiry executed by firing squad at the Fort d'Ivry.

ABBREVIATIONS

BCRA   *Bureau Central de Renseignement et d'Action:* the Free French wartime intelligence and sabotage organisation.

CCI   *Centre de Coordination Interarmes:* the title of the section of the French Secret Service working in Algeria.

CNR   *Conseil National de la Résistance:* National Resistance Council, the political and subversive organisation, working primarily in France, with the aim of preserving French Algeria.

CRS   *Compagnies Républicaines de Sécurité:* the French riot police.

DGER   *Direction Générale des États et des Recherches:* the initial post-war title of the French Secret Service.

DST   *Direction de la Surveillance du Territoire:* the French Security Service.

ENA   *École Nationale d'Administration:* the French National School of Administration.

FAF   *Front Algérie Française:* one of the movements formed in Algeria to preserve French dominance there.

FFL   *Forces Françaises Libres:* the wartime Free French Forces.

FLN   *Front de Libération Nationale:* the main moslem freedom movement in Algeria.

FNC   *Front National des Combattants:* a French ex-servicemen's organisation.

FNF   *Front National Français:* one of the pro-French movements in Algeria.

FTP   *Francs-Tireurs Partisans:* a French communist-inspired resistance movement during the war.

GLAM   *Groupe de Liaisons Aériennes Ministérielles:* Governmental Air Communications Flight.

GPRA   *Gouvernement Provisoire de la République Algérienne:* the provisional government (moslem) of Algeria.

MPC   *Mouvement pour la Coopération:* a French gaullist movement in Algeria.

MRP   *Mouvement Républicain Populaire:* a left-centre political party in France after the war.

OAS	*Organisation Armée Secrète:* the main French subversive organisation working for French Algeria.
OM	*Organisation des Masses:* one of the sections of OAS headquarters in Algeria.
ORO	*Organisation Renseignements et Opérations:* the intelligence and operations section of OAS in Algeria.
RCP	*Régiment de Chasseurs Parachutistes:* Light Infantry Parachute Regiment.
REP	*Régiment Étranger de Parachutistes:* Foreign Legion Parachute Regiment.
RPC	*Régiment de Parachutistes Coloniaux:* Colonial Parachute Regiment.
RPF	*Rassemblement du Peuple Français:* the gaullist party in France.
SDECE	*Service de Documentation Extérieure et de Contre-Espionnage:* the modern title of the French Secret Service.
SFIO	*Section Française de l'Internationale Ouvrière:* French Section of Workers' International.
UNC	*Union Nationale des Combattants:* a French ex-servicemen's organisation.
UNR	*Union pour la Nouvelle République:* an opposition political party in France.

TARGET
DE GAULLE

❧ PART ONE ❧

Dawn

CHAPTER 1

The Opening Shots

Late in 1944 Dakar had put out its decorations to celebrate the liberation of France. The port area was invaded by a motley crowd. Out to sea flags and pennants flapped in the breeze. The heat was stifling.

Slowly General de Gaulle climbed the portside gangway to the stern of the cruiser *Georges Leygues*; he was relishing this come-back, for four years earlier, as he neared Dakar on board the *Westernland* escorted by the Royal Navy under Admiral Sir John Cunningham, the French sailors of the *Richelieu* had received him with gunfire. At that time he had still been no more than a little 'renegade' general who had not even protested —at least not officially—when the British had destroyed the French fleet at Mers el-Kébir. The French sailors had not forgotten.

So on this morning, when all Dakar acclaimed Charles de Gaulle, the general could not suppress a sense of great satisfaction. There on the cruiser's bridge was the cream of the French fleet standing to attention.

The *Marseillaise* rang out. It was 11 a.m. De Gaulle stood stiffly to attention as the national anthem was played. Thirty yards away, a man slowly raised his rifle and laid his sights on the nape of the general's neck.

His name was Jacques C. He was a petty officer on *Air France III*, an antiquated escort vessel previously employed to help flying boats in difficulty on the Dakar–Natal route.

Jacques C was one of those who had not forgiven de Gaulle for Mers el-Kébir and who still regarded him as primarily responsible for the massacre of the French fleet by the British. He made no secret of his conviction that the general had 'sold himself to the Anglo-Saxons', a point of view assiduously cultivated by the Vichy authorities.

When Jacques C heard that 'the English stooge' was coming to Dakar, from which he and his fellows had chased the general four years before, he decided to kill him. He was the escort's master gunner, and com-

3

manded a gang of ruffians recruited into the navy for the duration of hostilities, some of them straight from prison. Such a crew bore little relation to traditional sailors; and they took little stock of gaullist sentiments. Jacques C himself was a hard nut; he thought it perfectly normal to kill a man who, in his eyes, was a traitor.

Looking at the positioning of the various vessels along the quay he observed that his old escort was quite close to the *Georges Leygues* and he calculated that from the forward look-out he would have a splendid view of the cruiser's bridge, where the general would be received. He took a rifle and installed himself in the look-out an hour before the ceremony.

With his eyes he followed the tall, slender, though slightly paunchy, uniformed figure of the head of Free France as he reached the bridge to the accompaniment of the bosuns' whistles and halted at the first bars of the *Marseillaise*.

Then, without a flicker of remorse, Jacques C lowered the barrel of his rifle and aimed for the base of the general's skull. A few seconds of concentration, and then his forefinger slowly closed on the trigger.

At this precise moment the steel door of the look-out opened. Taken by surprise Jacques C moved back from the porthole: Jean Le Guichet, the engineer petty officer, looked at him, thunderstruck at first and then understanding it all. He was not particularly surprised. He knew the feelings of the crew in general and of Jacques C in particular.

'You're mad!' Le Guichet shouted. 'Don't be such a fool!'

Jacques C, still holding his rifle, raised it towards Le Guichet—'Get out, or I'll shoot you before I shoot him!'

Jean Le Guichet, then twenty-four years old, now runs a big dance-hall in the north of Paris. He had never been particularly gaullist nor had he ever thought that de Gaulle should be killed. He tells the story: 'I knew Jacques well and he knew me well too—we had often been out on the town together. But he had forgotten that I had been his ju-jitsu instructor. I had him disarmed and motionless on the floor in two movements. He stared at me fixedly. The *Marseillaise* was over and de Gaulle was starting his inspection. It was now too late to kill him. I let go my hold. Jacques stood up and simply said, "You were wrong, Jean. You were wrong." I had made an enemy of him. But I had saved de Gaulle. And I am certain that I saved Jacques too, for he would have been caught and shot.'

This was the first assassination attempt de Gaulle survived. He was destined to wait for fourteen years for the second. Oddly enough, it happened in Africa again and during one of his great triumphs—on 4 June 1958.

A few days earlier the bankruptcy of the Fourth Republic had reached rock bottom. As René Coty, the President of the Republic, pointed out to the leaders, the government had only two choices: a Popular Front or an appeal to the man whom Jacques Duclos, the communist, called 'the usurper'.

On 28 May de Gaulle went to the former offices of the RPF (*Rassemblement du Peuple Français*—the gaullist party) in the Rue Saint-Dominique in Paris. There he received emissaries from General Salan, the Commander-in-Chief in Algeria, led by General Dulac. He told them that he wished to keep within the law. If he was given plenary powers, he would liquidate the system afterwards.

He studied Plan 'Resurrection' submitted to him by Dulac, a plan for the despatch of airborne troops to Paris, and ended by saying: 'If they do not want de Gaulle, then do what is necessary.'

That same evening de Gaulle received René Coty's emissaries in their turn. De Gaulle laid down his terms: investiture without debate and without his personal attendance, plenary powers without parliamentary control, suspension of parliament for a year and preparation of a new constitution by de Gaulle.

At 3 p.m. on 29 May André Le Trocquer, President of the Chamber of Deputies, read a message from the President of the Republic: 'In view of the threat to the country and the republic I have turned to the most illustrious of Frenchmen . . .'

De Gaulle had won. The Left was silenced. Only René Coty was still thinking clearly, saying in some disillusionment to Pflimlin as he handed in his resignation, 'The people of Algiers are going to have some surprises with de Gaulle. He will hammer them—and hard!' And he added prophetically, 'First because, as a good soldier, he will tolerate neither disorder nor insubordination but, secondly and more important, *because he does not believe in a French Algeria*. As far as Algerian policy is concerned he will go further than any government of this régime could have done and I bet that one day the French of Algeria, after having hung me in effigy, will regret overthrowing me.' But the French of Algeria did not take this realistic view of matters. They greeted de Gaulle's arrival as a victory.

On 4 June 1958 the general climbed out of the presidential Caravelle at Maison Blanche aerodrome. There was a crowd at the foot of the gangway; among them were to be seen Salan, Soustelle, Massu and the tall, bearded figure of Pierre Lagaillarde, president of the Algiers Students' Association.

During lunch in the Palais d'Eté, at which eighteen dignitaries were present, Massu introduced the members of the Committee of Public Safety to de Gaulle; the general responded: 'You have been both the torrent and the dam.' In the afternoon, while visiting the anti-aircraft cruiser *De Grasse*, he referred to Algiers as 'a great French city'.

Finally at 7 p.m. came a great popular assembly on the Forum. Amid fantastic and very Mediterranean enthusiasm de Gaulle and Salan appeared before the crowd. After a few words from Salan and Soustelle the general rose and went up to the microphones, to be greeted with a vast ovation lasting almost a minute.

He was plainly silhouetted in the telescopic sight of a rifle aimed at him from the other end of the Forum square at a distance of 150 yards. For the expert marksman concealed in the building opposite the *Gouvernement Général* he was a sitting target. The marksman was an Algiers antique-dealer aged about fifty, an old militant supporter of Pétain. If opposition to de Gaulle came from the Left in France, in Algeria it came from the Right.

In Algiers a small nucleus of ex-Pétainists, who had had their troubles at the time of the liberation, had remained intransigent on one subject: the return of de Gaulle implied the abandoning of the French Empire. They had not forgotten his speech in Brazzaville nor his various pronouncements on the colonial problem. Having done their utmost to prevent his return through the Committees of Public Safety, they had decided to take direct action when it became clear that de Gaulle would inevitably come back.

On 4 June 1958 a small group of some sixty students belonging to the *Jeune Nation* movement made it their business to boo the general during his triumphal progress; one of them even managed to spit in his face as he came up to shake hands. For their part, however, the old die-hards were determined to use the only certain method of preventing the abandonment of French Algeria which they were sure was coming: the elimination of de Gaulle on the very day of his arrival. One of them— the antique-dealer—volunteered. He owned weapons, including a .22 rifle with telescopic sights, and he had the opportunity to instal himself in an apartment facing the official building.

So, keeping back a little in order not to be seen, there he was, crouched in the semi-darkness, behind the cheering crowd. He was under no illusions about the gravity of what he was about to do; he knew that by a simple movement of his finger he could change the course of events. But he also knew that he had to do it. For de Gaulle would beat about the bush; he had not changed. Undoubtedly he would give forth some fine phrases but none of them would amount to a formal commitment. The man of Brazzaville would not be able to say that Algeria would remain French, that he had understood local feeling. Otherwise he would be undertaking a commitment which he would be bound to keep. Thirteen years of retirement had certainly not changed him. The best thing for Algeria was to do away with him.

The antique-dealer felt completely in control of himself. He was an experienced shot; his finger was steady and his eye sharp. Slowly he swung towards the general's head and held it in his telescopic sights. He had only to press the trigger.

At this moment there was silence and, in a ringing voice, de Gaulle proclaimed: 'I have understood you!'

The antique-dealer was dumbfounded. Gently he released the trigger pressure while an incredible roar rose from the crowd. Had he been mistaken? Suppose de Gaulle had changed! Suppose that, as he had just said, he had at last 'understood' what went on here! De Gaulle continued: 'I know what has gone on here . . . I see what you have wanted to do . . .'

The antique-dealer listened spellbound, his finger still on the trigger. 'I see the path you have mapped out in Algeria . . . brotherhood . . . one single category of inhabitant . . . a magnificent achievement . . . the door to reconciliation.'

The antique-dealer was thunderstruck. He placed his rifle against the wall and listened to the end of the speech—'France is beautiful, France is great, France is generous!'

So perhaps there was a chance. Perhaps the general was the man Algeria was waiting for. This chance, however small it might be, must be seized. The antique-dealer decided to let the general go. De Gaulle was never to know that this simple little sentence, 'I have understood you', not only guaranteed him power but also saved his life.

This stay of execution granted by one of their number did not meet with the approval of all the ultra right-wing militants in Algeria. Very soon it became clear that the speech in the Forum had been merely an electoral address. Analysis showed, moreover, that its tactical adroitness had been prodigious. De Gaulle had made no sort of commitment on Algeria's future. He had merely talked of 'reconciliation' and of 'Frenchmen with a full share'. But he had also talked in barely concealed terms of self-determination; his precise words had been: 'All Frenchmen, including the ten million Frenchmen of Algeria, will have to decide their own fate.' This summed up his whole policy. His choice of phrase had concealed the reality and by this means alone he had touched the hearts of the *pieds-noirs* (the French of Algeria) and so given himself the time to liquidate 'the system', as he had said to Salan's emissary, General Dulac.

A month later he was in contact with 'the rebels' in Tunis. By 17 June he was signing agreements with the Tunisian government although it was providing a base for the rebellion.

He had not changed. The militants of *Jeune Nation* and the ex-Pétainists of Marseille were convinced of the fact and they in their turn decided to put an end to his career when he visited the city, which he was due to do in November of that same year 1958.

The attack was to be made in the Rue de Rome during the drive from the prefecture to the town hall. The street was narrow and the crowd would be thick there. The party from *Jeune Nation* selected the dagger as their weapon. The idea was to create panic among the crowd by setting off thunderflashes and powerful smoke-bombs giving off vast quantities of smoke. In the confusion the party would rush the general's open car and assassinate him.

During the previous night the young conspirators positioned some thirty thunderflashes and smoke-bombs to be ignited in turn. The bombs were too large to be carried about without attracting notice at the time of action; the police, who would be out in force, might discover them and the alarm would be given. Everything was in place by dawn. De Gaulle was due to pass at 11 a.m.

At 9 a.m. a fearful rainstorm, such as sometimes bursts in the south, descended on the city, totally drowning the smoke-bombs. The attempt ended like a schoolboys' prank; what had been planned as tragedy finished as farce.

Serious business was not to begin for another two years.

CHAPTER 2

The Angry Sergeant-Major

At 8 p.m. on 4 November 1960, the curtain rose on the sort of theatrical scene the Elysée provides for television. After the regulation musical fanfare General de Gaulle was about to address the French—and the French were completely disconcerted by the vicissitudes of the moment. The year 1960 had been eventful: the death in a road accident of the author Albert Camus, Algerian-born and a Nobel Prize winner; Pinay's resignation; the barricades in the streets of Algiers; the detonation of the first French atomic bomb at Colomb-Béchar; the launching of the liner *France*; the Agadir catastrophe. Public opinion was divided: the Right was for a French Algeria; the Left had signed the 'Manifesto of the 121'.*

The French were not exactly blasé, but they had been swamped with official and semi-official propaganda and were simply sated with words, ideas, statements, rumours and claptrap. They had received the announcement of this further address by the head of state without enthusiasm.

Nevertheless, this particular speech was destined to be of prime importance for the further development of the Algerian drama. One short simple phrase, such as de Gaulle was apt to produce from time to time, was to become a veritable detonator in the Algerian powder-barrel.

'Indeed,' the general said that evening, 'as people say, we live in our times and these times, full of promise though they are, are nonetheless hard and dangerous.' And then, after one or two sweeping introductory remarks, he came to the point: 'Having resumed the leadership of France, I have, as you know, decided, in her name, to pursue a new path. This path leads, not to an Algeria governed from France, but to an Algerian Algeria.'

This was not the first time that the general had used the phrase. It had first been heard on Wednesday, 5 March 1960, during his famous

* A manifesto published in 1960 by a group of intellectuals calling on Frenchmen to refuse military service.

9

tour of the officers' messes, by the officers of the outpost of Azziz in Algiers province. The officers had been taken aback and the atmosphere had become frigid. This phrase had also opened the eyes of certain senior officers such as General Challe.

Repeated to the French as a whole it carried the weight of an official slogan. But this was only a beginning, for the general went on: 'This means an emancipated Algeria, an Algeria in which the Algerians themselves will decide their destiny, an Algeria which, if the Algerians so wish (and I think that they do), will have its own government, its own institutions and its own laws.' And then, like a signature tune, he let fall the shocking words 'Algerian Republic'.

Extremely violent reactions were to be expected; the general's entourage had done their best to stop him saying those dangerous words. It was too late; de Gaulle had recorded his speech and had not seen fit to pass the text to his staff. As soon as they discovered, a few hours before the broadcast, they tried to get the general to expunge the two fatal words.

De Gaulle was shaken and asked if it were possible to erase them. When consulted, the technicians of Radio France were quite definite; they could easily be expunged from the radio recording but not from that for television. It would be necessary to record the speech afresh. 'In that case,' said de Gaulle, 'I'll leave it be.'

Michel Debré and Paul Delouvrier, who knew what the reaction of the *pieds-noirs* would be, made one last effort: 'Your life is at stake, General. Think of the tour you are to make in Algeria in December.' De Gaulle simply replied: 'Don't keep on at me.' So it was decided: France was to abandon Algeria. The decision seemed irrevocable.

When de Gaulle had finished speaking General Challe turned off his television set, opened his diary and modestly wrote: 'From this moment I shall begin to think deeply about the sense of my continuance in the Army.'

De Gaulle accepted the inevitable trial of strength because he knew that he could count on the support of the 'silent majority' of Frenchmen. A few months before popular sympathies had been with the *pieds-noirs*; in May 1958 the great avenues of Paris had resounded with a memorable babel of car-horns all tapping out the celebrated 'Dit-dit-dit Dah-dah' signifying *Algérie française*. But the vast gaullist propaganda machine had then swung into action and had turned public opinion round. The *pieds-noirs* were portrayed as capitalists for whom the 'natives' had to sweat; the more militant of them could only be fascists. A solid popular consensus was necessary to bring the French, and even more the army, to accept those two ominous words 'Algerian Republic'. A firm grip had been taken on the army ever since March of that year when de Gaulle had said to officers of Algiers province: 'Ferhat Abbas is a washout. The independence of Algeria would mean the ruin of the country . . . France must not leave; she has the right to stay in Algeria. *She will stay.*'

During that same period, however, in an isolated post in Azziz, he had 'tried out' the expression 'Algerian Algeria'. The repercussions in the Paris press had made him furious and he had hauled Paul Delouvrier, his Delegate-General, over the coals for failing to 'put the censorship into action'.

As was to be expected, there was a lively reaction next day in Algeria, not only from the general public but also from the administration: several members resigned. For the government the most surprising reaction was that of the officers, some of whom gave public expression to their disagreement.

On 14 November there took place at Zeralda the funeral of ten men of the 1st Foreign Legion Parachute Regiment; they belonged to No. 1 Company commanded by Captain Sergent and had been killed in an ambush by the FLN (*Front de Libération Nationale*—the Algerian nationalist movement). On this occasion Dufour, the regimental colonel, gave vent to a veritable tirade interspersed with pious comment from Delarue, the chaplain.

Admittedly Colonel Dufour was not in high favour. He had had the temerity to refer to de Gaulle in public as a 'Joan of Arc' and at a Bastille Day parade he had ordered his men not to wear their medals. Nevertheless, his outburst set the fashion: Colonel Dufour had said out loud what many officers were quietly thinking.

In France reaction was more varied. Supporters of a French Algeria were in the minority—but they were determined men.

A handful of them, led by André Orsoni, the most decorated sergeant-major of the Indo-China campaign, decided to take a hand in public affairs and organise the kidnapping of the President of the Republic. This was no plan concocted during a late-night drinking session: Orsoni was no practical joker. He had enlisted in the Free French forces at the age of sixteen and had been with the British Eighth Army when it captured Tunis. Finding life too unexciting there, he had moved to London and enlisted as a parachutist in the Special Air Service. He had parachuted into France and then into Holland. Unable to settle down when the war ended, he continued his 'hot war' career in Indo-China and then in Algeria.

He had always been of above-average intelligence but he was also highly emotional and he became fired with the idea of French Algeria. On 27 January 1960, three days after the 'Barricades' rising (itself caused by the recall to France of General Jacques Massu), he went over to the insurgents lock, stock and barrel. He thus became the first man to desert from the army on Algerian soil—and all in the cause of French Algeria.

When the insurgents behind the barricades surrendered, he left them. Armed with travelling expenses of 80,000 francs provided by Pierre Lagaillarde's father, a barrister in Blida, he set himself up in Paris, living clandestinely under the name of Marcel Nouveau.

Still the complete extrovert, he went daily to the restaurant of the National Assembly where he lunched with Pierre Vignau, the deputy for Médéa, Jean-Marie Le Pen, member for Paris, or Bachaga Boualem, the Vice-President of the Assembly. He met all the gaullist celebrities, in particular Lucien Neuwirth who had been one of the champions of de Gaulle's return to power and whom he had known in London. The ushers of the Palais Bourbon saluted him deferentially; they naturally had no idea that he was being hunted by every police force as a 'particularly dangerous' deserter.

Orsoni was determined to go into action again in the cause of French Algeria and so he looked for a leader. His thoughts turned naturally to Jacques Soustelle who had been Governor-General of Algeria and who had made public his disagreement with the policy being pursued by General de Gaulle. He succeeded in obtaining an appointment with the ex-minister and went to the offices on the Champs Elysées occupied by Soustelle. A brawny attendant showed him into the sanctum.

'At that moment,' Orsoni says, 'I saw why everyone had nicknamed him "The Big Tom-cat". As you talk he listens to you with both fists clenched against his cheeks, looking fixedly at you with eyes half-closed. You expect to hear him purr.'

The first part of the interview was cordial. 'What can I do for you?' Soustelle asked.

'Well, *monsieur le ministre*, I am at present with a team of parachutists and all we ask is for some action.' Soustelle's eyes widened. 'We are experienced people,' Orsoni went on. 'We have made war and we know how to fight. We understand nothing of politics and we would like to have someone responsible behind us. That is why we thought of you.'

Soustelle hunched himself behind his desk. 'But, my dear sir, that is not my sort of war. My war is a political one.'

'You are wrong not to have confidence in me, *monsieur le ministre*. Has anyone told you who I am?'

'No.'

'I am Orsoni, the sergeant-major deserter of the Barricades.'

'Big Tom-cat' showed his claws. He got up, rang for one of his bodyguard and ordered him to show the deserter the tradesmen's entrance. So the interview ended with unexpected rapidity and Orsoni realised that French Algeria must look for some other 'historic leader'.

He found a parliamentary deputy from Algeria waiting for him in a café and told him the story. 'Be patient,' the deputy said. 'Some opportunity will present itself soon. Then you will be able to show the public that you exist. In fact why don't you kill some of the grave-diggers of Algeria—Lucien Neuwirth or Ali Mallen, the Arab deputy, for instance? They live in the Hôtel d'Orsay. Talk about it to your boys.'

The 'boys' were in agreement. Orsoni explained his plan: he would arrive at the Hôtel d'Orsay with one hand in plaster but in it would be concealed a silenced revolver. He would find Mallen, the deputy, and tell him that something serious was about to happen and that it was essential for Neuwirth to be present; Mallen must ask him to join them in the room. Orsoni then merely had to shoot down the Arab and repeat the performance when Neuwirth appeared. Orsoni's escape would present no problem in so busy an hotel. (Orsoni had presumably not studied ancient history for the trick of an arm in bandages had been used in AD 96 by Stephanus to enable him to approach and stab the Emperor Domitian. At least, that is what Suetonius says.)

In any case, all the members of the gang were agreed but they added one proviso: 'We must have money if we are to carry on; we have barely enough to eat. You must ask for ten million.'

That was the end of the deputy's friendship with Orsoni. He refused to advance a single centime.

This abortive plan merely emboldened Orsoni; he was once again in touch with an Algerian friend known as Fusil (who still prefers to remain anonymous) and he thought up an ambitious project to disrupt the life of France by terrorist action.

The Orsoni group constituted itself as the Nationalist Revolutionary Committee and made the authorities aware of its presence by exploding fifteen charges of TNT in one night in various squares of Paris. Having no slow-burning fuse but wishing to give the impression that his forces were numerous, Orsoni had worked out a delayed-action system using tinder; he had calculated its rate of burning to the centimetre. In this way one man could set off three bombs in three different places at some distance from each other. (Again there is a historical parallel here: the procedure was exactly the same as that used in 1800 by the conspirators who attempted to assassinate Napoleon in the Rue Nicaise.)

Their terrorist offensive having been comparatively successful, Orsoni and Fusil decided to strike at something more important. The ideal target naturally seemed to them to be General de Gaulle.

When de Gaulle's televised address brought the fiction of a French Algeria to an abrupt end, they hit upon the idea of kidnapping the general—an apparently crazy idea but perfectly logical in the context of the moment.

Orsoni says today: 'It was the radio we had in our hide-out which enabled us to listen to General de Gaulle. When he had finished and the

Marseillaise had been played, we remained speechless. We had no need for discussion; we were all itching to act.'

Although Orsoni's description was posted in every police station, he regularly met a small group who had one surprising characteristic in common—they were professional police officers in the Ministry of the Interior. It was part of the strength of these clandestine movements that they should be able to find supporters at all levels of power and in official agencies. It was also their weakness, however, for the risks of penetration were obvious.

Orsoni's friends showed enthusiasm for his idea. Like him they thought that the 'arrest' of the head of state—not his execution—would be calculated to change the course of events. The situation as regards French Algeria was not yet totally catastrophic. All could still be saved if the political authorities in France and the army in Algeria so decided.

Orsoni obtained his unexpected support because there was no question of bloodshed. Subsequently many people recoiled from something which could only be classed as sheer murder. 'Anything you like,' Colonel Rémy said one day, 'but not "that" ' ('that' being the physical elimination of de Gaulle).

Orsoni's friends passed him a detailed plan of the Elysée together with an enormous pile of photographs showing the entire building and taken from every conceivable angle. Armed with these photographs it was possible, as it were, to reconstitute the Elysée like a house of cards. Minute study of the plan and photographs would enable a raiding party to move about inside the building as if they had lived there all their lives.

For its part the army provided some essential components. Orsoni still had excellent contacts, particularly in certain regiments stationed in Melun and adjacent towns. A properly organised company with sections and sub-sections could be formed, totalling 220 men—all volunteers to kidnap the head of state.

All these people had to be transported and so another friend of Orsoni, who was a haulier in the Halles, agreed to provide covered lorries. Weapons and uniforms were also required since the 220 volunteers belonged to different services and it would have looked odd to see a sailor, a *chasseur alpin* and an airman sitting side by side. Moreover, to avoid arousing suspicion they all had to be on leave and so would not have their weapons available.

Again Orsoni could provide: Major d'Ars who was in charge of the mobilisation reserves in Vincennes and had 3,000 small arms and 3,000 parachutist uniforms in stock, agreed to make them available.

The plan of attack was prepared in the greatest detail; the capture of the Ministry of the Interior and the Elysée was due to take only eleven minutes. Through his police friends Orsoni knew precisely how many guards would be on duty on the day in question. Oddly enough, the number of guards had been reduced; the security system was only tightened up some time later. In 1960 the Elysée was guarded only by some ten men and the Ministry of the Interior by a mere handful. A determined and well-organised raiding party working quickly and professionally should have been able to occupy the buildings easily. Every man had been given his assignment, particular attention being paid to the Ministry of the Interior's secret communications' network which spanned the country.

To complete the operation a third building had to be occupied—the Prefecture of Police which was the centre of another large-scale communications' network. Orsoni accordingly paid a visit to ex-Police Commissaire (Inspector) Dides; naturally he knew the building well and his pro-Algerian sympathies were public knowledge. Orsoni was accompanied on his visit by Major d'Ars who was deaf in one ear and carried a hearing aid connected to an amplifier. Major d'Ars sat down facing Dides, turned a little button—which merely controlled the sound volume—and said to Dides: 'I am listening.'

Dides was a hard-boiled old policeman who had been dismissed in connection with the affair of the 'leaks' (the leaking to the Viet-Minh of a report on Indo-China by Generals Ely and Salan); he thought that there was some scheme afoot—particularly since he was facing an officer in uniform—that the conversation was to be recorded and that the Major was carrying a miniature tape-recorder. The conversation was a short one and the conspirators were forced to abandon capture of the prefecture.

Planning for the remainder of the operation continued, nevertheless. De Gaulle's arrest should be an easy matter.

The difficulties would begin, however, once de Gaulle had been arrested and the Ministry of the Interior captured. Orsoni explains: 'The general's arrest was not the major problem, which could be summarised in one sentence. What were we going to do then? Physically we should have had him but what about the political side? We were nothing but military toughs and we had no idea of politics. We needed capable people to exploit our "capture". A sergeant-major cannot run a country. This was why we thought of going to see General Faure.'

Orsoni was a disciplined soldier, brought up in the hard parachutist school; there, even more than in other regiments, the men were imbued with the notion that a hierarchy and sense of discipline constitute the main strength of an army. Orsoni could not for one instant conceive of assuming such grave responsibilities without referring to some superior. This attitude of mind was of vital importance and we shall find it recurring again and again during the struggles marking the end of the war in Algeria.

General Faure had been arrested in 1956 in connection with the 'Paris plot'. He was an ex-ski champion who had taken part in the Narvik operation;* he was a great friend of Michel Debré—at the time a fanatical supporter of French Algeria—and still had contacts in high places. His abortive *putsch*, in which connection famous names had been mentioned, had endowed him with a sort of halo which dazzled the conspirators. To avoid a last-minute arrest, which would have compromised the operation, Orsoni despatched Fusil, his 'associate', to visit General Faure.

The general gave Fusil a lengthy audience and seemed very interested. 'I must think,' he said. 'All this seems very good to me. Let us meet again on Friday fortnight.' There was great disappointment in Orsoni's camp. This delay seemed far too long, particularly since many people were now in the know and the secret risked being discovered.

It evidently had been. Twenty-four hours later Major d'Ars was suddenly posted to Algeria and the weapons in Vincennes were removed and dispersed. Without them Orsoni's men could not operate.

No one knows whether the leak came from one of the conspirators— one of them still seems highly suspect today—or from one of the members of the 'Paris plot' who had been informed by General Faure. A certain A—— who was a member of the plot is said to have been a gaullist agent and may have informed the government.

The fact remains that Orsoni called off all his men though he himself remained indefatigable and at once began to look for some fresh method of acting against de Gaulle.

'It was all the greater pity,' he laments today, 'in that we had accomplices inside the Elysée itself and in the Ministry of the Interior who would have opened the doors to us.'

Still at liberty in his gilded Elysée prison, de Gaulle pursued his Algerian policy without in any way weakening and never missing an opportunity to demonstrate his resolution.

On 22 November he withdrew Paul Delouvrier, his Delegate-General, from Algeria, although eight months earlier he had said to him: 'You are there for a long time.' In his place de Gaulle despatched Louis Joxe, his Minister of Education, whom he placed in charge of Algerian Affairs together with Jean Morin who became Government Delegate.

In his choice of Jean Morin, de Gaulle apparently took no account of the continuing friendship between the new Government Delegate and Georges Bidault who had been his superior in the CNR (*Conseil National de la Résistance*—the French wartime resistance organisation). Yet Bidault was continually making anti-gaullist pronouncements. In fact,

---

* In May 1940, as a follow-up to the Narvik naval operation, a combined force of Norwegians, Poles, French and British attacked the German garrison at Narvik in Norway and held it for a month.

de Gaulle's confidence was well placed: Jean Morin was a committed gaullist.

He had hesitated to accept the post. De Gaulle had given him a few days to think it over but Debré cut these short, saying to Morin: 'Do you imagine that you have time to think?' Debré's remark was so effective that the same evening Jean Morin flew off to a country which he did not know and which was to make life difficult for him.

CHAPTER 3

The Spanish Redoubt

Towards the end of November 1960 the 'Barricades'* trial opened in Paris. In the dock was a real cross-section of civilians and military; they were there because the French Army would not go along when it was a question of opposing the authorities. For the majority of general officers de Gaulle was a sort of historic monument labelled 'Do not touch'. Very soon, therefore, civilian reasoning ran as follows: If the monument is destroyed, the military will swing over to our side. This was to become their overriding idea for a period of several years.

The physical elimination of General de Gaulle was first seriously considered in December of that year. Some of the personalities in the 'Barricades' trial were on bail, their only obligation being to report to the court daily. They took the opportunity to hold several secret meetings together with a number of the ex-leaders of the *Front National Français* (FNF), the movement for French Algeria founded by Joseph Ortiz in 1959. All were agreed on the advisability of an assassination attempt when General de Gaulle next visited Algeria. Colonel Godard was placed in overall charge of the operation.

From the point of view of both sides Godard still remains today one of the most mysterious figures of the whole of this turbulent period. Yves Jean Antoine Noël Godard was born at Saint-Maixent on 21 December 1911; he was a regular soldier, a typical intelligence officer but also a remarkable man of action, as he had proved when mopping up guerrillas in the interior of Indo-China. His mission in life seemed to be that of an operational Chief of Police; he had commanded No. 11 Shock Battalion, the unit responsible for providing operatives for the SDECE (*Service de Documentation Extérieure et de Contre-Espionnage—* the French Secret Service); from 1957 to 1960 he had been head of the *Sûreté Nationale* (the CID) in Algiers. With such a record he was a natural as organiser of the planned assassination attempt on de Gaulle.

* See Chronology—24 January 1960.

18

Another colonel, Roland Scipion Annibal Vaudrey, whose name had been mentioned in connection with the 'Paris plot', was in charge of the on-the-spot details of the operation.

Since the army had apparently decided to employ two of its best men to ensure the success of an operation against de Gaulle, the civilians regained some of their confidence. They even thought it quite normal that the military should envelop themselves in the greatest secrecy in carrying out an operation later described by Degueldre as 'meticulous'.

Nevertheless, in true Mediterranean fashion, an undercurrent of mistrust still persisted. Some of the accused in the 'Barricades' trial accordingly thought it their duty to evade the police and take refuge in Spain in order to resume direct action. They knew that a large-scale military movement was under way in Algeria and that, when the moment came, the first reaction on the part of the police would be to put them back in prison. They therefore decided to follow Pierre Lagaillarde who had been the first to join General Salan in Madrid (the General had arrived there in late summer 1960).

Lagaillarde's successor as President of the Algiers Students' Association and theorist of the FNF was Jean-Jacques Susini. On 4 December he met Marcel Ronda (ex-commander of the territorial armoured units in Algeria) in a cinema on the Champs Elysées (*In Case of Bad Luck* was showing) and they arranged to leave in the immediate future.

Their departure was precipitate. At 2 a.m. Susini, who was lodging with his uncle Me Palmiéri in the Rue Jouffroy, was awakened by Dr Lefebvre (former leader of the poujadist movement in Algiers and an admirer of Salazar, the late Portuguese dictator), Jean-Maurice Demarquet, a parliamentary deputy, and Marcel Ronda. A military rising was about to take place in Algiers, they said, under General (Air Force) Edmond Jouhaud. Alain de Sérigny, owner of the newspaper *Echo d'Alger*, had left for Geneva in a private aeroplane, they continued. Colonel Jean Gardes, ex-head of the Psychological Warfare Section in Algiers, and Major Sapin-Lignières, commander of the Territorials of Algeria, had left Paris to see General Allard, commander of the French Forces in Germany, whose task would be to move on Paris with his tanks.

The conspirators were unable to contact Dr Jean-Claude Perez, former head of the FNF Action Section. Instead they went to Colonel Trinquier, who had succeeded Colonel Bigeard in command of 3 RPC (*3e Régiment de Parachutistes Coloniaux*—3rd Colonial Parachute Regiment). He also thought that the moment had come, saying: 'I believe this move is in earnest; I am with you.'

Colonel Trinquier took the wheel of Jean-Maurice Demarquet's Aronde; the others left in an American car belonging to Me Albert

Vignolles, one of the counsel for the defence in the 'Barricades' trial, as was Me Palmiéri.

Near Chartres there was a dramatic development: Colonel Trinquier suddenly made a U-turn, leaving the other fugitives to carry on.

Realising that their escape would be known as soon as the court opened next morning, the remaining three decided to bypass a number of places where the police would certainly be waiting for them. Instead of driving straight on south they turned off towards Royan where they knew they had a sure friend—Marcel Bouyer, an ex-poujadist deputy whom Susini had known in 1957 when he was establishing communications between the poujadists of Algeria and those of France.

It took them a week to cross into Spain. The entire Pyrenees frontier was closely guarded by the police and they were forced to use a guide who had taken resistance men across during the war. Finally one morning, unshaven, with their clothes in rags, and exhausted after an arduous climb through the mountains, they reached the Civil Guard frontier post at Cantelops and asked for political asylum. This was granted and they travelled on to Madrid by train. On the train a passenger lent them a transistor and over this they heard that the proposed army rising in Algeria had been cancelled.

Gardes and Sapin-Lignières were arrested at Strasbourg and, instead of visiting General Allard, they were back in the dock next day. Having heard that the rising was off, they preferred to return rather than spoil the psychological effect of the trial, which was being presented as the first official judgement on supporters of French Algeria.

Though many French officers at the time seemed to take pleasure in executing a sort of hesitation waltz, some, like Captain Sergent, had definitely made their choice, questionable though the attitude of the civilians seemed to them.

Pierre Sergent was what was known as a 'brilliant young officer'. While serving with the 1st Foreign Legion Parachute Regiment (1 REP) he had become emotionally involved in the Algerian drama; throughout his service in Algeria he had gone from one disillusionment to another, ending in the conviction that the policy of the de Gaulle government amounted solely to one of desertion. His greatest disillusionment had occurred when commanding No. 1 Company of 1 REP on the Tunisian rontier. He had discovered that a certain village was acting as an important training centre and arms depot for the guerrillas but he had been ordered to withdraw at once since the village defying the French was in Tunisian territory. A few months earlier he had been ordered to act against Frenchmen shouting '*Algérie française*'. The government apparently wished to protect 'the enemy'.

At the time of the 'Barricades' trial Sergent was on leave in Paris. He took the opportunity to meet certain friends, particularly Lagaillarde who was on bail in the house of a well known barrister. In this way he learnt that 'something' was being prepared. A few days later he found out what that 'something' was when he was asked to return to Algiers at once carrying an important message to General Jouhaud from General Salan (who had taken refuge in Spain a few weeks earlier in order to demonstrate his open opposition to de Gaulle). The message was laconic: 'You have the green light.'

Sergent's aircraft left Orly at 11 p.m. on Wednesday, 7 December. The day had produced a number of developments. There had been violent scenes in the National Assembly following a government declaration on Algerian policy. The announcement of the probable formation of an 'Algerian Republic' had been very badly received by many of the deputies. Moreover, the date of the referendum on self-determination for the people of Algeria had been fixed for 8 January. The question was: 'Do you approve the draft law submitted to the French people by the President of the Republic dealing with self-determination for the people of Algeria and the organisation of public authorities in Algeria prior to self-determination?'

The way the question was drafted was an example of de Gaulle's machiavellian political cunning, since it demanded from the French a single reply to two questions. The draft law dealt with two points: do you approve, on the one hand, of self-determination for a people and, on the other, of the policy of the government which is about to form an Algerian executive? It was perfectly conceivable that many men of good will would have liked to reply 'Yes' to the first question and 'No' to the second. Certain experts, forgetting the subtlety of the procedure, also commented that the second proposal automatically restricted the effects of the first, since it excluded the possibility of choosing a totally French Algeria.

The announcement of a referendum on these lines was bound to spark off revolt by the Europeans of Algeria, and even by certain officers who were also at flashpoint.

Accordingly next morning, 8 December, Captain Sergent presented himself to General Jouhaud. General de Gaulle was due to arrive on the 9th.

'Green light?' Jouhaud grumbled. 'Don't understand. Salan? Why doesn't he come here himself?'

Sergent realised at once that no preparations had been made to use force. But he had been in similar situations before. He was certain that the civilians at least were ready to act; he rapidly reached agreement with Jouhaud, taking it upon himself to convince the parachute regiments, without whose support any rising would be doomed to failure. He quickly obtained the necessary agreements. He could count on his own regiment,

I REP; there a certain Lieutenant Degueldre made it his business to convince the waverers. Moreover, ironically enough, the authorities had selected 18 RCP (*Régiment de Chasseurs Parachutistes*—Light Infantry Parachute Regiment) and 14 RCP to be on duty in Algiers; the commanding officers of these two regiments were both in the game.

On its side the *Front de l'Algérie Française* (French Algeria Front—FAF) went into action. This organisation had been formed on 15 June 1960 following General de Gaulle's appeal to 'the rebels'; the *pieds-noirs* had scented danger and had been determined to confront it. Antoine Andros, Dominique Zatarra and Camille Vignau, the FAF leaders, issued a call for a general strike. The FAF leaflet ordered: 'All life must stop. Civilian vehicles are forbidden to move. Shops are not to open on pain of being ransacked. Strike pickets in all businesses. From early morning the population should demonstrate in the centre of the city to show its indignation and disgust at the visit which General de Gaulle has the temerity to make to Algeria.'

This, undoubtedly, was the trial of strength.

De Gaulle and his entourage knew it. Information had come from Algeria that an assassination attempt would certainly be mounted against the general. Oddly enough, this was confirmed from another source—Israel. The Israeli secret service, which had highly effective listening posts among the Jewish population of Algeria, had got wind of an assassination attempt against the general. As soon as the secret service report was received the Israeli cabinet met and decided that Shimon Peres, the Minister of Defence, should pass the information to the French government. The French government at once made certain precautionary arrests and reinforced the team of gunmen detailed to accompany General de Gaulle.

The Israeli information indicated that the attempt would be made at the exit to Orléansville. When warned, the general simply shrugged his shoulders. As a precaution his gunmen each carried a second revolver strapped to the calf of the leg in case they should lose the first in a scuffle.

CHAPTER 4

The Algerian Powder-Barrel

By 8.15 a.m. on 9 December 1960 the presidential security service had done its usual conjuring trick at Orly: two identical Caravelles had been made ready in order to thwart any attempt at sabotage. A policeman stood every ten yards between the Elysée and the airfield.

The presidential Caravelle arrived at the aerodrome of Zenata-Tlemcen without a hitch. The general and his entourage boarded a helicopter which took off in the direction of Aïn-Témouchent, a sizeable town fifty miles from Oran, where the general's visit was due to start. It had been promoted to the status of sub-prefecture; there were 25,000 inhabitants, of whom two-thirds were moslem.

The general disembarked from the helicopter and entered his car escorted by two CRS outriders. His entourage, which included four marksmen (Comiti, Tessier, Sassia and Djouder), followed in other vehicles.

As de Gaulle left his car he received an unpleasant shock: a crowd of about 5,000 people was waving *Algérie française* placards and shouting 'Down with de Gaulle'. He merely made a gesture of vexation as he saw among the crowd a number of moslems armed with whistles piping out the famous 'Dit-dit-dit, Dah-dah'. It was 11.45 a.m., and it was raining. Without a glance de Gaulle went up the steps of the town hall, straight as a ramrod in his uniform. Joxe, Messmer, Terrenoire and Morin fell in behind him, followed by Generals Ely, Crépin and Olié. De Gaulle was scheduled to speak and everyone wondered whether he would. An officer tried to silence the crowd but the shouting only redoubled.

Inside the town hall the general received the dignitaries and officers of the sector. Outside in the pouring rain the crowd continued to bellow, held in check with some difficulty by a CRS squadron. Inside the building there was some casual conversation, and the general appeared more relaxed.

'People are getting excited over nothing,' he said, almost with a smile.

23

'We need action, not shouting, to create a brotherly Algeria where both communities can work together for the prosperity of their country.'

He took by the arm a moslem deputy, M. Mekki, and a European deputy, M. Lopez, brought them together and said: 'There is the Algeria of tomorrow.'

Outside the tumult continued. The general was about to emerge: what would he do? The bodyguards posted themselves at the door, hands on their Colt Cobras, ready to act, scrutinising the crowd from which the murderer's shot might come. The general came down the steps and abruptly veered towards the yelling crowd. He was at the mercy of any unknown assassin. Through the CRS cordon he was shaking the hands timidly held out to him. A woman shouted '*Algérie française*'. Still shaking hands, de Gaulle replied: 'But of course, madame.'

But the crowd went on yelling and whistling. Slowly the general went back to his car, the bodyguard remaining near the crowd. The general passed—within inches—the escorting CRS motor-cyclist who was level with the car door, and got in with a wry smile. The bodyguard gave a sigh of relief and went back to their own vehicles.

They thought that the moment of danger had passed.

They did not know (and presumably still do not know) that General de Gaulle had never been nearer to death. This was the precise moment at which he should have been shot down. And the man due to do the shooting was the CRS motor-cyclist of his own escort.

Géronimo tells the story today: 'I was on my motor-cycle, an SMEC Ratier 750, beside the offside door. The general was less than three feet from me as he got in. The bodyguard were looking elsewhere, towards the crowd. The general gave me a surreptitious smile. I gritted my teeth. I must have been white beneath my helmet—white with rage. I had only a single movement to make—draw my MAC 50 and shoot him down. I should have shot him from in front. But my hand stayed clenched on the butt. "They" had not wanted me to kill him that day.'

Géronimo is not a man given to boasting. He is a placid individual. With his tanned complexion and Mexican moustache he looks like Zapata. He had not joined the police force for the love of it, but because he was out of work. He was a *pied-noir* by origin but by temperament the very opposite of the average *pied-noir*; he never talked and his face seldom betrayed his feelings. His friends say that he would sometimes spend a whole day without saying a word. If no one says anything to him, he says nothing. He can feel deep friendship for someone but he does not show it. His placidity, however, is only skin-deep; his former subordinates compare him to a wild beast. For hours he would not move a muscle and then suddenly he would explode.

In December 1960 he belonged to No. 210 CRS Company, based at Aïn-Témouchent. Most of the men of No. 210 were *pieds-noirs* who had recently been transferred to Aïn-Témouchent as a disciplinary measure. Some of the men had mutinied and had levelled their sub-machine-guns at a prefect's stomach. To avoid a scandal the company had been moved. And this was the company detailed to escort the head of state.

In addition to two Land Rovers, de Gaulle's immediate escort consisted of three motor-cyclists, one clearing the way in front of the presidential Citroën Déesse, and two, one of them Géronimo, beside each rear door.

De Gaulle had referred to 'Algerian Algeria' and these two words had deeply shocked Hilaire Géronimo and his two accomplices. There was only one way to save Algeria—shoot the general down. Géronimo had volunteered to do the shooting. From his place at the rear nearside door he could not miss.

When de Gaulle got out of his car and went into the town hall with the crowd yelling behind him Géronimo seized the opportunity to vanish and call the Café Colbert in Oran where he knew that the leaders of the revolt were meeting at that very moment to prepare the demonstration against the head of state. He asked for confirmation of the order to execute de Gaulle.

'I will refer to the leaders at once,' replied Santini, the proprietor of the Colbert. 'Call me back in five minutes.'

'All right, but be quick about it,' Géronimo said, 'because I can shoot him down when he gets back into his car after his speech.'

He fumed with impatience. From the café where he was telephoning he could hear the shouts of the crowd through the half-open door of the telephone booth. Cautiously he took out his MAC 50 revolver; despite the rain it had stayed dry in the holster and Géronimo knew that it was in first-class working order—he had tried it out that morning.

At the end of a seemingly never-ending five minutes he called the Colbert again. The answer he received deflated him totally: 'No question of killing him now. Our information is quite explicit: de Gaulle is in fact in agreement with us. He wants to keep Algeria French. He is making his present statements in order to deceive the Arabs.'

Géronimo says: 'I knew the man at the other end well enough not to doubt what he said. I suspected that the military were behind it but I was too upset to say so to Santini. Instead I repeated: "I swear to you that I could not miss him," Santini replied: "No question of it; this is an order."'

So Hilaire Géronimo went slowly back to his motor-cycle. The two others looked at him questioningly; he gave them a wink, meaning No, it was not for this time. At that instant the general came out of the town hall and went off shaking hands in the crowd. Then he came back to the car, giving Géronimo an enigmatic smile as he approached and got in. The CRS motor-cyclist, with his fist clenched on his revolver, was saying to himself again and again: 'But it would have been easy.'

And indeed it would have been easy. Escape after the attempt presented no problem. Surprise would have been complete. Géronimo would have taken advantage of the inevitable disorder to dive into the crowd on his motor-cycle. The gunmen would have been hesitant to fire, for Géronimo had proposed to make off in the direction of the schoolchildren assembled at the exit to the town hall. He could have roared round the building without touching them and disappeared. The danger of subsequent discovery was minute; he knew the area like the back of his hand.

Géronimo was never in any trouble. The two others kept their mouths as tight shut as he did. They all remained with the company and were posted back to France in 1962, still in their blue CRS uniform.

In the emotional atmosphere of that period there was nothing surprising in the counter-order received by Géronimo. The most ludicrous rumours were going the rounds. When the OAS was formed Michel Debré, for instance, was long held to be a member of it. He was no such thing, although his convictions did lead him to defend French Algeria until de Gaulle drove him to repudiate it. At this time, therefore, there was nothing extraordinary in presenting de Gaulle as the clandestine leader of the supporters of French Algeria.

In fact, faced with so heinous a crime as an attempt on the life of the general, the FAF leaders in Oran, their subordinates and even more the military who were in league with them, simply had not the courage to say 'Yes.' 'A pity,' Géronimo still says. 'Just the word "Yes" and he would have been dead.'

This sort of hesitation was a characteristic reaction of both camps. When Colonel Argoud was kidnapped by the French Secret Service in Munich in 1964, he should have been done away with, but no one on the spot was willing to give the order. It is a sort of intellectual cowardice. The killing of de Gaulle would have been a historic assassination. Quite apart from the actual physical danger involved, there was the consideration of the future judgement of History—all the more significant because at the time there was no popular consensus in France. This type of reaction has always been a factor; in the past it has often paralysed action which could have changed the course of world history. Circumstances change; men do not.

Had de Gaulle been killed at Aïn-Témouchent the upheaval both in France and in Algeria would have been considerable. Most observers consider that the French Army would have swung over. The vast majority of officers were supporters of French Algeria, even though only a minority were prepared to commit themselves politically; the remainder were thinking primarily only of their pay at the end of the month.

People were also afraid of acting against the man of 18 June 1940. Against the background of the blatant mediocrity shown by the French ruling class he was apparently the only man capable of becoming the 'great leader'. Shortly before his posting back to France in 1960 General Massu arrived in Algiers and attended a meeting of *pieds-noirs* leaders; he said to them: 'You must realise, gentlemen, that I have actually seen Him. He is a leader. I have also seen Bidault. He is small and sick and his overcoat has a fur edging. You cannot replace de Gaulle by Bidault. Well then, *who have you got?*'

This same reaction was to be seen during General de Gaulle's visit in December 1960. The FAF had, to all intents and purposes, been disbanded but its steering committee was still in existence and in contact with the army. In all three provinces of Algeria there were teams of determined men willing to carry out a 'meticulous operation' against de Gaulle; such men were to be found particularly in the SDECE, known in Algeria as the CCI (*Centre de Coordination Interarmes*—Inter-service Coordination Centre) under Captain Benoît (cover name Louis Bertolini). However, each time the FAF leaders asked the colonels for the green light, the answer was 'No'.

Nevertheless, on three occasions during this visit General de Gaulle was within an ace of being killed without explicit agreement from the soldiers. There are always men ready to sacrifice themselves for their beliefs.

After his frosty reception at Aïn-Témouchent General de Gaulle—still with no inkling that death had been so close to him as he got into his car —returned to his helicopter. At 4.30 p.m. he arrived at Tlemcen—in a terrible hailstorm; even the weather seemed to be against him, yet despite it several thousand people were waiting for him. He made a brief speech, translated word for word into Arabic and punctuated with mixed applause and booing. Then, after a quick visit to the officers of the sector, he departed.

The visit continued at de Gaulle's usual tempo—a stop in every sector, a speech in the rain of which he seemed unaware, complete disregard of security measures, hand-shakings.

He seemed not to see the hostile placards or hear the angry shouts. Erect in his uniform, he passed on. His entourage was exhausted, anxious and at their wits' end when he dived into the crowd. His bodyguards, their hands on their revolvers, kept as close to him as they could, on the watch all the time for any suspect movement or one of the faces of the men whose photographs they had studied for so long. Even though the approaches had been policed, death could come from this crowd, be it Arab or European.

Jean Morin, the Government Delegate, was no better informed. The general had forbidden him to return to Algiers where revolt was in the air; 'Your place is at my side,' the general had said drily.

Morin was not afraid for himself but for the head of state, for if anything happened to him it would be a national catastrophe. Towards the end of the Saturday afternoon, taking advantage of a halt, Morin spoke on the telephone to Vieillecaze, assistant director in his office. '*Monsieur le délégué*,' Vieillecaze said, 'the intelligence service is quite explicit; an assassination attempt is being prepared for Orléansville. The information provided by the Israeli government checks with our own. A team of killers has left Algiers and is waiting for the general on the outskirts of Orléansville. That is all that I can tell you.'

This time Morin was really dismayed; he knew what the general's reaction to this would be—he would simply shrug his shoulders and carry on. Morin confided in Louis Joxe who also knew his man. 'Try it all the same,' Joxe said.

A few yards away from them the general was shaking hands . . . still more hands.

CHAPTER 5

In the Line of Fire

Joseph Rizza, known as 'Nani', is a small, thickset, broad-shouldered man with a thin moustache. He came from Bab el-Oued. He was in no way striking. He had passed unnoticed all his life. He was thirty-one years old. Nevertheless he was tough, a grim, secretive being. He was poor—a fitter for the Algerian Haulage Company.

When the rebellion started with the moslem rising of 1 November 1954 he had simply said: 'Something must be done.' Accordingly he collected a team of four of his mates and they gave as good as they got from the FLN killers.

He was a man of few words. His secretiveness and power of resistance were proverbial. Several times he had been arrested by the police but he would only say one thing—his name. The policemen got no more from him, even with the use of their 'methods'. His concept of total friendship gave him unquestioned authority over 'his men'. He himself was completely committed. At the time he was earning very little but he gave up his cigarettes and his aperitif to buy the essentials for his operations. He was an astounding marksman, quick on the draw, and he never missed.

When asked (with no officers present, for they did not appreciate this type of activist) to kill de Gaulle, all Rizza said was: 'When and where?'

Among the supporters of French Algeria were a number of Jews who knew that the departure of the European community would mean a veritable massacre for them. They were therefore at one with the *pieds-noirs* in carrying on the fight. Inevitably, however, they also included a number of Israeli intelligence agents. Undoubtedly this was how the plan to assassinate de Gaulle had come to ears of the Israeli government. The information was correct: Jo Rizza and five resolute men had in fact left Algiers to take up positions at Orléansville.

It was Jo Rizza who later blew up the notorious villa in Algiers occupied by the *barbouzes*.★

★ Undercover agents of the *police parallèle* who achieved a sinister reputation.

Orléansville is a town of 40,000 inhabitants, most of them poor; it lies at the foot of the Daha hills in the Wadi Fodda valley where a dam has been built. The approaches are easy. Jo Rizza had posted his men at the entrance to the town, at a spot where an approaching vehicle would be an easy target for marksmen as experienced as his team. They had a real arsenal with them—light machine guns, dynamite, revolvers and hand grenades.

Moreover Rizza was well informed—from the official intelligence service in which he had highly efficient contacts. He knew the route the official convoy would use. He even knew the exact timing, for the general liked to keep to a precise time-table. He was fully prepared. He had merely to wait with his finger on the trigger. He was completely calm, as always at the moment of action; so far he had never missed.

Jean Morin was sitting in the presidential Citroën Déesse beside General de Gaulle. The car began to move. In less than half an hour it would enter Orléansville. Morin was still hesitant; the imperious general seemed lost in thought. Morin could picture what would happen in a moment.

Then he made up his mind: 'General, I am extremely uneasy. I have just received very reliable information confirming the earlier warnings. An assassination attempt against you is planned at the entrance to Orléansville. I beg you to agree to a change of route. I also ask you not to stand up in the car as you arrive.'

That was all. He waited for the inevitable reply. To his great surprise the general looked at him almost with a smile: 'You don't have to ask me anything, Morin. You are the man responsible for the maintenance of order. Well then, you decide.'

Without losing a moment Morin shouted orders through the car window. A few miles from the town the convoy tore down a little mountain road, bypassing the built-up area, and roared up to the prefecture. The general's car stopped at the foot of the steps. The bodyguard took up position. The police closed ranks. The general disappeared into the white building where the officials were awaiting him; outside, the crowd, massed before the gates, continued to chant its hostile slogans under the nonchalant gaze of the soldiers on duty.

After five minutes Jo Rizza realised that something had happened. He sent one of his men to find out. On his return the matter was quite clear: de Gaulle would not be assassinated on this occasion. There were far too many police in the town for Rizza to try anything on.

'Come on, lads. Home,' he said calmly.

Without hurrying, as if on an exercise, the death squad stacked its weapons and climbed into a car to go back to Algiers by way of the mountains. The car was a grey Panhard and the petrol had been paid for out of the wages of an Algerian workman.

The general continued his crusade. On Sunday morning, after mass at Orléansville, he went on to drum up support among his soldiers (he knew that they formed the linchpin of his policy). He went to the airbase at Blida, to address four hundred officers of the Algiers Army Corps.

'France's victory over the rebellion in Algeria is won,' he told them. 'It can never be undone. The rising has given Algeria a new spirit which she did not previously possess. It must be seen in the context of the emancipation movement which is sweeping through the world.'

The silence was complete, hardly disturbed by the engine of a small blue and yellow reconnaissance aircraft wheeling round the edge of the airfield. The officers listened as their 'leader' explained his policy by means of phrases such as 'honour, conscience, our country' and so forth. In typical 'de Gaulle language' (and with good reason) he told them that he understood the problems they faced: 'Initially an Algerian Algeria needs its French minority which will be like leaven in the dough. It is therefore essential that the two communities work together—even if they are not inclined to do so of their own accord.' In conclusion he added: 'Politics are not the army's business. It is the army's honour, its duty, simply to serve. This it must do whole-heartedly; it must be exemplary. If, by some stroke of bad luck, it should fail to do so, all would really be lost for France.'

This said, he took his leave and moved towards the helicopters of his escort.

From his little blue and yellow aeroplane wheeling round the base the pilot observed the general emerge, surrounded by a mob of officers.

The aircraft's pilot was Christian P, aged thirty, of medium height and suntanned from the beaches of Moretti or the Madrague. He was of the bourgeoisie, a handsome philanderer, invariably surrounded by suntanned girls in revealing dresses. He liked good food and wine. Life had always been easy for him. No doubt this was why he was already a little blasé. He looked as if he had stepped out of a Françoise Sagan novel where the men while away their time in dinner jackets and drinking whisky. He had never had to struggle for his existence. Normally he would have succeeded his father in his business, married a girl of his own social standing and had a son who would have succeeded him in his turn—a pleasant life but colourless and with no surprises.

Suddenly the explosion took place: suddenly there was a reason for living, believing and hoping. There was also a sort of fear of losing everything. He was fired by Pierre Lagaillarde who, like Susini later, had the gift of inspiring a crowd and gathering around him men ready to stake everything for their ideas. He became totally committed to the struggle for French Algeria. His taste for the good things of life was matched by the enthusiasm with which he followed others into counter-terrorism.

When de Gaulle came to power Christian P was one of those who had no confidence in the general. In their view de Gaulle had not understood them; he would abandon them; he was the danger. The only defenders of French Algeria were the military, but they were hamstrung by de Gaulle. Their hand must be forced by doing away with the general. Christian P decided that he would be the man of destiny.

He was alone in his villa in Moretti that Sunday morning. He wrote a letter which he had gone over in his head a hundred times before, a letter for all the world to read. He left it on the stone mantelpiece. He drank a large whisky, but he was not afraid. He got into his Mini and went to the near-by civil airfield of Chéraga. His Jodel stood at the end of the runway.

He had not wanted his friends to be there. This was to be a personal affair, as good a way as any other of committing suicide.

Down to his left he could see the Mediterranean. It was calm and rather grey that morning. He headed for the Blida Atlas, aiming for the foot of the Chréa hills, for a little place which he knew well. He passed there every Sunday in winter with skis stowed on top of his car.

Now he could see the Blida military airbase. He switched off his radio. No doubt the control tower would be calling him. He circled round wide. His mind was made up. He had practised for hours at the controls of his Jodel, diving on trees or isolated buildings. He was quite calm. He banked his little aircraft slowly to put it on the right track—then he would open up, dive on de Gaulle's helicopter and crash into it with his tankful of petrol. He would sacrifice his life to liberate Algeria from the general.

There was a whole fleet of helicopters down there. Which would de Gaulle take? He would soon see. Seconds passed, apparently endless. Everyone had got in. The Jodel banked again so as to be on track.

At that very moment a whole cloud of helicopters took off all together. Christian had no notion which was the general's.

It had been a stupid failure. He moved off in a wide circle while the helicopters departed eastwards in formation. Then, suddenly sober and feeling the absurdity of the situation, he burst out laughing.

Next day (Monday) de Gaulle missed death again at Réghaïa, the military airbase near Algiers. This was the nearest de Gaulle came to the capital which had been in turmoil ever since he had set foot in Algeria. On FAF orders a general strike had been called leading to full-scale riots which 10,000 CRS men were unable to control. On all sides there were short violent clashes. The morale of the civilians was set fair: they had been told that the army was coming to their rescue. During the night of 10/11

December, 18 RCP under Colonel Masselot had in fact arrived. Captain Sergent tried in vain to contact Lieutenant Degueldre and 1 REP. Everyone, however, was full of confidence: the army was about to take the place of the CRS and they knew that, somewhere during his visit, de Gaulle would be struck down.

Suddenly everything changed: the moslems, alerted by some mysterious signal, entered the lists. As early as the evening of the 10th they were causing disturbances in the suburbs and starting to cut European throats.

In his memoirs General Jouhaud says: 'That very day Bernard Tricot, Secretary-General in the office of the President of the Republic, conferred in Algiers with François Coulet who was in charge of political affairs in the office of Jean Morin, the Delegate-General. Apparently their conversation turned towards the possibility of simple counter-demonstrations by the moslems with the slogan "Algerian Algeria"; they might have had a cheering effect on the head of state who was deeply wounded by his reception in the various towns.'

Whatever the truth of this, the moslem counter-demonstrations developed into riots with the CRS as spectators; the latter even went so far as to forbid Colonel Masselot to intervene with his troops. The moslems literally took over the city while the Europeans kept their heads down. Faced with this flood of humanity the FAF was forced to cancel its instructions; otherwise there would have been a real massacre. In any case, they preferred to leave the CRS—the morning's enemies—to deal with the Arabs, who were now entirely out of control. Admittedly some parties of Europeans did some shooting, but the restoration of order was now the job of the army which was formally ordered to fire on the crowd, whether moslem or European. Over the course of three days 112 Arabs and 8 Frenchmen were killed. The course of events was now irreversible and the two communities irreconcilable. The FAF was disbanded. Jouhaud and Sergent tried to persuade the army to come over to their side. It was too late. Sergent said to Colonel Masselot: 'We have not changed but we cannot improvise.'

Such was the explosive atmosphere in which the visit of the head of state took place.

On the Monday afternoon, while the general was on the way to the airbase at Réghaïa, a man emerged from a cheap apartment block in the Redoute quarter of Algiers, where he lived. He had bought his apartment on a twenty-year mortgage; he was sure that the French would stay in Algeria and had no hesitation in undertaking this commitment. He was tall with an ascetic's face and piercing eyes. He was 2nd Lieutenant Pierre Delhomme and he was on the way to his unit, Air Detachment 40, which was resting at Réghaïa where de Gaulle was expected.

33

Lieutenant Delhomme (Military Medal, *Croix de Guerre* Indo-China, Military Cross, 4 mentions in despatches) had given himself an assignment—to shoot down the general and all his entourage in less than an hour's time.

He was a *pied-noir* by origin, a determined man who had already risked his life. He had enlisted at eighteen and had been through Indo-China. Starting from the ranks he had gradually climbed the ladder; his physical courage and exceptional fighting qualities had brought him promotion to 2nd Lieutenant in the field, like Roger Degueldre. He had married a Vietnamese and had one child; he was deeply immersed in colonial problems. Most of the Indo-China *condottieri* suffered from a particular complex: that a part of France had been lost down there. In most cases this complex carried over to Algeria which they did not wish to lose either. In the case of Delhomme it had become an obsession.

At the end of 1960 Algeria was still his religion. Gradually an *idée fixe* possessed him: to kill de Gaulle because he was going to abandon Algeria; but he proposed to kill him in his own way—as a commando would, acting alone. He had confidence only in himself and his methods.

He had already decided to act once before—in March when the general had come to Algeria for his famous 'tour of the messes'. De Gaulle had visited the Aurès area and Delhomme had thought that he could get close enough to him in a little village east of Arris; the air detachment he belonged to was responsible for the security of the head of state who was due to land at an airbase. Fate and the headquarters staff decided otherwise that day. His platoon was posted on a rocky hillock overlooking the base and some half-mile from the runway; between his post and the base was an open slope and he would have attracted general attention had he come down. Moreover, his men would not have understood his desertion of them. In any case, on the runway he would not have been able to get near de Gaulle since he was due to speak to the officers and Delhomme was only a sergeant-major at the time. The thing would only have been possible had his platoon formed the guard of honour on the general's arrival.

So Delhomme had had to abandon his idea and simply watch the general arrive. In any case de Gaulle had not inspected the troops but had gone straight into a sort of hangar where the officers were waiting. Undoubtedly the general was not destined to die then. Nevertheless, Delhomme had been fully determined; he had not slept all night for thinking of what he was about to do and, although normally a teetotaller, he had swallowed down half a bottle of brandy to keep up his courage.

This first abortive operation had in no way changed Pierre Delhomme's determination. He merely waited for another opportunity. This came with de Gaulle's visit to the base at Réghaïa.

The fact that his platoon of Detachment 40 was stationed at the base enabled him to act without difficulty. He was now a 2nd Lieutenant and he thought that this time his men would form the guard of honour. In fact it was to be done by the air detachments of the base training camp, but Delhomme did not know this.

'In any case,' Pierre Delhomme says, 'I thought that I could go up to one of the men, ostensibly to check his turn-out. As an officer I was only entitled to carry a service revolver but on some pretext or other I could have borrowed a soldier's sub-machine gun. At that moment I had only to empty the magazine into de Gaulle, taking in his entourage as well since I thought them equally guilty. I know that it was a suicidal operation but I was definitely determined to sacrifice my life for a cause which I considered right. My sacrifice would not have been in vain.'

Once more fate decided otherwise.

When Delhomme left his apartment to go to the base he intended to go in his Dauphine, but it obstinately refused to start. He was thinking how to borrow a vehicle when rioting broke out in the area. Arabs were firing from the roofs on the men of 18 RCP who were chasing them. He helped the paratroopers for a time and then thought it better to abandon his plan and look after his family. His Indo-Chinese wife was not in Algiers; she had gone home to Vietnam to have her baby (a son). Delhomme's brother lived in the same district and he decided to join him in his apartment in Kouba.

Here it is worth jumping slightly ahead and following Pierre Delhomme's career through. This second disappointment did not shake his *idée fixe*. He took part in the April *putsch* as the most junior officer and, when the *putsch* failed, went underground. Together with Roger Degueldre he was one of the founder members of the OAS action commandos. At this stage he tried to mount a further operation with 'target de Gaulle'. He confided in a colonel of the SDECE asking for assistance to get back to France in order to kill the general. 'You are more useful here than in France,' the colonel replied. 'In any case, forget it; there are two colonels dealing with this business, one in Algeria and the other in France.'

Delhomme accordingly stayed in Algiers and became operations officer of the 'Hussein-Dey' commandos under Captain Montagnon. He was seriously wounded by two bullets in the back during an ambush laid by the *barbouzes*. On recovery he changed his cover-name from 'Canard' to 'Saturne'; then he followed Captain Montagnon into the famous Ouarseni *maquis* in the house of Bachaga Boualem, and there he was finally arrested.

On 2 September 1963 he appeared before a Military Tribunal. The prosecutor demanded the death sentence. Delhomme asked to speak and made the following statement:

'On 12 December 1960 Charles de Gaulle inspected the Air Force parachute commandos on the airbase at Réghaïa before boarding his aircraft. I and certain others were due to shoot down the head of this police state. Owing to indecision we let slip this opportunity of putting an end to the machiavellian activities of the tyrant and probably of saving Algeria. . . . In the autumn of 1960, having equipped a party destined to shoot Charles de Gaulle during his visit to the South-East, I showed lack of courage in failing to take part myself. As a result, although fully prepared, the operation was never attempted. So, having failed in my duty in the face of the infamous conduct of those upon whom the fate of French Algeria, my native country, depended, I deserve the death penalty, not once but twice. I rely upon the justice of God.'

He was sentenced to life imprisonment but was amnestied with the rest in August 1968. In prison he found faith in God and to this he now devotes all his energy. One cannot but acknowledge the sincerity of his conviction. There is no doubt that, had he been in a favourable position, he would not have hesitated to fire on de Gaulle. His two attempts are proof.

With that thought we return to 1960.

When de Gaulle returned to his office in the Elysée after his eventful visit to Algeria, he could be certain that henceforth his Algerian policy would go according to plan.

Admittedly he did not know that in fact he had escaped death four times. He had seen, however, that the moslem reaction had swamped the demonstrations of the *pieds-noirs*. He was more than ever determined to show his inflexibility and to hold the referendum on self-determination planned for 8 January.

His first action was to issue guide-lines to Michel Debré, his head of government, for his statement to parliament on 16 December. They were extremely firm: he had laid down his policy in his speech to the nation on 4 November and he proposed to pursue it in the teeth of any storm.

The storm wind was to blow again soon and once more it was the ex-sergeant-major Orsoni who was to raise it.

CHAPTER 6

Twinges of Conscience

André Orsoni had given prolonged thought to the reasons for the failure of his attempted kidnapping. Technically the operation had been perfect but it had collapsed as soon as there was any question of an overall policy. In other words, the great difficulty about kidnapping de Gaulle was that one did not know what to do with him once the operation had succeeded.

Orsoni's thought processes were simple. He reached the following conclusion: if you did not know what to do with someone, it was better to kill him. The problem would then disappear of its own accord and one could proceed to the next and inevitable stage, the rescue of French Algeria. But this amounted to regicide. The affair looked like being even hotter to handle than he had at first thought.

'I knew that I could not get away with it,' Orsoni says. 'Later I even heard that the police and the secret service knew of my plan. If I could strike quickly, however, I could produce a *fait accompli* and so save Algeria. What would happen afterwards was unpredictable. I should probably not have managed to save my skin, for my own friends would not have hesitated to offer me up as a sacrifice to public opinion. I accepted this and did my utmost to bring it off. I even lied to my own people, telling them that, if the operation succeeded, we had three hundred million to divide between us. Of course there was not a penny; no one had promised me even a sou. It's true; I deceived those people— just as de Gaulle deceived one and a half million *pieds-noirs*. Everyone was in agreement except one fellow called Lauzier; he was all for action but did not want to take part himself.'

Apparently Lauzier had some idea of what was going on after Fusil's visit to General Faure in connection with the kidnapping of de Gaulle. It is worth noting that at the time he was a member of the SDECE under Colonel Fourcaud (whom we shall find reappearing later in an unexpected rôle at the trial of the Pont-sur-Seine conspirators).

Mortified by their previous failure, however, Orsoni and Fusil decided to keep the location and details of the new operation strictly secret; the members of the commando were only to be told at the last moment when it would be too late for any of them to pass the news to some outsider.

Several times they drove together along the route used by de Gaulle on his way to Colombey, looking for the ideal spot for their attempt. Their choice fell upon a place which, they thought, lent itself admirably to a military-type operation; it was on Route Nationale 19, beyond Provins. It is an odd fact that, without knowing it, a year later the Pont-sur-Seine conspirators selected a spot only a few miles away.

What attracted Orsoni and Fusil was the lay-out of the trees bordering the road; a stretch of about 500 yards was marked by three trees at one end and two trees at the other; in between was a big heap of gravel under which a bomb could be concealed.

A very detailed plan was made for the operation. When the general's car came level with the heap of gravel, the bomb would explode; at the same time, however, the trees at either end of the stretch would be felled by charges laid at their base and connected to the same ignition system as that of the bomb. The convoy would thus be caught; a squad of eleven men armed with sub-machine guns and rifles would then finish off the survivors. Most of the group were former Resistance men who had kept their weapons when France was liberated.

'The main disadvantage of this procedure,' Orsoni says, 'was that everyone would be on de Gaulle's side but the people up there were taking no account of FLN atrocities.'

The bomb consisted of 90 lbs of TNT and 90 lbs of buckshot. Orsoni and Fusil spent several nights laying the wires; there were several hundred yards, all connected to a single ignition system and running to the bomb and the various trees.

A telescopic sight was laid on the heap of gravel; as soon as the convoy appeared in the sight—it generally consisted of three cars and four motor-cyclists—Orsoni would press the button and everything would go up.

The entire party was to assemble at a farm (l'Epinoche) lent by a friend and there await confirmation of de Gaulle's departure.

On the evening of 23 December everyone was in his place. A friend of Orsoni's was to telephone as soon as de Gaulle emerged from the Elysée. Lauzier was at Provins watching the road and as soon as the president's convoy reached the entrance to the town, he was to warn Orsoni and his men; they then only had to go to the spot, lay the charges—this would take only a few seconds—and wait for the procession.

At l'Epinoche all thirteen men were assembled in front of the wood fire in the great fireplace. Orsoni and Fusil calculated that the convoy should pass between 9 and 10 p.m. When the local church clock struck 10 Orsoni realised that something was amiss. The telephone remained infuriatingly silent.

At 11 p.m. he gave the order to disperse and went to find out what had gone wrong. He found the friend who should have telephoned busy putting up a Christmas tree for his six children.

'You never warned us?'

'No.'

'De Gaulle has not left then?'

'Yes, he has.'

'He used Route 19?'

'Yes.'

'Well then, why didn't you warn us?'

'I couldn't do it. I didn't want to be the one to give the signal for execution. You know, I was in London like you. Do you understand?'

Orsoni did understand. He knew that, like him, his friend had been an SAS parachutist in London when de Gaulle was still no more than the man who had issued an appeal to France on 18 June 1940. Of course the general had changed since then. He had become a politician and had opted for certain courses of action with which, particularly on the tragic subject of Algeria, many of his old comrades disagreed. But memories are memories.

Orsoni's nerves gave way; he broke down and wept—'I understand that you may not have wanted to warn us, that you may not have wanted him to be killed—for we wouldn't have missed him. But you should have made this decision *beforehand*.'

That evening, 24 December, at 70 mph de Gaulle passed a heap of gravel which could have changed the course of French history. It still keeps its secret today; some of the wires are still buried in the area.

After this setback the gang of conspirators dispersed. Pressure from the police was becoming increasingly severe and the conspiracy business increasingly uncomfortable.

Orsoni did not lay down his arms. For a time he thought of blowing up the Elysée via the sewers. But in fact no one's heart was in the effort any more; the few members of the underground who remained with him felt—with good reason—that they were politically isolated and in a hostile country.

When Orsoni was arrested, he said not a word. 'I did not even talk about my decorations,' he says today: 'Before me one of my friends had told the bench that he had the Legion of Honour and they put him down for twenty years. So what would happen to me with my seventeen mentions!'

CHAPTER 7

Birth of an Organisation

Outside France the repercussions of the events of December 1960 had been deplorable in so far as the supporters of French Algeria were concerned; if nothing else, they had enabled the Provisional Government of the Algerian Republic (the GPRA) to launch a major diplomatic offensive in the UN, with the Foreign Minister, Krim Balkacem, as spokesman. Nevertheless, these developments enabled the small group of exiles in Madrid to draw a certain number of conclusions.

These exiles were few but they were determined. There was, of course, Salan, firmly established in the Hotel Princesa with his ADC, Captain Jean Ferrandi. Then there were two young men: Pierre Lagaillarde, the leader, and Jean-Jacques Susini, the thinker.

These last two held long discussions. They were of the same generation and they felt close to each other; one had succeeded the other as President of the Algiers Students' Association. They had fought the same battles—13 May, the 'Barricades' on 24 January 1960, and, after a period of waiting in Spain, the abortive *putsch* of December 1960. Salan, 'the mandarin', came of another world, of another background. He was a republican soldier and would hear no word of revolution. Susini and Lagaillarde, on the other hand, thought that Algeria offered a chance of giving a violent heave of the helm to French political life. For whole days and nights they strode around Madrid mentally putting things to rights.

The army had drawn back in Algeria. In December it had, nevertheless, asked the FAF to take action. The FAF had nearly one million adherents who were supposed to come out onto the streets, requisition vehicles and even hold certain positions. Faced with the Arab flare-up, however, which had been more or less instigated by the authorities, the army had thrown in the sponge. It was therefore necessary to start from scratch.

Until the affair of the 'Barricades' the civilians had had confidence in the army. After the 'Barricades' they no longer had confidence, though they still hoped. By the end of December, however, they knew that there could be no counting upon the army.

So they hit upon the idea of an independent civilian organisation. The FAF had been disbanded and its leaders arrested or deported; there remained no one in Algeria—or at least so they thought—to resume the struggle and defend French Algeria. The two young exiles accordingly decided to form an organisation whose members would be civilians—or military deserters—and which would combine political thinking and terrorist action on the ground.

Late on a February afternoon, in Lagaillarde's apartment in the sky-scraper known as the Madrid Tower, Lagaillarde and Susini produced their plan.

'What shall we call it?' Susini asked. 'We must have a name apparently reminiscent of something. For instance, I suggest "Secret Army", as in the Resistance days.'

'I think we must have the word "organisation" somewhere in our title,' Lagaillarde replied. 'I would be happy with "Clandestine Organisation" or "Armed Organisation".'

For some time they juggled with these four words. When they left the Madrid Tower with dusk falling they had agreed on three letters which were soon to be on the lips of half the world—OAS (*Organisation Armée Secrète*—Secret Army Organisation).

As early as October 1960, however, others in Algeria had reached the same conclusion. They had formed a network totally separate from movements like the FNF (*Front National Français*—French National Front) or FAF (*Front de l'Algérie Française*—French Algeria Front) which worked in the open. This network proposed to do its fighting in the shadows.

It was run by two men. The first was a magistrate whose cover-name was 'Grandpère'; the second was André Canal, known as 'Le Monocle' or alternatively 'The Colonel', although he was a civilian—an industrialist, to be exact. One provided the brains, the other the brawn.

The first planned action undertaken by the new network was carried out by determined men collected by Canal; it consisted of the execution of Popie, a gaullist barrister and champion of Algerian Algeria. Maître Popie set himself up as the protector of Europeans in an independent Algeria but in fact he was playing the government game; in a television broadcast he had said: 'Five columns in one,' and 'French Algeria is dead.' This was enough to condemn him in the eyes of certain people. In addition, however, the lawyer's undercover intrigues led the new network to select him as their 'curtain-raiser'; he was said to be the agent in Algeria of Bernard Tricot, Secretary-General in the Elysée. After the 'Barricades' he had gone to see Alain de Sérigny, owner of the *Echo d'Alger* and had said to him:

'Monsieur de Sérigny, you will not be incommoded on one condition: sell your newspaper *to us*. We offer you 800 million. If you refuse we shall arrest you and take you to court. Your support of the insurgents and the statements you have made to the Algiers Students' Association are enough to earn you a severe sentence.'

It was true that the *Echo d'Alger* had undoubtedly taken the side of the insurgents. Its circulation in Algeria was enormous and it was a considerable embarrassment to the government.

Alain de Sérigny naturally refused this offer with disdain. Taking Popie's threats very seriously, however, he boarded a cargo-boat sailing to foreign parts. It was intercepted by a military patrol boat and ordered to heave to. Alain de Sérigny was arrested.

All this became known in Algiers. Popie was condemned to death by the new network, the execution order being signed by 'Grandpère' in person.

Claude Peintre and Dauvergne, two members of Canal's strong-arm squad, presented themselves at the lawyer's office in the Rue de l'Abreuvoir and executed him by stabbing.

At the same time, to give public demonstration of its existence, the new network engineered a series of explosions in the city, the most astounding being that at the Palais de Justice where 'Grandpère' functioned as an examining magistrate—'Plant the bomb after 8 p.m.,' he ordered, 'since I leave my office at 7.30.' (The identity of 'Grandpère' has never been revealed. At least the police do not know it, despite the most exhaustive enquiries. He was a man 'above suspicion' and he still is so since he is today president of a court in France.)

The appearance of this network in Algiers was significant in that it paralleled the intuition and the logic of Lagaillarde and Susini as to the necessity to crystallise and organise resistance to the authorities' Algerian policy. The instinctive nature of the reaction is all the more apparent when it is remembered that at the outset there was no contact between the 'Grandpère'–Canal network and the new-born OAS. Initially their actions ran parallel, neither knowing anything about the other.

In Madrid, however, when General Salan heard of the Lagaillarde–Susini plan, he accepted the presidency of the movement at once. Salan set much store by Susini's advice and often held private discussions with him. Susini looked upon Salan as a soldier and, the situation being what it was, showed no great enthusiasm in accepting him as head of a civilian organisation. Like Lagaillarde, however, he thought that the ex-C-in-C in Algeria constituted an essential figure-head for a new military revolt: the general who had already refused to cross the Rubicon on two occasions might be persuaded to do so at the third attempt. General Salan, of course, had no part in the military mafia which had formed in France and

Germany after the 'Barricades'. But his presence at the head of a powerful civilian organisation might carry the army along. Instinctively Lagaillarde and Susini had attempted to combine the principles of clandestine action as exemplified separately by two equally famous groups in Israel—the Haganah (more military and hierarchical) and the Irgun (more civilian and terrorist).

As soon as Salan had accepted, Lagaillarde and Susini drew up a plan of action. They knew what was afoot in Algiers through emissaries who were free to come and go. They first attempted to bring the 'Grandpère'– Canal network into the organisation now headed by Salan but the marriage did not take place at once. The new organisation first had to show that it existed and possessed genuine power. It was therefore necessary to form strong-arm squads on the spot receiving orders from Madrid. A general protocol of agreement was signed in Madrid under which all activist formations were to be absorbed into the OAS under Salan; a copy of the agreement was despatched to Lagaillarde's friends in Algiers who were still numerous and active. They welcomed the birth of the new organisation but still hesitated before enrolling. One group of underground fighters, however, did agree to act for the OAS, by distributing the organisation's first leaflet (it was pushed through all letter-boxes in Algiers during the night of 1 March) and then by carrying out the first terrorist actions bearing the signature 'OAS'.

The first 'specific' OAS order, signed by Susini and Lagaillarde, was passed to Algiers by Philippe Castille. Its subject was the immediate execution of Dr Pierre Merrot. Emissaries from Algiers had brought to Madrid files of information culled from the best possible sources (SDECE monitoring, tapped telephone conversations, copies of official orders, police files and so forth); many people's activities were therefore known. From these files the staff of the OAS selected that of Dr Merrot; he was President of the FFL and a personal friend of de Gaulle, who used the familiar *tu* with him (one of the few colleagues, apart from Marshal Juin, whom de Gaulle addressed in this way). A number of tapped telephone conversations proved that the information was genuine and showed that Merrot was one of de Gaulle's direct personal sources of information, in whom he had complete confidence.

Claude Piegts, a young *pied-noir* who ran a mineral-water business in Castiglione with his brother Roger, was commissioned to carry out the execution. The operation took place on the Castiglione–Algiers road. Piegts used a shotgun with a buckshot charge and fired on the doctor's Peugeot 403 from another car. But the cartridges were damp and so the buckshot lost its penetrating power. Dr Merrot was merely wounded in the chest and face.

The official enquiry produced no results at the time, though the police had their suspicions. Fifteen months later, on Thursday, 7 June 1962, Claude Piegts faced the firing squad, ostensibly for another assassination, that of Police Commissaire Gavoury. But he knew that de Gaulle had intervened with his judges in order to procure the death sentence and that when his defence counsel had gone to the Elysée to present a petition for clemency, de Gaulle had not uttered a single word.

In the visitors' room of the Santé prison Claude Piegts had said to his brother some time before: 'I know that I shall be shot. De Gaulle has never forgiven me for having made an attempt on Merrot's life.'

The net result of the first specific OAS operation was therefore a double failure: Merrot remained alive; Piegts died. Nevertheless, a course of planned, organised, determined action had been launched with the dual purpose of forming a clandestine army and organising a terrorist network.

While a group of exiles was spawning the new organisation, General de Gaulle, who was soon to be its target, was pursuing his policy by leaps and bounds—as if in a hurry to offload the burden of Algeria with the tacit approval of the silent majority at home.

He knew, too, how to talk to this silent majority. In a television interview on 6 January, two days before the referendum on self-determination, he described the struggle as 'absurd and outdated', spoke of 'chaos' in the event of failure of consultation and asked the French to give him a 'genuine massive Yes', the favourite weapon of gaullist terminology. France presented no problem; the French would vote all right. But voting was also to take place in Algeria and the significance of that vote would be great.

Jean Morin, the Government Delegate, was ordered to orchestrate official propaganda in the utmost detail. At great expense, leaflets urging the people to 'Vote Yes' were distributed in the remotest regions; films were shown in Arabic and Kabyle urging the moslems to vote; Algeria was closed to Frenchmen likely to campaign in favour of a 'No'. Jean Morin sent an 'urgent and most secret' note to all prefects and inspectors-general prohibiting persons liable to prejudice the 'normal development of the campaign and the poll' from entering or residing in Algeria. Specifically the note said: 'No considerations of reputation, influence, function, electoral mandate or ethnic origin will *a priori* constitute a reason for exemption from this measure of any person, however important.'

Naturally the army too was worked on. The overall result was satisfactory to the government: 75·26% voted 'Yes' in France and 69·51% in Algeria. As expected, Algiers, Oran and Bone voted 'No'. The moslems obeyed FLN orders and 41·22% of those on the voting list abstained. From the authorities' point of view, however, the essential was to get their 'Yes' even if some of the results had to be cooked. Major Camelin, for instance, was posted as a punishment because he had naïvely drawn attention to the fact that his ballot box contained more 'Yes' votes than there were voters on the list in his sector. History alone will judge whether General de Gaulle was right to embark upon his policy but he was certainly wrong to use such methods to achieve it.

The result was unarguable and apparently irreversible. It was bound to produce a violent reaction from all those who still believed in a French Algeria, a reaction which began with the generals' *putsch* and continued with a long series of assassination attempts against the head of state.

Certain people did not wait for the result of the **referendum which** they considered a foregone conclusion.

It must be emphasised that the members of the OAS were not alone in wishing that, in one way or another, the general could be removed from the scene of power. Politics resemble an iceberg: only the tip is to be seen; the rest remains submerged.

In January 1961 certain mysterious forces, whose influence extended into many fields (finance, politics, the army, the administration), showed their hand; probably they had long been at work under cover. The fact remains that on 5 January 1961 they apparently decided to take certain risks. (We shall see later what influence such groups, working in the name of a politico-religious entity, can exert upon the general politics of a country.)

The group which made a special impact on 5 January was closely connected with world catholicism; its composition alone is proof; most of them were ultra-nationalist Catholics. This group was known, somewhat misleadingly, as the 'Old General Staff'. It was this group which was behind the two major assassination attempts at Pont-sur-Seine and Petit-Clamart. Both attempts were directed by Lieutenant-Colonel Bastien-Thiry; but in conversation with his associates he continually referred to certain mysterious superiors. The 'Old General Staff' has contrived to preserve much of its anonymity. It knows that it is protected by the law of libel which prescribes punishment for 'any allegation or imputation affecting the honour or standing of the person or body to whom the action is imputed'.

Certain publicly known facts, however, may be recalled—as they will be later in this book.

By the beginning of January 1961, therefore, three forces existed, all of which aimed to eliminate de Gaulle who was damaging to their policy, in other words, to their interests:

1 First the 'Old General Staff' (inaccurately known as 'of the Army').
2 Then the French Army, which was hesitant and divided. In a letter to General Salan Colonel Château-Jobert (later head of the OAS in Constantine province) reported having seen Pierre Messemer, then

Minister of the Armed Forces, who apparently said to him that an officer could only serve the man who paid him. Château-Jobert's conclusion was: 'Basically perhaps Messmer is right.'

3 Finally, the supporters of French Algeria who were grouping and organising themselves.

The army was the most likely of the three to move in the immediate future; it included many who admitted to being violently anti-gaullist and who were clamouring for action. Three-and-a-half months later they were to prepare—and bungle—one of the greatest military *putschs* in French history.

The other two forces, however, were in turmoil. There was a certain osmosis taking place, for many officers who had been compromised in the abortive *putsch* of December had been posted back to France—a total of some thirty-five including Colonels Broizat, Godard and de Blignières. They frequently met under General Faure who chaired a sort of Military Committee known as the Military Committee 'of Paris', not to be confused with the 'Old General Staff'. The Committee was in constant touch with General Salan, primarily through an emissary, Arnaud de Gorostarzu, nephew of the great confessor to Pope John XXIII. He came and went between Paris and Madrid and, whenever he arrived in Spain, was immediately received by Salan; the only others present at these meetings were Captain Ferrandi (invariably) and Jean-Jacques Susini (frequently), the one acting as ADC, the other as political director. General Faure himself twice went to Madrid to see Salan. Since he did not wish to register in a hotel, he slept in his car.

Whenever a visitor arrived, Susini was summoned to the general by telephone. He lived in an apartment in the Calle Victor not far from the Hotel Princesa where the general lodged and beside the University campus, overlooking the Madrid Tower and the ruins of a barracks which had been the scene of furious fighting during the Civil War; Susini could therefore be on hand quickly. He was helped by the fact that he had a comfortable American car, a Nash, and two bodyguards from the Spanish Security Service. This arrangement had been in force ever since Colonel Eduardo Blanco, head of the Security Service, had summoned him one day together with Ronda and had said to them: 'We have heard that several Arab countries have despatched to Spain certain people who are hostile to you. We have accordingly decided to protect you and are placing at your disposal cars with chauffeurs and guards who will escort you wherever you want to go. The guards are armed of course.'

Lagaillarde, Salan and Ferrandi were all protected in the same way. The guards had orders not to leave their side and certain private meetings took place with a policeman, an expert in ju-jitsu, waiting patiently in the next room, his gun always within reach.

Everything was registered, docketed and watched.

The Spaniards did not provide money, however, and the exiles lived on contributions from Algeria. The emissaries brought such cash as had been collected—five hundred thousand francs, a million, two hundred thousand and so forth. It was all given voluntarily and without pressure of any kind. During its six months of exile the little group in Madrid received some six million (old) francs.

During one of his visits Arnaud de Gorostarzu was received by Salan in the office-lounge near the hotel's American Bar, where the general went regularly morning and evening. Susini and Ferrandi were present.

'General de Gaulle is due to visit the south-west,' Gorostarzu said. 'Some of my friends wonder whether this would not be an excellent opportunity of doing away with him.'

Salan replied to the suggestion by giving his full agreement in front of Susini and Ferrandi. 'How do you propose to proceed?' he asked.

'My friends propose to lay a remote-controlled mine on the road he will have to use near Mont-de-Marsan.'

There was silence. All were weighing up the prospects of the plan. Then Salan said, 'Reports I have indicate that 5% of these mines do not explode.'

Ferrandi, who had served with the general for a long time in Indo-China, nodded.

'That's correct,' he said. 'In any case, General, I have perhaps something better to propose. It is a method I have used myself. In defence of our posts in Indo-China we used to lay mines connected to wires laid across the paths and hidden in the sand. But the Viet-Minh soon found out how to defuse them. One of them crawled on his stomach pushing a small stick along the ground in front of him; as soon as he felt some resistance he knew there was a wire there. When I discovered the trick, I placed 75mm shells painted green in the trees on either side of the path and stretched the wires a foot or so above the ground. The scout met nothing with his stick but he himself came up against the wire and the whole thing went up. We could use the same method. We would merely have to connect the shells to a firing point some 200 yards away and in this way the operator would escape.'

'Let's go for this method,' Salan said.

'In any case,' Gorostarzu said, 'if we cannot lay on this operation, we have another in reserve. An ex-Legionnaire has suggested to us that he kill de Gaulle with a telescopic rifle. He asked for a reward of 40 million.'

Salan threw up his arms: '40 million? That's exorbitant.'

Gorostarzu cleared his throat—'We have already given him half.' Salan's arms stayed in the air.

'But,' Salan went on after a moment, 'are you sure of him? He could be an *agent provocateur*. The gaullist régime needs these continuous alarms and excursions to keep public opinion in a state of tension and provide justification for police measures.'

'We have confidence in him,' Gorostarzu said. 'We could not do otherwise. If he succeeds, it won't seem expensive.'

On 12 April de Gaulle visited the south-west and returned to Paris in the best of health.

Susini went to the Hotel Princesa where Salan was having lunch in the vast dining-room which was still almost empty—Spaniards do not start their lunch as early as 1 p.m. A magnificent standard-lamp was alight next to him and two waiters hovered around.

'Have you had lunch, Jean-Jacques?'

'No, General.'

'Then sit down and have lunch with me. Have you any news?'

'De Gaulle is back in the Elysée.'

'Of course. So the duck is still alive, Jean-Jacques.'

This last comment, which was to be repeated many times, was a reference to Robert Lamoureux' famous sketch telling how his father was unable to kill a duck. Ferrandi, Salan's ADC, frequently talked of it and it became a sort of standing joke during these evenings in Madrid.

CHAPTER 8

Four Generals

For the moment Salan was presiding at a distance over an emergent organisation; he did no more than listen to reports while his staff drew up plans. On the army net Paris was the centre of serious preparations, the OAS not yet being ready for political action. Salan was well aware of this; he was in touch with General Faure who, with the assistance of Regard, ex-secretary-general in the Algerian government and now treasurer of the department of the Seine, was preparing further action on the ground. It was to be on a large scale this time since seizure of power in France was seriously envisaged.

As early as February Salan despatched his first directive to the Paris Committee, appointing General Faure his representative in France for military matters and a certain 'Raphaël' for political questions. Paris accepted it politely, though with certain reservations regarding Salan who was too divorced from current problems.

Meanwhile increasingly important meetings were held at the Ecole Militaire (Military Academy) on Saturday afternoons—a day normally devoted to the training of reserve officers, so suspicions were not aroused.

General Jouhaud undertook to sound out a number of French politicians but all, from Guy Mollet to Maurice Faure, thought the problem insoluble. On the other hand, Jouhaud's contacts with certain officers in Algeria threw up a name which inspired confidence—that of General Challe. Even more than Salan, Challe seemed to be the man who could rally round him the largest number of French officers.

Challe had been Commander-in-Chief in Algeria and it looked as if he would not be difficult to convince. His last interview with Michel Debré towards the end of January had been dramatic. Challe had said: 'The government's policy will lead Algeria and then France to catastrophe.' He had also told the Prime Minister of his disquiet over de Gaulle's Atlantic and European policies. Debré had replied: 'The only possible policy on Algeria is that of General de Gaulle and there is only one man who can implement it—de Gaulle.'

Maurice Challe had ended the interview by asking Michel Debré to replace him as NATO Commander-in-Chief Central Europe and to accept his request to resign from the army.

Challe was therefore 'available'. Edmond Jouhaud undertook to convince him. On Sunday, 26 March, accompanied by 'Raphaël', he went to Lyon where Challe lived.

Two days earlier Challe had had a conversation on the state of morale in the army in Algeria with his ex-*chef de cabinet*, Colonel Georges de Boissieu (cousin of Alain de Boissieu, de Gaulle's son-in-law). Boissieu gave it as his view that the soldiers would follow him. Nevertheless Challe hesitated.

He knew what was expected of him but it was not in his nature to take such a decision lightly. He was worried over the use of force by the military. He would have preferred a purely political solution under which all the elected representatives would quietly have broken off relations with France; the military could hardly take action against calm, peaceful, resolute men. He had proposed this plan to what he called 'The Directorate'.

This 'Directorate' consisted of two members of parliament, three generals and an ex-cabinet member. Here again appears the mysterious force which, together with the 'Old General Staff', was destined to show the tip of its nose from time to time and master-mind certain of the assassination attempts.

Challe asked for time to think it over and arranged to meet the others again in 'Raphaël's' house on 29 March. In his memoirs Maurice Challe states that he took his decision after hearing General de Gaulle's press conference of 11 April, which he describes as an 'inhuman homily'. In fact he gave his agreement in his own house in Paris on 29 March in the presence of General Zeller.

On 8 April the final meeting was held in the Ecole Militaire when prospects were assessed. There were present Vanuxem, Godard, Broizat, Degueldre, Sergent, de Blignières, Argoud and General Faure. The decision was that the *putsch* be attempted.

One of the first to be informed of this decision was Salan, who was still in Spain. He immediately sent a directive nominating Challe as the 'military officer responsible'. It did not produce any marked enthusiasm from General Challe—'Very well,' he said, 'but I know what I've got to do.'

On 12 April Challe, Jouhaud, Faure, Zeller and Gardy fixed the date of the *putsch* for the night of 20/21 April. Among the first to be told were General Vanuxem, who arrived with an offer of two motorised brigades from Germany, and Georges Bidault, happy as a schoolboy to find himself back in the atmosphere of the wartime Resistance Council.

Movements began at once. Jouhaud was commissioned to find an aircraft for Challe and Zeller.

The army as a whole was not in the plot but the conspirators thought that the waverers would quickly join them once they saw the scale of the movement. The home country had not been forgotten; the capital was to be occupied by units from Orléans, Rambouillet and Auxerre.

On 20 April Challe's proclamation was drafted in Colonel Lacheroy's office in the Ecole Militaire; it was to be published on the great day. The vast machine was under way.

Salan himself was ready to move to Algiers with Susini. On receipt of a secret message ('The maid's room has been burgled') he would know that he could leave. Serrano Suner, Franco's brother-in-law, had promised to place an aircraft at his disposal.

Colonel Godard went to Algiers as a tourist by the normal aircraft. He had been due to remain in Paris but Challe preferred to have the ex-Director of the *Sûreté Nationale* with him and asked General Faure to replace him in the capital.

Captain Sergent and a number of other officers left Istres for Blida in a military aircraft. Colonel Argoud landed clandestinely in Constantine province.

Lieutenant Degueldre arrived at Orly a few minutes before take-off. He had been a deserter since December 1960. With his own special brand of calm audacity he told the CRS man at the gate that he was a sergeant-major on leave who had had all his papers stolen.

'As one NCO to another,' he said, 'you can't let me down. They'll register me as a deserter.'

The CRS man let him go.

A veritable shuttle-service had been organised between Istres and Algiers to carry all the participants in the *putsch*. Jouhaud had been in Algiers since the 16th.

One snag was the impossibility of finding an aircraft for Challe, which caused Jouhaud to order postponement of action by a day. The order was cancelled almost at once when an aircraft was found. The result, however, was a whole series of hitches which risked compromising everything.

H Hour was finally fixed for 2 a.m. on Saturday, 22 April.

It is an entertaining thought that all this fantastic deployment would have been useless had a handful of resolute men succeeded in carrying out their *coup*—placing a bomb in the box at the Comédie Française occupied by de Gaulle at 9 p.m. on Thursday, 20 April. He had gone to the Comédie with President Senghor to see a performance of Racine's *Britannicus*—the whole atmosphere of the play lent itself to an attempted political assassination.

51

The idea had occurred to certain ultra right-wing groups but they were unable to find a sufficient number of accomplices on the spot and were forced to abandon the plan.

In Algeria, however, things happened.

Everyone has his own description of the *putsch* of 22 April.

De Gaulle's was: 'An insurrectionist authority . . . a military *pronunciamento* . . . a quaternion of retired generals . . . a group of biased, ambitious and fanatical officers . . . their enterprise leads straight to national disaster.'

Challe said: 'I could not blithely accept that millions of Algerians of all communities be delivered with no form of safeguard into the hands of a totalitarian and terrorist authority; it was impossible for me to continue to back government policy.'

Jouhaud's comment was: 'We had no wish to be uprooted.'

Militarily the operation was not an unqualified success. Algiers was admittedly taken by the paras but the city was more or less isolated. The insurgents had forgotten one important detail: the main broadcasting station was not immediately taken over and it continued to transmit as usual. Degueldre and a party of civilians captured it during the morning and 'Radio France' took the place of France V—Henri X (whose acquaintance we shall make later in connection with the Mont Faron assassination attempt) became director. This early omission was a bad mark for the insurgents; neutralisation of all forms of communications media is Lesson No. 1 for any small-time *putschist*.

The second problem was that the army deliberately ignored the civilians. Officers showed a sort of allergy to the emergent OAS movement since its propaganda was still centred on General Salan who had still not arrived in Algiers. When a group of OAS presented itself at the Palais d'Eté to take over from the commandos, Major Forhan drove them away, threatening to have them arrested on the spot.

At the very start of the revolt, at about 2 a.m., Jean Morin, the Government Delegate, telephoned Paris. Geoffroy de Courcel took the liberty of waking de Gaulle—a bold thing to do. The general, however, realised the importance of what was happening. He summoned his principal associates at once to examine the situation. Messmer, the Armed Forces Minister, was away supervising the transfer of Lyautey's ashes to Morocco, so Debré drafted a communiqué which was broadcast by all French radio networks at 6 a.m. It was from this that the Algerians learnt of the success of the *putsch* since the first broadcast from 'Radio France' did not take place until 8.30 when Challe's proclamation was transmitted. It read as follows: 'Officers, NCOs, *gendarmes*, sailors, soldiers and airmen, I am with Generals Zeller and Jouhaud and in touch with General Salan with the object of keeping our oath to preserve

Algeria. A government bent on surrender is preparing to hand over Algeria to the rebellion. Do you want Mers el-Kébir and Algiers to be Soviet bases tomorrow? I know your courage, your pride and your discipline. The army will not fail in its duty and the orders I shall issue will have no other purpose. This headquarters reserves the right to extend its action to France and to re-establish the constitutional republic which has been so seriously compromised by a government, the illegality of which is obvious to the nation.'

For his part Colonel Godard put a gloss on this immediately afterwards; he would not tolerate, he said, 'any initiative apart from that of the army from any quarter whatsoever.'

So it was definitely a military *putsch*; the civilian organisations were clearly excluded. Subsequently Colonel Godard joined the OAS but he retained his natural mistrust of 'civilians'. He was commissioned to organise the execution of de Gaulle but continually postponed the operation; he could not, however, bring himself to agree that the more determined civilian members of OAS should carry it out instead.

Naturally, when the *putsch* took place the OAS civilians seized the opportunity to emerge from the shadows, all the more eagerly since, at his press conference of 11 April, de Gaulle had given the OAS a certain credibility by saying quite definitely that he was ready to abandon Algeria completely to the Russians or the Americans, wishing them 'much pleasure of it'.

The *pieds-noirs* felt confidence in Salan's organisation (though he had still not arrived in Algiers); for the army they felt a certain natural distrust since it had already let them down after the 'Barricades'.

The people of Algeria, moreover, soon realised that the army intended to keep its distance from the civilians. This was particularly clear when it refused a proposal by Dominique Zatarra, the ex-leader of the FAF, that civilians should join the conspirators' staff and that he should mobilise 25,000 men.

When, therefore, Salan and Susini arrived, the OAS, now fully aware of the situation, decided to play its own game. The situation quickly deteriorated. Many army units refused to follow these 'compromised' generals; the vast majority of the navy and air force were against them; the conscripts were obstructive. Finally, the only forces remaining 'in earnest' (de Gaulle, after all, had said: 'The most serious aspect of this affair is that it is not in earnest') were the Foreign Legion and the OAS.

Very soon, therefore, the situation swung in the government's favour. As Salan was about to leave for Algiers at 11 a.m. on Sunday, 23 April, Serrano Suner had been quite outspoken: 'Your affair is no good. Your generals in Algiers are not energetic enough. They have not had either Morin or Gambiez shot. Franco would have had no hesitation.'

Another cry of disillusionment came on the Monday morning—from

Colonel de Boissieu who was due to be Maurice Challe's chief of staff: 'Everything you are doing is excellent but I do not see what it is supposed to achieve.'

The radio stations of metropolitan France launched a major offensive, even announcing that Salan had committed suicide. They initiated a classic campaign, whipping up Algerian public opinion which was already torn this way and that. This was a transistor war.

By the Tuesday the *putsch* had collapsed. Faced with resistance and disaffection Challe contemplated giving himself up. Sensing danger Salan sent Susini to see him and the two remained closeted for a whole hour. On emerging from Challe's office Susini gave a little smile: Challe had agreed to continue the struggle; he had also approved a proclamation drafted by Susini. No sooner was Susini out of sight, however, than Challe's pessimism returned; after hearing a report from an officer to the effect that he could no longer count upon the civilian organisation, he decided to throw in the towel. He sat down in an armchair, lit a pipe and waited; Boissieu had left for Paris to arrange his surrender.

Captain Sergent drew his revolver and was about to commit suicide but Challe stopped him.

The most determined among the officers simply abandoned ship. Argoud and Gardy disappeared into the countryside and refused to give themselves up. Zeller put on mufti and vanished into the crowd. Salan and Jouhaud were escorted to Zeralda by the Foreign Legion and decided to go into hiding; on taking leave of Challe, who had accompanied them there, Jouhaud embraced him and Challe handed over such money as he had on him.

At 5.30 a.m. Coulet, the French *chargé d'affaires*, telephoned to Paris: 'Algeria is free. The rule of law has been re-established.'

CHAPTER 9

A Secret Letter to Kennedy

The *putsch* had lasted for only four days.

By 25 April 1961 there was, to all intents and purposes, no military faction on the side of French Algeria. The *pieds-noirs* now only had the OAS to rely on. At this period most of the *pieds-noirs* were for the OAS, just as in 1944 most Frenchmen had been gaullist. Accordingly, backed by a popular consensus, the OAS now expanded rapidly. In Madrid it had been a civilian organisation, a small minority group. The new OAS was the successor to an abortive *putsch* which had been solely a military affair. In a very short time it was to become a genuine terrorist organisation backed by a population which supported it. The real OAS, therefore, was formed in Algiers; the Madrid organisation was the 'historic' OAS. All those who set up the movement were in the Algiers underground, with the exception of Lagaillarde whom the Spaniards had not allowed to leave.

The success of the new OAS rested to a great extent on the fact that it was the expression of the despair felt by the European community, who more or less refused to leave Algeria. The word 'despair' is not too strong; many clung to what they considered to be their country, though knowing that, sooner or later, they would be hunted out of it. Some thought that they could succeed. Others knew that without some God-given surprise (a successful assassination of de Gaulle) or a political upheaval at home or the formation of a civilian army of *pieds-noirs*, the die was cast.

'To set our movement in perspective or explain its philosophy,' Susini says, 'I would say that at that point top priority was the struggle against the French Army. My view is that, although forced to leave Algeria in the end, we were beaten, not by the FLN but by the French Army, an army which obeyed the authorities. We were not as lucky as the Israelis; when the British Army left, the Jews found themselves alone facing the Arabs and they were able to defend the positions they held.

55

In our case we were facing, not an Arab army but 400,000 men of the French Army, of whom 60,000–70,000 were *gendarmes mobiles* [mobile security police] completely loyal to the authorities, as that élite force, the Security Police, invariably are. We had only one possible way out— to form an army of 50,000 *pieds-noirs* with the necessary weapons and take the risk of a frightful civil war. Undoubtedly many soldiers, unwilling to risk their lives against the FLN, would have been even more unwilling to do so against the French of Algeria. Had there been violent clashes between an organised and armed European community (a genuine civilian Haganah in Algeria) and the French Army, the crack units would have faced a terrible problem, a problem so tragic that they would eventually have swung over to our side. Unfortunately they would not have done so until there were 3,000 dead men on the field.'

This view was not shared by everyone. Some still placed their confidence in the army, despite the fact that it was undergoing a fearful purge.

After the *putsch*, therefore, the OAS, now rapidly expanding, laid down two objectives for itself—first, formation of an army of 50,000 (this was never achieved; it never reached more than 5,000); secondly the assassination of de Gaulle. This was still the linchpin; if this succeeded, the gate of history would be open. For both these purposes, of course, resources were necessary. Weapons and money were required before any firm organisation could even be thought of.

For weapons the OAS leaders turned to the Americans who had been in contact with General Challe when the *putsch* took place. Having been C-in-C Central Europe under General Norstad, Challe still had a number of firm friends in the Pentagon, where many senior officers had a personal aversion to de Gaulle. The *putsch* was over so quickly, however, that these friendships had had no time to bear fruit. It very soon occurred to the OAS to pick up the threads with the Americans whose representatives had been on the prowl in Algeria for some time.

As early as 1 November a member of the OAS sent an intelligence report to Salan and other OAS leaders; its code number was AFP/149 and it dealt with 'the attitude to TWA [code for OAS] of the United States'. Referring to the 'neutrality' of the USA in the Algerian affair, the report added that this neutrality 'would nevertheless be benevolent as far as TWA was concerned'. The report ended by indicating that certain American nationals had been sent back to the USA because 'they had interpreted their enforced neutrality in a manner prejudicial to TWA'.

One American national, Mr Rambeau, had been the victim of a bomb attack at 8.30 p.m. on 20 October and the consul apparently wished to know what Mr Rambeau was supposed to have done. He was prepared to report to his government if there had been 'police provocation on the part of the French authorities with the object of rousing anti-TWA opinion among American nationals'.

Before this another intelligence report, this time from the *Sûreté Nationale* in Algeria (No. 98 dated 26 October 1961), had been 'collected' by the OAS. It read: 'In order to counter FLN propaganda the OAS proposes to send representatives to the UN for the forthcoming debate on Algeria. ... The Associated Press is said to have agreed to distribute information on the OAS. Finally an American journalist is expected shortly in Algeria in order to report on this organisation which will take charge of him when he arrives.'

On 12 November came a further note from R-17 (Jean-Claude Perez) to R-15 (Gardy), R-16 (Gardes) and R-19 (Susini). This passed on information from an agent 'on the 149 level' (a territorial designation) giving the views of a secretary in the White House and indicating that Dean Rusk was extremely anxious to know what was really going on in Algeria. The secretary asked for any newspapers, leaflets, circulars, etc., which could be sent to him for information; he had also asked for 'a list of personalities who could profitably be contacted'. The note added that the American *Newsweek* of 28 October had published a photograph of the statue of Joan of Arc in the United States with the letters OAS on the pedestal.

On 25 November the headquarters of the Algiers region of OAS issued an investigation order (AFP 149—signed W 12) as follows: 'It is reported that the Jonson commando has reappeared. [It had already been detected during the summer of 1961 when the emergent OAS was trying to recruit members and organise itself.] It consists of Americans and Canadians in direct touch with the CIA and is trying to contact student circles. It is said to be offering weapons and perhaps money. This commando is extremely dangerous. Pursue enquiries discreetly and keep us informed.'

The interest shown by Americans in Algerian affairs was further illustrated by the transmission on American television of 6 November (CBS network) of an interview with General Salan.

In fact General Salan had received three journalists in his hide-out— Richard Kaalsen of CBS, David Grant-Adamson of the *Sunday Telegraph* and a correspondent of the Dutch *Volkskat*. The French government was furious and issued a minatory communiqué accusing the journalists concerned of 'complicity in an attack on the security of the State and on arrangements stemming from the President of the Republic's decision of 24 April 1961 concerning participation in and encouragement of a subversive enterprise against the authorities and laws of the Republic. In accordance with Article 23 of the decree of 2 November 1961 journalists guilty of this type of misdemeanour will forthwith be escorted across the frontier.'

The report which de Gaulle found on his desk explained that 'Richard Kaalsen recorded this interview on 2 November in a village about an hour by road from Algiers'. Ex-General Salan told him that the OAS was determined to prevent constitution of an independent Algerian state. He had then stated that there could be no question of discussion with de Gaulle because 'he has deceived us and has lied too much'. The report added that General Salan hoped that 'the United States would understand us and help us since basically this is a fight for liberty'.

On 26 November this interview was broadcast on Belgian television and the French government made a vigorous protest to the Belgian government. The same day the *Sunday Telegraph* published the interview in London, putting General de Gaulle into a fury. Grant-Adamson added that Salan had received him in an Algiers villa and that it had been quite easy for him to meet the head of OAS. (In fact the interview took place in a farm on the Mitidja in the district of Saoula.)

The interview made a certain impression in America, so much so that the French government reacted sharply both to the US Embassy in Paris and the Consulate-General in Algiers. In a note dated 29 November (Ref. No. W 28) William Porter, the Consul-General, said: 'Such protests would normally be considered unacceptable since, in the United States, freedom of expression is considered to be a major element of democratic theory.' Clearly the United States had a strong hand in refusing to be lectured by a government which was itself using every form of coercion in Algeria.

These various comings and goings culminated in a meeting between General Salan and the head of the CIA in France. The latter had gained contact with Lieutenant Degueldre who had kept his lines open to the SDECE via Colonel de Blignières. Degueldre had sent him to Susini who in turn had introduced him to Salan in his own apartment in an Algiers suburb—near the golf course overlooking the Fromentin *lycée*. The American was fully *au fait* with the Algerian problem, having married a *pied-noir*.

He arrived in Algiers 'officially', in other words he had been authorised by his masters in the Pentagon to pursue a certain policy. The Pentagon generals he represented were perfectly clear on the Algerian problem. In essence what he said to Salan and Susini was that the USA knew perfectly well that, if France were to move out of Algeria, her place would be taken by the Russians; and that they were convinced that the *pieds-noirs* could be successful in Algeria but that they would fail in France. It seemed, he said, that there must be a break between France and the French in Algeria and that some form of Franco-Moslem republic must be set up, provisionally—or permanently—separate from France.

The talks between the members of the underground and the American colonel continued while down below the police vehicles and half-tracks thundered by as usual. The American put a certain number of questions to Salan and Susini showing clearly that the United States knew perfectly well what the insurgents' intentions were, what they had achieved, their organisation and their prospects. They were 'rich'; probably the source of the information which the Pentagon needed was paid very well.

Finally he came to the point—'America can help you. What help do you want?' He knew the answer in advance. They wanted equipment for an army of 50,000 men, in other words 50,000 sets of conventional light infantry weapons together with a large-scale allocation of mortars and machine guns.

'We are ready to provide you with all this,' the American colonel said to Salan. 'Though we do not demand payment for this aid, we shall obviously make one condition. Here is the condition: we ask that you accord preferential treatment to American goods in an independent Algeria. We also ask for the opportunity to set up military bases in the Sahara, bases to accommodate inter-continental ballistic missiles.'

The insurgents had practically no choice. Such conditions are invariably accepted at the outset; later, when one is 'free', they can be called in question. As we know this is what happened in the case of the Evian agreements between France and the Provisional Algerian Government: they provided for a French presence in the Sahara and at Mers el-Kébir for a long period; as soon as Algeria was independent the agreement was repudiated by Ben Bella's régime and then by Boumedienne.

Salan accordingly accepted the American terms. The essential point was that he was going to be given the wherewithal to equip a veritable army and this would undoubtedly mean the salvation of French Algeria. Susini, always ready to finalise matters, took a sheet of paper and began to write in his neat hand.

By midday next day President Kennedy had the following letter on his desk:

Algiers, 12 December 1961

Mr President,
Our two peoples traditionally look to each other in moments of difficulty. Men of my generation, their hair greying after all they have suffered, do not forget all the Americans who, during this century, have laid down their lives in the service of your great country's mission and sense of right.

The beaches of Algeria still bear witness to this today and, twenty years ago, our sea carried to us the first waves of our liberators. How vivid this memory remains! Little is required to awaken among the Algerians, as they recall this page of history, all the emotions of nostalgia and of hope.

I have felt the need to tell you of this country's sincere friendship, as a man who expects no more for himself; I have carried my responsibilities and I had hoped to relax in the peace of mind born of duty done. Then, faced with the developments in Algeria, I have felt an urge to leave my retirement and come here to place myself at the disposal of all these good people who have had to suffer so many anguished years.

It was not possible to betray the self-sacrifice of our officers, to abandon these moslems and Europeans to the tender mercies of subversion. It was unthinkable that this country should be handed over to the dictatorship of a minority which has only been able to assert its grip on part of the moslem population of Algeria through the use of violence.

In the end, Mr President, necessity has led us to raise an ever larger force against a state which is prepared to disown our constitutional laws and which has ceased to try to defend freedom in Algeria on the empty pretext that it died in Berlin.

My sole object is to obtain the approval of all personalities in France, whether of the Right or the Left, who are anxious to ensure France's future in face of the arrogant mistakes made by a man immured in an ivory tower.

We have no purpose other than to re-establish the Republic in all its rights, a republic which, like your great democracy, will be able to reconcile freedom of conviction with the exercise of power. It will be the duty of this republic to respond to the appeals of our country, to guarantee the life of the nation and of society and to play its part in defence necessitating the integration of all Atlantic forces.

Within this defensive system American bases on French soil, particularly in Algeria, will clearly constitute the weapon of deterrence which Europe and Africa so sorely need.

Mr President, I have tried to bring to your ears the appeal of a man whose whole life has been devoted to the defence of those values common to us both.

May God ensure that right shall triumph. We will do our utmost to ensure that communism does not come here to turn yet another region of the world into an inhuman land where we should be strangers to our own destiny.

Raoul Salan

The letter was typed by Susini's secretary, Micheline (later to become his wife). It was signed by Salan and handed to the head of the CIA in France who despatched it by special USAF aircraft. It amounted to acceptance of the American terms.

The American representative considered that the principle was settled and that he could now turn his mind to actual methods of landing the equipment. The staff of the OAS therefore contacted a certain number of *pieds-noirs* who had experience of this sort of operation, having had a hand in the American landing on 8 November 1942. The plan was for some ten boats, each carrying 50 tons of armaments, to come from Portugal under CIA cover. They were to take advantage of a gap in the radar screen at a certain point on the Algerian coast and land their equipment on the beaches of Sidi-Ferruch. Roger Degueldre asked William Lévy, a captain in 2 RCP, to make himself responsible.

At this time Lévy was president of the SFIO (*Section Française de l'Internationale Ouvrière*—French Section, Workers International) in Algeria. Some time later, early in 1962, he was shot by a murder squad on orders from Degueldre himself—most disquieting reports on him had been received. Lévy was in fact denounced by one of his relatives; the report on this 'specific action' by the OAS says that he was working to hand Algeria over to the FLN and as a result 'was in collusion with the murderers of his own son who was executed by the FLN in the Rue Soleillet at Bab el-Oued at 7.30 p.m. on 23 June 1957'.

Although Lévy's connections with the FLN were acknowledged to be overt and confirmed, this particular 'specific action' had political repercussions. Lévy had been holding meetings in the Rue Négrier with FLN representatives and he was attempting to sow discord between the Jews of Algiers and the OAS. As soon as it was discovered that he was playing a double game, Lévy was shot by a member of the 'Delta' commandos, a certain B. As soon as the news of his death became known, the socialists of Algeria, hitherto comparatively favourable to the OAS, swung over to the side of its enemies. Sergent, who was in touch with Guy Mollet in Paris, was furious because the doors of the socialist offices were now closed to him. It was significant that, according to a contemporary document (undoubtedly genuine though the accuracy of its contents cannot be guaranteed) Gaston Deferre, the SFIO leader, at this point put up 5,000,000 old francs as aid to the anti-OAS networks formed by the 'National Association for the Support of General de Gaulle'; according to the same source François Mauriac contributed 50,000 old francs. The document in question came from the MPC (*Mouvement pour la Coopération* —Movement for Cooperation), a movement formed in Paris by Jacques Dauer, the left-wing gaullist, its representative in Algiers being Lucien Bitterlin, a radio director; the note was signed 'Raybois' and dated 5 December 1961.

Degueldre handed over responsibility for the landings to another of his associates and continued his preparations. A few days before Christmas 1961, when all was ready, a message was included in an OAS pirate broadcast intended for the CIA monitoring service. It read: 'The orange trees are in flower.'

Meanwhile, however, President Kennedy and his advisers had given prolonged thought to the famous letter from Salan. It might well change many things in the Mediterranean but it would also lead to all sorts of difficulties with France. Gavin, the US Ambassador in Paris, was consulted and was violently opposed. The President's advisers, always ready to do battle with the Pentagon military, backed his advice. Kennedy himself, who was never enthusiastic, ended by cancelling the operation. The Franco-Algerian republic had lost its last chance of becoming a reality one day.

Undoubtedly this equipment would have changed the situation and, had it reached the *pieds-noirs*, the Algerian problem would have reached another dimension.

Left to its own devices, the OAS, which had no money, was unable to buy from the usual arms merchants and had to make do with those provided by the military. The military were prepared to let the OAS commandos have light weapons but refused to supply any heavy equipment. The French army leaders undoubtedly had in mind a top secret note signed by de Gaulle and counter-signed by Michel Debré dealing with the position to be adopted by the French Army in the event of insurrection in the major Algerian cities; French troops were to be withdrawn at once and the city recaptured 'with tanks and guns'. This document, which fell into the hands of the OAS through sympathisers in the official intelligence service, explains why the military preferred not to see the OAS in possession of heavy weapons. The French Army was willing to help its 'lost' soldiers but it preferred to keep the strong cards in its own hand in case it was obliged to obey the political authorities.

The OAS did, nevertheless, acquire one valuable asset from the army in the shape of officers who deserted to it. They brought with them something the civilians lacked—a sense of discipline and organisation, though some of them naturally had little political sense.

The French Army itself was being subjected to a violent purge: 200 officers were relieved of their commands; 115 *pied-noir* members of the CRS were arrested; several generals were imprisoned including General Nicot, ex-*chef de cabinet* to Michel Debré, and General Faure; complete parachute divisions were disbanded as were 3 'air commandos' out of 5 (they were numbered 10, 20, 30, 40, 50). Meanwhile the OAS leaders formed a well-found clandestine paramilitary organisation.

CHAPTER 10

The 'Delta' Commandos

At the top of the OAS pyramid was General Salan, whose Number Two was General Jouhaud. The staff director was General Gardy (ex-Inspector of the Foreign Legion and fiercely anti-gaullist) assisted by Colonel Godard. There were three main divisions: a staff duties section (BS—*Bureau de structuration*) together with an organisation section (OM—*Organisation des masses*), a psychological warfare and propaganda division (APP—*Action psychologique et de Propagande*), and an intelligence and operations division (ORO—*Renseignements et Opérations*). Staff Duties and Organisation under Colonel Gardes also dealt with false identity papers and the collection of funds. Psychological Warfare and Propaganda was under Jean-Jacques Susini. His team, which included Colonel Broizat, dealt with propaganda, the drafting of leaflets and publications and with clandestine broadcasts. Finally, Operations and Intelligence were under Dr Jean-Claude Perez. Basically it consisted of action squads, the best known being Roger Degueldre's 'Delta' commandos, and of sector commandos, each under a captain.

Colonel Godard was also in charge of intelligence from within the army and was 'official' organiser of de Gaulle's assassination. This organisation was centred on Algiers but things developed quickly and it soon extended into Algiers province where Colonel Vaudrey had four captains under his orders. Jouhaud was alone at Oran, somewhat out on a limb. No one dealt with Constantine province.

A lively correspondence developed between these various organisations, everyone had a cover-name, sometimes several. Salan's cover name was 'Soleil' but he changed it several times since many letters went back and forth to various people in France and papers might fall into the hands of the police. (This actually happened on 7 September 1961 when the police arrested Maurice Gingembre at Maison-Blanche airport; he was carrying a series of important documents which, by cross-checking, gave the key to a whole list of cover-names.) To guard against just this risk, those concerned changed their cover-names with great frequency. At one time they even used female cover-names (Degueldre as 'Danielle', for instance, Godard as 'Françoise', Susini as 'Janine', Perez as 'Paulette' and so forth).

Salan became in turn 'Soleil', 'Eléphant', 'GBI', 'Francis', 'Santiago' and even 'Ferhat'. Jouhaud was successively 'Compagnon', 'Bertrand', 'Soleil Bis', etc. Sergent was 'Sierra' and 'Trujillo', while Godard became 'Buenos Aires' and 'Claude'. Many of these cover-names caused the police a great deal of trouble. For a long time they did not know who 'Verdun' was: they still do not know who 'Grandpère' and 'Raphaël' were.

The part of this organisation best known to the public at large was the operations section which gave birth to the celebrated 'Delta' commandos. They were the creation of an astonishing personality—Roger Degueldre. Of all the OAS fighters he was probably the most committed and he was to pay for it with his life. After the 'Barricades' he had told the colonels: 'I will go to the limit.'

When the OAS was formed he was thirty-six years old. He had been born in 1925 in Louvroil, a little village in northern France. He was of medium height (5 ft 10 in), hefty, with close-cropped brown hair, a hatchet face, small bright eyes and a sanguine disposition. He was a somewhat mysterious being who liked to leave others wondering about his life. When Jean-Pierre Ramos, head of one of the Delta commandos, asked him one day: 'Is it true that you were in the SS?' he merely smiled and did not reply. In fact during the Nazi occupation he had joined an FTP *maquis* (*Francs-Tireurs Partisans*—a communist-inspired resistance movement) at the age of seventeen. In 1945, although married, he suddenly disappeared, leaving his wife without a word, and joined the Foreign Legion under a false name, obviously as a private soldier. He was a very good soldier indeed and was promoted to officer rank in the field; his name became legendary. He was wounded at Dien Bien Phu where he saved the life of Colonel de Blignières, earning his eternal gratitude.

He was adept at getting out of tight corners and a good man in a brawl. In his book *Je ne regrette rien* (No Regrets) Captain Sergent tells of some of their joint escapades—and they are significant. He was intelligent, cunning and a born leader of men. Not until he became an officer did he resume his own name—he had enlisted under a false name saying that he was a Belgian subject. His qualities as a soldier were such that he succeeded in climbing the ladder of the military hierarchy—for the Foreign Legion to promote a man to the rank of lieutenant in the field when he has never been to a military college indicates that he is someone quite exceptional; both friends and enemies agree on that.

On arrival in Algeria he developed an almost physical passion for the country; the situation was a somewhat specialised one for the officers of 1st Foreign Legion Parachute Regiment were extremely politically minded (it was the only regiment which went over *en masse* to the side of the rebels without a single officer or NCO defecting). In many cases their determination was undoubtedly dictated by the French defeat in Indo-China. Like most officers of the French army Degueldre had sworn that France would never abandon Algeria—how many officers are there today who still remember this oath which, rightly or wrongly, they did not keep?

After the failure of the December 1960 *putsch*, on the occasion of de Gaulle's visit to Algeria, Degueldre was posted away from his regiment since he had been involved in the plot. On 11 December he refused the posting and went underground. After the abortive April *putsch*, of which he was one of the mainsprings, he became assistant to Jean-Claude Perez, head of Intelligence and Operations for OAS Algiers.

At this point he formed the first Delta commando (Delta signifying D for Degueldre), placing in command Albert Dovecar, a sergeant from I REP whom he particularly liked.

There were six Delta commandos. The first were formed with men from I REP; very soon, however, Degueldre was joined by a number of civilians and counter-terrorist groups who volunteered to form commandos. Examples were Jo Rizza, Jesus Giner and Gaby Anglade. Louis Bertolini also arrived: he was an important secret service agent (from the CCI, the SDECE's branch in Algeria) and he brought with him a veritable organisation which had been employed to construct files on all sorts of people. These files now passed to the OAS which was able to make good use of them.

One significant incident occurred. Louis Bertolini's team showed itself averse to being placed by the OAS staff under the orders of Degueldre. 'Very well,' he said, 'I will talk to them.'

In a small seaside villa at Pointe Pescade, a few miles west of Algiers, Bertolini introduced Degueldre to his men. 'I know what you have done,' Degueldre said. 'I know that you have been fighting ever since 1954, ever since the beginning of the moslem revolt. You think, no doubt, that I am not worthy to command you. Well, I will prove to you that you are mistaken. I will carry out one or two operations with you. Then you can judge.'

He then proceeded to carry out a number of operations under the eyes of the CCI counter-terrorists. They were impressed by his courage and speed of action and accepted him.

The Delta commandos consisted of very few men—six to twelve each. Subsequently other commandos were formed, dividing Algiers up into sectors and each commanded by a captain (the captains' 'soviet' consisted of Le Livain, Branca, Achard, Picot d'Assigny and Montagnon).

65

The commandos comprised some three hundred men in all. Under his direct orders Degueldre retained only six particularly tough commandos; they were authorised to act in any sector and could intervene if some team showed itself somewhat soft. Degueldre met his six Delta leaders every day in his mobile headquarters, handed them out intelligence bulletins and collected the results of operations. These meetings were extremely businesslike. Though kind and sensitive among friends, Degueldre was uncompromising and abrupt when in command. He often said to his commando leaders: 'If I see one of your men in a bar, I will shoot you unless you yourselves have shot the man before I next see you.'

When a new recruit presented himself saying, 'Lieutenant, I would like to do something active,' Degueldre would gaze at the candidate and then say: 'I give you thirty seconds to repeat that remark. Then you will go with one of my men and carry out an operation of this type. He will have orders to shoot you if you shrink.'

On several occasions the man withdrew his offer and returned to the ranks to await orders.

In fact Degueldre could take no risks. He himself, for instance, shot Michel Leroy, representative of the nationalist front in Algiers, who had joined the OAS as assistant to Colonel Gardes in the Organisation section. A number of overlapping reports convinced Degueldre that he was a traitor and he referred the matter to the headquarters staff. The verdict was death. He assembled Rizza's commando, summoned Leroy and coolly shot him down, saying to his men: 'There's what I have in store for you or what you will have in store for me if, one day, you or I turn traitor.'

Such severity did not mean, however, that he was not very close to his men. After the successful attack on the *barbouzes*' villa in the Chemin Raynaud on the night of 31 December 1961 to 1 January 1962, for instance, he chose to see in the New Year with his team rather than with his girl-friend Nicole Gardy, the general's daughter, with whom he was very much in love. He made a definite conquest of these men, who initially did not like him. His closest associates were: Jo Rizza, Gaby Anglade and Marcel Ligier, his 'Delta artificer' and expert shot (it was he who was later chosen by Louis Bertolini and Gaby Anglade to kill de Gaulle with a telescopic rifle during 'Operation Chamois' in May 1962). Ligier was under Degueldre personally and was only lent to different groups for particularly delicate operations.

At the head of his commandos Degueldre was therefore a high-level executive, but he was also a stern opponent of blind terrorism. He acted punctiliously, on orders from the staff. The victims were FLN militants, *barbouzes*, police officers and certain military officers. His 'success' rate was estimated at 98%.

At home, however, this man, who condemned a hundred human

beings to death daily, was kindness itself. He was frequently to be found with his girl-friend in the Susini house; the two men were close friends. Degueldre had complete confidence in Susini's intelligence and he was the only member of the staff whom Degueldre saw frequently; the others refused to admit him to their homes. 'Those people don't want to see me,' he would often say, 'because I have blood on my hands. They do not understand that I am not fighting for them but for French Algeria. My strong arm is essential to them.'

With those he knew well he was extremely thoughtful. At the end of a meal he would often get up and do the washing-up at the very moment when his commandos were slinking through the night, revolver in hand.

He had a sense of humour as was shown by his attitude to a certain *pied-noir* braggart, a dental student named TG. This student frequented the cafés, particularly the well-known Otomatic in the Rue Michelet below the University, boasting: 'Again this morning I said to my friend Roger, "Watch out. You're going too far. Listen to my advice." What's more he gave me a *laissez-passer* to France.' This talk came to the ears of Degueldre who thought it so dangerous to his organisation that he decided to go to the Otomatic for the first and last time in his life and rid himself of the over-garrulous student. He sat down close to TG who was at that very moment in the process of saying his piece. He had a guard posted outside as he invariably did when he went anywhere. He started up a conversation with the student who proved to be in particularly good form and gave an account of a recent 'interview' with the head of Delta.

Degueldre asked him: 'Do you know who I am?'

'No!'

Degueldre then laid his revolver on the bar and said in front of the entire flabbergasted company: 'I am Roger Degueldre.'

The student was so quick-witted, however, that he was by no means taken aback; he wriggled adroitly out of the awkward situation and even managed to make Degueldre smile in the process—Degueldre could no longer be angry.

On return to his headquarters he simply said to his men: 'I forbid anyone to touch a hair of TG's head. In the hell I live in he is the only man capable of making me really laugh.'

A head—the staff—and a strong arm—Degueldre—were not enough to establish the OAS firmly. It also had to have the sinews of war, in other words money.

The very word brings to mind the famous OAS treasure still shrouded in mystery today. As soon as the OAS had been formed its leaders began to think how to obtain the funds essential to its existence. There were several sources, particularly voluntary contributions from sympathisers together with a certain number of hold-ups, some of which produced several milliard old francs—far more than the various 'hold-ups of the century' which later became the talk of the town. Funds were also drawn from various sources, particularly financial or political groupings.

Colonel Raymond Gorel is known to have been the treasurer of the OAS. He was not the only one. Certain well-known people dealt with the movement's finances and they figure in various legal documents, such as those dealing with the case of Maurice Gingembre, then director of the Djebel Onk Company, who was arrested on 7 September 1961, on the eve of the assassination attempt at Pont-sur-Seine.

Maurice Gingembre answered Perez, his judge, as follows: 'As I have stated, on 7 August, at the request of Lagaillarde and Argoud, I agreed to deal with certain financial questions. I have said that I thought of obtaining money by forming a company which would have made available to me about eleven million per month, in other words five million for the clandestine newspaper, three million for organisation of the army and three million for miscellaneous expenses. I indicated to Colonel Godard that I should not be able to lay hands on the eleven million straight away and in reply to this he proposed that I despatch five million to Floride (Colonel de Blignières). I had to tell Sergent of this but I do not think that I told Blignières . . .'

This obsession with obtaining funds through more or less open channels goes back to the very first days of the OAS in Madrid when a curious Catholic organisation, unknown to the general public, appeared on the scene. The OAS and this organisation came into contact in various mysterious ways—like the ways of Providence.

CHAPTER 11

A Strange Intrigue

In Madrid there lived an aged exile of the 1945 war, who had been a major in Darnand's Militia (a French pro-Nazi organisation). He was a prince in his own right, and claimed to be a cousin of the Queen of England, and his grandfather had commanded one of the Czar's famous Guards regiments before, oddly, becoming one of the co-founders of *L'Humanité* (the French communist newspaper). He lived in a villa in Posuello del Argon in extreme poverty but he had retained his lordly tastes, even refusing to drink anything other than brandy at meals— when he had the opportunity.

During a lunch with Jean-Jacques Susini he mentioned one of their mutual friends whose ex-tutor had been a close friend of a French bishop. Chance, which arranges many things, brought Susini and this friend together and the friend expressed astonishment at the information possessed by the ex-President of the Algiers Students' Association. He nevertheless agreed to a meeting and the two lunched together at the Hotel Pyramides. Susini tells the story: 'I had a bad attack of 'flu and was suffering from that semi-intoxication which comes with a high temperature. I gave him an exposé lasting three hours and I thought it was brilliant. When I had finished—he had listened without saying a word—he simply murmured: "I have only one question for you—how much?" "It is not for me to answer that," I replied. "I am not the leader. It will be for General Salan to name a figure. If necessary I could work out something with Lagaillarde, but it is for the general to decide." The first sum advanced was about thirty million.'

A few days later 'Mr Good Offices' invited Susini and Ronda to one of the best restaurants in Madrid, the Horner, run by an ex-chef of the Czar. The conversation was lively and the 'friend' explained confidentially that certain sales of ferrous metals had taken place on orders from the Vatican which has always been good at running its commercial affairs.

'I am in a slight difficulty,' he then explained. 'The Catholic organising body in Paris, which is in very close touch with Colonel de Blignières, is opposed to this money being paid to General Salan who is a freemason and an atheist. For the moment the business is at a standstill.'

A series of contacts then began which showed Susini's ability as an unofficial diplomat. This chain of friendships and contacts quickly produced a result. It took the form of an initial payment of thirteen million which arrived in mid-March (before the *putsch*). At least for the moment, however, this money was not available to the OAS because, for various reasons, it journeyed from Madrid to Paris and then to Switzerland.

The important point to remember about all this is that there existed in Paris an extremely influential group of Catholics. While the OAS was sharpening its claws in Algiers and thinking of organising the assassination of de Gaulle, this group was working on its own in France, working under cover and eventually clandestinely backing the three most spectacular operations against the head of state, those of Pont-sur-Seine, Petit-Clamart and the Ecole Militaire. The most astounding fact is that there was no form of direct contact between the OAS and this mysterious group. The tip of the iceberg was only to be seen in that certain of its less exalted members, as we have seen, were allowed to call themselves the 'Old General Staff'.

It should be emphasised here and now that the staff of the OAS (except perhaps one or two members who kept their mouths shut) knew nothing of the preparation or execution of the Pont-sur-Seine attempt. In fact, after the abortive generals' *putsch*, the OAS was fully occupied for some time in organising and establishing itself and did not launch into preparations for an assassination attempt. Admittedly Colonel Godard was in charge of such preparations but, on the surface at any rate and to the astonishment of some members of the staff, he took no actual preliminary steps. Did he know of the preparations for the Pont-sur-Seine attempt? He has never spoken but it seems reasonable to suppose that he did, if one looks at one of the documents seized in the luggage of Maurice Gingembre on the eve of the attempt.

In a report dated 3 September, headed 'Coordination 3' and signed 'Tennessee' (cover-name for Maurice Gingembre) there appears the following: 'Buenos Aires [cover-name for Godard] is very much in favour, as we all are, of unity and a central organisation, the title of which he considers unimportant—it could be called "Central Civil and Military Committee" or "National Revolutionary Directorate"; this aspect does not interest him; he says: "I leave this question to those who carry some weight on the national level." In general terms it seemed to me that he was *disinterested* [italics in original] in what he calls speculations about political action in France, saying, "The only thing that matters *is to shoot down the Great Zora*. Never mind about the rest." As regards the succession he says: "Never mind about the window-dressers." As regards money he says: "Money poisons everything. However tell Floride [cover-name for de Blignières] that we are managing to send him five million per month from 5 September 1961. This will enable him to coordinate activities around him." He *pretends* [italics in original] to have no need of equipment, saying: "I have 15 tons of plastic and all the false papers I want. I have no need of anything." '

This report by Gingembre confirms that Godard was thinking of an assassination attempt against 'Great Zora', a phrase coyly interpreted by Perez, the judge, during his interrogation of Maurice Gingembre—'You have told the police that in fact this cover-name, Great Zora, indicated the President of the Republic.'

On 31 August 'Claude' (cover-name for Godard) sent a note to 'Guy' (General Gardy), 'Fleur' (Colonel Gardes), 'Pauline' (Jean-Claude Perez) and 'Janine' (Susini) which included the following: 'Balance [Colonel de Blignières] agrees on Objective No. 1 (Great Z) and says that he is dealing with the matter in earnest.'

Study of these various documents can only reinforce one's conviction that Colonel Godard was undoubtedly aware of what was going on in Paris. He had not acquired his reputation as an extremely secretive man for nothing—the other members of the OAS in Algeria knew nothing.

During this period—in other words before the Pont-sur-Seine affair—OAS activity in Algeria was intense. 'Officially' it began on 27 April, the day after the collapse of the military coup, with a bomb explosion followed by a leaflet: 'We have just suffered a set-back, not through our own fault but through that of the military leaders who had not the sense to use the potential which we represent. This set-back cannot be final. We are, of course, going back underground but we shall continue to act against the treachery of our rulers and their henchmen. . . . The latter can expect no mercy from us. Wherever we can reach them, we shall do so without mercy.'

This leaflet carried a signature destined to become famous on more than one count—'Le Monocle'.

This James Bond-type cover-name was that of a Frenchman resident in Algeria since 1940 and a fierce champion of French Algeria. He had gone to Madrid to offer his services to General Salan during the latter's lean period there. He was short, hefty, hard-faced and wore a black monocle, an oddity for someone living under cover. His name was André Canal and he was one of the first to initiate clandestine OAS action.

The first 'official' poster carrying the letters OAS did not appear on the walls of Algiers until 3 May. It read: 'All can yet be saved. Do not give up your weapons. Regroup into small sections. Shoot down those who try to arrest you. Set fire to official buildings. Kill all traitors, great or small. Sabotage the press and burn warehouses. Do not listen to the radio which is lying and inflammatory.'

As background to the forthcoming negotiations in Evian a round of explosions began.

Very soon the OAS had graduated from the stage of words and high-sounding phrases to the more serious business of executions. The slogan was: 'The OAS strikes where it wants, when it wants and who it wants.'

The first victim selected by the OAS was the senior police inspector (Commissaire) Roger Gavoury who had been given charge of the investi-gations into the OAS immediately after the *putsch*. He was a resolute opponent of French Algeria (he had already taken part in the secession of Morocco together with Gilbert Granval). As early as December 1960 he had opposed Colonel Masselot and taken the side of the moslems. General Jouhaud had said that he had 'remained suspiciously calm in face of the violence of the moslem demonstrations'. Immediately after the *putsch* he instituted a merciless hunt against the OAS which then condemned him to death and executed him 'officially'.

On the night of 31 May five men silently entered the little apartment occupied by the Commissaire in the Rue du Docteur Trolard. Leading the commandos was one of Degueldre's associates, Bobby Dovecar. One of his men was the son of a police officer. Gavoury was at once executed with a paratrooper's dagger.

The execution constituted a virtual declaration of war on the gaullists of Algiers. There was a great outcry and the OAS killers were accused of cowardice (in subversive warfare no holds are barred and both sides take advantage of the fact, as did the wartime resistance for different reasons).

A vast police machine was launched into action hunting Degueldre's men; in their behaviour, their actions and their contacts they had to exert an iron discipline. Their numbers grew, nevertheless, and they were reinforced by members of the Nationalist Front who became 'Commando Z'. This enabled official propaganda to label the OAS commandos as 'fascists', although in fact the right-wingers were only a minority.

Degueldre and his men were thus putting the OAS on the map with their bombs, their daggers and their revolvers. At the same time Susini's psychological warfare section worked up an intensive propaganda campaign with the help of Georges Ras, a journalist from the *Voix du Nord* who had joined the clandestine organisation, and Colonel Broizat. Two newspapers appeared: the *Centurion* (30,000 copies of which were distributed to officers) and the *Appel de la France* which ran to 70,000 copies—it must unfortunately be admitted that its general propaganda line was almost worthy of a totalitarian country.

OAS orders reached their largest popular audience, however, through their pirate broadcasts. These were made regularly on the television sound channel, starting on 5 August in Algiers and 5 September in Oran. These broadcasts caused the maximum irritation to the authorities who were forced to admit that these clandestine orders were obeyed to the letter.

Reaction was naturally savage and violent. The authorities used every weapon; with complete logic they distributed fake OAS leaflets and even engineered man-hunts which were firmly disowned by the OAS. An authentic OAS leaflet said: 'The OAS will not allow man-hunts. If necessary it will shoot down publicly those who are identified as instigators.'

The OAS believed that in certain cases communists were acting as *agents provocateurs*, as the chief of intelligence noted in a report to Paris.

Naturally, too, to a certain extent each side penetrated the other which explains why, in a confused Algeria, a certain number of events heralded the thunderbolt of Pont-sur-Seine.

There is no doubt today that the police knew much of what was going on inside the OAS; similarly the OAS knew perfectly well what was afoot in the plush offices of the gaullist authorities.

The underground even monitored de Gaulle's ultra-secret telephone conversations. For their part, the police infiltrated their stool-pigeons into the clandestine organisation.

Dominique Zattara says today: 'One of the failings of the OAS men was that they were too garrulous. In the early stages, when we were forming the first teams before the *putsch*, we would meet sometimes in one person's house, sometimes in another's. There was a representative of *Jeune Nation*; there was René Villard representing *France Resurrection* and five or six other 'safe' people. Twenty-four hours after the first meeting I was visited by a childhood friend who worked in the *Sûreté Générale*. He said to me: "Dominique, you have had a meeting. Here are the names of the people there and here is what you all said." And it was all correct!'

CHAPTER 12

The Bomb in the Sand

On Tuesday, 5 September 1961 a member of the *Union Nationale des Combattants* (UNC—National Union of Ex-Servicemen), whom we will call X, returned from holiday, leaving his wife and children behind. He was visited by one of his closest friends, a senior police officer who knew that he was active in the cause of French Algeria—'I have come to warn you that you are shortly going to be arrested. The Ministry of the Interior is aware of an operation due to take place in a few days' time. It is a very serious business, the attempted assassination of the head of state. We know that two generals, one colonel and two civilians are involved. You are one of the civilians.' He was referring to an assassination attempt which was to create quite a stir a little later.

The UNC man did not know the precise details of the affair; what his friend had told him, however, showed that, even if the police did not know everything, they knew enough to take a whole series of precautionary measures.

X knew the Paris underground well and so he warned the colonel mentioned by the police whom he had every reason to suppose was involved in the attempt. The colonel thus had time to disappear. Subsequently the police arrested two officers who had had no hand in the business, once more showing the inadequacy of their information.

Undoubtedly the idea of a large-scale assassination attempt intended to do away with de Gaulle took shape in the drawing-room of some great or influential family. So, once more, we revert to those mysterious forces already mentioned. As we have seen, at the core of these forces which were uneasy at the prospects held out by de Gaulle, was a certain Catholic organisation. This formed the focus, however, for a whole gamut of authorities and personalities connected with finance, industry, politics and literature. The roots of some of these components reach back to the famous pre-war secret organisation, the *Cagoule.** Moreover, in the ante-

* A terrorist organisation active 1935–40, *Comité secret d'action révolutionnaire* (Secret committee for revolutionary action). *Cagoule* literally means a hood with eye-holes or a monk's cape with hood.

74

room, as it were, of the supreme directing agency were to be found a whole host of sympathisers and, even more important, an activist potential ready to provide the tools for action.

In the first place it must never be forgotten that, in a country's politics, vast interests are at stake. It is worth noting, for instance, that at the period we are considering, when negotiations took place between the FLN and OAS, certain Swiss, German and Italian bankers were prepared to invest five thousand milliard old francs in Algeria. These same bankers subsequently offered their services to Ben Bella's government after it had been installed, the only difference being that the situation had 'slightly changed' and they were offering only three thousand milliard.

Secondly, crises of the magnitude of the 'Algerian drama' inevitably give rise to disillusionment, animosities and despair. Men in whom these emotions have reached passionate intensity form ideal material for enterprises from which cooler heads would recoil.

These two factors combined to produce what has been called the 'Old General Staff' of the army. In particular, in this 'Old General Staff' were to be found the survivors of the former *Cagoule*; among them were the men who belonged to the 'Capital O Organisation' of 13 May 1958 set up by Dr Martin, ex-secretary and right-hand man to Eugène Deloncle, the cagoulard leader. Another was Watin, whose cover-name was 'La Boiteuse' (the Limping Woman); he was an ex-member of the Algiers counter-terrorist parties connected with Robert Martel whose political mentor had been the same Dr Martin.

Several general officers, some still on the active list, were members of the 'Old General Staff'. One incident is enough to show how widespread were this organisation's ramifications and secret affiliations: during a certain secret meeting a general commanding a military district spread out on the great drawing-room table against which the members were leaning the Ministry of the Interior's top-secret map showing the strategic points to be occupied in the event of a *coup* in order to control and secure the Ministry's secret lines to the various regions and prefects in France.

The aims of the 'Old General Staff' were both simple and specialised: unadulterated nationalism (reaching back to Maurras as its source) and economic liberalism (based on the divine right of the great magnates). The complexity of the background influences at work was to be seen on the semi-metaphysical level where catholic thinking and the cagoulard influence met—and, it must be admitted, they were *a priori* fairly antithetical. Its relationship to the 'Capital O Organisation' awoke echoes of the 'Great East' (*Orient*), although in fact there was little connection other than similarity of title. Memories of the *Cagoule* were revived by the initiation ceremonies and semi-masonic secrecy which were part of its ritual.

But thoughts alone are not enough; action is also required. And to kill a man—for that is what the problem was—killers are necessary. At this point, therefore, an officer in whom the secret circle had complete confidence but who was certainly not a full member of the inner council, was commissioned to recruit a 'team'.

This was not easy for there was the utmost confusion among activist circles in Paris. There could be no question of bringing over to Paris men from Algiers; they were required on the spot and were fully occupied in organising themselves. It was better to leave them where they were so that they could try to salvage what was still recoverable.

In Paris a certain number of groups were working on their own and out of touch with each other. They included Orsoni's little group, as we have seen, and that of Captain Sergent who had installed himself in Paris on his own initiative and set himself up as chief of staff of the OAS in France.

The colonel responsible for recruiting the team to kill de Gaulle had no confidence in these little groups, some of which, as we shall see, were fighting among themselves. He accordingly decided to form a nucleus of reliable men who, in their turn, would recruit others.

Recruitment was carried out in the best clandestine tradition: each man considered sound was watched, tested and finally recruited according to a sophisticated system of compartmentation, with the result that the police subsequently had great difficulty in penetrating the network. Moreover, they never succeeded altogether, and were brought up short at the door leading to the 'Old General Staff'.

The process of recruitment of the killers began with a search for sympathisers. This was assisted by the police who have a mania for invariably arresting a suspect. In prison the suspect meets other suspects; on occasions some of these are stool-pigeons but others are 'recruiters' on the look-out for good men. This is what happened in the case of Armand Belvisi.

He was a *pied-noir* born in Tunis in 1926. He had enlisted at the age of seventeen and had fought in France. In 1947 he joined the police and was assigned to the Bey's escort. He was then involved in the hold-up of a Post Office truck on behalf of the French underground in Tunisia and sentenced to two years' imprisonment. On his release he worked in the counter-terrorist groups attacking the Néo-Destour and at the same time for the French Embassy's 'special services', alias the SDECE. He arrived in Paris on 15 December 1959 having been expelled from his country—uprooted and disorientated, but ready to go on.

He says: 'What struck me as I left the aircraft was people's placidity and indifference and then the dark façades of the houses.'

He soon found work in the Sejac garage at the Porte d'Orléans where he regained contact with his political 'friends' of the *Front National des*

Combattants (an ex-servicemen's association); one of its leaders was the deputy Jean-Marie Le Pen and it made no secret of the fact that its primary aim was to defend French Algeria. Belvisi's contribution to the *putsch* of 22 April was merely to transport 'someone' to Orléans without knowing whom or why.

After the *putsch* he joined an embryo circuit known as *Plume* but it had no future. One of its members belonged to the communist party and he told the whole story to *L'Humanité Dimanche* which published it on 28 May 1961, with the result that Belvisi was arrested at 6 a.m. on the following Monday.

He was released a month later and was back in serious business the following week. A man named Aubry presented himself at the garage and shortly afterwards introduced him to someone else whose name he would not divulge. This air of mystery was the spice of life to Belvisi.

On 24 June he was given his first assignment. He was handed a parcel containing two blocks of TNT each of 227 grams, two detonators wrapped in cottonwool inside a matchbox and some slow-burning fuse. The parcel was accompanied by a piece of paper on which was written 'Librairie Maspero, The Joy of Reading, 20 Rue Saint-Séverin'.

If the truth be told Belvisi's first job was a lamentable failure: the night watchman discovered the bomb in time and threw it into the street. From the recruiters' point of view, however, this test had given them their answer: the jail-bird who had been reported to them had shown himself brave and worth cultivating.

A few days later he was given a rendezvous outside the Alésia church. A stranger sat down beside him in his car and simply said: 'Drive on.' After a moment the stranger, without looking at him, began to talk: 'Are you prepared to take part in a major operation, Monsieur Belvisi? I cannot tell you what it is but, if you agree, I will put you in touch with the man in charge of the operation—one of our best.'

A meeting was agreed for the following Saturday: 'Outside the church of Sainte-Jeanne-de-Chantal at the Porte de Saint-Cloud. A man will be there at 9 p.m. He is tall, fair and wears a green mackintosh. Here is the password.'

At 9 p.m. Belvisi drove slowly up to the church and saw the man. He got out of his car and went up to him.

'Are you waiting for someone?' he asked.

'No,' the man replied.

'Sorry,' Belvisi said, 'but you look like a friend of mine called Germain.'

The man signalled him to follow and they got into a green Peugeot 403 parked not far away. The other man drove calmly, his face expressionless. After a prolonged silence he decided to talk—'I need you,' he said simply. He had a great air of authority. 'I am called Germain. That is all that you will know about me. As regards the assignment for which you have been chosen you will hear details of it this evening; the rendezvous is at midnight in a small village on Route Nationale 19 five miles after Brie-Comte-Robert in the direction of Troyes. As you leave the village you will see a black Citroën Déesse, registration number 5699 HZ 75; there will be three men in it . . .'

Belvisi was uneasy but happy. He was 'in the business' once more. As he left, Germain simply said to him: 'Great things are done quietly and Algeria is something great.'

Belvisi went to the rendezvous, but he had instinctively noted the registration number of Germain's car on his cigarette packet—he too was mistrustful.

As he left the village of Coubert, Belvisi's headlights showed up the Citroën, stationary with three men inside. Leaving his headlights on he went up to the driver, his hand in his coat pocket—'Excuse me, gentlemen, but I am looking for the Nogent road.'

'It's straight on,' the driver replied without turning his head.

'Thank you. Have you broken down?'

'No, we are waiting for a friend.'

'What a coincidence! I am too. He is called Manou.'

'Who sent you?'

'Germain.'

The driver turned his head, showing his face—'I'm Manou. Get in.' Manou was very swarthy, a Mediterranean type. When Belvisi was seated beside him he introduced the two others—'Dominique, Jean-Marc.'

Dominique was sallow with a small black moustache and tight lips. Jean-Marc was young and bright-eyed; he also wore a moustache.

Manou drove off towards Provins. (In fact, Belvisi's three companions were called Henry Manoury, Dominique Cabanne and Jean-Marc Rouvière.) For a long time no word was spoken in the Citroën. Then, at Ozouer-le-Voulgis, Manoury stopped and began to talk:

'The others know about our assignment. It is a great assignment. Germain has sufficient confidence in you for me to tell you about it; then you will be free to accept or refuse. We are to position a bomb here which will kill de Gaulle.'

Another long silence during which Belvisi considered the implications of the affair. The others had said 'Yes'. Was he going to refuse? He made up his mind—'I am with you.'

Manoury held out his hand; the two others smiled at him.

The date was 24 June, six days after the 18th, of sacred memory (1940).*

The car passed through the village and halted in front of a six-foot-high sand-heap on the left of the road. A few yards before it a lane led off at right angles towards the village. Manoury explained:

* The date of de Gaulle's first radio broadcast from London to occupied France.

78

'The bomb will be placed under this heap of sand. It will be connected by 400 yards of wire to the ignition system which will be at the foot of the tree over there in the field. Ignition will be by pressing a button actuating four batteries.'

The following nights were devoted to installing the system. Belvisi suggested that the wire be laid in the nettles from the tree to the lane, then along the lane to the main road and thence hidden in the gutter as far as the sand-heap. Everyone agreed and laying began.

During the night they were frequently disturbed by passing cars which swept the countryside with their headlights, but the wire was laid nevertheless. On the second evening Manoury announced that he was leaving them: 'I have got to go on holiday for a few days. This is a long-planned holiday and it would look odd if I did not take it. I will hand you over the equipment and the bomb and then it's up to you.'

Belvisi put the equipment in the boot of his car. The bomb was impressive and very heavy—over 150 lbs—a butane gas cylinder.

The first hitch occurred on the night of 30 June when they realised that they were short of about 30 yards of wire, Manoury having planned to run it straight from the tree to the sand-heap without making a detour. Belvisi asked Aubry if he could meet Germain and once more the meeting took place according to the best clandestine tradition.

'You think that this attempt has a real chance of succeeding?' Germain began by asking.

'I am sure of it,' Belvisi replied.

After discussion Germain promised to supply the additional wire and fixed a rendezvous two days later. Before leaving, however, he put his hand on Belvisi's shoulder and said simply, 'We are blood brothers, you and I.'

The next day Belvisi and Cabanne made a trip to the sand-heap to ensure that no traces of their work were visible by daylight. A shock awaited them: a road-worker was burning the grass along the verge of the lane and he was only some twenty yards from the point where the wire joined it.

The two men watched the roadman who, at around 6 p.m., collected his tools and departed on his bicycle; his fire had stopped about ten yards from the wire. At this rate the next day would bring catastrophe: the wire would be discovered, it would be traced to the bomb and the alarm would be given. The operation would be a failure and a fresh operation would be impossible for a long time to come since additional measures for the President's security would be taken.

At midnight, therefore, they returned to the spot and dismantled the whole arrangement. Belvisi put the bomb in his car and returned to his new ground-floor flat in Paris. He decided to hide the bomb in his cellar and snatch a few hours' sleep. He had an appointment at the prefecture of police in the morning. He had in fact been seized by an irresistible desire to know who Germain really was. Knowing someone in the prefecture of police who made out car licences for his garage, he had gone to see him: 'I have a small matter to ask you. This afternoon some fellow cut in on me near the Etoile and I would like to catch him. I took his number.'

'Come back tomorrow and I'll hope to have his name for you.'

In some trepidation, therefore, Belvisi went to the prefecture the next morning—into the lion's mouth so to speak.

'Have you got my information?'

'Yes. But I advise you not to tangle with that fellow. He is a most important gentleman—Chief Engineer in the Air Ministry. He lives at 13 Avenue du Lycée-Lakanal in Bourg-la-Reine.'

'What's his name?'

'Lieutenant-Colonel Jean-Marie Bastien-Thiry.'

When Belvisi next met Germain on 5 July he was happy in the knowledge that his 'chief' was a highly-placed person; this was therefore serious business. He never divulged that he knew who Germain was; Bastien-Thiry never knew that he had done anything so crazy and there were fortunately no repercussions.

Germain was sitting in a corner of the Café Biard at the Porte d'Orléans, very upright and with a somewhat distant air.

'I have decided to change the location of the operation,' he said. 'It's too risky down there. I have chosen a better place. From the firing point you can see the road for over 3,000 yards. How many reliable men have you got?'

'Three at least. Bernard Barbance, a friend who works with me in the garage, and two Corsicans I knew in the FNC.'

'In fact we must have enough people to post a party 300 yards from the explosion; then, if de Gaulle manages to get through the explosion, he will come up against two light machineguns, sub-machineguns and grenades. What do you need for this operation?'

'A black car, military registration plates and uniforms; men in uniform will get through more easily in the panic. I must also have a blank military movement order in case of a police check.'

'I think I can get you all that. I will refer to my superiors.'

Belvisi still remembers this last sentence today: it was vital as confirmatory evidence of the fact that the order to kill the general came from higher up than a colonel. Belvisi was silent and Germain asked:

'Anything else?'

'Yes.'

'Out with it, then.'

The tone was that of a commander, of a *grand seigneur*.

'Will Madame de Gaulle be in the car?'

Bastien-Thiry fixed the young thug with his deep blue, almost opaque eyes—'She will be.'

Belvisi had difficulty in continuing to look Germain in the eye—'But we have no right . . .'

The colonel cut him short: 'We have every right when the salvation of a country is at stake. Moreover we cannot do otherwise. Your scruples do you credit, Monsieur Belvisi, but just think: Madame de Gaulle never leaves her husband. How can we attack him without touching her? My superiors and I have considered this at length. It is the only possible solution and I deplore it, but it is the price of our success.'

The new place selected for the attempt was in the Pont-sur-Seine district, at kilometre stone 158 on Route Nationale 19, just before the village of Crancey. At this point the road is dead straight for 500 yards in the Paris direction and 1½ miles in the Troyes direction. On the right of the road was a fairly large sand-heap for sanding the road in case of ice conditions.

Route Nationale 19 had been chosen by another team, the members of which are still unknown; it worked directly under the 'Old General Staff'. It had conducted a scientific study of probabilities concerning the routes used by the general. Over a period of weeks observers had noted all the routes he used on his way to Colombey. There were four: one by the south motorway—Sens—Troyes; a second via Fontainebleau—Montereau—Nogent-sur-Seine; a third via Cézanne and Méry; finally, the fourth by Route Nationale 19. Checks made over a period of four months showed a 60% probability in favour of this last route. A final point to note: this study had been ordered immediately after the failure of the *putsch*, showing that the intention to kill de Gaulle was of long standing and originated in high places.

Belvisi set about collecting the weapons required for his 'reception committee'. Aubry introduced him to a mysterious character known as 'The Tunisian', who handed him two suitcases containing a Bren gun, three German sub-machine guns, one Sten, six grenades and a Colt 11/43 together with the necessary ammunition all wrapped up in newspaper. They came from 'the south-west' or to be more exact the Bordeaux area. It is probable that a plan for assassination in this area had been worked out by Arnaud de Gorostarzu using a party organised on the spot. It is not impossible that these weapons were a present from them.

During a rehearsal organised by Belvisi the members of the assault squad arrived late and one of them seemed too 'soft'. Belvisi told Manoury, suggesting that he take the place of the man concerned. Manoury did not like the idea and talked about it to Germain in such terms that the colonel decided to cancel action by an assault squad and rely on the bomb alone.

Manoury thereupon announced his departure for his 'holiday' and the others began laying out the system. Dressed in trousers, dark pullovers and elbow-length gloves the death squad began to burrow; they had to bury their wire in the beet fields so that it could not be seen. The difficulty was that they had to do so without light of any sort because the area was extremely open and any light would have been seen miles away—that risk was too great.

Two days later, on 12 August, Belvisi reported to Germain. 'What's more,' he said, 'I need quite a lot more material to finish off the bomb.'

Germain's eyes darkened. 'I don't understand. Manoury is the man responsible for this bomb and he was to construct it. He knows about explosives, so there is no need to worry. I thought that this bomb had been finished.'

'The casing is ready but the charge is not enough. I would also like to try out the firing system by doing a trial run.'

The try-out took place on 15 August, timed to celebrate the blockade of the Bizerta base by the Tunisian army. Germain had accepted the idea and had delivered to Belvisi two charges of 500 grams of TNT. They went off in the lecture hall of Tunisia House in the University grounds in Paris.

This success gave those in the 'Old General Staff' who were calling the tune the idea of organising a series of explosions, all on the same night and at the same time so as to give the impression that a real shadow army existed. In fact during the night of 22/23 August, at precisely 1 a.m., five bombs exploded in Paris—among their targets were the government minister Jeanneney, and Gabriel Robinet, owner of the *Figaro*.

On his return from this operation Belvisi's logic told him that the police would react by arresting a certain number of suspects among whom he was bound to figure, having been arrested before. Consequently it seemed imperative that he move his 150-lb bomb to some safe place. He removed it from his cellar and put it in the boot of a Simca Beaulieu belonging to his garage. He left the Simca in a street facing the garage where he could keep watch on it. He had placed the detonators in the glove compartment.

Naturally the police arrived at the garage next morning to collect him. Belvisi refused to go with them; they had no arrest warrant. While one policeman telephoned to his chief the garage proprietor tried to intervene:

'Leave the fellow be.'

'We are merely asking him to come. It won't take long.'

'Last time it was supposed to take two hours and he was away over a month.'

The two policemen hesitated.

Belvisi kept a cool head. He had in his pocket the keys of the Beaulieu containing the bomb and associated equipment together with nearly 100 lbs of plastic. From where he was he could actually see the Beaulieu.

'All right, I'll come with you,' he said, 'on condition that I can give instructions about today's clients to one of the other salesmen. Then I would like to drop in at my house, on the way, to warn my wife.'

The police heaved a sigh of relief and agreed.

Belvisi went up to Barbance who was one of his team: 'I have to go with these gentlemen,' he said. 'Here take the keys of the car over there opposite. A client is due to come and collect it; give them to him.'

Barbance gave an imperceptible sign that he had understood.

Back at home Belvisi contrived to have a few seconds alone with his wife while the police were drinking a glass of white wine.

'Barbance will call here this evening. Tell him this: "*You are to give the car keys only to Germain and to no one else.*" '

Once more Belvisi was taking a considerable risk, for if this remark had been overheard by the police that would have been the end of the whole affair.

At police headquarters Belvisi was subjected to a routine interrogation. Then, before being transferred to Beaujon, he was permitted to telephone a friend. He called Barbance: 'I'd be happy if you went along to see my wife this evening; her morale is at zero.' Barbance would therefore get the message.

While in prison at Beaujon, Belvisi met a number of people including a certain Captain Mertz who was to play a somewhat doubtful rôle and to whom we shall be referring later. After some days Belvisi demanded to be examined by a doctor since he was suffering from a bad attack of sciatica which had hampered him considerably on the night of the bombings. The doctor intervened to secure his release which took place a few days later.

Immediately he was free Belvisi called Barbance at the garage.

'I'm really happy to hear you,' Barbance said. 'What's more, there's someone here asking for you.'

'I'll take a taxi and come.'

It was Manoury who was asking for him. He was suntanned and still in holiday garb, having been recalled by a telegram from Germain telling him, in code, that Belvisi had been arrested. So he had left his tent on Canet-Plage, where he was resting, and had come direct to the garage—yet another rash move.

He was waiting opposite the garage. 'Where is the bomb?' he asked as soon as Belvisi came up.

'You are sitting on it!'

'What?'

'Behind you. In the car you're leaning on.'

'Isn't everything in place yet?'

'I'm terribly sorry but as far as I was concerned I was on holiday at Beaujon.'

The next day, 27 August, Manoury returned to the garage and—a further indiscretion—he was not alone: Rouvière, Cabanne and Martial de Villemandy, a new recruit, were with him. They decided to begin work at Pont-sur-Seine on the 28th.

It was Monday and at 9 p.m. there were a lot of cars about. Rouvière, Villemandy and Belvisi were waiting for Cabanne who was late. They were standing beside the Beaulieu at the Porte d'Orléans.

Suddenly a police car stopped opposite them and four policemen armed with sub-machineguns surrounded them.

'What are you doing there?' the sergeant in charge asked.

'We're waiting for a friend.'

'Is the car yours?'

'No, it belongs to the garage across the road there, where I work.'

'Papers!'

The car's papers were in the glove compartment. Belvisi put an arm through the window and opened it—it contained the detonator for the bomb still in its wrapping marked 'US Army'. Belvisi quickly took out the registration book and snapped the glove compartment shut. The policemen had seen nothing. The sergeant checked the number and then said: 'Open your boot.'

His electric torch lit first upon a propane cylinder—the bomb!

'It was all you could see,' Belvisi says today. 'It looked to me out of all proportion—enormous . . . gigantic.'

'What's that?' the policeman asked.

'It's propane. We have some welding to do out in the country.'

'And this wire?' It was the wire intended to connect the bomb to the firing apparatus.

'I don't know. It must belong to the garage. The mechanics must have left it there.'

The sub-machine guns were still covering the three men.

'And *that*?'

'That' was a large block of bakelite carrying a button which was in fact the firing mechanism.

'*That?* It's a battery used in the garage to check the electric circuits of cars.' This was all said in a relaxed, almost joking, tone of voice, as if it was just a chat between friends. The sergeant nodded.

'Very good. Thank you, gentlemen. *Bon voyage!*' and he added, 'Be careful.'

They got back into their car and disappeared, leaving the three men sweating.

The police never suspected that they had been so near the bomb intended to kill de Gaulle.

On his delayed arrival Cabanne found them still shaken. He loaded into the Beaulieu the canister of napalm which he had been commissioned to manufacture and they then drove the hundred-odd miles to Pont-sur-Seine without further hitch.

But another shock awaited them: a group of gendarmes was standing beside a Juva 4 which was stopped in front of the sand-heap! They drove slowly by without being stopped and, fearing that the secret had been blown, went and hid their bomb in the cemetery of the near-by village of Crancey, behind the imposing tomb of a recently deceased ex-serviceman.

They decided to find out why the gendarmes were so interested in *their* sand-heap before abandoning this spot which seemed to them ideal for the attempt. Quite uninhibited Belvisi and Cabanne stopped the Beaulieu alongside the gendarmes—'Good evening, gentlemen. Can we help?'

'No thank you; it's not worth it.'

They were in the process of checking the papers of a motor-cyclist. Ten minutes later they were gone—it was only a routine check; the secret had not leaked.

They could now begin to instal their equipment.

The first night they buried 150 yards of wire. On 31 August came the moment to place the bomb in position. Manoury had been in charge of its construction and he had delivered it to Belvisi. Apart from Manoury no one knew the name of the craftsman who had actually made it. It was a propane cylinder, type A1 and stamped CFR (Compagnie Française de Raffinage—French Refining Company). Manoury had confirmed that it contained just under 100 lbs of plastic but, since there was still room, the empty space had been stuffed with paper.

With the bomb in position in its hole in the sand, Belvisi fitted the main detonator into the aperture which had been made in the cylinder. He pushed the stem of the detonator as far as he could into the plastic; it only remained to connect the two wires at the last moment. Beside the bomb they placed the canister which contained 15 litres of napalm. When the bomb went off the home-made napalm would be sprayed over the road and form a real barrier of flame.

Once the apparatus was in place, it remained only to carry out some tests by connecting the end of the wires to pellets of fulminate of mercury instead of to the bomb. Martial de Villemandy, who was in charge of the actual firing, installed himself in a small thicket and Rouvière came down the road in a black Citroën Déesse travelling at 70 mph. The first time the car passed Villemandy had undoubtedly found the right timing mark since the pellets exploded as the car was level with them.

'First-class!' Belvisi said. 'Let's go.'

'Wait a moment,' Villemandy gasped as he came running across the field. 'I'm not sure I found the right mark. I'd like to make another test.'

He was sweating and was clearly nervous. He had been introduced
into the team by Manoury. He was young, skinny, constantly blinking,
with a hook nose and rimless glasses—an anxious being with fragile
nerves, as the sequel was to show.

The second test was conclusive. As soon as the headlights of the car
showed up a little tree some three feet from the sand-heap Villemandy
pressed the button and the pellets exploded as the car door came level
with them.

Belvisi then asked the others to move away and began to connect up
the bomb—a delicate and dangerous operation. He connected the two
wires to the detonator, wound adhesive tape round the whole thing, and
heaved a sigh of relief. It now remained only to connect up the firing
mechanism in the thicket, and the deadly contraption was all ready to
change the policy of France.

Germain let the party know that the operation was planned for
5 September and assembled them all on the 4th in an apartment in the
XVIth *Arrondissement* of Paris. He was as imperious and impressive as
always.

'Gentlemen,' he said, 'I repeat your instructions. Dominique will be
in the café Le Bon Roi Henry in Nogent-sur-Seine and Martial in the
Beau Rivage. A certain "Monsieur Paul" will call Dominique who in
his turn will warn Martial under the name of "Monsieur Raymond".
You will then take up position on the ground. When the convoy is in
sight Dominique, who will be in a car parked not far away, will flash
his headlights twice and will at once leave Route Nationale 19 for
Route D52 and disappear. Martial will press the button at the right
moment and will leave the scene on a motor scooter which will be there,
going back to his car which will be hidden much farther away.'

Villemandy cleared his throat.

'Is something wrong?' Bastien-Thiry asked.

'Why a scooter? I could get away much quicker in my car.'

'Out of the question. You will use the scooter. That is an order.'

The colonel rose and the others did likewise: 'Gentlemen, the fate of
France is in your hands. You are living a page of our history. I know
that you will be equal to your task. In the name of France I thank you.
Good luck!'

He went out buckling himself into his green mackintosh, erect and
dignified.

All was now ready. Bastien-Thiry had provided a real relay of observers
starting at the gate of the Elysée. A couple of middle-aged 'strollers' were
to warn the second link in the chain as soon as the presidential convoy
left the palace. The real problem was to know in which vehicle General

de Gaulle was travelling, for the presidential security service, under Commissaire Ducret, invariably changed the order of the four limousines at the last moment and they were all identical.

The general's car was driven by his favourite chauffeur, Francis Marroux, with Colonel Teisseire, the general's ADC, beside him. A second limousine carried Dr Delamare, the general's personal physician, and the detectives. The third limousine was kept for personnel of the 'Official Journeys' service and the fourth, known as the 'ghost vehicle', for the police. The order of the convoy was fixed by Ducret at the last moment.

The watcher who saw the convoy leave the Elysée was to telephone the first relay post and say: 'I am ringing on the subject of the apartment. I have found one. It is on the third floor.' This meant that the general's car was No. 3 in the convoy. This information was to be passed down the chain until it reached Villemandy who would then know which car was his target. To guard against the risk of a change in the order of the convoy—always a possibility—an additional piece of information was to be passed, the number of the general's car. The watcher was to say: 'The apartment must be paid for in cash.' He was then to name a figure, as, for example, 801,000 francs. If the noughts were left off, and each of the remaining digits increased by one, this figure should give the number of the president's car—912, for instance, as was in fact the case.

On the afternoon of 5 September, Bastien-Thiry's D Day, Cabanne and Villemandy went to their posts in their respective cafés. All was ready. It was raining.

Belvisi was waiting at the garage for a telephone call telling him of the success or failure of the operation.

The hours passed but the telephone remained silent.

At about 9.30 p.m. Cabanne rushed into the garage like a tornado, his hair standing on end, and announced: 'Martial has cracked.'

All had gone well as far as Cabanne. As soon as he had been alerted from Paris he had called 'Monsieur Raymond' at the Beau Rivage but there had been no 'Monsieur Raymond' there; Villemandy was not at his post. Thinking that he had misunderstood and had gone direct to his little thicket, Cabanne stationed himself as agreed beside the road and gave his signal when he saw General de Gaulle's car coming. The convoy roared past the sand-heap and there was no explosion.

The next day, 6 September, Villemandy bravely admitted that he had taken fright. Just that. The jitters, paralysing jitters such as have afflicted even the strongest characters.

Bastien-Thiry gave much thought to the problem and together with Manoury (who had again returned very suntanned from Canet-Plage) decided to keep Villemandy in his place for the next attempt. Word was passed to the rest of the party.

On 8 September Belvisi was called to the telephone—'I am coming along for bridge as we arranged,' a voice said. This was the code announcing that General de Gaulle was once more leaving for Colombey that evening and that the assassination attempt would therefore take place. This time it *had* to succeed.

The most astonishing fact was that, although the killers' plan was now under way, General de Gaulle himself did not yet know whether he would be able to go to Colombey. In fact the conspirators' headquarters had taken a gamble—that de Gaulle would feel a physical urge to go and meditate beneath the trees of La Boisserie as he always did when things were not going the way he wished.

The liquidation of Algeria was not going according to plan; the OAS was fomenting disorder on the spot; the Evian negotiations were marking time. Difficulties had arisen between the French and Tunisians on the subject of Bizerta. Paris was being shaken by bombs and had turned into a city held in a state of siege by its own police. The farmers of Brittany were in revolt. The latest reports on Algeria seemed to indicate a veritable conspiracy against the authorities. Even the government was half-hearted, for ministers were divided. The calm and tranquillity of the forest of Colombey were more essential than ever to the general; it was in this peaceful atmosphere that he had invariably prepared his major decisions. Bastien-Thiry and his 'superiors' *knew* it and felt sure that he would take advantage of the fine weather to escape. They ordered their troops into position even while the general was still hesitating.

It was not until 5 p.m., after he had received Louis Joxe, the Minister for Algerian Affairs, that he made up his mind.

'Colonel Teisseire, I will leave for Colombey at 7.30.'

'Very good, General.'

Immediately there was a flurry of activity in Commissaire Ducret's presidential security service. The *gendarmerie* was alerted to clear the route; the Prefect of Chaumont was warned; the intelligence service was informed.

Commissaire Ducret was not anxious. His arrangements had been tightened up (all the 926 culverts on the Paris–Colombey road had been blocked up) and a veritable army of men and equipment stood ready for mobilisation. A radio network covered the entire distance all the time and it included all the vehicles, all the hospitals and all *gendarmerie* headquarters, not to mention the police, who were several hundred strong. In all, nearly 1,000 men were on emergency alert. Logically Commissaire Ducret had every reason to feel confident. He would not have been had he known that an officer of colonel's rank was passing information to the conspirators from the Elysée itself—the apple was rotten at the core.

At precisely 7.40 p.m. General de Gaulle came down the steps of the Elysée, followed by Madame de Gaulle. Francis Marroux, the chauffeur, closed the right rear door behind the general. Madame de Gaulle settled down beside her husband; Colonel Teisseire sat in front in the 'hot seat' beside the driver who moved off slowly towards the gateway.

In the next car were Commissaire Ducret, Dr Delamare the general's personal physician, and one gunman. The third vehicle, a Citroën Idée, carried the police of the *Garde Républicaine*.

The convoy, with two motor-cyclists ahead (even further ahead was a phoney convoy which was already waiting for the real one at Boissy-St-Léger), passed at walking pace in front of a few people standing aimlessly on a street corner. One of them moved off and, at about the time the procession reached the Place du Châtelet, he went into a café and snatched up the telephone. The operation was under way.

At 8.45 p.m. Cabanne de La Prade went to the telephone booth in the Bon Roi Henry.

'Monsieur Paul here.'

'I have found you an apartment. It is on the first floor but you will have to pay 801,000 francs'—in other words, de Gaulle was in the leading vehicle of the convoy and its number was 912.

Cabanne leapt into his own car and went off to join Villemandy at the Hotel Beau Rivage. The two cars moved off towards the scene of operations; Cabanne's headlights showed Villemandy moving towards the little lane; he stationed himself at the junction of Route D52 and Route Nationale 19; he now only had to watch for the convoy in his rear mirror.

Martial de Villemandy was nervous. He had been suffering from toothache all day. He arrived opposite the bush where the moped was hidden; he slowed down and hesitated. He was supposed to leave his Neckar at this point and use the motor scooter to reach the thicket some 300 yards away; that had been Bastien-Thiry's formal order. But Villemandy thought that he would be able to get away more quickly by car; he accelerated and dived down the little rutty track leading to the thicket.

He coupled up the firing mechanism and waited crouched under the trees, his field-glasses round his neck leaving the case on the ground.

Francis Marroux, behind his wheel, kept his eyes on the road. He knew it well. He also knew that the general behind him had his eyes on it too. The car was doing 70 mph. The road was straight.

Suddenly there was a frightful noise; a cloud of oil and sand erupted from the darkness. The car veered over to the left. Marroux tried to keep it straight but a wall of fire rose in front of him—the entire road was flaming. He trod on the accelerator and the car surged forward. 'Faster,' the general said.

The Déesse dived into the flames. It passed through the wall of fire and went on its way, still accelerating. In his rear-view mirror Marroux saw the barrier of fire recede. He clung to his wheel. He could also see the general, still just as erect and calm. Madame de Gaulle was equally motionless. Marroux instinctively looked at the car's clock: it was 9.35 p.m.

A few minutes later the presidential Déesse entered the Air Force barracks at Romilly and stopped. Marroux got out and examined it. The offside headlight and rear light were broken but otherwise it was intact. The general got out in his turn and without a word got into another car. Colonel Teisseire came up to him and asked: 'Is all well, General?'

'Yes. Let us go on.'

Escorted by three Air Force vehicles the car went on its way towards Colombey.

The France of de Gaulle was continuing on its way.

'When I saw the general's car disappear,' one of the gunmen said later, 'I thought that it had blown up.' The two other vehicles had had to stop in front of the wall of fire.

A general alert was issued at once. *Gendarmerie* motor-cyclists and vehicles dashed out of every barracks in the region. In a few minutes road-blocks were established on all the roads around.

The initial investigation was made by Houdet, Lieutenant of *Gendarmerie*. The roadway was covered with sand, oil, debris, melted tar and pieces of metal. The banks of the road were burnt. Half-burnt slabs of plastic were strewn about over several yards. Fragments of the bomb were found.

When he saw Cabanne flash his headlights twice Martial de Villemandy suddenly felt quite calm. A few seconds passed seeming like an eternity. Then the little tree which was his mark was suddenly illuminated. Without hurrying he pressed his button. Everything went up.

Villemandy got up, trembling now, and feverishly got into his car. He fiddled with the controls. Finally the car started. He knew that he had only a few minutes. In the distance he could see vehicles stopped at the edge of the flames and figures running in all directions. The track was terribly bumpy and the car pitched from side to side. Suddenly he missed a bend and his front wheels sank into the mud. He tried to reverse but nothing happened. He lost his head. Quickly he realised that he was not going to get out; his wheels were spinning. At that moment Villemandy felt his hair rise. Through the window, which was down, came a voice inches from his face: 'Shouldn't come this way, young fellow. Leastways not by night.'

It was a farmer called Pillet who lived near by—'I'll help you.'

With Pillet's help the Neckar was put back on the road. Villemandy, however, realised that he could not allow the man to go since he might well meet the *gendarmes*—'Come and have a glass of something. At least I owe you that.'

At the Café Centre in Pont-sur-Seine they ordered white wine. Villemandy, still overwrought, began to talk. He even referred to the explosion —unnecessarily.

'An explosion? That's what it was!'

While Villemandy went on drinking his white wine to restore his courage, Pillet and a friend went to see 'that'. They were immediately surrounded by *gendarmes*.

'You have seen nothing suspicious?'

'No. Only a fellow who had got himself stuck in the little lane. We have just drunk a glass with him in the Café Centre.'

At the café the suspect was not to be found. The *gendarmes* searched the village in vain. They returned to the café and the first man they saw at the bar was Martial de Villemandy who had realised that he could no longer leave the area since it was completely cordoned off.

He became embroiled in explanations and then, realising that he was cornered, admitted everything. The *gendarmes* discovered his field-glasses which exactly fitted a case found in the thicket—Villemandy had forgotten it in his haste.

So the police now held one of the conspirators. Pont-sur-Seine was a double set-back.

CHAPTER 13

Revelations

The rapid success of the police in the Pont-sur-Seine affair must be ascribed to chance and the clumsy behaviour of one of the conspirators rather than to perspicacity on the part of the sleuths.

As we have seen, the police did suspect that something was afoot. They alerted all the informers they had been able to infiltrate into the OAS but none of them could obtain any high-level information, only impressions and probabilities. Accordingly, the French government, using its multifarious and more or less well coordinated forces, decided to cast their net wider. This in itself amounted to an admission of impotence in face of the increasingly numerous incidents by which the OAS was demonstrating its existence.

The organisation of the clandestine movement had been tenaciously continued. On 2 September General Salan had issued from his secret command post in the Mitidja a special instruction carrying the number '1' and setting out the movement's organisation chart.

'There must be only one and the same secret army organisation for the whole of Metropolitan territory and Algeria–Sahara,' he wrote.

Accepting the *de facto* existence of an OAS at home, he nominated two representatives in France: a military representative, 'Verdun' (General Vanuxem) and 'Raphaël', a senior treasury official, for whose real name the police are still searching today.

On the same day Salan despatched a note to Captain Sergent defining the limits of his activities. The note was top-secret and entitled: 'Guideline note with a view to establishment of a plan of action.'

At the same period efforts were being made to bring into the fold the exiles in Madrid headed by Lagaillarde and Argoud. This was primarily the work of the industrialist, Maurice Gingembre (referred to earlier), managing director of the Djebel Onck Company, who travelled frequently between Madrid and Algiers. In a report drafted on 3 September, Gingembre said:

'The purpose of my journey to Tegrecigalpa [Algiers] was to see Santiago [Salan], hand him a letter from Michigan [Argoud] and persuade him to go to San Francisco [Madrid] by explaining the situation to him. . . .'

Gingembre's travels were known to the police since they were in a certain sense official. The police decided to arrest him when they judged that he would be carrying interesting documents.

At 4 a.m. on 6 September Jean Juillard, senior inspector of the *Sûreté Nationale*, went to No. 97 Boulevard Pitolet in Algers-Saint-Eugène where (in the words of his report) 'according to information communicated to us there existed a hide-out for leading personalities of the clandestine movement known as "OAS" and in particular for M. Ferrandi. . . .' The police information came from an informer named Pino, an ex-Foreign Legionary of Italian origin who styled himself the OAS representative in Tiaret. With this cover he had even succeeded in meeting General Jouhaud but without discovering his hiding-place. Working on instructions from Colonel Debrosse, commander of the *Gendarmes Mobiles* in Algiers, however, Pino had succeeded in having Albert Garcin, Salan's liaison officer, arrested. In Garcin's notebook Debrosse had discovered Ferrandi's address together with the code which would ensure that the door was opened. Hence Inspector Juillard's operation on 6 September.

In fact Ferrandi had been shadowed for several days in the hope that he would lead the police to Salan's hide-out but he had succeeded in giving his guardian angels the slip. Colonel Debrosse had therefore decided to try an operation in both Algiers and Oran. His men lit upon the hideout of Colonel Godard who had taken French leave. In the apartment occupied by Ferrandi (under the name of Catinghi) they found only a female ex-member of Salan's staff, Noëlle Luchetti, who was arrested. During their search, however, the police laid hands on important documents.

Among the papers confiscated in Colonel Godard's hide-out Colonel Debrosse found proof of Maurice Gingembre's activities. He was accordingly arrested at 10.15 p.m. on 7 September as he came off the Paris aeroplane at Maison-Blanche, Algiers.

In Gingembre's luggage the police discovered:

a note from Sergent to Godard;
a pass dated 1960 in the name of Georges Bidault, with the following in manuscript on the back: 'With confidence, 7 September 1961, G. Bidault';
a note signed 'Tennessee' (Gingembre);
various intelligence dossiers;
various notes and letters addressed to Godard from Salan;

a letter from Argoud to Salan;

a note from Godard including the following vital sentence: 'Balance (Blignières) agrees on objective No. 1 (Great Z) and says that he is dealing with the matter in earnest.' 'Great Z' (Great Zora) indicated General de Gaulle and so this discovery confirmed that something was afoot with de Gaulle as its target;

a report signed Sierra (Sergent) to Claude (Godard) handed to Gingembre by Sergent a few hours before his departure.

Gingembre and Sergent were close friends and the managing director of Djebel Onck frequently invited Sergent to his sumptuous house in Seine-Port. For Sergent, living in hiding in Paris and almost totally impecunious, Gingembre's arrival was providential. He was Colonel Argoud's representative in certain financial and political circles in Paris and he had helped Sergent and his men financially, providing them with the funds they lacked. He had even promised them a great deal more. Sergent was somewhat uneasy at Gingembre's nonchalance vis-à-vis the police; by living openly he thought that he would not be suspect.

On 7 September, the very day of his arrest in the evening, Gingembre had met Sergent in the Café Du Coq in the Place du Trocadéro. He had come from Spain carrying letters and pamphlets. After some hesitation Sergent had given him his mail for the Algiers headquarters just before Gingembre had leapt into a car to go to Orly.

The arrest of Gingembre proved to be good business for the police. They had laid hands on a whole host of highly important papers giving an insight into the organisation of the OAS and the list of cover-names used by its members.

It must not be forgotten, however, that the object of this police offensive was to obtain information concerning an assassination attempt against de Gaulle which seemed to be imminent. The result was not what the police expected: they had obtained confirmation of the attempt, but they still did not know the place, the date or the names of the perpetrators.

The curiosity of the police was due to be satisfied next day, however, because it was on 8 September that the general's car was almost blown up at Pont-sur-Seine and on the same day they succeeded in laying hands on one of the conspirators who, as a result of incredible stupidity, had allowed himself to be captured.

Naturally, it was essential that Villemandy be made to talk and he was handed over to the expert in the *Sûreté Nationale*. The interrogator quickly realised that the nervous, highly strung young man who faced him would not hold out for long. In fact, late that night Villemandy collapsed.

At the same time the Algiers police were continuing their searches and enquiries. They arrested many people and during their interrogations they were quite prepared to use extreme methods. Noëlle Lucchetti, for instance, was badly beaten up and Madame Salasc, long a liaison agent (under the name of Catherine Brune) for Colonel Godard, and wife of a well-known gynaecologist, was subjected to torture characteristic only of a totalitarian régime, including even the notorious bath-tub method. These tortures, it should be noted, were condemned by many and the press made much of them.

On Sunday, 12 November 1961, for instance, Pascal Arrighi, a Corsican deputy, caused a serious incident in the National Assembly by calling Pierre Messmer, the Minister of the Armed Forces, a 'liar'. In connection with the Salasc affair Messmer had attempted to clear a certain officer. Arrighi concluded his statement by saying: 'I ask you to realise the feelings which any citizen is likely to have towards a minister who covers up a torturer.' In support of his statement Arrighi produced depositions from reputable medical men who had examined Madame Salasc a few days after her 'little conversation' with this officer and his men. Professor Lagrot had even drafted an official report in which he listed the 'cruelties' to which she had been subjected. This report, dated 15 September 1961, spoke of 'torsion of an ovarian cyst' produced by a state of trauma and necessitating immediate 'surgical intervention'; of very many lacerations 'on the face, around the right eye and nose, on the left arm and forearm, on both thighs and both legs'; and, in particular, of 'two slanting lacerations on the thighs below the buttocks, symmetrical and apparently produced by the same method'. Professor Lagrot also referred to a 'cerebral trauma necessitating an electro-encephalogram'.

The policemen disputed the evidence. Finally the government, which was highly embarrassed, despatched its own expert who examined Madame Salasc in the presence of various doctors who had signed a protest following the statements of the police. The expert's eyes were opened and he even asked Madame Salasc whether she had been subjected to sexual assault; she stated that she had no knowledge of it.

In short it was regrettable that, in their search for information concerning an assassination attempt against de Gaulle, the police should have disgraced themselves by using methods worthy of the Nazis and should be protected in so doing by a colonel of *gendarmerie*. In face of the accusations made by members of the National Assembly and the press Pierre Messmer's feeble protestations, attempting to explain the accusations as 'a vulgar political manoeuvre', cannot invalidate the truth. It may be thought that those who made the attempt on de Gaulle's life were not particularly praiseworthy, but the use of torture against women by a government which ceaselessly proclaims its devotion to the great principles of justice, can hardly expect to be applauded by historians.

In any case these methods proved unproductive. 'No one will talk,' General Jouhaud noted, 'except Gingembre who will be persuaded into making certain revelations.'

These 'certain revelations', however, amounted to a real 'spilling of the beans' if one takes the trouble to re-read the minutes of Gingembre's interrogations, first by Inspector Gaston Boue-Lahorgue in the Tagarins barracks in Algiers and then before Judge Perez in Paris where he had been transferred.

Maurice Gingembre gave details of his contacts with all the members of OAS whom he knew; he even gave the real names of those whose cover-names he knew. Nevertheless, he tried to clear as many people as possible. The judge said to him: 'In this report you indicate that ex-Colonel Godard said to you that the only matter which counted was "to shoot down Great Zora". You have told the police that in fact this cover-name "Great Zora" indicated the President of the Republic. We would remind you that an assassination attempt against General de Gaulle took place on 8 September.' Maurice Gingembre's reply was as follows: 'I have confined myself to repeating what Colonel Godard said to me; what I can confirm is that neither Lagaillarde nor Argoud nor Sergent nor Blignières nor I was ever in favour of such action.'

For his part, Raoul Salan contrived to have a letter bearing his signature published by Le Monde on 15 September 1961; it included the following:

> Have not the depths of ignominy been reached when the story is spread that I, Raoul Salan, twice a Commander-in-Chief in the field, might have been the instigator of an attempt to murder the head of state! I would not besmirch my military past nor my military honour by ordering an assassination attempt against a person whose past belongs to our nation's history. During the German occupation both the lives and the belongings of erring Frenchmen were attacked, but in no case did the Resistance assume the right to attempt to assassinate the head of state whom France had selected. Like Marshal Pétain, General de Gaulle took office by the will and with the confidence of the nation. . . .

This historic passage was quoted at General Salan's trial and perhaps contributed to saving him from the death penalty. It would be an infallible guide to General Salan's thinking in so far as his opposition to an assassination attempt against de Gaulle was concerned, did we not know that this famous letter to Le Monde had been written—and amended—by Jean-Jacques Susini's own hand, the idea being that it might possibly be of help to Salan in the future. 'The Pont-sur-Seine attempt has failed,' Susini thought. 'Why endorse it?'

So the Algiers police were marking time; they obtained no real information from Gingembre concerning the assassination attempt. The Paris police, however, had more luck with Villemandy who cracked early in the morning and told all. Those involved in the Pont-sur-Seine attempt were now known and were hunted pitilessly; a series of arrests were made on 9 September. Arrest warrants were issued against all those who seemed to fit the cover-names elicited from Gingembre's mail. 'Verdun' (General Vanuxem) and 'Cannes' (thought to be General de Crèvecoeur) were arrested. Authors, professors and Colonel de Blignières were hauled in. An enormous spider's web was thrown over Paris; the city was literally held in a state of siege by the police.

The search naturally concentrated on the 'stars' of Pont-sur-Seine, whose names were now known to the police although, despite his confusion, Villemandy had covered their tracks as best he could.

Belvisi managed to escape two policemen who descended on his garage. Jean-Marc Rouvière was caught at home—no one had warned him. Barbance was arrested in the Dordogne in the house of a girl-friend where he was hiding. Cabanne de La Prade succeeded in crossing into Belgium but was arrested in Brussels for vagrancy (!) and extradited to France where he was sentenced to life imprisonment. Manoury was arrested only 50 miles from Colombey-les-Deux-Eglises. He had 'gone back into business' in Lyon, carrying on his clandestine activities; one day his car broke down and he had to stop at Langres in Haute-Marne, where he was arrested almost by accident.

Belvisi alone slipped through the net. This fact undoubtedly accounts for the story about the murky rôle he was reputed to have played, but which is disproved by the logic of events.

CHAPTER 14

The Mystery Explosive

The great problem which still puzzles students of the Pont-sur-Seine assassination attempt is the reason for its failure. Everything had been worked out and organised to guarantee success. Villemandy had pressed his button at the right moment to within a tenth of a second; ignition had occurred when it should. But the bomb did not explode; the napalm produced a curtain of fire but half-burnt slabs of plastic were found strewn all over the road.

The first idea which occurs to any student of these troublous times is that a third party had penetrated the circuit and had doctored the bomb. One thinks, of course, of the French secret service, the SDECE, which undoubtedly had wind of the affair and could have intervened.

This story does not hold water. The bomb contained nearly 100 lbs of plastic and was connected to a canister containing twenty litres of napalm. No secret service in the world could have taken the risk of allowing such a device to explode at half-cock beneath the wheels of the president's car. We must therefore look for some other, and infinitely more subtle, form of intervention by the SDECE.

It is best first to eliminate the other theories, in particular that based on the supposition that the detonator failed to function properly. The report drawn up at the request of M. Henry Théret, examining magistrate in the High Court of the Seine department, by two highly qualified experts is illuminating on this subject. This report by 'national experts' as they are entitled, is signed by Henri Forestier, chief engineer of the Paris Municipal Laboratory and head of the Explosives Division, and Marc Wilmet, Commander of the Legion of Honour, Doctor of Science and senior lecturer at the Ecole Polytechnique (College of Military Science). This report shows that, when 'empty', the bomb weighed 72 lbs and could only hold a maximum of 150 lbs of plastic. Even with 95 lbs of explosive it was very heavy and considerable effort was required to handle it.

The experts then considered what would have happened had the bomb exploded:

'The distance between the bomb and the vehicle is estimated at 4–5 yards. As a result, had the charge functioned normally, it would have been enough to cause serious damage to the vehicle resulting, at the very least, in serious injury to the occupants. Phenomena of this nature do not automatically produce results precisely in accordance with forecasts, however, and the above is stated subject to the proviso that the explosion took place precisely at the moment desired [which it did] and that the results of trials were regarded as entirely valid.'

In other words, and taking into account the probable side-effects described in the report (blast, the 'considerable' effect of fragmentation, stone splinters, crater 20–25 feet in diameter, etc.), General de Gaulle would have been killed at Pont-sur-Seine, had the bomb exploded.

But, the report continues, 'the results of the explosion' and in particular the discovery of bomb fragments and slabs of explosive 'prove with certainty that the phenomenon did not follow the lines of the tests mentioned above. . . . There was, therefore, no "explosion" in the proper sense of the word but a process of "deflagration" of the explosive. . . . Part of the plastic "deflagrated", thus disturbing the mechanism of the bomb, projecting non-ignited slabs of plastic, bursting the adjacent jerrican and igniting the liquid which it contained. The blast effect was much less than that which would have resulted from an explosion and the displacement of sand was comparatively small. . . .'

The report then analyses the way in which the bomb was fused using an American electrical detonator. Fusing was 'undoubtedly very defective', the experts say; they stress, nevertheless, that the electrical preparations were 'most thorough' and that the current available was 'more than adequate'.

The experts then attempt to explain the 'non-explosion' of the bomb, referring to an inadequate homogeneous charge, an inadequately resistant casing, etc. They also refer, however, to the 'high coefficient of self-excitation of plastic', this coefficient being determined by the airspace separating two adjacent slabs. They mention tests carried out with 50-gram slabs separated by an airspace of 20 cms which produced three detonations against three 'failures'.

Reading this report with its diffident, though learned, explanations it is difficult to imagine that a perfectly good American detonator, when inserted into nearly 100 lbs of plastic, would not have produced an explosion in view of plastic's 'high coefficient of self-excitation'.

The explanation must, therefore, be sought elsewhere. The clue lies on page 5, line 17 of the report—'dependent on the physical state of the explosive. . . .' Here lies the real reason for the failure of the attempt of Pont-sur-Seine.

The first step is to consider the highly unusual rôle played in all this by a highly unusual person—Colonel Fourcaud. His name only appeared officially during the trial of the Pont-sur-Seine conspirators which opened at Troyes Assizes on 29 August 1962.

The press had moulded public opinion and everyone expected to see in the dock a set of vile killers with horrifying faces and boorish manners. What they saw were men of the world—brilliant, polished, elegant, smiling.

In essence they said: 'This was a "phoney" attempt. It was organised by the gaullist authorities for the glorification of de Gaulle. Even the arrest of Villemandy was planned—why would he have hung around near the spot if he had not wished to get himself arrested? In any case we were all acting under the orders of "Monsieur Simon".'

In support of their statements one of their counsel produced a letter signed by the mysterious 'Monsieur Simon' in which he admitted that he was acting on government orders and had himself handed the bomb to Manoury. Pursuing its offensive the defence demanded evidence from two of the régime's major dignitaries, Jacques Foccart, secretary-general in the Elysée, and Alexandre Sanguinetti, specially employed in the Ministry of the Interior. For good measure, they also demanded to hear Colonel Fourcaud, long a senior officer of the SDECE, though no longer in the secret service at the time.

Jacques Foccart naturally denied all knowledge of the accused and in particular of persons not present, whose names only were known—Aubry, 'Germain' and 'Simon'.

Alexandre Sanguinetti similarly denied all such knowledge. Under pressure from the defence, however, he was forced to admit responsibility for the despatch to Canada of a captain called Mertz with a ticket provided by the Ministry of the Interior. Sanguinetti explained:

'His wife was Canadian and had found him a job out there. Accordingly we jumped at the opportunity and sent him out to get rid of him. If I had a chance of providing a ticket for all the OAS men I know, I would willingly do so.'

Undoubtedly Mertz must have been a highly embarrassing person to merit such an expenditure.

Now Armand Belvisi had made Mertz' acquaintance during his second tour in Beaujon. It has since been said that Mertz was sent there to mix with the numerous activists under arrest and try to collect information. It may be thought, moreover, that Mertz, holder of the Resistance Medal and the Legion of Honour, was the sort of man in whom Belvisi might confide—and at that time Belvisi was the possessor of a terrible secret: he was the only man who knew the location, in some Paris street, of the bomb destined for de Gaulle. Even 'Germain' (Bastien-Thiry) did not know.

Mertz belonged to the SDECE where he had worked direct under Colonel Fourcaud who was later to give evidence at the trial and disconcert the judges. There is, therefore, one possibility: Mertz may have succeeded in gaining Belvisi's confidence and Belvisi may have let slip some information on the bomb; Mertz may have told his masters in the SDECE and Colonel Fourcaud. The establishment's craftsmen may then have got to work while Belvisi was still in prison. Once the bomb had been cleverly neutralised Belvisi would have been released in time to pursue the operation in accordance with 'Germain's' plans.

This version is perfectly plausible (more fantastic things have been done). It would explain why the bomb did not 'explode' on D Day. The secret service might then have been prepared to let matters ride in order to increase General de Gaulle's popularity; he would once more be considered to have 'the luck of the devil'.

Looking at the facts, however, this story hardly holds water either. Admittedly, Belvisi was considered to be a somewhat blustering fanatic who might be prepared to divulge secrets if someone had gained his confidence. All his earlier behaviour, however, proves that he was not merely a man committed to 'French Algeria' but that he was also extremely suspicious. His determination to find out the identity of 'Germain' (who proved to be Bastien-Thiry) is enough to demonstrate this.

Armand Belvisi says today: 'I know that all sorts of stories have gone round about my meeting Mertz. In fact I was at Beaujon for three days and I saw a lot of detainees there. We talked. As far as I was concerned, Mertz was undoubtedly a supporter of French Algeria. I could not describe him otherwise. It is possible that we had stool-pigeons amongst us. We knew that and we took care. If I had talked to Mertz about Pont-sur-Seine, the reaction would have been inevitable; "they" would not have taken the fearful risk of simulating an assassination attempt and allowing nearly 100 lbs of plastic to go off five yards from the general's car. "They" ran the risk that we might check and fix the bomb again to ensure an explosion. Then, when the attempt had taken place and had officially failed, "they" would have arrested Bastien-Thiry, the head man, not merely the "extras". It is true that I managed to escape but I paid the price. I should certainly not have been retrieved by the same "organisers" in order to prepare the Petit-Clamart attempt and I was one of the leading lights of that.'

It is at least probable that Belvisi may have indicated that something was up, without giving any names or details. This may have acted as an alarm bell and would explain the feverish police activity just before Pont-sur-Seine. They arrested numerous suspects, initiated enquiries in all activist circles and arrested Gingembre on the eve of the attempt (the precise date of which they did not know).

No one can be sure that Captain Mertz was the stool-pigeon. What is certain, however, is that on the afternoon of 8 September, *the very day of the attempt*, Mertz took an aeroplane for Canada and that his ticket was handed to him by Alexandre Sanguinetti, then a close associate of Roger Frey, the Minister of the Interior.

Since Mertz' rôle remained obscure, the evidence most eagerly awaited was that of Colonel Fourcaud himself. He brought an air of mystery and adventure into the Troyes trial.

Tall, lean and good-looking, the colonel made a great impression on the jury. He had been deputy director of the SDECE and had known de Gaulle well in London, where he had served him, although he did not like him.

'This is clearly provocative action on the part of the authorities,' the colonel announced. 'In my view it was an operation organised to restore de Gaulle's prestige and he was badly in need of it at the time. This is not the first time that this sort of operation has been engineered for political reasons—from the Ems telegram to the Vaillant ʋomb. I definitely have the impression that the attempt was phoney.'

Coming after the mysterious 'Monsieur Simon' the colonel's views dumbfounded the jury. They did not accept the plea of the Public Prosecutor (who was demanding the death sentence) and allowed extenuating circumstances in the case of all the accused.

Manoury was given twenty years' imprisonment, Belvisi and Rouvière fifteen years, Barbance ten years. Cabanne de La Prade was sentenced to life imprisonment *in absentia*.

At first sight Colonel Fourcaud's rôle would seem to be that of a secret service technician who came to give his opinion (tainted with deep-rooted anti-gaullism). It is in fact far more complex than it appears.

In February 1946 Colonel Fourcaud was appointed deputy director in charge of intelligence in the SDECE. Henri Ribière, deputy for Allier, was nominated director. The same list contains the name of Pierre Sudreau who was appointed deputy director in charge of administration.

Colonel Fourcaud's mother was a Slav. He had been one of the first Frenchmen to instal himself in London in 1940. He was essentially a 'man of the shadows'. His activities were invariably those of a secret agent. During the war he was sent on a mission to France to see certain members of the *Cagoule*. He was arrested by the Vichy counter-espionage service and then released. He subsequently fought in the Resistance, was wounded and taken prisoner but then escaped. He was an extremely brave man and had great personal charm but he also had a pronounced taste for intrigue. Fourcaud was counting on becoming sole director of the secret service but he clashed with his chief, Henri Ribière, to whom he was continually presenting fanciful plans.

Fourcaud had a hand in the celebrated 'leaks affair' which, it will be recalled, originated from the disclosure to the Viet-Minh of the contents of a report on Indo-China by Generals Ely and Salan. The names of Generals Revers and Mast had been connected with this but Fourcaud had defended them. He was nevertheless forced to leave the service and undoubtedly this still rankled. He still had many secret service friends, however, and subsequently made for himself a sort of parallel career.

Everything indicates that, in the OAS *imbroglio*, Fourcaud saw an opportunity to take his revenge when the moment arrived. To prove this, note should be taken of an important document numbered '55' in the OAS secret files and dated 26 October 1961 (in other words six weeks after Pont-sur-Seine). This lifts the veil on Colonel Fourcaud's activities. The document is in fact a report sent to OAS headquarters in Algiers (where it was received and registered) from an ex-graduate of the École Nationale d'Administration (School of Administration). It refers to Colonel Fourcaud, Captain Mertz and Lauzier, whose dubious rôle in André Orsoni's planned assassination attempt at Provins has already been mentioned. Each of these people is referred to by a number corresponding to his real name in the official OAS code list.

The following are the significant passages in this report:

'Immediately after his arrest 4372185 [Lauzier], through his defence counsel, was able to warn 557–534617 [Madame Martin]. Through her he asked Colonel 81745376 [Fourcaud] to follow the matter up.

'From the outset Colonel 81745376 [Fourcaud] had supported clandestine action on the part of 4372185 [Lauzier] who was an old friend, providing him with the first 100 lbs of plastic enabling him to demonstrate OAS presence in Paris. He also assisted with information, personal files and contacts and he finally put at 4372185's disposal the members of what might be called a personal team which had been working with him for a long time—2155 [Joss], Captain 5762 [Mertz] and myself.

'Colonel 81745376 [Fourcaud] has agreed to take the place of 4372185 [Lauzier]. He has nevertheless asked 557–534617 [Madame Martin] and Doctor 815624 [Victor] for the following:

1 Formal appointment
2 General directives
3 A plan of action if possible
4 Opportunity to report

'In view of the precarious nature of communications between France and Algiers resulting in almost total isolation, I have proposed to the colonel that I should try to send him a responsible OAS officer in order to [only the most relevant clauses are quoted here]:

2 Report on the structure adopted by Colonel 81745376 [Fourcaud] for the organisation under his control.

3 Report on operations envisaged in the immediate future and obtain agreement on the advisability of these operations.

8 Organise direct contact between Colonel 81745376 [Fourcaud] and OAS headquarters in Algiers. To establish this contact I have asked 2155 [Joss], who knows him personally, and also the colonel himself to contact Madame 934675 [Gardes] and this he has done.

'Since I am now dealing with material requirements, I report that Colonel 81745376 [Fourcaud] has ordered me to request:

1 9 mm guns
2 Silencers to be fitted to them
3 Mauser carbines
4 Explosives
5 Lead-covered fuse
6 One 60 mm mortar with about ten bombs (the colonel was particularly insistent on this point) . . .

. . . [Other significant paragraphs followed]

1 Colonel 81745376 [Fourcaud] asked me to emphasise that two-way communications should be established (he asks me to report that we have here six suitcase sets but that, if radio communications are to be established, wave-length and frequency must be given).

2 He asks to be informed when he can come and make personal contact. I am busy obtaining papers for him and they will be ready shortly. He says that, if you wish, he could also go to Spain. He asks to be informed where and when contact could be made in Algiers, Oran or Spain.

3 We are *extremely anxious* [italics in original] to be put in touch with OAS elements now in Paris, particularly Y 08 [Sergent]. On this subject I will recover from Oran, where I sent them, the documents of which I spoke to Pauline [Dr Jean-Claude Perez] about a so-called OAS brigade. This is probably a provocation, hence the importance of knowing exactly who is accredited by Algiers and of exposing the *agents provocateurs*.

4 Colonel 81745376 [Fourcaud] asks that his membership of OAS be officially confirmed to him.'

This report, which is authentic, clearly shows that Colonel Fourcaud was undeniably in contact with the OAS; he himself asked for membership on 26 October 1961. It also appears that he *provided the first 100 lbs of plastic*. Finally the report shows that at that period his OAS contacts were practically nil and plastic was provided to *demonstrate the OAS presence in Paris*.

The conclusion is obvious: it was Colonel Fourcaud who provided the

95 lbs of plastic used in the bomb (the report mentions 100 lbs as a round figure) and he gave them to Manoury via one of his own men, who may well have been Lauzier.

The authors of this book have, moreover, discovered a certain ex-officer who wishes to remain anonymous. This officer was deputed by Fourcaud to house the machinegun which was to fire on de Gaulle's car if it escaped the bomb at Pont-sur-Seine. When this man gave Fourcaud full information on the plans for the attempt, he was ordered not to make himself a member of the assault squad—and accordingly he refused. As a result the second section of the Pont-sur-Seine operation (the machine-gun attack) was abandoned by Bastien-Thiry; in this he was advised by Manoury who, unless further information is forthcoming, must be assumed to be the man in contact with Colonel Fourcaud.

Bastien-Thiry relied totally on Manoury for the production of the bomb. Manoury turned to Fourcaud through one of the latter's men. The bomb was manufactured and handed over to the conspirators with Fourcaud's agreement.

There is an important detail here, however: Fourcaud did not wish de Gaulle to be killed. He did not like him but he was loath to assassinate him. In London one day de Gaulle had said: 'Fourcaud, I know that you are devoted to me, but if I asked you to shoot Pétain, you would refuse.'

Fourcaud had looked smilingly at de Gaulle: 'That's correct, General,' and he had added, 'The opposite is also correct.'

Fourcaud was probably attracted to the Pont-sur-Seine attempt by the 'lesson' which it would teach de Gaulle. He hoped to cut him down to size and show him that he was not as invulnerable as he thought. Then he also wanted his little personal revenge. Hence his far-reaching 'flirtation' with the OAS, his request for 'regular membership' and his participation by proxy in the Pont-sur-Seine operation.

The document quoted above proves indisputably that Colonel Fourcaud possessed neither weapons nor explosive since he was asking Algiers for them. Yet he provided the 95 lbs of plastic used in the bomb. The answer is that he had had this plastic for years; it came from Resistance stocks; it was old and semi-decomposed.

The man commissioned by Fourcaud to provide the plastic and manu-facture the bomb was a craftsman. Moreover Forestier and Wilmet, the experts, have admitted that the electrical preparations were 'very thorough'. They were unable to establish the 'physical state' of the explosive (their own expression), since the slabs found (some 20 lbs) were partially destroyed or had been affected by the fire.

So Colonel Fourcaud emerges as the *deus ex machina*, the man who pulled all the strings from behind. His appearance at the trial, in a commanding rôle, undoubtedly saved the accused from the maximum penalty by lending credence to the theory of the mysterious 'Monsieur Simon', said to be the organiser of the entire 'party'.

'Monsieur Simon', of course, never existed except in the imagination of the accused, though the source of their inspiration was probably a good one. At the time there was nothing so illogical in the existence of this 'Simon'. With striking unanimity the accused stated that 'Simon' had been present at a meeting with Foccart in Sanguinetti's office and that he had decided to mount a psychological offensive to open de Gaulle's eyes to the danger constituted by the OAS. Foccart had asked 'Simon' if he knew of a group which could carry out the operation and it was thus that Manoury was canvassed. The story was not illogical and the support which it received from Colonel Fourcaud paid off.

It seems probable that Bastien-Thiry never knew the precise rôle played by Colonel Fourcaud in this affair. We only know that 'Germain' bitterly regretted having entrusted manufacture of the bomb to Manoury —the latter had always maintained that he was an expert in these devices, whereas in fact he knew nothing at all about them and had to use the services of a mysterious expert who came straight out of Fourcaud's conjurer's hat.

The explanation of the failure of the Pont-sur-Seine attempt is not to be sought in the incompetence or mendacity of some individual; it is to be found in the mind of Colonel Fourcaud who betrayed nobody while betraying everybody.

One final detail to illustrate the rôle played by Colonel Fourcaud at this period. An OAS staff meeting was held in Algiers, as early as August, at which Colonel Godard proposed (the minutes of the meeting exist) that a 'chief' be appointed in France to head all the organisations; he put forward officially the name of Colonel Fourcaud. Godard even sent a long report to Salan in which he guaranteed Fourcaud's loyalty. Salan, who mistrusted the secret service on principle, refused and Fourcaud's OAS career ended there.

Godard's report was dated 20 November 1961—two months after Pont-sur-Seine.

CHAPTER 15

Rumours

When Martial de Villemandy pressed the detonator button of a bomb which might have upset French policy for a long time to come, the fate of Algeria had apparently been decided. By the referendum of 8 January 1961 the principle of self-determination for the Algerian people and the establishment of an executive in Algiers had been accepted. Pursuing his policy of accelerated disengagement, de Gaulle had opened official talks with the Algerian rebels, first in Evian, then in Lugrin.

In fact, on coming to power in 1958, even while giving his solemn promise that Algeria would remain French, he had already established secret contact with these same rebels in Tunis. The left hand did not know what the right hand was doing.

Oddly enough, however, one of his problems was the money required for this policy. Under no circumstances could the national accounts include a heading: 'Contacts with the Algerian rebels.' He decided, therefore, to use the secret vote, discreetly entitled 'Special unaccounted funds'. When he opened the till, however, he found that his predecessors in the Prime Minister's office had emptied it. The funds had been used up completely but, since they were 'unaccounted', no one could cavil at that.

In fact every year a bizarre, long-established ceremony, generally unknown to the public, takes place in the Prime Minister's study. A great log fire crackles in the huge fireplace. The master of the house receives a group of mysterious functionaries whose duty it is, each in their respective ministry, to keep the accounts of the secret funds. Each has noted outgoings and receipts in his own fair hand. Entries are, for instance: 'Paid to Colonel X—10,000 frs' or 'Paid to Ambassador Y—150,000 frs'. Each of these functionaries is bearing a fully up-to-date list of all monies disbursed. The Prime Minister, flanked by the holders of the main portfolios, then makes a little speech on the following lines:

'Gentlemen, I have assembled you so that you may present to me the accounts showing the use made of the special funds placed at the disposal of the various ministries. All I wish to do, however, is to thank you for your excellent conduct of these accounts and assure you of the complete confidence which I have in you. I therefore ask you to burn here and now the documents which you have brought with you.'

One by one the secret accountants of the State burn their lists. Thus each year milliards go up in smoke. De Gaulle's predecessors had pursued the ritual to its logical conclusion.

Early in July 1958 a special aircraft landed at Algiers airport and an official car whisked away a special emissary from Paris. His name was Pierre Brouillet. General Salan, at that time the government's Delegate-General in Algeria, was highly intrigued by this mysterious visit and he received the emissary forthwith, his ADC, Captain Ferrandi, being present.

Pierre Brouillet, an ex-ambassador, was at this time director of de Gaulle's Private Office, with Georges Pompidou to help him; he was one of the general's two confidants. De Gaulle was then still only Prime Minister (he was not elected President of the Republic and the French Community until 21 December 1958).

What Brouillet said to Salan in effect was this: 'General, we know that Robert Lacoste, your precedessor here, left you certain special funds. Six hundred million is made available to the government of Algeria annually and you still have approximately half of that. You have been more fortunate than we have, for the Matignon safe is completely empty. Now we are in the process of establishing secret contact with the rebels in Tunis and we need money. We have not even a centime to keep the Private Office running and we have not the time to wait. What can you do for us?'

Salan was an old hand. Although now aware of the new and unusual destination for this money, he felt that basically it would serve an Algeria which was still French. He asked Ferrandi to bring out the cheque-book. Then he signed a cheque drawn on the Algerian treasury for nine million; its number was 383912. Then he made out a second cheque for thirty million; its number was 383913. The two cheques were cashed through the Rothschild bank. They enabled the de Gaulle government to maintain a delegation in Tunis whose duty it was to enter into discreet talks with the rebel leaders.

The talks did not become official until 1961. The story is well known: at first they broke down because the French government refused to give up possession of the Sahara. The Provisional Algerian Government's negotiators, certain that the French would abandon this claim, refused to continue discussions. They were right; the conference had barely ended when Louis Joxe stated that 'the problem of sovereignty over an area so sparsely populated and so sterile as the Sahara is not vital'.

There was, therefore, no longer any reason for the Algerian 'rebels' to continue to boycott the negotiations, since the de Gaulle government, with the tacit agreement of the majority of Frenchmen, had announced its desire for total disengagement. This is not to say that it was right or wrong; it is merely an historical statement.

On three fronts, Algiers, Paris and Madrid, a handful of resolute men were fighting this policy of total abandonment.

In Algiers the OAS under General Salan had become an effective clandestine movement, invisible but ever present. It squared accounts with its enemies and flouted the authorities, even going so far as to steal their television masts and use them for pirate broadcasts. These broadcasts were taken very seriously by the Government Delegate; in the Algerian budget for 1961 (Vote 41–01, article 2) a sum of 250 million francs was allocated 'to finance the jamming of pirate broadcasts'.

In Paris several scattered groups were known to be working for French Algeria. Captain Sergent was trying to build up a movement but he was practically alone and did not know what the other groups were doing. The government hunted them all ferociously and gave proof of its determination by condemning Generals Salan and Jouhaud to death *in absentia*; Challe and Zeller were expeditiously sentenced to life imprisonment. The existence of the OAS was, nevertheless, confirmed by the publication in July by *Le Nouveau Candide*, a government newspaper, of extracts from the 'note-books' of Colonel Godard who was somewhere in the Algerian underground.

Salan was extremely vexed by this newspaper article. He remembered that on the night of the *putsch* he had seen Godard hand a revolver and a note-book to Marie Elbe, a journalist of the *Journal d'Alger*. Jean Ferrandi noted: 'She was obviously scared, not by the note-book but by the revolver, and hastened to hand everything over to her colleague Jean-François Chauvel of *Figaro*. The note-book must have been passed from hand to hand and finally ended up with Georgette Elgey who has just made use of it, as we know, by publishing it in *Le Nouveau Candide*.'

The article produced no special revelations; it formed part, however, of a high-powered government campaign aimed at presenting the OAS to public opinion as allied to fascism. Occasionally there came a discordant note: Jacques Soustelle, for instance, gave an interview to *Carrefour* in which he explained his reasons for leaving France 'for the second time' and prophesied 'a general civil war' if de Gaulle 'gave everything away to the FLN'.

In Madrid a hard core of activists led by Colonel Argoud and Pierre Lagaillarde urged establishment of 'unity of command' of the clandestine movement.

Such was the situation when, about midday on 9 September 1961, the news broke of the fresh abortive assassination attempt against General de Gaulle at Pont-sur-Seine. It was broadcast on the radio and repeated in the evening newspapers. The affair had been kept secret for fourteen hours.

The attempt may have been a semi-surprise for the government but it was a total surprise to the OAS in Algeria. The members of the clandestine movement's headquarters, who were in theory in command from Dunkirk to Tamanrasset, heard of the affair over the radio like everyone else.

At a staff meeting which was called at once, everyone looked crestfallen; no one knew who were either the instigators or the perpetrators of the attempt. Not a single member of the staff was in the know except perhaps Colonel Godard who, in any case, affected surprise. One may hazard a guess, however, that he had had wind of the affair through the numerous contacts he still maintained in Paris. It should be remembered that, before the April 1961 *putsch*, when he had been posted to Melun, Colonel Godard had sent a letter to Jean-Jacques Susini in which he asked whether there was a team of men available capable of mounting an assassination attempt against de Gaulle.

Another surprising fact was that Captain Sergent did not know. The attempt had been made, so to speak, under his nose and he had had no wind of it—which gives some idea of the prevailing lack of cohesion between the various clandestine movements in Paris. Any rational and impartial observer might be justified in thinking it all pathetically laughable.

Be this as it may, the abortive attempt against the head of state presented the government with an opportunity to reinforce de Gaulle's halo as a man protected by Providence. Naturally it also provided an excuse to intensify repression and take measures designed to save the threatened Republic.

Using the powers given to it by Article 16 of the constitution, in particular extension of preventive arrest to 15 days, the government continued with arrests and interrogations in an attempt to discover the truth about the attempt; it was not destined to discover it and has never done so. The judiciary—fully independent of the authorities, as we all know—assisted with enthusiasm in this inglorious chase.

Severe diplomatic pressure on the Spanish government succeeded, on 6 October, in obtaining the arrest of the OAS leaders resident in Madrid; they were deported to the Canary Islands on 26 October.

On 12 October Bobby Dovecar, one of Roger Degueldre's direct subordinates and leader of 'Delta No. 1', was arrested. Colonel Debrosse's policemen only just missed Degueldre himself, for the location of the Delta headquarters had been given away by Roger Giono, a member of the commandos known as 'Fines Moustaches' (Silky Moustache), who had also been arrested. Giono was interrogated by a policeman 'friend'; he had cracked and Degueldre had only just had time to take to his heels, having been warned by Jean-Pierre Ramas, one of his commando leaders. Bobby Dovecar paid the price—he was executed as a result of the 'information' extracted from Giono.

On the government side people were somewhat alarmed since all sorts of contradictory rumours were circulating. About this time information was received that Susini was preparing an assassination attempt against de Gaulle on the occasion of his visit to Corsica. The island was placed in a genuine state of siege. In fact Susini was fully occupied in running the OAS in Algeria and never had any intention of making an attempt on the life of the head of state, though that does not imply that he did not wish to do so.

General de Gaulle accordingly visited Ajaccio on 8 November in the midst of a crowd consisting primarily of his sympathisers and whole boatloads of police who had been landed on the island. At 2.45 p.m. he left Campo Dell'Oro aerodrome and at 3.45 landed on the naval airfield of Palivestre near Hyères.

Naturally, once more, he did not suspect who was watching him.

CHAPTER 16

Four Seconds at Hyères

The weather was inauspicious. Heavy clouds hung over the ruins of the old castle towering above the ancient town of Hyères on the hill of Castéou.

The procession, which included Berthet, the prefect, Admiral Cabanier and M. Decugis, the mayor of Hyères, moved slowly along the line of the Salins and entered the town under the railway bridge.

The town had put out its flags. Behind the barriers an average crowd, interspersed with policemen, some obvious and others less so, welcomed the general who acknowledged with a salute. The procession moved down Avenue Edith Cavell and then Avenue Gambetta. The palm trees shivered in the damp cold wind. The procession reached the Place du Portalet, the main square of Hyères and then turned to the right along the town's main highway, the Avenue du Général de Gaulle.

Standing in his presidential car the general waved to the crowd jostling on the pavements. The car moved slowly towards the town hall, a little way on on the right. The houses were decorated and beflagged as the police had requested. The convoy moved past the shops almost at walking pace.

In the shadows behind the closed shutters above a shop selling women's underwear crouched a man. He lay full-length on a cupboard, holding a Mauser repeater rifle. His eye was close to the sight. From his perch, where no one could see him from the street, he saw General de Gaulle, standing erect in his car, come into his line of vision. He followed the general's head with his foresight. His finger was on the trigger. His target was only 14 feet away—impossible to miss. It remained in his line of fire for four seconds. Then the general's head disappeared. The man had not pressed the trigger.

The man who, at 4.12 p.m. on 8 November 1961, had General de Gaulle in the sights of his Mauser for four seconds, was Albert Spaggiari. 'It was an ideal opportunity,' he says. 'I could not have missed him. Because of the angle no one could even have fired back at me from the street. I was aiming through the closed shutters. I could have fired several shots. Four seconds is a long time for a man who is used to a gun. He was as good as dead. Unfortunately I had only positioned myself there for fun. I could not fire; I had not been ordered to.'

Once more the spirit of discipline had been on the side of de Gaulle.

In 1961 Spaggiari was twenty-nine years old. He had served in Indo-China in the 3rd Colonial Parachute Battalion. He came from Nice.

After Dien Bien Phu he was involved in an affair labelled a 'hold-up' by the military; actually it was a soldiers' brawl in which his entire platoon took part. Like the rest of his platoon he was sentenced to four years' hard labour, deportation and loss of military rank—an odd punishment for a private soldier who had no rank anyway. He returned from Indo-China in the bilge of the ship and in irons.

On his release he spent two years in Senegal, returning to France in 1960 to find the Algerian problem raging. He at once took the side of French Algeria and, encouraged by friends equally determined to do something, departed for Spain in a Citroën 2 cv. In October 1961, a few weeks after the Pont-sur-Seine attempt, he presented himself at Pierre Lagaillarde's house in the Calle José Antonio.

Lagaillarde welcomed him with open arms—any new arrival from France was welcome. There was nothing suspicious about him. Spaggiari explained that he was going to live with his mother in Hyères and that he would await orders there. He asked for no contact with anyone. All he asked was that someone should arrive saying, 'There is such and such a thing to do,' and he would do it.

'Very good,' Lagaillarde said. 'I will get in touch with you. I advise you, however, if you can, to buy an ambulance. You will then be able to move about much more easily without arousing suspicion and you could be very useful to us.'

On leaving Madrid, Spaggiari knew that the ex-deputy for Algiers was aware of his address and would get in touch with him when he was needed.

After a journey of some twenty hours in his little 2 cv Spaggiari arrived at his mother's house in Hyères in the middle of the night. At breakfast next day they were chattering. She told him that the police had appeared the previous day. In view of his past history Spaggiari thought that they had come for him. In fact they had only come to ask his mother not to close her shop on 8 November and to decorate her house on the occasion of General de Gaulle's visit to Hyères.

Spaggiari immediately had the idea of killing the general. He had just arrived from Madrid where he had talked about the Pont-sur-Seine attempt with Lagaillarde. Lagaillarde, it must be admitted, had not shown himself enthusiastic about the idea of assassinating de Gaulle but he had agreed that, if de Gaulle had been killed on the road to Colombey, much would have changed and Algeria would probably have been saved.

Albert Spaggiari, therefore, immediately planned the ideal assassination. To reach the town hall the general would have to pass in front of his mother's shop since it was on the main street. Above the shop was a vacant apartment which could only be reached from the shop; it had no separate entrance. Behind it was a tiny courtyard, six feet square, and opposite the two rear windows of the apartment was an empty lodging previously used by a couple who worked as *concierges*. One of Albert's games as a boy had been to jump from one apartment to the other. Once having carried out his assassination, therefore, he had only to jump into the building in rear and disappear. He would have plenty of time before the police reacted.

This was therefore the ideal assassination: he was certain to hit de Gaulle and he had the time to make his escape. He had a fortnight in which to prepare. He had two weapons, a No. 40 sub-machine gun and a 7·92 mm Mauser repeater. After rehearsing behind the shutters he decided to use the rifle and keep the sub-machine gun for his escape. He planned to leave his Lambretta scooter in front of the building at the rear through which he would escape. In a few minutes he would be able to reach the hills which he knew like the back of his hand.

The plan was practicable. The security services were not expecting an attempt at this time or place. Every security service in the world knows that, whatever the precautions taken, the real danger comes from the lone gunman—as proved in Dallas when President Kennedy was assassinated. Like Lee Oswald, Albert Spaggiari had time to escape— there would have been several seconds of inevitable confusion on the part of the police. His experience and his qualities as a marksman left no doubt about the outcome of the operation. De Gaulle could have been killed on that chilly afternoon underneath the shivering palm trees.

As soon as Spaggiari had decided to kill de Gaulle in order to save Algeria, he took his little Citroën and dashed to Italy. He went to the main post office in Ventimiglia and despatched a letter to Lagaillarde in Madrid, using a false name; it was a registered letter and he threw the receipt stub away a few days later. He signed himself 'Gambier', the name agreed with Lagaillarde a few days earlier. In this letter he explained his plan, which seemed to him foolproof and perfectly practicable. He explained that he had everything required on the spot and only needed one thing—the order to carry on. Then he returned to Nice where he lived in No. 56 Route de Marseille. He put his weapons in order and tested them—they functioned perfectly.

The days went by and Spaggiari received nothing from Madrid. After waiting a week he despatched a second registered letter. Still no reply.

Yet he was sure that they had reached their destination; they had not been returned to the *poste restante* in Ventimiglia which he had given as an address.

On the day of de Gaulle's visit to Hyères he was back with his mother, having checked that there was still no reply and that his letters had not been returned.

Today he knows that Lagaillarde did not wish de Gaulle to be killed. He had news of Lagaillarde several weeks later. A courier arrived and said: 'I come from Lagaillarde. We know that you have an ambulance; it should be used to move a printing press which is in a certain villa.' At once Spaggiari collected one or two friends who bore a grudge as he did. They saw at once that the printing press was quite useless and came to the conclusion that the emissary from Madrid had deliberately wished to 'sink' them for no good reason.

In fact, Albert Spaggiari saw the man concerned again; he could not possibly have come from anyone else since only Lagaillarde knew Albert's plans and his address.

'Later,' Albert Spaggiari says, 'I was given away by one of the men whom I had with me. He was an extraordinary type, a real expert thief; he knew every conceivable method of breaking down a door or opening a safe. He had done six months on the Russian front in the French volunteer contingent and was arrested by the police when on the run. The police proposed a deal: either he denounced some of his mates who would be given no more than three months or he would serve the full six years due to him. Believing the police to be honest, he had no hesitation in giving us all away; he even told them where my weapons were hidden. The police only took my No. 40 sub-machine gun; fortunately my Mauser was hidden in the house of another friend. I was sentenced to four years in prison and I did three and a half. I only regret one thing —not having received the order to pull the trigger when de Gaulle passed underneath my window.'

Not knowing that for a space of four seconds he had been so close to death, de Gaulle concluded his visit without a hitch. After a speech at Hyères town hall he went to Toulon. Then next day he visited Draguignan, Le Muy, Fréjus and Saint-Raphael before returning to Marseille in pouring rain.

During a reception held in his honour in the prefecture of Draguignan he gave vent to one of his famous remarks. A deputy from the department asked him somewhat sarcastically: 'General, what do you think of this organisation which would take your life and which is known as OAS?'

De Gaulle replied drily: 'OAS? Never heard of it!'—and turned his back. Admittedly he did not know that, a few hours earlier, the Madrid branch of OAS had granted him an advance reprieve.

PART TWO

High Noon

.

CHAPTER 17

Internal Feuds

On his return to Paris from the south at 9.40 p.m. on 10 November de Gaulle found a political situation which infuriated him. During the debate on the government's Algerian policy in the National Assembly on 8 November no fewer than eighty deputies had voted in favour of François Valentin's amendment on the mobilisation of eight annual classes in Algeria. It had immediately been dubbed the 'Salan amendment' and had caught the public attention. A number of members, including Pasquini, Lefèvre d'Ormesson, Vincinguerra, Domenech and Le Pen, had made speeches amounting to a violent indictment of government policy in Algeria.

A few days later, on 16 November, the 'Vincennes Committee' which comprised the main supporters of French Algeria, among them Bidault, Lauriol, Bourgès-Manoury, Cornu-Gentil, Coste-Floret, Devraigne, Duchet, Lacoste, Malterre, Moatti, Morice, Soustelle, etc., met in the Mutalité.* The meeting was a great success; Jean Dides paid tribute to the generals imprisoned in Tulle and made an inflammatory speech.

De Gaulle realised that he must react at once. He had Dides arrested on a charge of conspiring against the Republic and insulting the head of state and on 22 November he dissolved the Vincennes Committee.

So there was no longer any real opposition in France. De Gaulle could pursue his policy in the certainty that he had outlawed those who did not think as he did on the subject of Algeria. His opponents were therefore left with only one form of action—armed revolt and subversion.

At this point there arrived in France an astonishing personality destined to act as a new broom in the OAS underground in Paris. He was André Canal, 'Le Monocle', and he carried an *ordre de mission* signed by Salan which amounted to a full-scale repudiation of Sergent's activities and those of the organisation he was attempting to form in France under the name of OAS France.

* A public meeting hall in Paris.

119

'We no longer recognised Sergent,' Captain Ferrandi explains. 'What we had against him was that, like Argoud, he had vanished from Algeria without saying where he was going. For us Sergent had become a stranger.'

In fact to OAS circles in Algeria the Sergent group seemed to be doing nothing at all. From the other side of the Mediterranean the efforts made by the ex-Captain from 1 REP to form a force in France looked futile. OAS headquarters knew that the Sergent group had had nothing to do with the Pont-sur-Seine attempt. These views were summarised in a note sent to Sergent by Salan dated 1 December; it was a real indictment of the Sergent group's 'lack of authority' and 'personal line of action'.

Canal's credentials, therefore, signed by Salan and dated 2 December, might have been thought to indicate that the head of OAS wished to restart effective action in France. In fact his motive was quite different.

The real reason for Canal's departure from Algeria was that Jean-Claude Perez, head of the Operations and Intelligence division (ORO) of OAS Algiers, had become afraid of his activities. Perez had learnt that Salan was lodging with Canal; knowing 'Le Monocle's' forceful character he thought that the latter would quickly supplant him as head of ORO. Pretending not to know that Salan was living with Canal, Perez issued a series of threats and deluged the headquarters with reports indicating that Canal should be removed.

General Salan was upset by this situation; if Canal were removed he personally would be in danger. He did not wish to clash with the staff of the OAS or create dissension in its midst. He decided, therefore, to cover Canal's departure for France by entrusting him with a somewhat vague mission. This was the famous 'Mission III' which, in the event, Canal enlarged and even exceeded.

Canal's first task was to ask General Valluy to become the leader of the OAS in France. The second part of his mission was essentially practical —fund-raising. With his fighting instinct he soon turned his mission into a commando-recruiting campaign. He immediately clashed with Sergent who had an initial meeting with him at the end of December. (Sergent's comment on hearing the new arrival's cover-name had been: '*Le Monocle?* Why not James Bond?')

On 17 December, before this meeting, Canal had come into contact with one of the Pont-sur-Seine conspirators, Armand Belvisi. This was the first genuine official contact between the OAS and any of the participants in the attempt organised by Bastien-Thiry and the 'Old General Staff'.

Via Philippe Castille, the man who had fired a bazooka at Raoul Salan's office in Algiers in the winter of 1957, Belvisi received a message through the post-box system (four people each received one quarter of a letter which they slipped through the letter-box of a fifth person who was the addressee). The message instructed Belvisi to place himself at the disposal of General Salan's emissary in France, a certain 'Victor Petit' known as 'Le Monocle'.

One of Belvisi's girl-friends was to instal herself in front of the Café de la Paix in the Place de l'Opéra, open a copy of *Jours de France*, draw a monocle round the eye of the film-star pictured on the cover and then order a cup of tea.

On meeting Belvisi, Canal showed him his credentials written in Salan's own hand. The document read as follows:

1 I commission the holder of this document, of which there is only one copy, to be my representative in France for purposes of action and finance.
2 His mission is entitled 'France III'.
3 He will coordinate all circuits now in existence under the authority of OAS. Those unwilling to place themselves under his authority, equivalent to my authority, automatically exclude themselves from OAS.

General Raoul Salan
Supreme Commander OAS
Signed: Salan
Algiers, 2 December 1961

When Canal met Sergent on 29 December he again displayed his credentials. An attempt to combine the two movements failed and thenceforth a state of semi-war existed between the two groups, each going its own way.

On his side Sergent brought off one or two spectacular operations such as the attack on communist party headquarters in the Place Kossuth. This he did with the help of Lieutenant Bernard who had come over lock, stock and barrel to the OAS a few days earlier bringing with him the equipment of his entire platoon which was training in the Lille area.

On his side 'Le Monocle' displayed great energy in recruiting personnel and organising explosions in Paris. On 4 January 1962 he despatched one of his commandos under the orders of Belvisi to raid a branch of the Société Générale. In February another branch of the Société Générale was raided in Champigny-sur-Marne. One of the members of the commando carried out a third raid on his own account. Canal had him executed in Meudon woods—they were fighting for an ideal, not for personal gain.

Realising that he was not going to be able to lead or control the 'Mission III' team, Sergent tried to use force. He arranged a meeting with Canal, the object being to do away with him.

The meeting was fixed for 8 p.m. on 3 March in Le Mysin, an American bar in the Rue Vineuse. Being suspicious, Canal arrived with some half-dozen men including Hubert Paldacci, Nicolas d'Andréa (it was he who owned a villa in Algiers run by Lucien Bitterlin—cover-name 'Dulac'—which blew up a few months later taking with it twenty-one *barbouzes* of the MPC [*Mouvement pour la Coopération*—a gaullist movement]), and an impressive personage, soon to become famous at Petit-Clamart, Georges Watin known as 'La Boiteuse' (The Limping Woman). Belvisi was also present.

For his part, Sergent had sent a gang consisting of Lieutenant Marbot, Georges Marchal and Captain Glasser, General Gardy's son-in-law and Sergent's personal assistant.

'Captain Sergent would like to see you *alone*,' Glasser said to Canal.

'Out of the question.'

'Very well. I will go and get orders. No one is to leave this spot.'

Guns were out and everybody waited.

Hours passed but Glasser did not return. About 1.30 a.m. Belvisi announced his intention of leaving.

'If one of you moves a step,' Marchal said, 'I'll shoot.'

Watin had not moved a muscle. Canal wore a distant air. The slightest movement would have been enough to turn the meeting into a shooting match.

At 7 a.m. Sergent's men, worn out with keeping their guns trained on the members of 'Mission III' and uneasy at the lack of news from Glasser, let Canal and his friends go.

About 9 a.m. Glasser returned with an operation order signed by Sergent. It was an order to arrest Canal and demand that he 'account for himself'—in fact a formal order for his execution.

While the supporters of French Algeria were engaged in these antics in France, the French government was pursuing its policy of 'disengagement' in Algeria culminating with the signature of the Evian agreements on 18 March.

In the name of France the French delegation, with Louis Joxe in the chair, recognised Algeria's independence. The new state would have ten million inhabitants including 1,600,000 Europeans and its frontiers included the Sahara. A cease-fire was to come into force next day, 19 March, and a referendum was to be organised in Algeria for the following 1 July. This time only one question was to be asked: 'Do the Algerians wish Algeria to become an independent state cooperating with France?'

From this moment the situation in Algeria was irreversible. There could be no doubt about the result of the referendum—the moslems formed the overwhelming majority and would reply 'Yes'. 'Self-determination for the people of Algeria', however legitimate it might sound, was in fact a piece of casuistry: one and a half million men were not asked what they wanted. The Europeans of Algeria were caught between eight million moslems and fifty million Frenchmen and they could only bow to the inevitable—like the population of Togo. Their lot had been settled by others. This is the explanation of their revolt and their violent efforts to change the fate imposed on them.

The motive of the assassination attempts against de Gaulle before the Evian agreements had been to save French Algeria. After the Evian agreements their purpose was only to pay off an old score with, of course, possible repercussions on French internal politics.

From the point of view of the authorities the struggle against the OAS took a similar twist. Before Evian it had been a political struggle against an organisation which advocated a policy different from that of the government. After Evian the OAS became, in de Gaulle's eyes, a sort of gang whose leaders were regarded as veritable bandit chiefs to be punished as evil-doers. French justice was meted out rapidly and, whenever it had an opportunity, the judiciary obeyed the orders of the government.

The 'paying off old scores' aspect was to be seen in the decision concerning an amnesty taken immediately after the Evian agreements. Members of the FLN were amnestied on 22 March and members of the security forces on the 23rd. Members of the OAS, however, were *not* amnestied, which resulted in the strange situation that French forces, assisted by the FLN, continued to hunt the French of Algeria who were merely supporting a policy which Michel Debré, the Prime Minister, had proclaimed for years.

This is not the place to argue the rights and wrongs. An opinion can only be formed in the light of the facts.

De Gaulle's rigidity on the subject of the amnesty became almost pathological. On 4 April 1962 G. de Benouville, a UNR (*Union pour la Nouvelle République*) deputy, tabled a motion in the Assembly calling for the amnesty granted to the moslems to be extended to French citizens. He was disowned by his party and his motion was shelved.

No amnesty was granted until 1968 and then purely for political and electoral reasons. No sooner was the ink of Evian dry, therefore, than the government's object became the elimination of those who opposed the agreements, both the underground fighters of the OAS and civilian sympathisers.

On 26 March, for instance, the army had no hesitation in firing on a crowd in the Rue d'Isly, Algiers; there were dozens of dead and hundreds of wounded. Christian Fouchet, the new High Commissioner, spoke of a 'shocking tragedy' and held an *agent provocateur* to be responsible. As far as de Gaulle was concerned he gave a television address that very evening, during which he said not a word about this savage repression although all radio listeners had heard the firing and the screams of the victims.

The same day General Jouhaud was arrested in Oran, thus giving the government an opportunity to demonstrate its 'firmness'. The wheels of justice, normally so slow, turned rapidly: nineteen days later Jouhaud was condemned to death.

Preliminary examination was completed by 3 April, more or less a record for so-called 'serene' justice. On Monday 2 April, while Thiriet, the judge, was interrogating Jouhaud, an official arrived to tell him that the date of the trial had been fixed for 11 April. So Jouhaud had only seven days in which to prepare his defence and that in a stifling unlighted cell. This was 'not very fair', General Jouhaud noted, and it must be admitted that he was not far wrong. He had to be disposed of extremely quickly—public opinion expected this demonstration of firmness from the authorities.

De Gaulle gave a brief interview to Charpentier, Jouhaud's defence counsel. He listened to him for a few minutes and then dismissed him with the words: 'I have heard you.'

In fact, he had not listened. Jouhaud's execution had to take place. General François Petiot, commander of the Versailles sub-division, was summoned by General Vezinet, Military Governor of Paris.

'Jouhaud has to be shot. You are responsible for making the arrangements.'

Petiot was shocked by this order and refused. He was at once placed under close arrest for thirty days—officially because he 'did not feel able to carry out an order stemming from a legal sentence'. General Vezinet dotted the i's—'the order concerned the execution of General [Air Force] Edmond Jouhaud'. When interviewed by Messmer, the Armed Forces Minister, Petiot explained: 'Salan has already been arrested and has been accorded extenuating circumstances. To execute Jouhaud would be a travesty of justice.'

To which Messmer replied: 'It is the decision of the court which could be a travesty of justice.'

The authorities continued their efforts to find a firing squad. The Navy was prepared to conform and furnished its contingent. General Hugo, commanding No. 2 Air Region, was shattered but obeyed. Next day, the execution having been postponed, he handed in his resignation, followed by Colonel de Saint-Péreuse, his staff officer.

Faced with this resistance de Gaulle agreed to postpone the execution and even allowed Jean Foyer, the Keeper of the Seals, to present Jouhaud's plea to the Court of Appeal. Foyer was the target for one of de Gaulle's major outbursts but he nevertheless succeeded in obtaining a further postponement of the execution, planned for the next day.

At 2 a.m. on 7 June Jouhaud was awakened in his cell in Fresnes by much coming and going in the passages; he thought that the moment had come but no one arrived. A little later he heard over the radio that it was Claude Piegts and Bobby Dovecar who had been shot at the Trou d'Enfer.

Paradoxically, Jouhaud's life was saved by Georges Pompidou. For reasons which were doubtless political the Prime Minister firmly opposed the General's decision—'Remember the execution of the Duc d'Enghien, General. This would be an error even more than a crime.'

'He must be executed,' de Gaulle growled.

'In that case, General,' Pompidou said, 'I would rather go.'

'Well then, Pompidou, you must go.'

'That I am ready to do, General, but I should warn you that I shall not do so alone. Five ministers will go with me including Giscard d'Estaing, Pisani and Foyer.'

This was the end of the famous governmental solidarity on which de Gaulle insisted so strictly. The general realised at once that he was beaten. Jouhaud would not be shot.

'Very well, Pompidou. I will let you know my decision.'

The general made Jouhaud wait a long time for his reprieve. Each morning Jouhaud expected death—an exhausting period of waiting. Finally de Gaulle was mollified by the results of the elections on 25 November and ultimately consented to sign the reprieve on 28 November, 229 days after the sentence.

It would have been at the very least strange had Jouhaud been shot when General Salan, his immediate 'commander', had managed to save his skin. Salan had been arrested a little less than a month after Jouhaud, on 20 April 1962, Good Friday.

From the beginning of 1962 Salan had been living in an apartment at the corner of Rue Desfontaines and Rue Daguerre in Algiers. He lived there almost in isolation with his ADC, Captain Ferrandi, seeing only a few intimate friends. He had become a sort of secluded Buddha, ever present, the symbol of the revolt. He invariably rejected the advice of his friends who urged him to escape to Portugal where he would have been sympathetically received. He was determined to remain with his followers hoping for some sort of political arrangement with the supporters of Messali Hadj which would enable the Europeans to stay in Algeria.

On Friday 20 April Salan came down from his fifth-floor apartment to the office which he had rented on the ground floor. He had a meeting with a man named Lavanceau, an ex-parachutist sergeant-major, sent to him by Jacques Achard. Salan and Ferrandi welcomed Lavanceau. The area seemed quiet and Salan's bodyguard had noticed nothing suspicious in the streets. Lavanceau had just handed over his 'letters of credence' when there was a knock at the door. Ferrandi looked through the peep-hole and saw several men outside.

Lavanceau was in fact a *Sûreté* agent who had been under instructions from Commissaire Parrat for several months. He had succeeded in penetrating the OAS circuit, even deceiving Jacques Achard, the former sub-prefect.

After Jouhaud's arrest Salan had realised that his turn might come. As early as 1 April he had signed a communiqué nominating Georges Bidault 'Head of OAS' in the event of his disappearance. This directive was not received with any very marked enthusiasm by Bidault; it was a somewhat embarrassing present. The ex-Prime Minister really only wished to preside over a revived National Resistance Council.

CHAPTER 18

The Deltas Go into Action

Salan had personified the 'spirit of French resistance'. With his arrest the OAS had lost its standard-bearer. A fortnight earlier it had lost its sword: on 7 April Roger Degueldre, leader of the 'Delta' commandos, had been arrested.

For the OAS this arrest was a greater catastrophe than that of Salan. Degueldre had in fact been the heart and soul of the clandestine organisation and he had undoubtedly succeeded in instilling into his teams organisation, toughness and efficiency.

Salan's arrest, which took place a few days later, was in fact only the culmination of a small-time police intrigue. It ought never to have succeeded had the higher levels of the 'shop' been better organised. A clandestine commander-in-chief should not be so accessible to someone he does not know and should not arrange to meet him twice in the same place.

The circumstances of Roger Degueldre's arrest were quite different— it was due to an extraordinary accident. The Delta leader was far too well protected and did not make such crass mistakes as those just referred to. The background to Degueldre's arrest was the fate of a group of ex-Foreign Legionaries who were caught in the *maquis* in Orléansville province. They were subjected to third-degree methods in the Hussein-Dey police school (where the methods of coercion used have unhappily become notorious) and they 'spilled' the address of another group of ex-Legionaries who were hiding in Maison Lafont above Algiers University.

OAS headquarters, warned by its police informers, immediately passed the word to the Algiers group of ex-Legionaries to evacuate their hide-out at once; it was also an important arms depot, even containing a 75mm recoilless gun.

The Legionaries accordingly prepared to depart but were in no great hurry about it—as one becomes used to living underground one relaxes and tends to consider oneself invulnerable. They were therefore arrested in their turn and their arsenal was captured.

A new round of interrogations started in the Hussein-Dey police school. One of the Legionaries revealed to his interrogators that his 'boss' was a man answering to a Spanish name and that he had gone with him one day to No. 91 or 93 in the Chemin de la Robertsau.

The police launched a 'shot-in-the-dark' operation; two Black Marias and some fifteen gendarmes took up position in the area. One of the windows of No. 93 had its shutters closed; the *gendarmes* dashed up the stairs, broke down the door with their rifle butts and burst into a totally empty apartment, the occupants having left a month earlier.

The *gendarmes* did not know that Susini had established one of his command posts only fifty yards away and that at that very moment a meeting was being held in Dr Perez' apartment in No. 91. Present at this meeting were Jacques Achard, most of the sector commanders and Roger Degueldre. The meeting realised that the police were after something in the area. But they were used to that—Algiers had long been an 'occupied' city. Some of those at the meeting decided to stay in a hide-out which had been constructed inside the apartment itself: a bookcase swung out, the section of wall behind it was movable and could be pushed back a yard on a system of rails allowing access to the next-door apartment.

Jacques Achard decided to go out despite the *gendarmes*; he considered his papers to be 'cast-iron'. In fact, he successfully passed through the police cordon and vanished into the town.

'I will do the same,' Degueldre then said. 'My papers are as good as his.'

His papers at that time were in the name of Joseph Esposito and they showed him as an inspector of primary education. He was all the more certain that this identity was valid since there was in fact an education inspector named Esposito.

Hardly had he reached the street than a policeman blocked his way. 'Papers, please,' and then, without even looking at the documents he went on, 'Lieutenant Degueldre, come with us.'

Degueldre was taken to the *gendarmerie* barracks of Tagarins. He knew that his adventure was at an end. He was hauled before Captain Lacoste who was in charge of his arrest.

'Sit down,' Lacoste said.

'No point, I have nothing to say to you. Undoubtedly I shall be shot, but you will not finish your tour of duty in Algeria. Anyway the day is not over; you will find out as soon as my men are alerted.'

They were alerted and very quickly too, for this sort of news was all over the town in a few minutes. Jean-Jacques Susini tells the story:

'We were very soon warned. I went at once to the Deltas' mobile headquarters which at that time was on the stairway of the Rue Victor-Margueritte in the centre of Algiers. We held a meeting on the spot. The first problem was to find out where Degueldre had been taken and how to get him out. We knew that, like others of our number, the Delta leader would be shot very quickly. We therefore had to mount an operation to liberate him using all our resources. If we could free him it would be a double victory, from the point of view both of action and psychological warfare. We busied ourselves with collecting equipment and alerting our commandos, while our informers fanned out into the city to try to find out where Degueldre was. He could be either in the Tagarins barracks or the Hussein-Dey police school.'

Towards midnight an informer in the SDECE brought the news that Degueldre was no longer in Algeria.

Captain Lacoste had taken to heart Degueldre's threats about what his commandos might do. He knew that they were capable of mounting, very quickly, an operation involving dozens of heavily armed men; it would be a genuine pitched battle. He ordered the Delta leader to be moved to Rocher Noir by helicopter. Thence a special aircraft took him to France.

For the Delta commandos Degueldre's arrest was a catastrophe. The weight he carried had not really been realised until he was no longer there. His absence was felt even more sorely by a woman, Nicole Gardy, with whom Degueldre was very much in love. Nicole's first thought was to continue her lover's work by taking control of the Delta commandos. She asked Gaby Anglade, one of the commando leaders, to take over. Anglade refused but suggested a sort of composite directorate consisting of himself, Jo Rizza (the man who had made the abortive attempt at Orléansville in December 1960), Nicole Gardy and Polo Nocetti. The latter was aged about thirty (but going somewhat bald); he was an assistant radio announcer and had long been a member of the counter-terrorist network. He was in charge of the Deltas' administration. So the Delta commandos (as a result of numerous arrests there were now only four totalling thirty-five men) continued in action, though their situation was becoming increasingly difficult owing to police pressure.

Nicole Gardy naturally thought first of all of organising the escape of Roger Degueldre. Susini, who was a great friend of Degueldre, approved the idea in principle, though views differed as to the method. Having done time in the Santé prison, Susini knew the ways round and considered that action by force would not succeed. He suggested that contact be made with the underworld and with certain Corsican warders. Money was required to buy up this little lot and Susini brought all his weight to bear on Colonel Gorel who had full authority over all OAS finances.

A meeting was held on the evening of General Salan's arrest and Susini obtained from Gorel a credit of 100 million which was to be passed from Algeria to France through a certain company along the 'Explosives Route'.

'Nicole,' Susini says, 'was determined to go to Paris with a commando consisting of the best Deltas. I did not agree with this method and would have preferred to negotiate with the underworld which had good contacts in the prison community. But women often react emotionally and fast. Without saying a word to me or consulting the headquarters, she left for Paris with five of the best Deltas; she left only Jo Rizza in Algiers to ensure continuity.'

When Susini heard of this, he could not help smiling. He had discussed a similar move with Roger Degueldre himself only a few months earlier. Degueldre was not prepared to stand by and watch the Paris groups failing to eliminate de Gaulle; when the Pont-sur-Seine attempt failed he had suggested that he take charge himself. He was to take with him Felicien Gardiola, known as Kiki, Jo Rizza, Gaby Anglade and Jacques Susini to handle the political side of the operation which was planned for December 1961. They were to be joined by Louis Bertolini—also known as Captain Benoît—who had most valuable contacts in the SDECE.

'We will show the Parisians how to carry out a good assassination,' Degueldre had said. 'I want you all to be completely ready for action. In the first place you must do some very intensive shooting practice. You must be able to score a bullseye on a pinhead at thirty yards.'

Every day the team went to a deserted quarry at Draria and for several hours a day the five men practised while still continuing to 'do duty' in Algiers. They became experts with the 22 carbine and the revolver which they fired from every known position. The attempt planned by Degueldre was to be made at Colombey, actually in the church.

One morning, after the normal Delta meeting when operations were allotted, Degueldre asked the other four men to wait. 'Shooting practice is at an end,' he said mournfully. 'The de Gaulle operation is cancelled. You can fall out.'

'Roger gave us no explanation,' Jo Rizza says. 'And we did not ask for one. He was very strict; if he said, "Tomorrow morning here at 6.30," one was there on the dot without knowing what one was going to do. We never referred to this matter again.'

The explanation was simple. Degueldre was in close touch with Colonel de Blignières and so with the 'Old General Staff'. When he had tried to organise his arrival in Paris he had at once clashed with the 'Old General Staff' which looked askance at the arrival of so high-powered a team as that of the Deltas. When Colonel Godard was informed by Paris he opposed the plan at once and wrote a very firm letter to Susini telling him to 'stop playing at soldiers' and 'mind his own business'. Godard, it will be remembered, had been officially commissioned by the OAS head-quarters in Algiers to organise an attempt against de Gaulle.

So, when he heard that Nicole Gardy had left with her best Deltas to try to get Degueldre out of prison, Susini looked upon it as an ironic twist of fate and did his utmost to help his friends.

In great secrecy Louis Bertolini obtained air tickets and the commando landed in Paris a few days after Easter. All had false papers which were perfectly in order; Gaby Anglade even had a police identity card in the name of Gabriel Laurent.

Before getting down to business the conspirators were tempted, on this spring Sunday in Paris, to take a stroll along the great boulevards. The shops were decorated and their display windows lighted. The good-humoured crowd seemed to have no conception that a merciless war was in progress on the other side of the Mediterranean.

Suddenly Kiki clutched at Gaby's sleeve and pointed to a newspaper kiosk. Gaby's heart stopped; in an enormous headline *Minute* proclaimed: 'Suicide commando against de Gaulle—the Elysée in a state of alert.' The news was given in further detail on page 2: 'Two Delta commandos are said to have arrived in Paris via Spain at the end of last week. Each consists of some ten men who are specialists in individual assassinations. Their mission is to strike down the Head of State even at the cost of their lives.'

Admittedly there were inaccuracies but there was also a considerable element of truth in this. Object No. 1 of the Anglade-Bertolini commando was to organise the escape of Roger Degueldre but Object No. 2 was to organise an assassination attempt against de Gaulle.

Since OAS headquarters in Algiers did not even know of their mission, they might well wonder how *Minute* had been so accurately informed of their arrival. In any case, this incident made the Delta team even more cautious and they were now suspicious of a newspaper which pretended to be on their side.

One point in the *Minute* article which was perfectly correct was the description 'specialists in individual assassinations'. Gaby Anglade, the commando's leader—he shared this position with Louis Bertolini—could in fact be described as a marvellous professional in planned specific action. He was in a way Roger Degueldre's favourite, since he was the most intelligent, the smartest, the quickest on the uptake and acted without bluster. He was very good-looking and, although still quite young—he was barely twenty-six—his hair was going grey, which earned him many female admirers and also the nickname of 'Silvery Gaby'. His upbringing had hardly marked him out to be one of the activist leaders of the OAS. His father was a militant communist and, as a boy, he had been brought up to sell communist newspapers on Sundays singing two bars of the International. When the Algerian war began he chose to defend his country rather than the principles of Karl Marx.

Louis Bertolini was also a good professional. Dark, of medium height, placid with a suntanned complexion, he was both discreet and efficient. For a long time the police only knew him under the name of 'Captain Benoît' which he had used when organising agents for the French Secret

Service. Ever since 1954–5 there had been small groups of *pieds-noirs* in Algiers who felt that the army was not being sufficiently tough with the Algerian terrorists, particularly at the start of the revolt; they had accordingly taken reprisals themselves. Finding that these counter-terrorist groups were both brave and efficient, the French Secret Service had considered using and controlling them in order to carry out operations which could not be publicly acknowledged. Their first organiser was Lieutenant Gaby Alleman but then there were one or two scandals such as the bazooka affair when General Salan was nearly killed, or the outrage in the Rue de Thèbes when a European counter-terrorist commando, on orders from the official intelligence service, placed a bomb in the Casbah, killing some twenty people. Alleman was relieved of his post and replaced by Captain Benoît, alias Louis Bertolini.

At this point Bertolini came in contact with men like Gaby Anglade, Jo Rizza and others who were working in Bab el-Oued long before there was any question of OAS. Bertolini was a shadowy figure and one of the most useful men in OAS. He was the source of the famous intelligence dossiers originating from the official intelligence service on which action by the OAS commandos was based.

Having recovered from the shock of the *Minute* revelation, Anglade and Bertolini set about drawing up their plan of action. Their first object was to get Degueldre out of the Santé prison. Felicien Gardiola (Kiki) and François Lecat, known as Fanfan, were despatched to Marseille to meet certain Corsican members of the underground who had contacts among the prison warders.

While these ambassadors were in Marseille, Anglade, Bertolini and of course Nicole Gardy contacted Roger Degueldre in prison through certain mysterious but reliable channels. On hearing of the arrival of Anglade's commando in Paris, Degueldre's first reaction was to order him 'to get the hell out of Paris' and back to Algiers, where he could be more useful to the cause. Degueldre would have preferred the commando concerned with getting him out of prison to be a purely military one; he did not wish his 'boys' to take risks in this operation when the military could deal with it.

The commando had, of course, fixed themselves with excellent lodgings. Bertolini, who was simply on leave, went to a hotel. Nicole Gardy, Gaby Anglade and Marcel Ligier lived in a flat in the Rue du Docteur-Finlay (XVth *Arrondissement*) rented by Louis Rizza, Jo's brother.

They set about establishing contact with the OAS in France, whose representative Algiers considered Captain Sergent to be. Gaby Anglade says: 'What surprised us most was that we were on duty twenty-four hours out of twenty-four whether there was a curfew or not, whereas these gentlemen in Paris took long week-ends from Friday to Monday.'

After various vicissitudes they succeeded in arranging a meeting in the square facing Saint-Augustin with d'Armaniac, assistant to Captain Curutchet, then head of the Intelligence and Operations organisation of OAS France. The men from Algiers were astonished at the air of mystery assumed and the number of precautions taken by the Paris men.

Anglade put his requests to d'Armaniac: 'We have come to get Degueldre out. Our first requirement is weapons. Then we need support —planks and cars.'

D'Armaniac shook his head—'I have great respect for Degueldre but unfortunately we have no weapons. Logistic support seems to me difficult, if not impossible. But don't worry. We are preparing an assassination attempt in earnest against de Gaulle and our "death squads" are ready for action.'

'That's great news!', Anglade said; he was always ready for action, as is shown by the fact that he had taken part, with Jo Rizza and Marcel Ligier, in all the major OAS *coups de main* in Algiers. 'All we ask is to join your team. Ask Algiers about us. You will see that you can trust us. We do not ask to be in command or provide the second-in-command. Give us something to do and it will be done.'

D'Armaniac refused—'No, it's out of the question. You are not known in the area. Let us finish with de Gaulle and we will use you afterwards. As far as Degueldre is concerned, all I can do is to give you plans of the tunnels and sewers in the Santé prison. We'll meet again later.'

Throughout the remainder of the Delta commandos' stay in Paris they never managed to meet Sergent's emissaries again.

The interview with d'Armaniac, however, merely strengthened the Deltas' determination to attack de Gaulle. Kiki and Fanfan Lecat had returned from Marseille with bad news: the Corsican underground refused to help, even for money. Some of the Corsicans belonging to the prison service had advised strongly against the operation; they considered it impossible, since Degueldre was too closely guarded by the police.

Though downcast by the realisation that they must abandon their plan for getting their leader out of prison, the Deltas immediately turned their attention to their No. 2 target, de Gaulle.

Since they could not rely upon their Parisian counterparts, they decided to mount the operation themselves; they knew that, from his cell in the Santé, General Salan would approve. A meeting between Bertolini and Nicole Gardy took place in the Hotel Astor (the owner of which later became father-in-law to Captain Ferrandi, Salan's ADC). General Salan had passed word to the Deltas to take good care of Nicole Gardy, not to frequent bars and above all to 'see what they could do with de Gaulle'.

A briefing was then held in the Rue Finlay flat. Its conclusion was that the first necessity was to obtain weapons since there were none on the spot; then the details of an assassination attempt could be fixed.

Some fifteen alternative plans were considered. One of the strangest was the poisoning of the communion host in Colombey church. De Gaulle took communion every Sunday and the affair could be quickly arranged. For men as expert as these it would have been easy to change the host in the pyx shortly before mass. The obvious objection, however, was that there was no certainty that de Gaulle would be the first to take communion; the effect of cyanide was shattering and if the first communicant collapsed, the service would be stopped and de Gaulle would not be affected.

Another idea was to doctor the butane gas containers delivered to La Boisserie, as the village of Colombey had no gas supply. This method also appeared too uncertain; it was in fact improbable that de Gaulle would be anywhere near the container when it exploded.

Yet a further plan was discussed—to make use of the medical group which invariably accompanied the general when he travelled. This section of the convoy attracted the least attention; it would be relatively easy to kidnap the members of the medical section and replace them with Deltas who would then be able to operate at close range.

After exhaustive study of all the possibilities by expert technicians the Deltas finally agreed on two plans.

The first was immediately christened 'Operation Chamois' since the idea was to kill de Gaulle with a telescopic rifle fired from a window opposite the Elysée; a bazooka would also be used to put the security personnel in the Elysée courtyard out of action. A telescopic rifle was chosen since Marcel Ligier, despatched to Paris by Paulo Nocetti, had just arrived from Algiers and he was the No. 1 Delta marksman.

Ligier was an ex-parachutist from Indo-China who had been in many battles before joining the Delta commandos. He was a Parisian but had become totally committed to French Algeria. He was cautious, methodical and his nerve was incredible. He was a real professional in the handling of weapons and explosives and a genius at manufacturing bombs; he had once even succeeded in booby-trapping a gold ingot. He could use any form of weapon from mortar to revolver. With a telescopic rifle he never missed.

The first step was to study the area round the Elysée and find, for instance, a hotel room with a view on to the main flight of steps. While the team on the spot proceeded with this task, Bertolini went to Algiers to look for light weapons. Meanwhile Anglade discovered that Fanfan Lecat was being hunted by every police force; his photograph was in every policeman's pocket and on the wall of every police station. Anglade at once decided to send him back to Algiers with the task of despatching a telescopic rifle and a bazooka.

Once alerted, Susini busied himself with the transport of the telescopic rifle from Algiers to Paris. He used for the purpose an extremely forceful woman who kept a flower shop in Algiers, wife of an ex-resistance man named Norbert Gazeux. Madame Gazeux was quite used to carrying explosives, plastic or weapons to Marseille. She was incredibly bold and did this sort of thing with a smile. She had numerous contacts and succeeded in transporting the rifle (stripped) without a hitch. She left it in an automatic left-luggage compartment at Orly airport where Louis Bertolini, who had been on the same flight, merely had to collect it.

As far as Fanfan Lecat was concerned, on arrival in Algiers he looked for Jo Rizza who was carrying on the business of the Deltas in the city. He found him in La Bressane, a restaurant he frequented in the Boulevard Saint-Saens. He was preparing for a mortar 'excursion'.

'I thought you were in Paris.'

'Gaby sent me back. They need a bazooka.'

'I've got one hidden. Let's go and get it.'

Having collected the bazooka, the next problem was to get it over to France. Armed with a note from Paulo Nocetti, the Deltas' administrator, Jo Rizza and Fanfan Lecat went to M. Pietrabiana, goods manager for Air Algeria, who agreed to help. He arranged a meeting in a garage opposite La Bressane; a tall blond chauffeur would arrive at the wheel of a Peugeot 403 and take delivery of a case containing the weapon.

Jo Rizza prepared the case himself. He laid the bazooka on a bed of straw with its two rockets well wrapped in cotton-wool. The whole case was then packed with straw. Having closed the case Rizza fixed to it a fine label on which he laboriously wrote: 'Port jet for Caravelle. Deliver to Technical Service Orly.'

The chauffeur arrived at the appointed hour and the case departed on its way. It was midday.

'Excuse me,' Jo Rizza said to Fanfan Lecat. 'I must leave you. I have to go and shoot off a mortar.'

'I've plenty of time. If you want a hand, I'm your man. I could hand you the bombs.'

'All right. I have three men with me already but you won't make too many.'

The commando took up position near the Tagarins barracks on the Blaine–Pascal road and began to fire. Twenty-five bombs hit the security forces' barracks creating great confusion. Then came the withdrawal. Rizza and Lecat went back to the hide-out from which they had taken the bazooka and put away the mortar together with its cleaning-rod and two bombs which they had been unable to fire because of the return fire of the police. Then they went to La Bressane to drink an aperitif like a couple of old regulars.

'I must go,' Lecat said. 'I'll be in touch with you. *Ciao.*'
'*Ciao.*'

Ten minutes later the café proprietor's wife came running: 'Monsieur Jo! Your friend, the one who was with you just now; he's just been arrested by the *gendarmes* at a road block.'

Rizza calmly put down his glass, went out and got into his car (he always paid for the petrol himself even when on duty); he went to the flat where Lecat and Jean-Lou Bianchi had been hiding. Not having a key, he broke open the door with his shoulder. At this moment he sensed someone behind him and his revolver was out in a flash. But he did not shoot for it was Capdelière, one of his own men who lived in the neighbourhood and had seen Rizza's car pass. Together they emptied the studio of everything—five sub-machineguns, six grenades, four 38 revolvers, one telescopic sight and even two mattresses.

This studio, located in the Lafayette building on the Boulevard Saint-Saens, had quite a history; it had hidden Ligier, Susini and Degueldre before Lecat and Bianchi.

An hour later the *gendarmes* visited the studio in their turn. They found only one word written on a window-pane in lipstick—'Greetings'.

Next day Gaby Anglade arrived at Orly airport by taxi. On the concourse a man was waiting for him—as agreed. Without a word they went off to the freight terminal. They had known each other since childhood and had been at school together; then, as chance would have it, one of them had taken a job in the technical service of Air Algeria.

A few days earlier Anglade had asked his friend: 'If a package arrives here, can one get it out?'
'Of course.'
'You wouldn't ask me what was inside?'
'I wouldn't want to know.'

At the freight terminal the package passed through customs without difficulty; since it came from Air Algeria in Algiers and was consigned to Air Algeria Orly, it was quite normal that an employee should take delivery of it; moreover it was labelled 'Caravelle jet' and so the helpful customs officials assisted in loading it; they did not wonder why a Caravelle jet weighed so little.

At 1.30 p.m. a taxi left Orly for the Rue Finlay. All was going well.

That morning Gaby Anglade and Louis Bertolini had paid a visit to a mysterious person in an office of the company which ran the 'Explosives Route'. The 100 million promised by Colonel Gorel was due to have arrived via Morocco. It had not arrived but they nevertheless left with ten million old francs.

Anglade says: 'Of this sum we only spent 100,000 francs on the purchase of several butane containers to be used in constructing a bomb.

Nicole Gardy and I had money of our own so there was no point in using the money sent by the Organisation which might well be required for something else sooner or later. Bianchi and Ligier, however, were broke; I gave them each 50,000 francs. The rest, 9,800,000 in other words, we hid in an armchair in the Rue Finlay flat. It was a very pretty Louis XV armchair and we took the seat apart very carefully. The flat had been rented furnished.'

'Operation Chamois' could now begin.

CHAPTER 19

Sitting Target

The team was ready. The equipment had been received. The only formality remaining was to fix a date. A good day seemed to be 20 May when de Gaulle was due to return to the Elysée in the evening after a tour of west-central France. He would get out of his car and go up the steps of the Elysée which meant that for ten to fifteen seconds he would be a perfect target for an expert marksman posted in a top-floor room opposite the Elysée. The choice of the firing point was therefore vital.

They agreed to try from the Hotel Bristol which is situated in the Rue du Faubourg-Saint-Honoré, not far from the entrance to the Elysée. Louis Bertolini, who was still quite legitimately on leave, took a room on the top floor of the hotel looking out onto the Elysée. Together with Anglade and Ligier he examined the possibility of firing at de Gaulle's car with the bazooka, since all three had realised at once that the Elysée steps were not visible from the window. The only possibility, therefore, was to fire at the vehicle as it entered, always provided that they knew precisely in which vehicle of the convoy the general was travelling. It was obviously risky since the marksman, however good he might be, would be at a distance of about sixty yards.

There was another possibility. The bazooka had a backsight and could therefore be used for high trajectory fire like a mortar. Provided the precise spot at which the bomb should fall could be discovered, an expert could hit it. This again was chancy, however, particularly since an observer would be required to give the signal to fire.

'We were not very keen on this plan,' Bertolini says. 'Then, while strolling along the pavement opposite the Elysée like any other passers-by we noticed that on that side all the windows of the houses were brilliantly illuminated. In particular the windows of Louis Feraud, the couturier, were all lit up. Gaby and I both had the idea simultaneously—go in, hold everyone prisoner during the operation and shoot under excellent conditions. Then, looking at the coming and going at Feraud's, we soon came to the conclusion that it was too risky—a woman had only to scream and the guards on duty thirty feet below would have been alerted. The idea was still a good one if we could find someone living alone in the neighbourhood.'

They found him next morning after chatting to an ex-member of the Women's Services named Geneviève who had been Salan's secretary in Indo-China. She told them:

'At No. 88 Rue du Faubourg-Saint-Honoré, exactly opposite the Elysée, there is a little studio belonging to a Russian painter called Portnoff. He is very old but is always delighted to welcome visitors interested in his paintings. His studio is on the fourth floor.'

From the old artist's window the view was splendid. The Elysée steps lay spread out in all their magnificence beneath the eyes of Bertolini and Anglade who had suddenly turned into enthusiastic art-lovers. They exchanged a glance of satisfaction while the eighty-year-old artist proudly showed them round his collection. The two young thugs, apparently captivated, took the measure of the spot while making flattering comments and asking the prices of the various pictures. While Bertolini was taking good note of the incomparable view offered by the two windows, Anglade was chatting to the old man—'Do you live alone here?' he asked, at the same time looking round for a cupboard in which to imprison the artist after binding and gagging him when the moment came.

Everyone agreed that it would be essential to duplicate—Ligier would fire the bazooka, at which he was an expert, and Anglade would use the telescope rifle. During a conference in the Rue Finlay flat all details were settled. A van was to be hired and from it two men would emerge in overalls and carrying pictures; their task was to put the artist out of action and, if necessary, anyone else who might be there. As soon as de Gaulle arrived the fireworks would begin.

'I was to fire first,' Anglade says. 'As soon as the general got out of his car I was to fire the telescopic rifle. At the same time Ligier was to fire the bazooka at him. I was then to drop the rifle and reload the bazooka so that Ligier could fire at the guard post. Meanwhile Kiki was to block the entrance by spraying it with sub-machinegun fire, pinning the guards down while we went down the stairs and jumped into a car which Louis would have ready at the second exit, for the building *also* had an exit at the rear.'

Bertolini adds: 'I had arranged for several cars driven by men from the SDECE—or, to be more accurate, from the Algerian intelligence service. They belonged to fringe groups and would have ensured our escape into Germany. The cars would have carried official registration plates so that they could force their way through any possible road blocks. I had all the official papers I required.'

During the conference, however, Marcel Ligier put forward an idea:

'Since de Gaulle is making a tour of central France, why not kill him during his tour? It would be easier.'

The others did not think so. During a tour the presidential security service was on the *qui vive* and enormous precautions were taken.

'Then why not at the Gare d'Austerlitz during the turmoil of his arrival?'

For form's sake they went to the Gare d'Austerlitz, where the station-master, Forsioli, was a *pied-noir*. Without making themselves known they examined the station and very soon reached the conclusion that a properly planned operation would be difficult in view of the number of people who would be there. Their professional conscience was so active that they even looked at a room in a small hotel opposite the station on the pretext of possibly taking it for a friend from the country.

Eventually they concluded that undoubtedly the idea of the old artist's apartment facing the Elysée was the best. But Ligier was pig-headed; he went on: 'On my way back to Paris I saw a little deserted wood near Etampes. Since Benoit has brought us a dozen sticks of cheddite, fifty yards of wire and a box of detonators . . .'

So off they went to consider this fresh possibility. They were well informed through Captain Caputo, an ex-engineer officer, who was in touch with a highly placed person in Citroën which maintained the Elysée vehicle park. So they knew de Gaulle's precise route. They knew that he was to take a special train from Limoges and arrive in Paris at 7.50 p.m. on 20 May. As Etampes is only some thirty miles from Paris they could calculate to within a few minutes the moment at which the presidential train would pass the little wood. It was tempting. It also had the advantage of doubling the chances of the operation succeeding. Two men could blow up the railway line while four others dealt with the telescopic rifle operation in front of the Elysée.

'Twelve sticks will not be enough,' Anglade said.

'Let's buy some butane gas bottles like the ones used for camping,' someone said; 'when it explodes butane is seven times as powerful as plastic.'

Next morning, 19 May 1962, the eve of D Day, they allocated the various commissions between them: one was to buy the gas bottles, another electric batteries, a third some wire and a fourth the necessary spades. They put all the equipment in the boot of the car hired by Bianchi.

At about 2 p.m. Anglade, Bertolini, Ligier and Bianchi left for Etampes to see if the railway track could be effectively booby-trapped. If it was possible they proposed to return that night, arranging to meet the others about 9 p.m.

All were in a serious mood, as always when action was imminent. They turned on the car radio which ground out the usual music. Suddenly, when Etampes was in sight, a special communiqué announced that Fanfan Lecat had been arrested in Algiers and was said to be involved in preparing an assassination attempt against de Gaulle.

All four were used to setbacks of this nature. Nevertheless they suddenly felt discouraged. The arrest of Fanfan Lecat might give the police the necessary clues leading to them.

'Impossible,' Anglade said. 'Fanfan does not know our addresses. I only met him in the Café d'Angleterre, on the boulevard, and, as a precaution I have never set foot there again. We are all right.'

They went on with the job. They were all tough and knew how to suppress their feelings.

After passing through the little wood under the guidance of Ligier, they found that the railway had six tracks at this point; there was no telling which of them de Gaulle's train would use.

'No matter,' Bertolini said. 'Let's put the bomb in the middle. The train will go up just the same. We'll come back tonight.'

By late afternoon they were back in Paris. Anglade ordered Bianchi to drop them at the Rue Finlay where the others were.

'Just let me go to my hotel in Rue Richer. My wife's waiting for me there. I'll only be a moment and then I'll take you all to Rue Finlay.'

The others agreed. But they could find nowhere to park and drove round the block once and then a second time. Since this seemed likely to continue, Bianchi stopped on a street corner. He got out and went towards his hotel. Automatically Anglade slipped across behind the wheel; they might have to move off very quickly and it was best to be ready for anything. Ligier and Bertolini were in the back. The street was perfectly calm.

Suddenly all hell was let loose. Several police cars emerged from all directions, sirens wailing, and blocked every exit. Anglade was about to jump out of the car when he felt a cold object on the nape of his neck and a voice said: 'Don't move.' None of them had a gun with which to defend themselves. They remained there motionless for a quarter of an hour. Then Commissaire Bouvier arrived with another commissaire. Both got into the car and forced Gaby Anglade to drive off towards the Quai des Orfèvres.

The three men were furious—twenty-four hours later and de Gaulle would have been dead.

During the journey the Deltas asked themselves what had put the police on their trail. They were used to life in the underground and had taken every possible precaution. They racked their brains but could not think of even the smallest error which they might have made.

Commissaire Bouvier himself told them the truth when he was quite sure that he had found everything out. The first clue had emerged with the arrest of Fanfan Lecat. He had been taken to the sinister Hussein-

Dey police school and interrogated forthwith. 'Who's your boss?', the police had asked him. Fanfan thought quickly; his boss was Jean-Lou Bianchi, with whom he had been living; he knew that Bianchi was in France and so out of range of the police; he could therefore give away his name and also his hide-out in Algiers since it was empty. As soon as he had given the name and address the police took him to the bed-sitter which they duly found empty. They searched it and found some apparently unimportant papers. Nevertheless one letter caught their eye; it was an affectionate letter signed 'Tania'—Bianchi's fiancée. The real reason for Jean-Lou Bianchi's departure for France had been his marriage. This, of course, the police did not know.

Bianchi had wished to get married as soon as possible and had gone to his immediate master, Paulo Nocetti. 'And you ask me that when everything's at sixes and sevens,' Nocetti had exclaimed.

'My fiancée lives in Toulouse and I simply must go there to get married.'

'All right. I'll authorise you to go but I'll give you a rendezvous in Paris where you can meet Gaby Anglade. He may need you.'

So Bianchi went first to Languedoc to get married and then started his honeymoon by joining his fellow-warriors in Paris.

The letter discovered by the police was simply that of a girl in love. It gave no particular information except one little line in the top left-hand corner—Tania's address in Toulouse where she lived with her father, Dr Peretti. At once the Algiers police sent a telegram to the Toulouse police who called on the doctor on 15 May 1962.

'You're out of luck,' the doctor said. 'My daughter and son-in-law have left for Paris.'

'We would very much like to contact them. Nothing serious, I assure you. Would you by any chance know how they left?'

'Oh, yes. They hired a car in Villeneuve-sur-Lot.'

The police quickly found the car-hire firm which gave them the type and registration number of the vehicle together with the assumed name under which Bianchi had hired it. The police machine went into action checking hotel registrations.

For his part, Bianchi met Anglade as soon as he arrived in Paris and was immediately asked, 'Are your papers in order?'

'They're perfect.'

'Where are you living?'

'I was to sleep in a cousin's house but he's not there.'

'If your papers are watertight, you can go to any hotel.'

Bianchi took a room in a hotel in the Rue Richer and saw Anglade again next day. He had bad news: he had gone to a night-club and had lost all his papers. As a precaution Anglade told him not to contact the others and arranged to meet him again on the 19th. They went to Etampes together and, as we have seen, on their return Bianchi asked that they go via his hotel to pick up his wife and pay his bill.

As soon as he entered the lobby he realised that something was not right. He tore up the stairs two at a time and, as he opened the door of his room, was greeted by 'Hands up'. His wife had already been arrested. It was the standard trap. The police, only three of them, took him down into the hall. One of them glanced through the door and saw the car, the number of which he already knew. He saw that there were three men in it. He telephoned at once to Commissaire Bouvier who initiated large-scale action.

Meanwhile Nicole Gardy, Félicien Gardiola and Eugène Castaldi were becoming uneasy at the failure of Gaby Anglade's team to reappear; they had promised to be at the Rue du Docteur-Finlay apartment at about 9 p.m. Thinking, however, that the others had decided to remain on the spot in Etampes in order to booby-trap the railway, they went peacefully to bed.

At 7 a.m. Eugène Castaldi went to the little café where they often foregathered. The proprietor had seen no one. Their only other point of contact was Jean-Lou Bianchi's hotel in the Rue Richer. They decided to go there. Nicole Gardy and Félicien Gardiola stayed some thirty yards from the hotel and Eugène Castaldi went in alone. He asked the receptionist whether M. Bianchi was there.

'One moment, please.' She took up the telephone and said: 'M. Bianchi? Someone is asking for you. Very good, sir. M. Bianchi's coming down.'

It was, of course, the police who came down. They arrested Castaldi on the spot and he emerged from the hotel under escort and handcuffed. Nicole Gardy and Félicien Gardiola watched from a distance.

'Come on, we must clear the apartment,' Nicole said.

They dashed back to the Rue Finlay, collected their belongings and the money but left the case containing the 'Caravelle jet' which was too heavy to carry. Moreover, Nicole was pregnant and very near her time. For them the struggle was over—they vanished.

At the Quai des Orfèvres Commissaire Bouvier and his assistants, Poiblanc and Pujol, soon achieved results. Fanfan Lecat's interrogation, which had put them on the trail of Anglade's team, had told them that the Deltas had gone up to Paris to organise an assassination attempt against de Gaulle. They already knew a great deal and it was not long before they knew the rest. The man who gave them most trouble was Gaby Anglade.

'You call yourself Laurent? We know that your identity card is false.'

'I do not deny that. I was condemned to death by the FLN and I provided myself with false papers in case I should be arrested by them.'

'You came to Paris to organise an assassination attempt.'

'I came to look for work, for I know that Algeria is finished.'

'Your name appears on the OAS organisation chart which I have here.'

Bouvier showed him the document which had been found in a Delta hide-out in Algiers.

'The christian name of one of the OAS leaders is "Gaby" like yours.'

'Mine is Gabriel. Anglade? Never heard of him. There are fifty of them in Algiers.'

'We know that you are a member of the OAS.'

'That's correct. My only duty was to drive people about.'

'Who?'

'Salan, Jouhaud, Susini, Perez.'

'How was it done?'

'I was in the transport business and I know the town very well. I was in a garage. The telephone would ring and someone would ask for a car to be at such-and-such a spot or such-and-such a house. I would go there and take the person where he wanted to go without asking questions.'

Bouvier was floored. Gaby's story seemed logical. But the police knew the truth; they merely lacked proof. The others continued to deny everything. In the car at the moment when they had been arrested Anglade had said to Ligier and Bertolini:

'Hold out. The others will certainly carry out the operation instead of us.'

They did hold out. But even the cleverest let slip one or two little details which, added together, give the police their information.

One morning Anglade was taken to a room in the centre of which was something which made his heart stop—the case containing the 'Caravelle jet'. So the police had found the Rue du Docteur-Finlay apartment. Then came another blow: he was confronted with the Air Algeria employee who had passed the package through customs.

'We know everything, Anglade. We know that you are in fact Gabriel Anglade, known as "Silvery Gaby". We know what you have done since you have been in Paris. You planned to blow up the railway track near Etampes and shoot at the head of state. Here is your equipment. Here are the bazooka and the telescopic rifle. You would have killed hundreds of people at Etampes. You are criminals. It is Bertolini who was the leader and organised it all.'

Anglade realised that, bit by bit, the police had found out all they wished to know. They had found the apartment and the weapons. They knew the men involved. He must at all costs clear Bertolini who had bravely taken responsibility for the entire operation and was in danger of the firing squad.

'Very well,' Anglade said. 'Since you know everything, I have nothing to add except that I was the leader of the operation.'

The case was allotted to the Court of State Security and the files were sent to the military legal department. Marcel Ligier accordingly found himself in the office of a certain Captain Dassonville of Military Security. Ligier recognised him:

'May I know your name?' he asked.

'I am the one who asks questions here,' the captain replied drily. 'You have only to answer when I question you.'

'I only asked because you are very like someone I knew in Indo-China who was not very proud of himself at the time. It was in 1952 or 1953. He was in a forward post, about to be captured and executed by the Viet-Minh. He squealed for help and sang pretty small. I arrived with my commando, cleared the area and saved the life of this man to whom you bear such a resemblance that it must be you. And today you have the nerve to interrogate me?'

The captain looked at him without a word and rang for the orderly— 'You can take him back to his cell.'

Ligier never saw him again during the preparation of the case.

All were sentenced by the Military Security Court for their two planned operations. Anglade and Bertolini, who were both held to be leaders, were given fifteen years' imprisonment, as was Jean-Lou Bianchi, against whom there was also another charge; Ligier was sentenced to ten years and Castaldi to five.

So the operation mounted on Paris ended in fiasco. De Gaulle was still alive. Had not the Delta commando, however, been neutralised by a curious combination of circumstances, it would probably have been otherwise and the general would have been killed on the steps of the Elysée. All the police admitted that the operation had been remarkably well planned and that it had every prospect of success.

As for Roger Degueldre, whose escape had been the original object, he was in prison without hope of reprieve. The Anglade commando, his last hope, had vanished. Alone he confronted the authorities who were determined to do away with him.

'Shoot "that thing" for me,' de Gaulle had said.

'That thing' appeared before a military court which quickly condemned him to death. On 29 June Lieutenant Degueldre was moved to the condemned-cell area of Fresnes, where General Jouhaud already was and whence Sergeant Dovecar and Claude Piegts had been taken to be shot on 7 June. Degueldre was under no illusions; he knew that he would be shot. He remained completely calm, however, so relaxed that his warders were astounded. His secret was a simple one; he had invented a 'double' for himself and it was this 'double' who was in prison and about to be shot. He himself, the real Degueldre, was in the scented hills of the *djebel* or the white streets of Algiers which were emptying even at this moment, disgorging into the port hundreds of thousands of people, the shipwrecked mariners of French Algeria.

On 5 July, in the evening, the governor of Fresnes prison arrived to tell General Jouhaud, himself under sentence of death, that the Delta leader was to be shot in the morning.

When woken at 2 a.m. Degueldre showed no surprise. 'I was expecting you,' he said simply to the officials who were trying to hide their emotion.

While dressing he talked quietly: 'I bear no grudge against you, Mr Judge Advocate Gerthoffer. I am merely sorry for you that you should have had to do this. I have no regrets. I can even say that I am proud to have served under the orders of General Salan and General Jouhaud, whom you will no doubt soon be visiting at this time of night. Let's go.'

At the Fort d'Ivry he confronted the firing squad in parachutist's uniform. He opened his tunic and there was a French flag covering his chest. With their rifles aimed the soldiers of the firing squad were trembling with emotion. Some of the rifles were lowered. The NCO in charge, his eyes almost closed, gave the order to fire. The first salvo rang out.

Degueldre fell but he had only been wounded by a single bullet; he was still alive. The soldiers had fired wide. The NCO took a grip of himself. It was his duty to finish off the condemned man. He held his revolver to Degueldre's temple and fired. But the shot had not been a steady one and did not achieve its object. Degueldre was still alive. He was in terrible pain but could still be saved; none of the shots had been mortal.

Seven minutes later a doctor arrived. Then the NCO made three further attempts to administer the *coup de grâce*. Each time the shot missed. Another revolver was called for. Eleven minutes had gone by before the final *coup de grâce* was administered. It had been a long process of butchery, very long, unpardonably long. One can only say, as did Degueldre's defence counsel: 'The French Army normally shoots straight.'

To the very end Nicole Gardy, the woman in love with Degueldre, had hoped against all reason to save him. A few days earlier she had sent a heart-rending letter to Jean-Jacques Susini in Algiers:

My dear Jean-Jacques,

Roger will be sentenced on Thursday by the new military court. There can be no doubt about his fate and there is no certainty that, between now and then, we can succeed in doing what we want. Elizabeth will explain to you what we are expecting from you and you can have full confidence in him. I myself am fully confident that you will do what is necessary and Roger thinks as I do.

We have a son, Philippe, born on Saturday. He is the living image of Roger. My love to you.

Nicole.

Before his death Roger Degueldre had written a little note in his cell to General Gardy, father of Nicole and grandfather of their son:

'Tell him that I died for France.'

CHAPTER 20

Exit a Conspirator

On 15 May 1962 a small man in civilian clothes and with greying hair was in the dock before the Supreme Military Tribunal. He appeared calm and relaxed. Nevertheless his fate was settled; by all the rules he would be sentenced to death and shot. Yet he was France's most highly decorated soldier—Military Medal, Grand Cross of the Legion of Honour, *Croix de Guerre*, Medal for Military Valour, American DSC, Interallied Medal, British CBE. In 1962, at the age of sixty-three, he was France's first living soldier to have been Commander-in-Chief on active service both in Indo-China and Algeria. He, Raoul Salan, had helped de Gaulle to power with his cry of 'Vive de Gaulle' on 15 May 1958. Now, almost four years later to the day, he was to be condemned because he had thought better of this cry and had pursued his ideal of a French Algeria.

From the outset of his trial Salan had no illusions. He put matters quite clearly in his preliminary statement:

'We soon realised that this attempt [he was referring to the bazooka affair] was connected with a major plot aiming at my assassination. Its instigators are those who are today demanding capital punishment for me.'

During the trial the news arrived of the arrest of the Deltas who had come to Paris to kill de Gaulle with a telescopic rifle. In Algeria, however, the OAS continued to terrorise. Streets in Algiers were on fire and running with blood. The leader was in prison and a demonstration must be made. Everyone thought it a mere formality. All observers agreed that Salan would be condemned to death. When the Military Tribunal returned to court after its deliberations everyone expected the final scene to be enacted.

On the first three counts the judges pronounced Salan guilty; to everyone's stupefaction, however, on the sixth count the reply was: 'By a majority the court considers that there were extenuating circumstances in favour of the accused, Salan.' There was a chorus of cheers; people hugged each other in public; they danced; they accosted total strangers; the *Marseillaise* was played.

The only man to remain quite still, completely calm and distant, was Salan himself despite the fact that his skin had just been saved.

When he heard the news de Gaulle was furious. He felt cheated of his legitimate revenge. His reaction was the same as Napoleon's when he heard that General Moreau, the rival who had plotted against him with Cadoudal, had been sentenced to two years' imprisonment. 'These miserable judges told me that Moreau could not escape capital punishment,' the First Consul had said in a fury. 'And then all they do is to sentence him as if he had been stealing handkerchiefs.'

Salan's sentence was heavier than that of a handkerchief-thief—life imprisonment—but it was nevertheless, in a sense, a rebuff for de Gaulle who reacted spitefully: he ordered that General Jouhaud, who had been condemned to death, although he was only Salan's second-in-command, should be executed in two days' time. The fact was announced over the radio and all preparations were made for this illogical sentence to be carried out. We have already seen how Jouhaud was saved from being shot—Pompidou and five of his ministers threatened to resign.

De Gaulle's second reaction was designed to show that he considered the chapter closed: he ordered the disbandment of the Military Tribunal. Most of the OAS leaders had now been sentenced, except for Degueldre whose fate had been settled beforehand, so the Military Tribunal had no further *raison d'être*. Apart from a few final convulsions the Algerian affair was at an end.

The general's appreciation of the situation was correct. Moreover it tallied with that of the OAS leaders still in Algiers. As early as 27 May the daily OAS pirate broadcast revealed that the heads of the clandestine organisation had been forced to concede that Algeria would not be French.

'Peace can only return to this country,' the OAS spokesman declared, 'if all those who consider Algeria to be their genuine home agree among themselves. Otherwise Algeria will go down in chaos. Secret contacts are being made between the OAS, the provisional executive and the FLN. Do not lose either hope or courage.'

The first contact between the OAS and the 'rebels' had taken place on 10 May 1962. On 18 May Jean-Jacques Susini and Colonel Broizat met Abderhaman Fares near the village of Alma. Their first concern was postponement of the date for the referendum on self-determination which had been fixed for 1 July.

'After Salan's arrest,' Susini says, 'we were forced to concede that Algeria would be independent. This was the subject of a dramatic conversation between me and Colonel Godard. I said to him: "We do not agree. You are the oldest and most senior officer. You take command

and I will join a Delta commando." Godard shook his head. "No," he replied, "it is too late now. You keep the strings. You must now carry these negotiations with the FLN through to the end. If you succeed, I shall say that you are a great man. If you fail, I shall say that you are a traitor." I then said to him: "I am ready to stall these negotiations. Have you an alternative solution?" "The only possible solution is to keep the pot boiling with these negotiations," Godard replied, "and move to insurrection on 1 July." His idea would have been a good one if we had been able to implement it. "What with?" I asked. "We have nothing any more. Even our commandos have no weapons. At this moment we have precisely 35 mortar bombs left. We have practically no ammunition for our sub-machine guns or revolvers. The height of irony is that we, the OAS, have run out of plastic." '

It was in effect the end. A letter written by Salan from prison set the seal upon it: 'My friends who have stood by me over the last two months should know that they have my complete agreement in accepting the fact that fighting must cease,' and he added: 'Faced with the choice between an exodus and life in the country of their birth, I advise Europeans to remain in their country.'

His advice was not followed. A piteous exodus began. Under a leaden sky endless queues moved slowly towards the port where the boats were filled to their gunwales; Algiers was left empty, echoing to the shouts of the moslems. People were killed, wounded, trampled on, clubbed with rifle butts. As if to underline the general's ill-will, the police searched the exiles' scanty luggage to ensure that it concealed no gun. They did not know that even the Delta commandos were out of ammunition and could no longer fire.

Equally, however, they did not know that the men of OAS had methods of leaving Algeria which did not involve queueing for two days to find some small corner on a ship like the *Kairouan*. The OAS had always been able to count on extremely reliable secret lines of communication; they could move anybody and anything across the Mediterranean. So, under the very noses of the police, an incredible colonels' quickstep took place. Colonel Godard himself, though sentenced to death *in absentia*, departed in a French Air Force aircraft. Serving officers and OAS officers were, so to speak, in league. From Colonel Dufour to Colonel Château-Jobert everyone travelled quite peacefully, thanks primarily to certain senior officers of the Navy and other services.

The sections of the OAS which left Algeria at this time did so in uniform and with official documents, thanks to under-cover assistance. Between 15 June and 1 July all the OAS action groups left in good order, echelon by echelon, following a carefully prepared plan to the letter. During all this time the *gardes mobiles* and the CRS were ripping open the shabby bags of émigrés who had lost everything. Some sections of the OAS even took their cars back to France with their weapons (without ammunition) concealed in the boot. The OAS radio squads alone left with 25 cars and 7 trucks. Not a single sub-machinegun was left on Algerian soil.

The French government had said again and again that it estimated at 100,000 the number of Algerian French who would ask to be repatriated. By 20 June the figure was already 650,000. By 1 August it had reached 1,400,000 including moslems wishing to remain French and the Jews to whom the Arabs had given twenty-four hours' notice to leave. In fact, the last of them left Algeria on 29 June on board the *El Mabrouk*.

On 1 July Algeria officially became independent. Only four indomitable men remained in Algiers: Susini, Dominique Liedo, Salan's ex-chauffeur, Colonel Broizat and Jean Garcia, Susini's secretary, today a radio announcer in Geneva.

Susini was not yet prepared to give up. As the days went by, however, the Provisional Algerian Government (the GPRA), with which he had negotiated, tended to lose ground to the Liberation Army (the ALN) which arrived victorious with its brand-new weapons without having fired a single shot. Susini was hunted all over the city but this clandestine genius slipped through the net every time. Not until he was certain that the ALN was definitely in charge did he decide to leave Algeria. On 30 July, his twenty-ninth birthday, he landed in Italy.

The OAS no longer existed. Its place was taken by the National Resistance Council (the CNR) under the chairmanship of Georges Bidault.

Algiers having failed, Paris tried to take up the running. In less than four months there were some ten assassination attempts against de Gaulle culminating in the affair of Petit-Clamart on 8 August 1962. They were not the work of OAS France, however—few members of the Paris branch even knew about them.

At this point the French network had been to all intents and purposes destroyed or neutralised by the police. 'Mission III', its most active component, had lost its leader when André Canal, 'Le Monocle', was arrested on 4 May. An anonymous telephone call warned the police that the head of 'Mission III' was due to meet one of his men at 4 p.m. on the steps of Batignolles church. (The call can only have come from someone well informed on 'Le Monocle's' doings, no doubt a member of some rival group.) Disguised as furniture removers, the police attempted to capture Canal but he fought back savagely and managed to escape. He ran down the Rue Legendre and was on the point of escaping and disappearing into the crowd when a lorry driver, hearing the shouts of the police and thinking that they were chasing a thief, brought him down with an expert tackle.

He was brought before Commissaire Bouvier and searched. On him was found a letter, signed by Salan and written in the Santé prison, in which Salan asked Colonel Gorel to make 100 million available to Georges Bidault to continue the struggle.

The police were disconcerted to find that something was still under way—a considerable sum of money was involved. They became increasingly vigilant and this no doubt had something to do with the arrest, already described, of Gaby Anglade's Delta commando a fortnight later.

With Canal's arrest there remained one man—who had now lost his spearhead—Colonel Jean-Marie Bastien-Thiry.

CHAPTER 21

Change of a Codename

At this point we must return to the early months of 1962 in France, to a man destined to be the leading figure in developments for some time to come—Bastien-Thiry. After the Pont-sur-Seine fiasco in September 1961 he had continued with his war. He was still obsessed by his determination to do away with de Gaulle. To his mind, as to the minds of the 'Old General Staff', de Gaulle's policy was leading France to political disaster. Bastien-Thiry was trying to mount a fresh operation. He was primarily looking for men.

Still erect and still enveloped in his strange green mackintosh, Bastien-Thiry had not changed. He had merely exchanged his cover-name of 'Germain' for that of 'Didier'.

In March 1962 he heard that Belvisi had reappeared in Paris. He immediately arranged to meet him.

At 4 p.m. one day, just outside the Café Corentin at the Porte d'Orléans, Belvisi met Bastien-Thiry who was on his way in. The colonel passed on without recognising him, for Belvisi's face had been completely changed by plastic surgery. Belvisi caught him up, planted himself in front of him and looked him straight in the eye. Bastien-Thiry took a second or two to recover; then: 'It's incredible. Even I did not recognise you.'

The two men then talked in a white Simca 1000 lent to Belvisi by a lady friend. Belvisi recounted his adventures since Pont-sur-Seine. He had travelled to Spain; then he had met Canal, for whom he was working at this moment. Early in March he had been moving a consignment of arms in a Peugeot van and, owing to some blunder, the vehicle had blown up outside No. 9 Rue Félix-Faure. He had been badly burned about the face but had nevertheless succeeded in escaping in the confusion; he had been taken in by some doctor friends who had looked after him and had ultimately given him a new face in the best American gangster-film tradition. In his apartment the police had discovered 400 lbs of plastic, 143 grenades, 60 assorted bombs, 6 machine guns, 2 sub-machine guns,

3 carbines, 1,700 grams of gelignite, 10 revolvers, thousands of rounds of ammunition, chargers and bazooka rockets.

'The newspapers said that you had been killed in that explosion,' Bastien-Thiry said. 'I am very glad to know that you escaped. Have you any plans?'

' "Le Monocle" has one, my friend. He is preparing to assassinate de Gaulle.'

'That could be interesting. Can you arrange for me to meet him?'

The meeting between Canal and Bastien-Thiry took place on 24 March, the day before General Jouhaud was arrested in Oran. It was fixed for 3 p.m. and as usual Bastien-Thiry was punctual to the minute.

When 'Le Monocle' did not appear, Belvisi became uneasy and, leaving the colonel on the pavement, went into the café. It was empty except for a priest leaning up against the counter. Belvisi was about to go out again when the priest turned and said simply: 'Good day, my son. Are you looking for someone?' It was André Canal who was using this disguise.

'Have a drink of hot chocolate; it's good here.'

'No, thank you, Father. I'm in a hurry; a friend's waiting for me outside.'

'In that case, my son, I won't keep you.'

The three finally met in Bastien-Thiry's car and drove round the Bois de Boulogne.

The two understood each other at once. Both were brave, determined and strong. They had no need to talk much before reaching agreement.

'There are many risks but we must take them.'

'That's what I think.'

'Belvisi will act as liaison between us,' Canal went on. 'Ask him for what you want. You can trust him.'

'I know. I already know him. See you soon.'

'See you soon.'

It was 3.45 p.m. Belvisi later noted in his memoirs that at this moment 'the count-down for Petit Clamart began'.

A few days later Bastien-Thiry asked Belvisi to meet him again in order to introduce him to an officer who would be the colonel's personal representative for the operation. So, in the quiet Trocadéro gardens, there entered upon the scene of the future tragedy of Petit-Clamart a little highly strung, alert man—Alain Bougrenay de la Tocnaye. Belvisi knew his name; he had recently gained notoriety by an adventurous escape from the Santé prison on 1 February 1962.

Alain de la Tocnaye came into the business with an astonishing history behind him. In his memoirs, entitled *Comment je n'ai pas tué de Gaulle* (How I failed to kill de Gaulle), he says of his family: 'For seven hundred years my family has struggled against the centralised and increasingly totalitarian state.' He then lists the members of the family: Olivier who crusaded in the 12th century; Jehan who fought against Charles VI; Pierre who went to the help of the Duke of Brittany; Gilles who became one of Henri IV's courtiers; Jacques-Louis who refused to take the oath to the Convention and emigrated; Henri-Marie who refused to take the oath to Napoleon III; Arthur-Marie-Anne who distinguished himself at Magenta as an officer of the papal zouaves. His own entry he recorded as follows: 'Alain, an officer who served in Algeria; was condemned to death by the gaullist revolutionary bourgeoisie on 4 March 1963 and amnestied on 10 July 1968.' He was therefore a sort of aristocrat crusader who had never accepted that the prerogatives of the nobility should be sacrificed on the altar of *la Patrie*.

In his slim body, with the face half-hidden behind wire-rimmed spectacles, there was astounding energy and an unsatisfied desire for a cause to defend. He found this cause in French Algeria and he committed himself to it with enthusiasm. The result was that he was arrested as a deserter, being found in a hole at the bottom of a vineyard in October 1961 by a soldier of the 1st Algerian Artillery Regiment who was obeying a call of nature.

After six weeks in the Maison-Carrée detention barracks he was transferred to the Santé prison where he had only one idea in mind: to escape and continue his crusade. In his cell he raged against the stupidity of the men who had made the attempt at Pont-sur-Seine. In his eyes whoever had organised this attempt was merely a 'hair-splitter'. To kill de Gaulle why not use 'the good old methods of our grandfathers', he thought.

People seldom escape from the Santé. But la Tocnaye took courage from the example of Léon Daudet who had got away with it in the 1930s, thanks to considerable inside help. La Tocnaye's help came from the Operations Section of Captain Sergent's OAS France.

A visitor's pass intended for la Tocnaye's uncle was falsified and as a result Tocnaye was visited in his cell by a real make-up expert who disguised him as an old man and increased his height by fixing false heels to his shoes. Then, pretending to be his own cousin and armed with a false visitor's pass, he emerged from No. 6 prison block. He successfully passed the first check-points. To circumvent the final barriers he carried an attractive-looking baby belonging to the wife of a prisoner. He made the baby bawl by pinching its bottom and so succeeded in distracting the attention of the guards who let him go at 5.08 p.m. on 1 February 1962.

It must be admitted that this was a highly successful escape from a prison supposed to be impregnable. La Tocnaye thereupon took the cover-name of 'Max' and tried to contact a friend named Jean Bichon whom he knew to be anti-de Gaulle and whose role is still somewhat obscure and little known.

Max and Jean Bichon had met on 23 April 1961 at the time of the generals' *putsch*. They had been introduced to each other by Michel de Labigne, a young lieutenant in the 1st Foreign Legion Parachute Regiment. They had talked at length during long journeys which they had had to make by air as liaison officers in Algeria and had realised that their views were very similar, if not identical. Both were fanatical Catholics.

Max managed to regain contact with Jean Bichon through a certain priest who pulled many strings from behind the scenes. What he did not know was that the man used by the 'Old General Staff' to recruit Bastien-Thiry and as the high-level organiser of the Pont-sur-Seine attempt was Jean Bichon.

Just at the moment when la Tocnaye emerged from the Santé, Bichon had been reactivating Bastien-Thiry (now 'Didier') for a fresh attempt against the head of state, though he realised only too well the difficulties of recruiting new men. Knowing Tocnaye's views, Jean Bichon naturally introduced him to 'Didier' who took him on at once. This was the way in which la Tocnaye and Belvisi were brought together to organise the Petit-Clamart attempt.

La Tocnaye noted: 'The man referred to as A . . . [Armand Belvisi], undoubtedly looks like a Mediterranean, or to be more exact a Southern Italian, type. He makes broad sweeping gestures and could be made to weep easily. He must be a good-hearted chap but is the sort to create a drama and indulge in dirty tricks—a bit of a small-time con-man. I am surprised that Didier seems to have such confidence in him.'

On his side Belvisi recorded: 'One would think that he had come out of a medieval book. He looks at people and things with a superior air; he is proud of his name, his ancestors and the fact that he comes from the Vendée. He would like to reconquer the French Empire. He is anti almost everything, swirling his cape and doffing his plumed hat. This was the first time that I had seen him but I did not like his haughty manner. I think my feelings were reciprocated. And here we are, the two of us, responsible for bringing off this operation!'

It was a real case of oil and water—they had every reason to loathe each other. But they were together in a good cause and la Tocnaye kept his feelings to himself.

From the time of their first meeting the two men had a single purpose: to discover the ideal spot to kill de Gaulle by direct automatic fire. They knew that, since Pont-sur-Seine, de Gaulle went to Colombey by aircraft of the GLAM (*Groupe de Liaisons Aériennes Ministérielles*—Ministerial Communications Flight); he was only vulnerable while in his car between the Elysée and Villacoublay, and between Saint-Dizier and Colombey.

Leaving nothing to chance, Bastien-Thiry recruited teams of nationalist students to record de Gaulle's movements in detail each weekend. At the same time he kept in close touch with a senior permanent functionary in the Elysée who informed him whenever de Gaulle was to travel. Thanks to this informer in the general's office he even knew the secret code used by the security guards in the presidential convoy.

On 22 April, two days after Salan's arrest (a factor in accelerating his decision), Bastien-Thiry told his friends that, after prolonged study of the reports received, he had fixed the location for the attempt. The students' reports showed that the general's route was less frequently changed in the direction Villacoublay-Paris; that normally used was Porte de Chatillon—Place d'Alésia—Avenue du Maine—Les Invalides —Pont Alexandre III.

The most remarkable fact was that the presidential convoy consisted of two vehicles only and that it adhered to the traffic rules. Bastien-Thiry's informers knew their subject so well that they could even forecast the timing to within a few minutes. The informer located near the military airfield of Saint-Dizier had had great difficulty in pinpointing the moment when de Gaulle became airborne; there were always two aircraft with a ten-minute interval between take-offs, and one could not tell which was the general's. Not until the departures had been observed at least half a dozen times was the truth discovered: the plane which was not de Gaulle's took off very steeply, whereas that carrying the head of state rose slowly taking every precaution to ensure the security and comfort of its illustrious passenger.

As soon as Bastien-Thiry had announced his decision, Belvisi and la Tocnaye held a meeting to work out the details of the operation which was to take place in the Avenue du Maine. La Tocnaye was forced to admit that, of the two of them, the 'Southern Italian' was the more effective; in fact Belvisi provided all the logistical support for the affair. This was not calculated to put 'The Knight' in any better humour.

Armed with four (false) identity cards provided by his master 'Le Monocle', Belvisi first hired four vehicles in four different garages—a Simca Montlhéry convertible, a Peugeot 403 covered van, a Peugeot 403 saloon and an Estafette. This last was modified to enable the rear door to be opened from the inside and the windows were painted white so that no one could see inside.

'Le Monocle' also provided the weapons. 'Mission III' was the only group to possess a stock. Neither Bastien-Thiry nor Jean Bichon nor even la Tocnaye could supply anything.

These weapons—two machine guns, five sub-machine guns, three revolvers with ammunition and some grenades—were placed in the van. Belvisi had the original but effective idea of parking it in front of a CRS barracks at the Porte de Châtillon sports ground. For several weeks, therefore, the weapons selected to kill de Gaulle were under police guard.

Equally most of the men were provided by 'Mission III'. They were: Georges Watin, known as 'La Boiteuse', Serge Bernier (alias 'Murat', born 10 July 1933), Lazlo Varga (a blond blue-eyed Hungarian who had fought the Russian tanks in Budapest), Lajos Marton (also Hungarian and an ex-MIG pilot), Yula Sari (yet another Hungarian who had fought in Indo-China), Louis Honorat François de Condé (known as 'Petitou'), three ex-parachutists, Alain 'The Pipe', Gérard 'The Sergeant' and Christian. Each was first introduced to la Tocnaye and then to Bastien-Thiry who explained his battle plan, ending by saying:

'We now only have to await the right moment to act. I think that this time we have made sure that luck will be with us. We must hurry before anything irrevocable takes place. Thank you, gentlemen.'

The right moment arrived on Sunday, 27 May. The Elysée informer confirmed that de Gaulle was due to return to Paris that day.

The entire team knew the plan of attack by heart. The vehicles were to be stationed in the Avenue du Maine before the Rue de la Gaîté, the two vans with the machine guns and sub-machine guns in the middle. La Tocnaye would be in the rear vehicle and would warn Belvisi by walkie-talkie radio. Belvisi in the leading vehicle would then crash into the first car that passed so as to produce a traffic jam. The presidential convoy, which would by then have passed la Tocnaye, would thus be halted level with the vans which would then open fire. La Tocnaye would hurl grenades through his sunshine roof to prevent the security guards approaching.

On receipt of the message from the Saint-Dizier look-out the men went to the various cafés allotted to them. While de Gaulle was still somewhere in the air, they were drinking coffee either to conceal their impatience or to calm their nerves. Finally, the second message came—from the look-out at Villacoublay: 'De Gaulle has just landed.'

They got into their vehicles and moved off, crossed the Place d'Alésia and began the drive down the Avenue du Maine. The traffic was fairly thick. This could only help the operation; a traffic jam would make easier both the shooting and the escape of those involved.

On reaching the Rue Vercingétorix, Belvisi in the leading vehicle was surprised that he had had no news from la Tocnaye in the rear vehicle. According to the timetable, which had been checked a hundred times, de Gaulle's car ought to be approaching. He called la Tocnaye on his walkie-talkie: 'What's happening?'

'Nothing in sight.'

'Sure?'

'Sure.'

On reaching the Rue de la Gaîté, where de Gaulle's car ought to have passed them, Belvisi called Tocnaye again:

'Still nothing?'

'Still nothing. I don't understand it.'

The four vehicles, including the two vans containing the men and machine guns, continued as far as the Invalides and then dispersed.

The plot had failed because a look-out stationed along the route had not observed that de Gaulle had returned to the Elysée another way.

Setbacks of this nature often result in the quarrels within a team boiling over. Belvisi and la Tocnaye, the two opposites, were only waiting for some excuse to clash and produce the blow-out. As André Canal, the head of 'Mission III', had now been arrested, la Tocnaye considered that Belvisi no longer represented anything and that he should return to the ranks. On the pretext of the failure of the Avenue du Maine attempt (which would certainly have been a murderous one had de Gaulle passed that way), la Tocnaye gave Belvisi to understand that he should no longer be the sole caretaker of the equipment and should hand over the weapons.

The argument took place at the Porte de Châtillon on a cold rainy Monday, the day after the failure in the Avenue du Maine.

'These weapons are not safe in the Estafette,' la Tocnaye said. 'We will put them in a lock-up where they will be secure.'

'So far everything's been all right. I don't see why I can't go on keeping them.'

'Will you please hand them over to me at once.'

'These weapons belong to Mission III and Canal gave me responsibility for them. I am keeping them.'

'Canal has been arrested and Mission III no longer exists.'

'That is not what I think.'

Faced with the 'Southern Italian's' calm resistance, 'The Knight', though mad with rage, thought it better to break off the quarrel at that point.

'We will see about that tomorrow—here at 9 a.m. precisely.'

'As you wish.'

Belvisi went off to report his quarrel to the man who had succeeded 'Le Monocle' as head of Mission III. He was known as 'Dr Victor' and, since he was never in any subsequent trouble, we will let him remain anonymous. Victor immediately ordered Belvisi to put the weapons in some secure place and to take two bodyguards with him in the morning, Gérard and Christian.

Having stowed the weapons in one of Mission III's hide-outs, Belvisi went to meet la Tocnaye.

'The Knight' arrived together with Georges Watin and Serge Bernier, formerly allies of Belvisi.

'The weapons?' la Tocnaye asked through the car window.

'They are in a place of safety.'

'Where?'

'In a place I know.'

Watin suddenly opened the car door and sat down next to Belvisi. He was not in a joking mood.

'Where are the weapons?' he asked again.

In the rear seat of the car Gérard and Christian had their hands on their guns.

'The weapons are hidden,' Belvisi replied calmly. 'They are available to Didier but they remain my responsibility.'

La Tocnaye realised that this interview could lead nowhere.

'Come away, Georges.'

'We'll settle this,' Watin growled.

'When you like.'

La Tocnaye was white. 'In any case Didier wants to see you—2 p.m. at the Debilly footbridge.'

'I'll be there.'

The footbridge was deserted. The sky was grey. The trees were dripping. In the river below, the yawning barges lay along the quay like great whales.

Three men walked slowly along the damp footway—Belvisi in front, Gérard and Christian slightly behind. Suddenly they stopped; from the other end of the footbridge three men were advancing to meet them. One of them limped slightly. The man in the centre was small and walked with short jerky steps—la Tocnaye. He was followed by Watin and Bernier.

The two groups stopped simultaneously some ten yards from each other. All had their hands in their mackintosh pockets. It was exactly 2 p.m. No word was spoken. The six men remained motionless.

Suddenly they turned their heads. A man dressed in a greenish-coloured mackintosh and a battered felt hat came hurrying along, making the footway clatter. He passed la Tocnaye and stopped exactly midway between the two groups. His face was calm and serious. He radiated an air of authority. It was Colonel Bastien-Thiry. He signalled imperiously for the six men to come closer.

They came. Watin still had his hand in his pocket. Bastien-Thiry frowned. He did not appreciate quarrelling between his men. He turned to Belvisi: 'I am listening to you.'

'They want to have me out of the team,' Belvisi said. 'My leader, André Canal, has placed me at your disposal as a member of Mission III. I have brought you equipment, men and weapons. I have done all I can for the success of the operation. Now I am being asked to go.'

Bastien-Thiry tossed his head, still looking Belvisi in the eye: 'No one but me has the right to decide anything. Belvisi, you will stay with us.'

Then, turning to la Tocnaye, he continued in a somewhat mellower tone: 'Without Mission III's men and weapons, we could do nothing.'

He remained silent for a moment and then drew himself up. 'Let us have no more of this sort of thing,' he said drily. 'I will not tolerate it a second time. Is that clear?'

No one answered. It was clear. All seemed to have grasped what their leader had said. Suddenly they started: one of them was having the temerity to speak—Serge Bernier: 'I can find you as many men like him as you want. Since he is making a mess of things, let's do away with him.'

Bastien-Thiry went pale; his nostrils twitched. Slowly he fixed his light-blue eyes on Bernier and said in a low voice: 'Never let me hear words like that again. Never!'

He took a step to the railings and gazed for a moment at the Seine flowing below: 'I want to see you all tomorrow at 2.30 at the Convention metro station.'

He departed towards the other end of the footbridge, his martial step ringing on the footway.

When he had disappeared the first to move was Watin; he turned his back on the others and departed in his turn with his slightly limping gait. Belvisi and his two friends moved off towards the other end with a simulated air of relaxation. La Tocnaye followed Watin. Bernier remained there alone, motionless, his hands in his mackintosh pockets, watching Belvisi and his two bodyguards vanish. His head whirled with vague pictures of a cowboy film-scene. But in this case the guns had not spoken. It was somehow a cowboy film gone wrong.

CHAPTER 22

Twists of Fate

The day after the meeting on the footbridge, Wednesday, 30 May 1962, fate provided a considerable boost to Alain de Bougrenay de la Tocnaye's ego.

At about 2 p.m. Armand Belvisi left the apartment where he was living at No. 3 Rue de Sontay, near the Place Victor Hugo in the XVIth *Arrondissement*. It had been lent to him by a journalist sympathiser who worked for French Radio and Television.

The sun had returned to Paris. Belvisi was in a hurry, not wishing to miss his appointment with Bastien-Thiry. In the apartment (it was well furnished with big red curtains) he had left Anne, one of his girl-friends who was busy arranging his papers.

At precisely 2.30 p.m. he stopped his car near the Convention metro station. He saw Bastien-Thiry's car at once. La Tocnaye was sitting beside the driver. Further away, under the metro sign, Watin and Bernier were pretending to be tourists trying to find their location from the metro plan. Without a word Belvisi climbed into the back of 'Didier's' Peugeot.

'I wanted to see you two alone,' Bastien-Thiry said, 'because our cause must be placed above personal feelings. Success is all that counts. Do you agree?'

La Tocnaye replied at once: 'Agreed. Let's forget everything.'

'Agreed,' Belvisi said in his turn.

'Good. Tell your friends that you have made it up. General meeting in three days time, 2 June. We will fix the final details of our operation. Shake hands.'

La Tocnaye held out his hand. Belvisi put his hand out slowly; his face did not register any great enthusiasm. With this handshake the three men parted.

Half an hour later Belvisi parked his car near the post office in the Avenue de Longchamp where he had to go to send money orders to the hirers of the cars. He noticed that three men in a black Ariane were taking a surreptitious interest in him. Despite the crowd he saw two of the men get out of the car and follow him, one on each pavement. Their way of going about things indubitably indicated that they were policemen.

Belvisi was astounded. Who could have known that he was going to that post office? Yet he was clearly expected. No one knew his address and he had not been followed to his meeting with Bastien-Thiry, otherwise everyone would have been arrested then.

'How had they found me?' Belvisi asks in his memoirs. 'How long had they been following me? These questions are still unanswered today. Yet someone knew the truth. But who?'

Belvisi thought that the only method of escape was to run. He took a deep breath and dashed off followed by the others who began shouting: 'Stop him.' He put everything he had into this frantic dash, his object being to get back to his apartment and barricade himself inside for long enough to destroy his compromising documents. In particular, discovery of the hire cards of the vehicles would mean that the commando could do nothing without being discovered.

He got there and successfully barricaded himself inside while police rushed up from every direction and cordoned off the building. They were already knocking at the door.

'I have 400 lbs of explosive. If you try on anything at all, I'll blow the lot up.'

The knocking ceased and a voice said: 'Don't do that, you fool. You can't get away. Open up.'

'Get out or I'll blow up the building.'

The police withdrew to confer. Belvisi took advantage of the situation to start burning all his papers, assisted by Anne. Names, codes, covernames, addresses, registration numbers of vehicles—all turned to ashes on the gas flame.

Leaving Anne to stoke the fire, Belvisi, in order to give her time to finish, put on a parachutist's uniform, a present from a captain in the 1st *Chasseurs* Parachute Regiment. He then took from a cupboard a Canadian sub-machine gun and a handful of grenades. He half-opened the shutters; there was a considerable crowd in the surrounding streets and steel-helmeted police on all the roofs.

He fired a burst into the air. The police replied immediately, firing at the windows of the apartment. Three grenades, two high explosive and one tear-gas, spread confusion among the carloads of police. They despatched a picked marksman up the service stairs but he missed and fled.

There remained a bundle of OAS leaflets which Belvisi threw out of the window. Meanwhile down below the Fire Brigade arrived as a reinforcement.

The telephone rang and after some hesitation Belvisi answered.

'Can you hear me? I am Commissaire Bouvier. You haven't a chance.'

'I have enough to blow up the whole area.'

'And risk killing innocent people?'

'Have them evacuated.'

Belvisi hung up nervously. But Bouvier was pertinacious; he called back: 'I know you have a woman with you. I give you my word that she will come to no harm.'

'Call me back in ten minutes.'

During this time Anne had succeeded in burning the last papers. There remained only an identity card—a false one—and the report which Belvisi had written on the preparation of the Avenue du Maine attempt. This was meant for the OAS and proved that Mission III had participated in the operation, the code-name of which was 'Charlotte Corday'. He raised some nails of the carpet and slipped the papers underneath. . . . They were to remain there for ten years.

Now he could give himself up. The telephone rang. It was 5.55 p.m.

'I am ready.'

'Give me your word of honour that you will not be armed.'

'I give it.'

A few seconds later a flood of policemen burst into the apartment. They searched for explosives without finding anything.

'Where's the plastic?'

'There's never been an ounce of plastic here,' Belvisi replied tranquilly.

Commissaire Bouvier was red-faced with anger; he had been conned. However, he could console himself with the thought that he had arrested a dangerous man who had been hunted ever since the Pont-sur Seine attempt.

Belvisi's exit, in camouflage uniform and surrounded by an army of police, took place before thousands of spectators and dozens of journalists. The historic photograph was published in the evening papers.

Belvisi had made the most of his exit but he nevertheless missed the operation upon which he had set his heart—the killing of de Gaulle. Operation 'Charlotte Corday' took place without him. He was sentenced to fifteen years imprisonment and only emerged from detention at Saint-Martin-de-Ré in 1968.

Belvisi's arrest seems to have made comparatively little impression on la Tocnaye. He does not even refer to it in his memoirs, merely noting that with the 'defection' of the 'Southern Italian'—whom he also calls the 'Flowered Shirt'—the commando had lost both weapons and men.

La Tocnaye naturally first addressed himself to the search for weapons. His first contact, as he says in his memoirs, was the 'manager of the

Orléanist den' who was responsible for storing arms for 'the great night'. This man, whose clientèle, he says, were 'vergers, bigots and strict gaullist dowagers', gave him a flat refusal. He then paid a visit to a certain colonel who immediately opened a cupboard and took out two sub-machineguns and eight clips of ammunition. For his part, Georges Watin went to see some cousins living in the south-west and they agreed to give him some weapons they had been holding.

As far as men were concerned, Bastien-Thiry's party gained a high-class recruit—Jean de Brem, a sensitive poet blown off course by the Algerian upheaval. Through him and Louis de Condé certain young people joined the group, bringing to full strength the handful of students whom Bastien-Thiry had been recruiting since the beginning of the year.

As we have seen, these young people were initially made responsible for the reconnaissance phase, being distributed at various points on the routes used by de Gaulle from Paris to Villacoublay and from Saint-Dizier to Colombey. From the outset, however, it had always been visualized that they would have a part to play in subsequent operations. They were responsible for providing hide-outs and cover for future operations. They reported personally to Bastien-Thiry once a week; he was known to them as 'Colonel Didier'.

'We thought that he worked for the Ministerial Communications Flight [the GLAM],' one of them (who is now a barrister) says today. 'Very soon, however, we realised that he was working in the Air Ministry since he always arranged to meet us near the Porte de Versailles or the Convention metro station. Had we wished to give him away, we could easily have identified him. This gives some idea of the atmosphere of confidence that there was between us. He radiated calm and dignity. He would listen to our verbal reports and then make us repeat them; he never took notes. Then he would go off in his green Peugeot.'

From the beginning of March Bastien-Thiry asked his students to begin the rehearsal phase. The technique to be rehearsed was that of firing on de Gaulle's car from a moving van.

One of the students (now a senior industrialist) says: 'In order to rehearse realistically we hired a Citroën Déesse and drove it down the motorway as if it had been the head of state's car. We did this near Ris-Orangis. We reached the stage when we could do it in our sleep.'

Another duty of the students was to conceal the weapons. A third one (now a doctor) says: 'Belvisi brought us a consignment. He had arranged to meet us at the Place du Trocadéro and arrived with a truck-load of apples under which the arms were hidden. We stored them in the apartment of a friend who was a student like ourselves. On the Friday before Palm Sunday everything was ready. That day the whole set-up was located on the road between Saint-Dizier and Colombey; there were teams of observers near telephones, vehicles with men and guns, etc. But we were wasting our time; de Gaulle took a helicopter at Villacoublay. Another attempt was made on 21 April, the day after Salan's arrest. Again it went wrong in the same way. From this time on things ran almost on a standard timetable; the party was in position every Friday and every Monday. Every time something did not work.'

Then, in about mid-June, de Gaulle went off to visit Franche-Comté and Jura.

CHAPTER 23

A Put-Up Job?

In mid-1962, faced with increasingly violent opposition, the French government needed to assert its authority. The vital referendum on self-determination in Algeria was due to take place on 1 July. It was absolutely essential that this referendum should be a government victory; it would thus definitely assert its authority over the French. To those around him de Gaulle made no secret of the fact that, if the referendum went against him, he would resign.

The supporters of French Algeria tried to bring a motion of censure against the government. It was defeated on 6 June despite the fact that, the day after the 15 May press conference, the MRP (*Mouvement Républicain Populaire*) ministers had left the government, banging the door behind them.

The government, therefore, needed to arouse public opinion to ensure that the vote was favourable. It could think of only one good weapon in its psychological armoury, which, moreover, it used whenever possible or necessary—fear: fear of disorder. 'Me or chaos,' the general said one day, knowing that the tide of the country was with him.

If, therefore, on some public occasion, during a journey for instance, a nice little plot against the person of the head of state could be discovered, the thought of the risks to which he was continuously exposed might make the French realise what a disaster his loss would be. If he were to vanish, subversion and disorder would be the order of the day everywhere. It is difficult to see any other motive for the announcement of the discovery of a plot in Vesoul on 14 June 1962, the very day before the general was due to visit that city. If the enormous headlines in the newspapers of the time be compared to the actual facts, it is difficult not to believe that this was part of a propaganda campaign. The facts are few indeed.

It is true that a network did exist in Franche-Comté as in other areas but it was not particularly active. Before the President's arrival the police went through the area with a tooth-comb and, miraculously,

167

announced that they had uncovered a plot to kill the head of state. During the last four days before the visit they arrested certain people said to be extremely dangerous. Roger Frey himself, the Minister of the Interior, held a press conference at 8 p.m. on 15 June at the Vesoul prefecture, flanked by his assistant Alexandre Sanguinetti, his Director of Security and various official functionaries. He announced that four 'killers' had just been put under lock and key: a woman named Liliane Gattrieci, a radio electrician named Georges Bourgary and one or two minor characters. The leader of the plot had fled and was driving round in a green Peugeot 404, registration number 843 CB 25, his pockets stuffed with dynamite with which to kill de Gaulle.

Chance—so often on the side of the police—had arranged that in the glove compartment of the car of one of the conspirators should be found a complete list of the members of the circuit organised by Marcel Bouyer, the ex-poujadist deputy. The circuit included barristers, doctors and businessmen. The papers confiscated also showed that twenty-one killers from Algiers had contacted the circuit in order to organise an assassination attempt against de Gaulle in the area. They also produced details of the way in which the 'OAS killers' proposed to get rid of de Gaulle. They had telescopic rifles, bazookas, bombs, grenades and even a somewhat novel method—dogs carrying delayed-action bombs and trained to go where the conspirators ordered them; these booby-trapped animals were to be loosed on to the official platform from which de Gaulle would speak. The police had also found the radio set used by the conspirators; it was in the possession of Jean-Jacques Dupont, son of the film-producer.

On the day of the general's arrival a vast force of police was mobilised under the eyes of the astonished journalists. They dutifully produced eight-column headlines: 'Despite threats of assassination de Gaulle continues his visit to Franche-Comté.'

A real commotion occurred at 5.30 p.m., when de Gaulle was only twenty minutes away from Vesoul. A particularly sharp-eyed CRS thought he saw the notorious green Peugeot 404 with a villainous-looking individual behind the wheel. The decks of Vesoul were cleared for action —the killers were there! Security was tightened further with police on all the roofs.

No one was found of course and de Gaulle completed his visit without incident or threat.

Marcel Bouyer's OAS undoubtedly existed. If, however, it is true that it had *envisaged* an attack on de Gaulle, it had not *organised* anything. The discovery of this plan by the police was no more than an episode in the psychological warfare from which the government drew its strength.

France-Soir's headline—'The OAS commando in Vesoul proposed to loose on the Head of State booby-trapped dogs guided by ultra-high-pitched whistles'—was one of the trappings of this psychological war.

CHAPTER 24

Action Stations

De Gaulle may not have been running any great risk at Vesoul on 15 June but a week later he was to run one which was much more serious.

Though living underground, Louis de Condé was still in touch with the aristocracy and through him Bastien-Thiry heard that General de Gaulle, incognito, was due to attend the wedding of a 'well-connected' young lady. It was to take place on the La Martillière estate in the little village of Rebrechien, some ten miles north-east of Orleans. The information came from the best possible source and everything indicated that de Gaulle would actually go to this wedding—a quite exceptional decision. The ceremony was due to take place on 23 June.

Bastien-Thiry immediately despatched his team of students to study the area in detail and as discreetly as possible. The estate where Madame Jean-Marie Reveroles lived was in the depths of the country.

'We made a complete reconnaissance of the place,' says the student who is now a barrister. 'The omens were very good. We had various routes for escape, all of them easy. An ambush would have been all the easier since the general's journey was not an official one. It had not been announced and so the security precautions would not have been very great. All we had to do was to intercept the convoy on its return from the ceremony. The most intriguing fact was that we had one of our men on the spot.' And what a man! It was Bastien-Thiry himself.

He had in fact succeeded in obtaining an invitation to the wedding. The most surprising fact of all was that he had obtained it through an actual member of General de Gaulle's family—at least that is what he said at his trial, though he may have done so out of bravado.

The commando accordingly took up position on the route which the presidential convoy must follow. Observers were posted to give warning as it passed various points. Fingers on the triggers of their sub-machine guns, the men of the commando waited in their vans for the signal. On this late morning in summer the heat beneath the canvas covers was intense.

They had no opportunity to pull the trigger. Once more, without knowing it, de Gaulle thwarted their plans. He went to La Martillière by helicopter. The commando saw the airborne convoy pass overhead. They had to make do with the radio 'flashes' telling of this unannounced trip.

This further setback may have cost Bastien-Thiry's men a week but it did not discourage them. Two days later, on Monday 25 June, they were in position in Meudon wood. The referendum on self-determination in Algeria was due to take place on 1 July; there remained only five days to change the course of events by eliminating de Gaulle.

Yet a further setback. The two observers stationed on a forest track above the Chemin des Gardes saw de Gaulle's vehicle through their field glasses and gave the agreed signal. Down below, however, one of the commando's vehicles was discovered by two police cars which gave chase. La Tocnaye only just had time to give his pursuers the slip and, meanwhile, the other vehicles of Operation 'Charlotte Corday' dispersed.

This succession of misfires left de Gaulle alive to pursue his policy and on 3 July he recognised the independence of Algeria. Bastien-Thiry's men were forced to postpone any further attempt for a month. The secret informer in the Elysée told 'Didier' that de Gaulle did not intend to travel between Colombey and Paris during July.

The members of the team took advantage of this to try and find fresh weapons and also take a little rest. La Tocnaye left for the Tarn. Bastien-Thiry went to Switzerland for a few days.

None of them remembered that de Gaulle would necessarily return to Paris for the sacrosanct ceremony of 14 July. This he could not miss. The commando could have made a further attempt on the Villacoublay–Paris road. With a little ingenuity the fireworks might have gone up as de Gaulle was driving down the Champs-Elysées before the parade.

Though the idea had not occurred to Bastien-Thiry's men, it had occurred to someone else. He was neither an officer nor a descendant of the crusaders and he was polite enough to reveal his plan to the police a week before the parade.

This man, whom we will call Dominique, was Corsican by origin, dark, of medium height, dark eyes, sallow complexion.

On Saturday 7 July he decided to go to a gangster film. As he emerged from the metro in Montmartre two men caught up with him and slipped handcuffs on him. They were two members of the criminal police who had been following him for a while. His photograph and his name figured on one of those lists of suspects over which every good sleuth should cast his eye each evening before going to sleep.

He was taken to the local police headquarters and interrogated by a commissaire. Finding that he was dealing with the criminal police, Dominique tried at once to place himself on the political net.

'I have nothing to do with common crime,' he said. 'I am a member of a commando which is to kill de Gaulle on 14 July.'

Everyone went to action stations and Dominique soon found himself facing the men of Commissaire Bouvier, the man who had arrested Belvisi a month earlier.

'So you were going to kill the head of state on 14 July?'

'That's correct.'

'Not by yourself, I imagine.'

'Of course not.'

'What's the name of your leader?'

'I've forgotten.'

The police were expecting as much.

'Well then, since your memory fails you, we will send you back to the criminal police. They want you for a hold-up in Algiers which has nothing to do with politics. You'll get twenty years. Take him away.'

'Wait a moment.'

'Is your memory returning?'

'If I talk . . .?'

'Sometimes certain files get lost between Algeria and France. A lot of people were being repatriated in those days.'

'You promise me?'

'I promise nothing. Talk first and then we'll see what we can do.'

'Very well. My chief is called Jean-Paul Gras. I and others of his commando were to hurl grenades at the general's car during the 14 July parade.'

Dominique then told all—in his own way. He first spoke of his immediate master, Jean-Paul Gras. He had been a 2nd Lieutenant in the 3rd Colonial Parachute Regiment which, a few years earlier, had been turned into the 3rd Marines commanded by the famous Colonel Bigeard. Gras had deserted during the summer of 1961. He had then joined the OAS and had been placed under orders of Jacques Achard, the former sub-prefect who had been a member of General Salan's staff when the latter had been C-in-C in Algeria. Jean-Paul Gras had become assistant to Claude Dupont, Jacques Achard's operational agent responsible for Bab el-Oued.

On 28 June Dupont and Gras were ordered to leave Algeria. They took ship for Marseille with their men and then reassembled in Paris with their weapons. After the upheaval of their hurried departure but now finding themselves together again by chance, the commando did not really know what to do. Jean-Paul Gras tried to contact OAS France but could not do so forthwith. He and his men had found a hide-out and they decided to go into action on their own. They decided, in principle, on a planned operation against de Gaulle on 14 July. When the general returned from the Arc de Triomphe, after laying the traditional wreath, and moved towards the official rostrum between the Rond-Point and the Place de la Concorde, the commando would attack his car with grenades, mingle with the crowd in the ensuing panic and disappear.

The story seemed sufficiently plausible to Commissaire Bouvier for a vast police operation to be launched. Determined to prove his good faith, Dominique had given numerous details including the names of all members of the commando. A furious hunt for them was initiated but the police had no information about them and no photographs; they had left their hideout in Paris and the police did not succeed in finding them.

Accordingly on 14 July the police array was formidable. Thousands of them, some summoned from the provinces, lined the route, watching the faces of the spectators for one or more people liable to hurl grenades at the presidential convoy. To the vast relief of the police no grenade was thrown.

In fact none was ever meant to be. This the police discovered on the following 27 November when they arrested Jean-Paul Gras in No 4. Rue de l'Exposition in the VIIth *Arrondissement*, the house of one of his *pied-noir* friends, Marc Thibault. In the apartment the police found a dozen sub-machine guns with clips of ammunition and some OAS leaflets. There was little doubt about Gras' intentions.

Immediately on the arrest of Gras the police passed word to the press that they had laid hands on the leader of the commando which was to hurl grenades at the head of state's car during the 14 July parade. When told of this accusation Gras was so taken aback that he burst out laughing: 'It's a joke.'

'You know perfectly well that it is not.'

'Who can have told you a ludicrous story like that?'

Faced with this statement the police realised that something was not quite right. They soon came to the conclusion that they had fallen for a fairy-tale invented by Dominique to escape a common law sentence.

The facts were that, a few days before his commando left Algeria, Jean-Paul Gras had carried out an operation against the Pelissier barracks in Algiers to liberate one of his men, an NCO who had been arrested by the police. During the operation, which was successful, a common criminal (none other than Dominique in fact) who happened to be in the same cell, was also freed, although he had nothing to do with the OAS. Jacques Achard and Jean-Paul Gras reviewed the case of this involuntary escapist and, not wishing to hand him back to the police, decided to make him a provisional member of the commando. In this way Dominique, who was no more than a hooligan turned OAS member, found himself in Paris with the rest. The others were taking no great risk; they had no police files. Dominique, however, had a criminal pedigree; his details were in the pocket of every member of the crime police. Hence the rest of the story. Although he had in fact invented the planned attack on the Champs-Elysées on the spur of the moment, it had actually been mentioned, among other ideas, by Jean-Paul Gras when the commando was looking for something to do.

The explanations given by Jean-Paul Gras were so convincing that no case was brought against him for this attempt. The police had been had and a vast man-hunt had been undertaken to no good purpose. Nevertheless, partly as a result of Dominique's 'revelations', Jean-Paul Gras had acquired a police file. His photograph had been found in the army records and had been distributed with the following comment:

'Gras, Jean-Paul, born in Gap 23 September 1939. Reserve 2nd Lieutenant. Deserter from 3 Marine Regiment. From 2 July 1961 in a relatively important position in the CNR. Arrest warrant issued on 22 November 1961 by M. Hontaa, examining magistrate of the Permanent Armed Forces Tribunal in the Algiers zone. Guilty of desertion within the country in peacetime.'

The police alert on 14 July and the resulting manhunt had just calmed down when the members of Bastien-Thiry's commando returned from their holidays at the end of July. It was probably as well for them that they had been away from Paris; had they been there, their inevitable comings and goings would hardly have escaped the notice of the police whose nerves were very much on edge as the day of the national festival approached.

Be that as it may, in order to keep their hands in, 'Didier's' team of youngsters and some of the old hands made two further attempts at the end of the month—both abortive.

On 6 August la Tocnaye returned to Paris, suntanned after a particularly good fishing holiday on the Tarn; he met Bastien-Thiry who had just returned from Switzerland. Their simultaneous return was no accident. General Eisenhower was due to visit Paris on 8 August and General de Gaulle would obviously come back from Colombey to welcome him.

At 7.30 a.m. there was little traffic at the corner of the Rue de Vaugirard and the Rue de la Convention. Many Parisians were on holiday; the metro was not disgorging its usual crowd. A van was parked opposite the metro station, a yellow Renault Estafette. At the wheel was a young man, aged about twenty, reading a newspaper. He seemed to be waiting for someone. Two policemen passed without noticing him; they could not be expected to know that the young man was called Lazlo Varga and that he had an American carbine hidden under his seat. Equally they did not know that three men were hiding in the back of the Estafette and that they had one sub-machine gun and two machine

173

guns—they were Pascal Bertin, Guyla Sari and Lajos Marton, the ex-hero of Budapest.

A Fiat Neckar was parked a little further away. At the wheel was a man, aged about forty, looking like a commercial traveller; he was arranging some papers and looking at a map. It was Bastien-Thiry.

At about 9 a.m. a small man, who seemed in a hurry, came up to the driver of the Fiat and spoke a few words to him. Bastien-Thiry nodded and pressed the starter. The little man—la Tocnaye—crossed the street and opened the door of a white-roofed Citroën Idée. He took the wheel, while another young man got into the back and a third person—who limped slightly—got in beside the driver.

'We have just had a call from our observer at Saint-Dizier,' la Tocnaye said. 'De Gaulle's aircraft has left. We will position ourselves opposite the Boucicault metro station. There is a café there which our informer at Villacoublay will ring to tell us that de Gaulle has landed and that the convoy is on its way.'

At about 11 a.m. the Villacoublay informer called reporting the departure of the presidential convoy by Route No. 1: Meudon Wood—Pont de Sèvres—Avenue de Versailles—Quai de Passy—Place de l'Alma—Elysée. The count-down had begun.

Bastien-Thiry's plan, which they had rehearsed a dozen times on the ground, was a simple one. The general's route and that of the commando intersected in the area of Pont Mirabeau 'where the Seine flows'. The commando was then to cross the bridge and drive slowly down the Avenue de Versailles, allowing itself to be overtaken by the presidential convoy. Fire would be opened from the rear of the Estafette as soon as the general's car had been 'framed'.

The three cars—the Idée leading followed by the Estafette with Bastien-Thiry's Fiat bringing up the rear—drove slowly down the Avenue de Versailles. According to the timetable de Gaulle's car would soon be there.

Suddenly things started to happen.

Bastien-Thiry's car, in the rear, was stopped at a traffic light and at that moment the presidential convoy, led by two motor-cyclists, came dashing up. But instead of turning down the Avenue de Versailles as it usually did, it continued down the Quai Louis-Blériot and disappeared under the eyes of Bastien-Thiry who was taken by surprise by the speed of developments. He could do nothing and simply noted down the time, 11.18. He also noted that de Gaulle was in the leading Déesse, that the second was full of security police and that the third, driven by the general's chauffeur, was empty.

The impetuous la Tocnaye grasped the situation at once. He accelerated and tried to weave his way through the traffic to catch up the presidential convoy which he could still see in the distance. The

Estafette was quickly left behind but la Tocnaye's Idée managed to catch up. It passed the police vehicle and almost came level with de Gaulle's car. La Tocnaye could see the general's hair and his sleeve.

Georges Watin, with his sub-machine gun on his knees, quickly wound down the window. Louis de Condé did likewise in the back with la Tocnaye still trying to edge up to the President's car which was travelling fast despite the traffic.

As he was almost level with the general's limousine and his two marksmen were about to raise their guns a Citroën 4 cv, driven by an agitated young man, squeezed itself between de Gaulle's Déesse and la Tocnaye's Idée. Despite all la Tocnaye's efforts he could not edge it out of the way.

Watin and de Condé were ready to fire. 'Shall we let fly?' Watin growled.

'No!' la Tocnaye yelled. 'We are at too much of an angle. There would be too much mess. And then we couldn't get away.'

On reaching the Trocadéro tunnel la Tocnaye abandoned the chase. 'And it's only our seventeenth attempt,' he groaned.

It was not to be the last.

CHAPTER 25

Codeword 'Charlotte Corday'

The 'Petit-Clamart' assassination attempt is now part of French history, like that of Damien on Louis XV, or that by Saint-Régent and de Limoelan on Napoleon in the Rue Saint-Nicaise.

Apart from the dramatic fact, not easily forgotten, that a man who had never shed a drop of blood was shot (Damien, too, was hung, drawn and quartered for striking once with a penknife), the Petit-Clamart affair had all the characteristics of a western.

The star was an international figure: Charles de Gaulle, the haughty omnipotent potentate who would grant no pardon. Surrounding him was a ubiquitous and implacable police force. On the opposing side the 'baddies' consisted of a handful of penniless men, some of whom could not even raise a metro fare to escape after the attack, but all inspired by complete determination to kill 'the tyrant'. The best Hollywood script-writers could not have produced a better scenario.

The film opened on a scene of magnificence: the courtyard of the Elysée at 7.40 p.m. on 22 August 1962. The presidential Déesse was parked in front of the great stairway and footmen were hurrying about. The general's chauffeur was holding open the rear left-hand door of the car for Madame de Gaulle to get in.

The general came down the steps with two uniformed officers: Colonel Teisseire and Colonel de Boissieu, his son-in-law.

Francis Marroux, the chauffeur, opened the right-hand rear door. As the general was getting in Colonel de Boissieu bent down to him:

'Father, I am going to spend the weekend at La Boisserie. It's hardly necessary for Colonel Teisseire to go with you; I could act as your aide.'

'Of course.'

Colonel de Boissieu made a discreet sign to Colonel Teisseire who saluted. Then he got in beside the driver.

The Déesse moved off majestically behind its two outriders. Followed by a second black Déesse, it emerged from the Elysée. One or two passers-by stopped to see the President of the Republic pass. One of them, who seemed particularly interested, hurried into a nearby café, went straight to the telephone and dialled a number.

In the Trianon Bar on the broad, almost deserted avenue of Petit-Clamart the telephone rang. The proprietor answered:

'Who's that? M. Perrin? Hold on. Here's the call you were expecting, sir. Go into the box and pick up the receiver. Hold on.'

A fairly tall, dark man with bright blue eyes closed the door of the telephone booth.

'M. Perrin here.'

'The national representative has taken Route No. 2. There are two cars. He is in the leading one, number 5249 HU 75. Two outriders. Good luck.'

M. Perrin hung up. He felt perfectly calm. He looked at his watch; it was 7.45 p.m. In no great haste he left the café. Dusk was beginning to fall in the great avenue. Colonel Bastien-Thiry, alias 'Didier', had crossed the threshold of history.

In Monique Bertin's bed-sitter on the third floor of No. 2 Avenue Victor-Hugo in Meudon the air was thick with smoke; some ten men were waiting there. Some were playing bridge; others were reading. One man was standing at the window; the curtains were drawn, but through a crack he was keeping watch on the street.

On the pavement below a man stopped, glanced surreptitiously up towards the window and unfolded a newspaper.

'The signal,' the observer at the window shouted.

At once the men of the commando got up quietly and went towards the door.

'Not all at once,' the smallest man in the group ordered.

'OK, Max.'

Max went out first followed by a round-faced broad-shouldered man. Down in the street he went up to a Simca 1000 which was parked near by. Bastien-Thiry was at the wheel.

'He should come via Avenue de la Libération on Route Nationale 306. Good luck.'

'This time we're all right.'

An Estafette and a Peugeot 403 van passed.

Max went to an Idée 19 and got in with the round-faced man and another thick-necked man with a slight limp: Jacques Prévost and Georges Watin. 'Max'—alias Alain Bougrenay de la Tocnaye—moved off in his turn. The Simca 1000 had already disappeared.

When he came out onto the Avenue de la Libération, la Tocnaye could see Bastien-Thiry who was already out of his Simca and had posted himself at the junction of the avenue and a small side-street, a few yards from a bus-stop. He was carrying a newspaper.

Further on towards Villacoublay, on the left of the road, the Peugeot 403 van was manoeuvring to get into position. At the wheel was the greenhorn of the team, Pierre Magade, a young *pied-noir* with a rather pronounced squint. Beside him were Louis de Condé and Pascal Bertin, brother of the girl who had lent them her apartment in Meudon. Their task was to block de Gaulle's route.

Still further on, some 250 yards from Bastien-Thiry and just before an Antar petrol station, the yellow Estafette, number 650 DM 89, stopped, facing away from Paris. Inside were five men: Lazlo Varga at the wheel, Serge Bernier in command, Gérard Buisines and the two Hungarians, Sari and Marton.

It was slowly getting dark. Bernier could hardly see the figure of Bastien-Thiry who seemed to be very far away. It was 8.05 p.m.

A hump in the road restricted Bernier's view of on-coming vehicles through the Estafette's half-open sunblinds.

One or two vehicles passed with their sidelights on.

A courting couple was quite close to the Idée in which were la Tocnaye and the two sub-machinegun experts.

It was 8.08 p.m. A bus passed, almost empty.

The Idée was parked in the Rue du Château and was not to come into action until the first shots had been fired. Its duty was to block the route of de Gaulle's car if it had not been stopped already.

Jean-Pierre Naudin was patrolling the area in a Citroën 2 cv lent to the conspirators, at the same time as the apartment, by Bertin's sister. After passing Naudin the presidential car would be seen by Bastien-Thiry who would give the signal. It would then be 'received' by the marksmen in the Estafette and 'finished off' by the passengers in the Idée.

There was not a loophole in the plan. Everything had been foreseen, precisely worked out and rehearsed. Every detail had been carefully calculated, examined, discussed and finally agreed. The weapons themselves, so laboriously collected, had been tried out. The commando had been awaiting this moment for months.

When the moment of action arrived, however, when it was actually approaching them at 60 mph and would be with them in a few seconds, everyone had the same small doubt: 'And supposing it goes wrong again.'

Bastien-Thiry himself was quite calm. His mind was at peace. If he had decided to kill de Gaulle, it was only for the common good. His own life counted not at all. As he noted later, he felt himself to be 'the defender of all those millions of men and women who have suffered physically, mentally and materially from the abominable, high-handed and unjust policy which has been pursued'. Ambition was not his motive, otherwise he had simply to continue his career; at thirty-five years of age he had reached the summit of his profession (military engineering) and was a

Chevalier of the Legion of Honour. Scientific circles regarded him as the 'French von Braun'; he was accepted and esteemed by the Americans, although he had received scant recognition in France for his invention of the famous ground-to-ground No. 11 rockets. He was acting simply for the sake of others. His only worry was his family, his wife Geneviève and his three daughters. What would happen to them if he disappeared? Perhaps she would remarry one day, as the wives of La Rochejacquelin and de Charette had done—and scandalised Napoleon. His father was another worry. Would he understand why he had done it? Would he realise that his reasons were altruistic and disinterested? Bastien-Thiry dismissed these sombre thoughts. This was the time for action; he must not allow his thoughts to wander. Standing near the bus-stop, he gazed into the gloom from which the black Déesse would emerge.

Further on la Tocnaye was not so calm. Seated behind the wheel of his Idée—which had been stolen that morning since they had run out of money for the hire of vehicles—he mulled over his various problems. For him the affair was not crystal clear. He was expecting a bit of sand in the works. His mind was at rest, of course. He had confided everything to his father confessor, who had followed him out saying: 'Peace be with you, my son . . . and good luck.' He too was certain that his cause was just and that he was fighting a good fight. He need not blush before his ancestors. He was hounding the heretic—like Olivier the crusader or Jehan, the great captain who had fought against the stupidities of Charles VI. He was on the right side of the barricade. He could take comfort from that certainty. But he was not so sure of the others. Had they the nerve? Admittedly everything had been minutely worked out— as far as was possible.

'Georges,' he said suddenly to Watin, 'where are the Molotov cocktails?'

'They're in our boot with the Mark 2 grenades.'

'Have they got grenades in the Estafette as well?'

'Yes, Max. They also have plastic and flares. It's all wrapped up in the boot.'

'I'm sorry that Didier did not want the 403 van to take part directly.'

'Didier knows what he's doing.'

'Anyway, I hope that our escape vehicles are all in position.'

Prévost took a hand: 'Condé and the two youngsters, Naudin and Bertin, have dealt with that. The Fiat Neckar is at the entrance to Meudon wood on the Place du Tapis-Vert. The blue Estafette which we hired is in the Rue Charles-Daubry. The white saloon we stole this morning is at the corner of the Route du Pavé-Blanc.'

Watin spoke: 'No need to get so worked up, Max. Everything's running quite smoothly.'

Max looked at him. Seated beside him, Watin radiated calm and strength. His conviction and his nerve were always unshakeable. To the very end the gaullist police never caught him. For six years he was the Ministry of the Interior's nightmare and was labelled 'Public Enemy No. 1' like a Chicago gangster. He was built for the job—thick neck, hair growing low on the forehead, small hard eyes, the shoulders of a furniture remover, squat and brawny; he would have made a good rugger hooker. His most remarkable characteristic was his limp—a fact which was to cause slight problems with the police for most of the lame men in Paris. Incredibly, though, it never led to his downfall. He was never arrested.

Watin was the typical *pied-noir*. He had been born in Algeria and was a qualified agricultural engineer. He soon abandoned agriculture for subversion, however, long before de Gaulle had decided to relinquish Algeria. He was expelled from Algeria by the police in 1960. He was in the firing of the 'Barricades'. In Paris he immediately re-established contact with supporters of French Algeria and soon became assistant to Canal ('Le Monocle'), head of 'Mission III'. He was involved in practically every assassination attempt and every raid. His courage and daring became legendary.

Looking at him as he sat in the passenger seat, solid, calm, radiating strength, with his gun on his knees, looking like a beast of prey ready to spring, la Tocnaye felt reassured.

In his rear-view mirror la Tocnaye could also see Jacques Prévost— equally calm, a similar squat figure giving the same impression of strength, a typical fighting type. He had been a telecommunications engineer and had had good prospects in this profession when he felt the need for adventure. He enlisted for Indo-China and then fought in the OAS. It was he who had been commissioned to blow up the Sahara oil-wells. His failure or near-failure—only two wells caught fire—was due to the fact that he was ordered not to proceed, as happened also in other cases we have looked at. Jean Bichon had met him by chance in a café, where he was calling himself Lieutenant de Brémonville, and had re-cruited him for Operation 'Charlotte Corday'. He and Watin knew each other well: they had fought side by side on the barricades in Algiers.

All three listened to the night noises, ready to pounce at the first sound of firing.

From the back seat of the Estafette Bernier was keeping the road under observation through field-glasses, his sub-machine gun beside him. Serge Bernier, also known as Bernard, was in some respects the opposite of Watin. He was tall, slim and blond with astonishingly clear blue eyes. But he was another fighting type; he had had a brilliant career during the Korean war but never talked about it. He was a calm, reliable man.

Through his field-glasses he was trying to see Bastien-Thiry near the bus-stop but could make out nothing except a hazy silhouette.

No one in the Estafette said anything. Marton, the veteran of Budapest, looked at his luminous wrist-watch. It was 8.10 p.m.

At this precise moment Bastien-Thiry saw two outriders in the distance, approaching fast. At once he unfolded his newspaper in the direction of the Estafette.

Bernier saw nothing. Bastien-Thiry was too far away and the newspaper could not be seen. In vain Bastien-Thiry gave his signal a second time; the Estafette was half blacked out and the night was too dark.

Bernier scanned the road desperately. Suddenly he saw two motor-cyclists, followed by a black car, appear only sixty yards away. He immediately opened the rear door of the Estafette, shouting to the others: 'Come on!' Then he opened fire.

He had been taken by surprise both by the arrival of the convoy and its speed. His sub-machine gun blazed, followed almost at once by Buisines' machine gun firing from inside the Estafette. Kneeling against the right-hand side of the van, Sari sprayed the President's convoy which did not appear to swerve even an inch off course.

Bernier joined Marton in front of the Estafette and went on shooting at the convoy which drove on at top speed.

At this moment a pedestrian, apparently absorbed in his own thoughts, passed close to the Estafette without noticing that he was in the middle of a shooting affray.

'Hi, you!', Bernier shouted calmly. 'You're in my line of fire.'

The unknown looked up, apparently found this quite normal and simply said: 'I'm so sorry.'

Then he edged across towards the hedge bordering the pavement and went peacefully on his way, still deep in meditation.

It was all over very quickly—a matter of a few seconds only. Though thrown into some confusion, the convoy, nevertheless, drove on into the night.

On hearing the first burst la Tocnaye started: 'That's it! Let's go!'

He threw the car into gear and moved out. But at the very moment that he reached the avenue, de Gaulle's Déesse passed at full speed, seemingly off balance, lurching drunkenly; the nearside front tyre had blown. It just failed to hit a Panhard coming towards it and passed it with only a couple of inches to spare on the offside. With his fantastic skill Francis Marroux, the general's chauffeur, had once more saved de Gaulle's life. The car rolled, zigzagged and skidded but it kept driving on at full speed. The hail of fire from the Estafette had not slowed it down.

Like a madman la Tocnaye turned down the avenue, tyres screaming.

The offside door was still open. He had moved off so suddenly that Watin had not had time to shut it and almost fell out as the car swung round. La Tocnaye managed to hold him in while Watin, one leg trailing on the road loosed a magazine from his Sterling at the drunken Déesse.

'I can see them,' la Tocnaye yelled.

De Gaulle did not seem to have moved. A figure was jumping up and down in the Déesse—it was Colonel de Boissieu leaning over towards his parents-in-law.

Watin was still firing. The rear window of the Déesse splintered.

'Georges, you're dead on!'

Suddenly the Sterling was silent. 'Hell!' Watin shouted; 'I've got a stoppage. Drive on, Max.'

At this moment de Gaulle's escort car cut in front of la Tocnaye's Idée, just missing the bumper. The fantastic chase continued at 75 mph. It began to rain. The pursuers' Idée was practically touching the escort car. In his rear-view mirror la Tocnaye saw the outriders zigzagging; one of them was trying to draw his gun.

'Look out behind,' la Tocnaye shouted. 'Jacques, shoot at their tyres.'

'My Schmeisser's out of action.'

'Take my Monopole. Watch out, it's cocked.'

Watin, who had managed to put in another magazine, turned and began spraying the outriders; the bullets struck sparks underneath their tyres. Then they were gone, swallowed up by the night.

The escort car was still in front of them, driving at full speed but there was no one to be seen inside; they could just make out the driver, bent over the wheel.

La Tocnaye put his foot right down but the Idée was losing ground; the two Déesses were more powerful. They were pulling away, although de Gaulle's car was still swaying dangerously. The driver was undoubtedly a maestro; since Pont-sur-Seine this was the second time that he had saved de Gaulle's life.

In the distance, lit up by the headlights, Watin saw a collection of people.

'Look out, Max. The cops have put up a road block.'

Realising that the game was up, la Tocnaye turned sharp right a few yards from the road block, tyres screeching once more. He dived down the little Café de l'Aviation street heading for the motorway interchange. He turned left again and they were on the Verrières road.

'What hellish luck!' Watin growled. 'I only fired eight rounds from my second magazine.'

'Still, I think you got him, Georges.'

In the back of the Idée Prévost had his ear to a transistor; he was listening on the police wavelength: 'There we are. The alert's been given.'

'I hope the others have managed to get away.'

'Are we going via the Pont de Sèvres?'

'They won't have had time to put out road blocks; it takes them at least ten minutes.'

La Tocnaye slowed down. A black Peugeot 403 passed at full speed.

'The Meudon police,' someone said.

The police went on their way, not realising that they had just passed the assassins' car.

On the Pont de Sèvres there was a blockage and la Tocnaye had to drive at walking-pace following a line of cars—was it road works or had the police already established a road block? It was not a road block and the Idée disappeared into Boulogne. In a little street in Passy it stopped. The three men got out; the road was practically deserted. They dived into a building and rang the doorbell of a flat.

The door was opened by an extremely pretty young woman named Ghislaine. She was white with emotion. She kissed all three men without a word. Then she said: 'He got away. I heard a news flash on the radio. Apparently he said: "It was a close thing this time." He has taken an aeroplane to Saint-Dizier.'

Once more 'he' had got away. It was dispiriting. They said nothing for a second or two. Then the habits of the underground asserted themselves:

'Don't tell me that you took your gloves off.'

'One forgets. You're right. We might have left fingerprints in the car.'

'There might also be some cartridge cases.'

'I'll deal with it.'

La Tocnaye went down, sat behind the wheel of the Idée and wiped it carefully. Then he wiped the doorhandles, both inside and outside. He drove off to leave the car somewhere. He thought it fun to stop near a police station and, having checked that no cartridge cases were lying about, he left the car and went back to Ghislaine's flat on foot.

Bastien-Thiry and Jean Bichon had arrived meanwhile and were holding a council of war. La Tocnaye was furious—'To make a mess of an opportunity like that,' he growled.

Bastien-Thiry looked at him calmly: 'These are the fortunes of war.'

'No, Didier. If you had not refused to let us have a second van, we would have had him. It was a great mistake.'

'I don't think so, Max.'

'In any case the signalling system didn't work. If Bernier had seen the signal, they would have moved and blocked the convoy's road whereas in fact the convoy came on them at full speed. The machineguns couldn't come into action as planned. As far as I was concerned, my car would hardly go and, what's more, Georges had a stoppage. Hellish bad luck!'

Watin felt that the moment had come to calm him down: 'In any case,

Max, you saved our lives. Your turn at the Café de l'Aviation got us away. We would never have been able to get off the motorway.'

Bastien-Thiry was still quite calm. He was trying to weigh up the situation. His first reaction was philosophical: 'I wonder why dictators so often have good luck. Hitler had moved away from the table and was behind a pillar when von Stauffenberg's bomb went off. Napoleon would have been blown up by the bomb in the Rue Saint-Nicaise if his coachmen hadn't been drunk that evening and set off at full gallop. Perhaps it's the hand of Providence which punishes the people who fall into the grip of such men.'

Prévost put down his glass and said: 'I hope the others have got away.'

'If they have, they'll be under cover by now. Call Bernier. His telephone's not being tapped.'

La Tocnaye dialled a number, let the telephone ring three times and then hung up. Then he dialled it again—this was the code. Bernier came on the line and confirmed that he had not seen Bastien-Thiry's signal. The party in the Estafette had been taken by surprise by the arrival of de Gaulle's car and had not been able to operate as planned.

As far as Bernier's party was concerned, once the presidential convoy had disappeared into the night pursued by la Tocnaye, they got back into the Estafette and went towards Tapis-Vert where the Fiat Neckar was parked near a bar. The cross-roads were quiet but the men were jumpy. The Fiat refused to start and they had to push it. When it eventually started, they realised that they had forgotten the machine guns which were still in the Estafette. It was too late to go back for them: police checks might already be in operation.

In fact the CRS were putting up a road block just before the Porte de Versailles as they arrived and, for good measure, the lights went red, bringing them to a halt.

Bernier had not lost his self-control. He laid the barrel of his submachinegun on Varga's shoulder (Varga was driving) and calmly waited for the CRS officer to arrive. As the officer leant in he found the muzzle of a gun a foot from his chest. He neither jumped back nor said a word. He gazed at the passengers in the car, looked down the barrel of the gun for a moment or two, straightened up slowly, took a couple of paces back and calmly waved them on. No one has ever known whether he merely had no wish to die or was a sympathiser. (It is also possible that he took the occupants of the Fiat for *barbouzes*; he might well have found it inconceivable that de Gaulle's would-be assassins would be so bold as to drive around Paris half an hour later with their guns still on their knees).

Since other road blocks might now be established on the main boulevards—and these would be more difficult to circumvent—they decided to park the car in a small street, the Rue des Périchaux near the Porte de Vanves.

On arriving at the ticket-office of the metro station near by, Varga and Bernier discovered that they had no money. Marton bailed them out and so they escaped.

Just at this moment a police patrol saw a badly parked Estafette along-side the pavement at the Tapis-Vert crossroads. The police approached it, sub-machine guns at the ready. They found two machine guns and one sub-machine gun. They radioed the news through at once but other ears were listening on the police net and so various radio sub-stations could give their listeners a special news flash a few minutes later.

The Fiat was not discovered until next morning. The police found two sub-machine guns and a US carbine in its boot.

For the police a great manhunt now began. Dropping everything else, they set themselves to find the men who had had the temerity to shoot at de Gaulle—without hitting him, for yet once more the general was safe and sound, and once again it was a case of *le canard est toujours vivant* ('the duck is still alive'—General Salan's celebrated remark about de Gaulle). This time, however, death had been very close.

De Gaulle must be given credit for being almost totally uninterested in his own safety. During the shooting in front of Notre Dame on Liberation Day he had been the only one to remain standing when the entire crowd threw themselves to the ground as the gunmen started firing from the roofs. His whole life was dominated by the conviction that he was a historic personality. The scorn with which he regarded those responsible for his safety was proverbial—'I am doing my job,' he would say. 'You do yours. De Gaulle is not to be kept under a glass case.'

On the evening of 22 August, while Marroux was driving him to Villacoublay, his thoughts were elsewhere. For him the Algerian affair was over. His political analysis had led him to think that the higher interests of France lay in the total abandonment of Algeria to the forces of revolution. He was unmoved by the resulting drama in the lives of more than a million uprooted Europeans—that was the price which had to be paid. When he signed the act recognising the independence of Algeria on 3 July, the general thought that he was bringing this unhappy affair to its final end—'Algeria, that's finished'. He could now move on to his great international designs, his principal purpose being to inflate the French frog to the size of the American buffalo. With this in mind his external activities multiplied: he despatched his diplomats to the four corners of the earth, commissioning them to intrigue, intrigue again, throw spanners in the works, oppose.

In July he had received Chancellor Adenauer, the only man to under-stand his thinking. A Franco–German alliance, if it could be brought about, would change the face of the world. Possession of a strategic nuclear force, moreover, would finally give France a seat among the Great Powers, on a level with the other two giants. In this he was sure that he could win. An anti-government motion of censure on a draft law allocating supplementary credits for the strategic force had been defeated in the National Assembly on 16 July. So he had been given the green light for the manufacture of atomic bombs and that would give both the men of the Kremlin and those of the Pentagon something to think about.

Turning to more immediate matters, that very afternoon of 22 August, before leaving in his car, he had presided at a cabinet meeting for which he had recalled ministers from their holidays—primarily to underline the fact that he was the master. He had not really had a great deal to say to them that day. He had merely referred to his forthcoming visit to Germany at the invitation of his friend, the aged Chancellor. He had not breathed a word about his great plan—the election of the President of the Republic by universal suffrage. It would be time enough to tell them about that when the moment came. He had left them worrying about the alarming reports of the installation of Soviet rockets in Cuba; but that was a matter for the Russians and Americans—let them work it out.

While his car was tearing through Petit-Clamart, he was suddenly aroused from these meditations by the voice of his son-in-law who was sitting in front beside the chauffeur: 'Father, get down!'

Almost simultaneously the chatter of automatic weapons stabbed the darkness.

De Gaulle looked calmly in front of him; in the headlights he could see figures and guns spewing fire. At once Francis Marroux accelerated, the big car beginning to swerve. Bullets hit the coachwork with a dull thud. Madame de Gaulle, sitting beside the general, seemed to have seen nothing. She preserved a calm as olympian as his own. In the front seat, however, Boissieu was jumping up and down: 'Keep to the middle,' he shouted, 'and keep driving!'

With his eyes starting out of his head he saw a car appear in front of them; the swaying limousine only just avoided it.

Boissieu then realised that the assailants' car was following them, still spitting fire.

'Father, for God's sake get down,' the colonel shouted once more.

This time the general did as he was told and Madame de Gaulle did likewise.

A fraction of a second later the rear window splintered, glass falling all over the general who got up and looked back. 'That's too much!' he said, still as calm as ever; 'they're following us.'

Marroux went on at full speed, though he could not stop the car zigzagging. Suddenly their pursuers vanished. The firing stopped. The car tore into Villacoublay like a whirlwind. Still trembling, Boissieu helped first his mother-in-law and then his father-in-law out. The general wiped the glass splinters from his coat with the back of his hand, scratching one finger slightly so that, when he wiped his face, he left a small streak of blood on his cheek. Then, to Boissieu's astonishment, he moved off, quite unhurried, to inspect the Air Force guard of honour which was presenting arms. He only showed his feelings when in the aircraft and after it had taken off.

'Their operation was badly organised,' he said to Boissieu. 'Their shooting was hopeless. They were no experts. But I congratulate you; in moments of crisis there is a ring of command in your voice.'

And suddenly, to everyone's surprise, he took his son-in-law in his arms and kissed him.

'Whisky!' he said to the steward. 'And some beer for my wife.'

Something very exceptional must have happened for de Gaulle to wish to regale himself with British liquor.

CHAPTER 26

An Expensive Obsession

The next morning, 23 August, Bastien-Thiry, Jean Bichon and la Tocnaye thumbed through the newspapers. All the headlines were devoted to the assassination attempt. Reading the articles, they were inevitably struck, yet again, by de Gaulle's incredible luck.

There were numerous photographs of the President's car. It had been hit six times. Two tyres were burst, one front and one rear. One bullet had entered below and to the left of the figure '5' on the registration plate, had passed through the boot and lodged in the left side of the rear seat. Another bullet had holed the front door; yet another had punctured the petrol-cap cover and lodged in the rear seat. The bullet which had shattered the back window had passed $4\frac{1}{4}$ inches above the top of the back seat. Had de Gaulle not taken cover, he would have been hit. The police reconstructed the trajectories of the bullets using lengths of string and it was impossible to sit down without touching a string. Yet no one had been hit.

The security guards' car had been hit four times in the chassis— Watin had only fired to stop it. The motor-cycle belonging to Ehrman, one of the outriders escorting de Gaulle, had been hit on the offside luggage-carrier; the other outrider found a bullet in his helmet.

The same 'luck of the devil' had even taken care of the 'extras' on the scene. The Panhard into which de Gaulle's car had nearly crashed and which was right in the line of fire, was driven by a M. Fillon. He and his family emerged unharmed from the fusillade apart from a scratch on the forefinger caused by a splinter from his steering wheel which had been hit by a bullet.

All around Petit-Clamart the police and press discovered bullet-holes in buildings, shop-windows and even hulls of boats displayed for sale. A television store at the corner of the Rue Charles-Debry had been hit twenty-six times. The Le Trianon café had been liberally sprayed with bullets; a group of men playing *belote* there saw their drinks knocked over by a bullet, and yet none of them was hit. (The café has since been renamed Le Trianon de la Fusillade in memory of this great day.)

The only casualty—except Bastien-Thiry who subsequently paid for the attempt with his life—was Robert Lombard, head of the *gendarmerie* in Colombey: he collapsed with a heart attack on hearing the news over the telephone.

The police collected about a hundred cartridge cases.

Not only had the attempt failed but de Gaulle had emerged as an even more impressive figure. He seemed to be protected by Providence which was clearly no longer on la Tocnaye's side as he had thought. This was no doubt the reason why the police seemed so anxious to give journalists a wealth of detail. It certainly did not herald any very secret investigations.

Bastien-Thiry, Bichon and la Tocnaye consequently had all the data on which to make an appreciation of their operation.

'I see what went wrong,' Bastien-Thiry said. 'We must not make the same mistakes in future.'

'In future?'

'At our next attempt.'

He really was incorrigible, never wavering for an instant from his ultimate goal. He had just failed—only just; every police force in France and all the ancillary services were practically exhausted and here he was already thinking of beginning again and of succeeding this time.

The Petit-Clamart setback, however, had cooled la Tocnaye's ardour. 'Before starting again,' he said, 'we must let the police calm down for a time. After last night's escapade we ought to send our men to Spain at once.'

'Paris is the best place to hide,' Bichon objected.

La Tocnaye blew up: 'We shall all be arrested. You're joking. All you want is to have them available so that you can make the same mistakes again. We must have money, forged papers and the resources to send out of the country the three Hungarians, Bernier, de Condé, Bertin and Naudin. Georges Watin and I will stay together. Do you agree to help them escape, yes or no?'

'All right,' Bichon sighed. He was clearly not convinced but had no wish to clash with the impetuous 'Knight'.

'Prévost can be responsible for getting Buisines, Constantin and Magade to Spain,' la Tocnaye went on. 'As for you, Didier,' turning to Bastien-Thiry, 'you may have been seen giving the signal and might be recognised. You ought to go to your family in Switzerland.'

'No question of that, Max. We must start action again as soon as possible. Anyway it is our only chance of extricating ourselves.'

'I agree that we must begin again, but we must do it with new weapons. And in any case it should be much later, when all this has blown over.'

This time Jean Bichon seemed to agree with la Tocnaye:

'Max is right. You are over-confident, Didier. I know the police who will be in charge of finding us and they are tough nuts. They will follow their clues through to us.'

'They won't find me. They have no reason to suspect me.'

'Do as you like,' Bichon said finally. 'Max and I will go to the country for a few days.'

In fact no such manhunt by the police had ever been seen. Maurice Bouvier, head of the criminal police, had been given a formal order by Roger Frey, the Minister of the Interior: 'We have got to get them. You have a fortnight to find them.'

The entire crime squad, reinforced by all other police forces, was put on the job. The famous police 'routine' got under way. One million cars were checked in two days—without any results, of course.

Starting from the vehicles used in the attempt, the Estafette and the Fiat Neckar, it was discovered that a man named 'Duprat' had hired several vehicles in Compiègne, Joigny and Amiens. This line of enquiry, however, yielded nothing.

As three stolen vehicles had been found in the XVth *Arrondissement*, the police made a house-to-house check to see if they could pick up a clue. Still no result.

All cafés between the Elysée and Petit-Clamart were visited systematic-ally by the police to check whether any suspicious person had been at the bar on the evening of the attempt. Again the result was more or less a blank. There was a vague clue, however: a certain M. Perrin had taken a telephone call in one of the cafés at the time of the attack. A meagre little piece of information, seemingly of no importance.

Finally a further team of police conducted enquiries in Meudon, in the actual area of the attempt.

The days went by and investigations were still at a standstill. At the end of the telephone Roger Frey, who called four or five times a day, was becoming impatient. For him it had become a personal affair. He was dreaming of the moment when he could go into de Gaulle's office and say to him: 'We've got them, General.'

For the moment the police could do no more than patrol the pavements night and day. Bouvier only slept a few hours a night. He wasted an infinity of time in checking the hundreds of telephone calls and letters from helpful people, as always happens in this sort of affair.

At last, on 30 August, Bouvier came upon the first link in the chain. The team dealing with the man who had hired vehicles under the name of Duprat discovered that he had been booked for a traffic offence a few days before the attempt by a local constable. When summoned, the constable in fact remembered that his 'client' had seemed somewhat odd; he was a small red-headed man behind the wheel of a Fiat Neckar—one of the vehicles used in the attempt.

A quick search in the files on the OAS produced two individuals answering to this description. One of them had already come to their notice at the time of the Pont-sur-Seine attempt: he was called Louis de Condé. This seemed to be a good clue, but it yielded nothing. Louis de Condé, always supposing that he was in fact 'Duprat', could not be found. A general search warrant was issued to all police forces but it gave few details: 'De Condé, Louis, known as "Petitou", alias François Duprat, born 1 January 1939 in Paris (XVIth *Arrondissement*).'

At the same time the files on known activists were being studied. They showed that an ex-secretary of the *Mouvement Populaire du 13 mai* was living in Meudon, at No. 2 Avenue Victor-Hugo, almost on the scene of the attempt. She was called Monique Bertin.

Having discovered the name of a girl who might have some connection with the attempt, the police at first proceeded to question people in her *quartier*. The *concierge* of the building and Monique Bertin's neighbours were asked: 'Did you hear anything on Wednesday, 22 August, about 8.10 p.m.? Had you seen anything suspicious in the neighbourhood beforehand? Strangers . . . etc?'

Suddenly one of those questioned came up trumps: he remembered having noticed several cars not belonging to the area parked outside No. 2 Avenue Victor-Hugo, in particular a yellow Estafette with the windows smeared with white paint. Bouvier felt that this time he was on to a good thing. Others had also noticed that Monique Bertin's brother often came to see her 'with his buddies'. One witness even said that one of these buddies limped.

Georges Watin! The name sprang to Bouvier's mind at once. It must be the elusive Watin who had always contrived to slip through his fingers but who was nevertheless involved in all the major coups. A photograph of Watin was called for. Yes, that was indeed one of the men who had visited Monique Bertin.

The girl was arrested at the door as soon as she returned from work. She protested complete innocence and had no difficulty in appearing truthful since *she did in fact know nothing about the assassination attempt.* Her brother had told her nothing. She was so innocent that she was quite prepared to say that she was meeting him in a library at 6 p.m. that very evening. It was by then 6.20.

Bouvier rushed to a telephone and alerted the Quai des Orfèvres which despatched three police cars at once. On returning to his office he found Pascal Bertin there. He had been kidnapped by the police as he was patiently awaiting his sister. He was searched. On him were found numbered stickers used to camouflage the registration numbers of vehicles, papers which left no doubt that he had been involved in the assassination attempt and even the key of an apartment, the address of which Bertin refused to divulge. He refused resolutely to talk and so the enquiry which had seemed to have got away to such a brilliant start, came to a full stop once more. Commissaire Bouvier could do no more than continue his routine checks and wait for the stroke of luck which sometimes comes the way of the police.

The stroke of luck took the form of two *gendarmes*—each with whistle, sub-machine gun, regulation moustache.

The day had just dawned on Route Nationale 7 at the entrance to Tain-L'Hermitage in the department of Drôme. The *gendarmes* had spent the night checking cars at a temporary road block. They had been ordered to stop and check all Renault cars driving towards Paris.

They were just about to take down their barriers and go home to bed when they saw a red Dauphine registered in Algiers (9A). In it were three men. One answered the description of the deserter for whom they were looking—crew cut and pronounced squint. But he made no fuss about admitting the fact: 'That's right. I am a deserter.'

The other two, whose papers were in order and who pretended not to know the deserter saying that he had simply thumbed a lift, were allowed to go by the gendarmes. After a whole day's interrogation by the local police inspector the deserter eventually admitted that his name was Henri Magade and that he belonged to the OAS.

'And of course you were at Petit-Clamart,' one of the *gendarmes* said as a joke.

'Yes, I was there.'

The *gendarmes* were thunderstruck. They had caught a big fish. Magade was rushed to Paris and brought before Commissaire Bouvier. He did not hold out long, for the head of the criminal police knew how to grill a suspect. Magade was no match for Bouvier and he let fall many names. He referred to Watin of course, and to Max, and to a Lieutenant de Brémonville who drove a Chevrolet Bel-Air registered in Algiers, and to Alexis who had hidden him in the house of his father-in-law, a retired general who lived in the Rue de Vaugirard. Who was the leader, Bouvier asked. A certain Didier.

Action stations for the criminal police.

This time the clues were numerous. Bouvier, who had been very talkative on the day following the attempt, now worked in the greatest secrecy. The conspirators must not know that some of their number had been arrested. Not a word was said to the press.

A squad was despatched to the house of the retired general who was quickly identified—General Venot, living at 185 Rue de Vaugirard. His son-in-law, Alexis Ducasse, a friend of Louis de Condé who had helped the conspirators, was arrested in the provinces. Every policeman in Paris was ordered to look for a Chevrolet Bel-Air registered in Algiers. This time investigations were really under way. Roger Frey could breathe again.

CHAPTER 27

The Dénouement

When he realised that the entire gaullist police force had been mobilised to find the regicides of Petit-Clamart at all costs, la Tocnaye went through his list of contacts to find someone who could hide him and certain other members of his team. His thoughts turned immediately to a foreign diplomat whose acquaintance he had made through a United Press journalist in Algeria and who had promised him one day that, in the last resort, he could provide him with a hide-out offering the advantage of extra-territorial status.

'I promised you and I will keep my promise,' the diplomat said to him over the telephone. 'But I can only accommodate two people.'

La Tocnaye proposed that Watin should go with him and Watin accepted at once. Long experience of life in the underground had taught him that, if one did not wish to be caught on the street, the answer was to avoid the street. He therefore took up residence in his voluntary prison and decided not to go out for a long time.

La Tocnaye, on the other hand, had no sooner arrived than he announced his intention of going to see some friends.

'You're wrong, Max,' Watin said to him. 'You'll get yourself caught.'

'I simply must find some safe way of getting to Spain. I can't do that here. And anyway I'm not a child; I'll take care.'

'You're wrong to think they're fools, Max.'

'So far we've been cleverer than they have.'

Full of self-assurance la Tocnaye went out several times. Soon he came back with good news: via Ghislaine he had contacted a civil airline pilot who could take time off at any time. The pilot agreed to take two people to Spain in a private aeroplane; they would take off from a private airfield near Paris and hedge-hop to the frontier to keep under the radar screen.

'I've managed to telephone a friend in Spain,' la Tocnaye added. 'He will come and collect us at the place we land. We only have to warn him of our time of departure.'

'Bravo,' Watin said. 'And now don't move any more.'

'That's impossible. I have a meeting with Didier in an hour's time.'

Once again la Tocnaye left his hide-out. In Paris he found Bastien-Thiry and Bichon studying the schedule of de Gaulle's activities.

'What are you looking for?'

'The moment at which we could make another attempt.'

Both, particularly Bastien-Thiry, were thinking only of the next attempt, which *must* succeed this time. La Tocnaye realised that nothing would dissuade them and so decided that he would see to 'his' men on his own.

He succeeded in finding Bernier who was hiding with Louis de Condé. From them he learnt that Bertin should still be in Paris, as should the three Hungarians. (Bertin had already been arrested but naturally none of them knew that yet.)

'I'm in the process of organising a way of getting us across to Spain. I'll let you know time and place. Meanwhile go out as little as possible and hold yourselves in readiness to leave.'

To show that this order did not apply to him la Tocnaye went back to see Ghislaine in Passy. From her he learnt that Prévost had returned from Spain and was trying to contact him.

'Tell him to be at the Dupleix metro station at 11 a.m. tomorrow morning, 5 September.'

Dupleix is an above-ground station, comparatively little used, where it is easy to see if one is being followed. La Tocnaye duly met Prévost there at 11 a.m.

'I'm just back from Spain,' Prévost said, 'and I have made all arrangements to get our friends out. I have even been given money for it.'

'Excellent. What's happened to Buisines and Magade?'

'I left for Marseille with them. I myself hired a car to go to Spain, but they thought it better to go on to Nice. I have no news of them since.'

'I don't like that. All the police are on the look-out and they risk getting caught. I am counting absolutely on you to get Bernier and the others out of France as quickly as possible.'

'OK. Meanwhile come and have lunch with me at my place in the Rue Chappe in Montmartre.'

'You're mad to go back there.'

'I have to. In the first place it's in the name of de Brémonville. And, secondly, I have hidden there the three Matt 49 sub-machine guns, the Sten and the Sterling we used the other evening.'

'All right. We'll go there, take it all and hide it in a cache I have.'

'My car's parked over there.'

Opposite the station the shining chrome of a Chevrolet Bel-Air registered in Algeria was visible to all concerned.

'What! You still have the nerve to drive around in that?'

'What a funk you can be, Max. No one will connect it with anything. If it makes you happier, though, I'll dump it afterwards.'

After a good bachelors' lunch Prévost and la Tocnaye stowed the weapons into an old suitcase and placed all compromising papers in a briefcase. Then, having put it all in the Chevrolet's boot, they moved off.

It was now 5 p.m.

As they were about to turn into the Rue Berthe a car suddenly swung out from the line of parked vehicles and blocked their road. In a flash half a dozen policemen were round the Chevrolet, revolvers at the ready. One of the police put his gun to la Tocnaye's forehead shouting: 'Watch it!'

The attack came so suddenly that la Tocnaye had no time to snatch his P 08 Luger from the side-pocket in which he had put it.

At the local police headquarters the two men were searched. In addition to their papers the 300,000 francs which la Tocnaye was carrying were confiscated and he never saw them again. The police even took his rosary. Faced with this final insult, la Tocnaye could only murmur: 'The will of God be done.'

For the moment it was the will of Commissaire Ottavioli of the crime squad that mattered. La Tocnaye, of course, refused to say anything other than: 'I am M. Guillet and I am on my way back from Spain where I met M. de Brémonville.'

At midnight Commissaire Bouvier came on the scene. He brought with him a green hat adorned with a feather: 'Your hat, monsieur. You were seen wearing it over at Petit-Clamart.'

A stroke of luck—the hat was too big for la Tocnaye.

Bouvier accepted defeat. La Tocnaye was more explicit: 'I have nothing to do with Petit-Clamart. It is true that I belong to the OAS. My real name is Alain Bougrenay de la Tocnaye. I have nothing else to say.'

'As you like.'

After a few hours' sleep on the floor of an office near by, la Tocnaye asked to go to the lavatory. In the corridor he had a shock: he saw Constantin, Bertin and Magade who, however, pretended not to recognise him. La Tocnaye immediately saw where his duty lay: he must assume his responsibilities and not leave his men to take the rap. He asked to talk to the Commissaire of the Division: 'I have a statement to make.'

'I am listening.'

'First I would like to have my rosary back.'

'It will be returned to you.'

'Here is my statement. I am the instigator, the organiser and the leader of the Petit-Clamart operation. From this moment I shall refuse to answer any questions put to me during the fifteen days' detention which I must undergo. You can have my head. That should be enough for you. Please now leave me in peace.'

Only three days later, as la Tocnaye was being led down the famous passage on his way to headquarters he happened to see Bastien-Thiry—handcuffed. He passed him without a glance, heart beating fast and in the depths of despair.

Commissaire Bouvier's investigations had undoubtedly been conducted with consummate mastery. Admittedly they had had their share of luck but all policemen know that that must be one of the ingredients.

The few names dropped by Magade had been followed up at once. After the arrest of Alexis Ducasse (General Venot's son-in-law) and Pascal Bertin, Bouvier had concentrated on finding the Chevrolet Bel-Air registered in Algeria. Since both the registration number and the colour might have been changed, he decided to have all Bel-Air Chevrolets in Paris checked by two plain-clothes policemen.

This method was successful. About 2.30 p.m. on 5 September a white Chevrolet registered in Algeria was located in the Rue Chappe. Bouvier immediately despatched a 'tough' team to intercept the owner or owners when they came to collect it. They brought off a double coup: Jacques Prévost and Alain Bougrenay de la Tocnaye were arrested.

Bouvier felt that he was now on the right track: in his office in the Ministry of the Interior Roger Frey started to smile again.

In the second bed-sitter occupied by Prévost the police found a note-book full of telephone numbers. The addresses concerned were visited. As a result, Constantin, who had contracted out of the Petit-Clamart operation because he had 'flu, was arrested in his turn. Bouvier's sleuths only missed Louis de Condé and Serge Bernier by an hour; when la Tocnaye did not return, they had thought it better to decamp.

The police routine was also under way in the search for the three Hungarians. The files of all the four thousand Hungarian refugees in Paris were checked. Their landlords reported three of them as missing. The file on one of them showed the name of his girl-friend. She was a barmaid. (A good filing system is the basis of all good police work.) A few hours later Varga was arrested: he was hiding in the house of a genuine countess in Versailles. Bouvier's list of trophies included another capture: Buisines was arrested in Marseille having been given away by an informer (who was shot for his pains nine years later).

There remained the big fish—Didier.

None of those under arrest would talk. Moreover, apart from la Tocnaye, none of them knew his real identity.

Bouvier had only a vague description of Didier. He must be about forty years of age and was certainly an officer; he seemed to work some-where near the Boulevard Victor. Bouvier asked Military Security to provide him with a list of senior officers who might possibly answer to the vague identikit portrait which had emerged from numerous patient interrogations (casually and without the prisoner suspecting, Bouvier had obtained numerous little indications which all added up).

A few hours later Military Security sent Bouvier an envelope. In it was a single photograph, that of the man who seemed to answer to the description given. Bouvier read its accompanying file: 'Jean-Marie Bastien-Thiry. Born in Lunéville (Meurthe et Moselle) 10 October 1927. Military College of Science [Ecole Polytechnique] 1948–1950; Air Force Staff College. Promoted Engineer 2nd class 1 April 1951; promoted Engineer 1st class 1953. Posted to Air Force Technical Service (Guided Missiles) 15 October 1954. Chevalier of Legion of Honour for flying duties 30 October 1961. Military Chief Engineer 2nd class with rank of lieutenant-colonel 1 January 1962. Married February 1955 to Geneviève Lamirand.'

Bouvier was uneasy. Admittedly he was sure that the description given was correct. The minute details provided by the men whom he had questioned all pointed in the same direction; there was no jarring note. On the other hand, Military Security had only provided him with one single file. He decided to show his suspect's photograph to the others. La Tocnaye, of course, refused with disdain to recognise anybody: 'I recognise nobody and have nothing to say.'

The others reacted in certain small ways. Two of them definitely recognised 'Didier'.

Bouvier now merely had to go into action as discreetly as possible—one does not arrest a lieutenant-colonel, graduate of the Military College of Science, as if he had stolen an apple from a barrow.

At dawn on 17 September a large force of police took up position near the villa in which Bastien-Thiry lived in Bourg-la-Reine. When he emerged, strapped into the inevitable green mackintosh, the police went quietly, almost shamefacedly, up to him—they would not have been so obliging in the case of someone less eminent in the hierarchy of bourgeois society.

Inside the villa, away from the prying eyes of passers-by, less polite methods were employed; the police went through it with a fine tooth-comb, turning back carpets and emptying cupboards. They brought very little back to Bouvier—two harmless address books and some notes on professional matters. But there was also a scrap of newspaper on which was written 'M. Perrin' with a telephone number. This name meant something to Commissaire Bouvier. He hunted through the pile of statements and records and eventually found it. It was the name of an unknown personage who had taken a telephone call on the evening of the shooting and very close to the scene. Bouvier at once despatched two police officers to Petit-Clamart with Bastien-Thiry's photograph. The café proprietor definitely recognised 'M. Perrin'.

Here was the proof. Bastien-Thiry was nailed. Moreover, the scrap of newspaper on which the name was written was dated the day before the assassination attempt—a policeman had spent an entire day checking the Paris press.

Calmly, almost casually, Commissaire Bouvier told Bastien-Thiry what he had discovered.

For hours 'Didier' refused to talk, fiercely denying any involvement in the assassination attempt. When Bouvier had finished his explanation, Bastien-Thiry tossed his head.

'Very well,' he said, 'I am ready to take responsibility. But I would first like an interview with a priest. Then I will talk.'

'I understand,' Bouvier murmured, almost sympathetically.

When Roger Frey, Minister of the Interior, heard that the leader of the conspiracy was under lock and key and prepared to confess, he was happy. At last he would be able to go into the general's office and tell him, with due modesty, that in less than a month he, Frey, had succeeded in discovering the would-be assassins.

But, as he thumbed through Bastien-Thiry's 'confession' together with the various reports indicating the existence of some vast conspiracy, he had a better idea. He would take the entire dossier to a cabinet meeting, bring it out in front of them all and give the general and his admiring colleagues an account of his triumph, with proof there for all to see. The general would undoubtedly produce one of his famous (and rare) comments—'That is very good, Frey'—and his friends would be white with envy. He would become the régime's new Fouché.

'I will keep the dossier to show it to the Cabinet,' Frey said. And he added, not without ulterior motive: 'That is very good, Bouvier.'

On leaving his office in the Ministry of the Interior Frey decided to secure the documents in the brand-new safe which had been installed for him that very afternoon. It was a well-nigh unbreakable safe, heavily armoured and capable of resisting oxy-acetylene, acids and plastic. The locking device was ultra-modern. The firm had sworn to him that it was the world's most modern safe. Here was a magnificent occasion to inaugurate it; in this safe he would lay the dossier on an already historic assassination attempt, with which his name would be coupled by posterity. Accordingly, in the presence of his secretary, the Minister of the Interior placed the dossier in the safe, took the key from the steel door, closed it, put the key in his pocket and decided to grace with his presence a social evening to which he had been invited.

Next morning he went early to his office in Place Beauvau. He intended to read the dossier in detail so that he could reply to any underhand

question which some envious colleague might put to him. He was in his
ministry by 8 a.m. He took out the key of his safe and realised at that
instant that he did not know the combination. He telephoned his secretary
at once: 'But, *monsieur le ministre*, I do not know it either.'

Action stations in the Place Beauvau. The Republic was in danger.
The director of the firm which had sold the safe was hauled from his
bath and brought post-haste to the ministry.

'I am glad to see you, monsieur,' Frey said. 'You can help me open this
safe which you have put in for me.'

'I do not know the combination, *monsieur le ministre*.'

'Nor do I.'

The two looked at each other in astonishment.

'But after all,' the minister said somewhat haughtily, 'if you, the
director, do not know the combination of your own safe, who does?'

'You, *monsieur le ministre*. We deliver safes, but it is the client who
decides on the combination as he wishes. As soon as the door is closed,
the combination becomes inoperative and no one other than the client
can open the safe.'

Frey was becoming aware of the magnitude of the disaster; his triumph
was immured behind an impenetrable wall of steel.

'There is nothing for it,' he said. 'We must open it with oxy-acetylene.'

The director smirked slightly; the quality of his products was soon to
be attested by a minister.

'But, *monsieur le ministre*, our safes are proof against oxy-acetylene.'

'Can one use explosives?'

Slightly irritated, the director explained:

'That sort of method is useless, *monsieur*. Our safes are unbreakable.'

Frey appeared to be lost in prolonged thought. His entourage, who
had somehow been alerted and had come running in despite the early
hour, looked at him uneasily. The cabinet meeting was due in two hours'
time and the general was as punctual as an alarm clock. They had two
hours to open that safe.

'Anyway,' the minister stormed at his private secretary, 'you might
have told me that one had to set the combination.'

'*Monsieur*, I thought that in a matter of this importance you would set
it yourself so that you would be the only one to know it.'

Frey was not going to have his triumph. He was not going to be able
to brandish under his colleagues' noses the hand-written confession of
the leader of the conspiracy. Then he had an idea—he called Commissaire Bouvier: 'Commissaire, bring me at once the copy of the Bastien-
Thiry dossier.'

The commissaire was taken aback: 'But, *monsieur le ministre*, I gave you
the only copy I possess, the original with the ink hardly dry.' (Bastien-Thiry
had insisted on writing his confession himself and there was only one copy.)

Total impasse. Suddenly one of the office staff coughed to attract the minister's attention: 'I am perhaps going to say something stupid. . . .'

'Then don't say it,' Frey roared.

Then he thought better of it: 'In the present situation, say it all the same.'

'We have in our employ a police officer who is a specialist on safes. He's always much in demand and so far no lock has held out against him.'

'What are you waiting for? Go and find him.'

'P'tit Louis'—this was his nickname—had never been asked to do such a thing—crack the safe of a Minister of the Interior under the eyes of the minister himself.

A curious ceremony then began. Everyone held his breath. The man pressed the tips of his fingers together and then applied his stethoscope to the lock. Minutes went by. The minister, who was in a highly nervous state, made a noise and thought it better to go out. 'P'tit Louis' continued to sound the lock, working with infinite delicacy. His career depended on his skill. He was sweating. Fifty minutes before the opening of the cabinet meeting—forty-five minutes. Frey put his head through the door. Everyone signalled for silence.

There were now only ten minutes before the general would enter the cabinet room where all the ministers were doubtless already assembled. Suddenly the door of Frey's outer office opened: '*Monsieur le ministre,* come quickly.'

Frey dashed in. 'P'tit Louis' was standing in front of the safe—open! Frey snatched up the bulky dossier, crossed the Place Beauvau at the double, dived into the Elysée, opened the door of the cabinet room and laid the dossier in front of him. At that moment the folding doors at the end of the room opened and General de Gaulle made his entry.

CHAPTER 28

Death in Suspicious Circumstances

The Ministry of the Interior had good reason to put out its flags. The police investigations had been a success. The assassination attempt had taken place on 22 August and it had been able to announce that enquiries were finished at the cabinet meeting of 19 September.

In fact they were not finished.

Admittedly Bastien-Thiry, the head of the conspiracy, was under lock and key and had confessed voluntarily. La Tocnaye, his commando leader, was also in prison, rosary in hand. Prévost, Buisines, Bertin, Varga, Constantin, Magade and Ducasse, were also safely out of the way. But neither Jean Bichon, nor Bernier, nor Condé (a descendant of the Duc d'Enghien), nor Marton, nor Sari, nor Naudin, nor, above all, the redoubtable Georges Watin had been captured, despite a vast effort on the part of every police force.

In particular there was one murky affair: that of Niaux.

As we have seen, routine police operations often produce results. Following distribution of the photographs of the members of the commando who were still at large, the police went the rounds asking the standard question: 'Do you know this face?' The manager of the Hotel de la Poste in Dinan stated that he recognised two of them. In fact, he thought he remembered three men spending a night in his hotel towards the end of June. He found the names in his police register; two of them meant nothing but the third caused police eyebrows to rise: Murat, a name mentioned during several different interrogations. The manager recognised the photograph of this man; he also remembered that one of the other men had a peculiarity: he limped slightly—the elusive George Watin. The hotel manager also remembered—his memory was first-class where the police were concerned—that the man Murat was about thirty, tall, blond, with blue eyes and that he had telephoned someone in the south-west.

While the hotel manager searched in his telephone register, the police held a council of war. Undoubtedly Murat was a cover-name for Serge Bernier; the description fitted exactly. As far as the other was concerned it was obviously Georges Watin, known as 'La Boiteuse'. The third man, a small jumpy individual, was not on their list (and for good reason—he was under arrest). Paris would know, however, they thought.

'Here we are,' the manager announced. 'Here's the number he called, in Lauzun, Lot-et-Garonne.'

Less than an hour later Maître Larrieu, magistrates' clerk in Lauzun, was arrested and taken to Paris. The local police were not merely playing Sherlock Holmes. This was an affair of state and all suspects were brought before the great men in the Quai des Orfèvres. The little clerk did not stand up to Bouvier for long. He soon produced the name of the man for whom he acted as 'post-box'—a certain Major Niaux.

Bouvier entered this new name in his notebook. He knew that the conspiracy had numerous supporters and he was no longer surprised at the standing of the men who made their appearance in the course of his enquiry.

Henri Niaux was a respectable soldier. He had failed Saint-Cyr but had been promoted major in the field, serving in Indo-China, Morocco, Tunisia and Algeria. He had been forced to resign from the army for refusing to receive de Gaulle when the latter visited the Signals Depot in Agen, of which Niaux was in charge. He became manager of an insurance agency but continued to help his friends working for French Algeria; he kept open house for anyone on the run or escaping from the clutches of Colonel Debrosse's *gendarmes* in Algiers.

At about 8 p.m. on 14 September Niaux was brought before Bouvier in police headquarters; he asked for time to think before accepting his responsibilities as an officer. Bouvier, who did not treat this type of man like a common criminal, proposed that he either rest in an armchair or sleep in the headquarters. Niaux chose to sleep there.

At approximately 8.30 a.m. next morning there was panic in the corridors. The warder had just found Major Niaux hanged in his cell from a sort of rope he had made from his shirt. Commissaire Bouvier may have acted as an honest policeman but there were others involved on the fringe of the enquiry whose rôle will one day be exposed by history. However this may be, on the morning of 15 September Major Niaux was found hanged in his cell.

A disturbing fact was that, when Madame Niaux was summoned to remove her husband's body, she found it completely naked. Moreover, she had been asked to 'bring some clothing'. She was convinced that her husband was not the type of man to have committed suicide and so she laid a complaint with the authorities. The court decided that it was suicide but, after several years of litigation, eventually admitted that there had been 'some negligence' and awarded fifteen million old francs in damages and costs to the widow.

But we must return to the major affair. The preliminary examination in the case of the Petit-Clamart assassination attempt could now begin. And indeed it did begin—with a flourish of trumpets, for de Gaulle was determined to make an example of these particular criminals. As in the Salan affair, the trial was no more than a legal formality. The problem and its solution were both in the hands of the general, and he had decided that the conspirators should be executed. In Colombey on the evening of the attack de Gaulle had said to Colonel de Boissieu, his son-in-law:

'I find it odious that my wife should be shot at. There will be no hesitation; I cannot grant a pardon.'

Without even knowing the men or their motives and although no one had actually been hit, de Gaulle had condemned them before the courts (*his* courts) had had their say. The court concerned, however, was no normal court: it stood outside the established judiciary.

The conspirators were in fact to be judged by the 'Court of Military Justice' which had been constituted by a decree dated 1 June 1962, a week after the end of the Salan trial, to replace the 'High Military Tribunal'. This was the 'emergency judiciary' which had already sentenced Degueldre and Canal to death. The latter had escaped execution only by a miracle and thanks to energetic delaying action by his defence counsel. Oddly enough, although there was no appeal against the decisions of this court, its validity could be contested before the Council of State. As a last resort, therefore, defence counsel for 'Le Monocle' (Canal), in the certainty that de Gaulle would pursue his desire for revenge to the bitter end if he had any prospect of doing so legally, applied to the Council of State.

On 19 October 1962 the Council of State (undoubtedly the only major organisation which refused to bow to the head of state) took a decision declaring the famous Court of Military Justice illegal 'in view of the importance and gravity of the infringements of the general principles of the penal code contained in the decree which established it'. André Canal was therefore in the uncomfortable position of a man condemned to death by a court which did not exist. In any case he could hardly be executed, since that would be nothing less than murder, as it had been in the case of Degueldre.

De Gaulle, acting in character, nevertheless took no notice of this decision by the highest authority in the country and decided to commute Canal's sentence to one of imprisonment for life. 'Le Monocle' received the decision with a shrug of the shoulders. From beginning to end his attitude had been one of perfect dignity. From the outset and with an air of finality he had refused to talk to anyone and had told his judges that he had nothing to say. When he was amnestied in 1968 he came out of prison just as calm, just as distant and just as silent.

The Canal affair, which had, so to speak, illegalised the Court of Military Justice, was an embarrassment to the head of state in his final settlement of the Petit-Clamart affair. He could not conceive that *his* judges would refuse him *his* verdict, which the ordinary courts might perhaps have done. He therefore had to have *his* court and so, on 15 January 1963, he promulgated a law which had the (unique) quality of being retroactive; it therefore legalised decisions which the Council of State had pronounced null and void. The next day, 16 January, a decree laid down that the Petit-Clamart conspirators would be brought before this court sitting in Vincennes.

There was, of course, no appeal against sentences awarded by this court. They were executive decisions, possibly mitigated only by the presidential prerogative of mercy—entirely contrary to the principle enunciated in the general Declaration on the Rights of Man (which France is one of the few countries to have refused to sign).

There was only one loophole for defence counsel: continually to raise points of order in an effort to prolong the trial until the date on which the court would be legally dissolved. This did not disturb the government in the least; on 20 February 1963, while the trial was in full swing, it promulgated a further law prolonging the existence of the court. General de Gaulle's pertinacity and spite were equalled only by that of the National Resistance Council and the OAS, whence the assassins had come.

Early in 1963, even before the Petit-Clamart trial had opened, two further assassination attempts were made against the head of state. The first was on 19 January 1963 in a big hotel on the right bank when de Gaulle attended the General Assembly of graduates of the National School of Administration. The second was on 15 February 1963 when he was about to visit officers of the Ecole Militaire.

Before dealing with these two operations, however, for the sake of continuity, we had better conclude the story of the Petit-Clamart affair.

CHAPTER 29

Death of a Banker

The composition of the Court of Military Justice was a matter for the government. The President was General Gardet. A few days before the trial one of the members of the court, when out to dinner, said quite openly: 'La Tocnaye? No problem—he must be shot.' Another of the members might have been thought to have provided some guarantee of 'objectivity'—at the time of the *putsch* he had been arrested and roughly handled by parachutists. The same applied to the third member who announced beforehand that he would judge 'according to the dictates of discipline'.

Counsel for the prosecution included Reboul, legal adviser to the Court of Appeal; he had been promoted lieutenant-colonel for the occasion and 'mobilised' as a Judge Advocate General. His presence on the side of the prosecution produced a number of heated exchanges, as a result of which one barrister was suspended for three years.

The part of Public Prosecutor was first played by M. Sudaka followed by M. Gerthoffer assisted by M. Floch (who during one session found himself challenged to a duel by Maître Richard Dupuy, one of the barristers. The Armed Forces Minister forbade M. Floch to fight it out and he was merely handed a certificate of non-appearance).

The trial took place at the Fort of Vincennes, surrounded by a large force of police. Of the three hundred witnesses put forward by the defence the judges only accepted about a hundred—why waste time when the outcome was decided anyway? After the anticipated tirade from Maître Gerthoffer the various counsel spoke in turn—Maître Jacquet, Maître Coudy, Maître Wagner and Maître Dupuy. At the session of 4 March 1963 the latter referred to the illogicality of the amnesty law of 22 March 1962 which exonerated from crime the moslems and pro-FLN Frenchmen but not Frenchmen fighting for the maintenance of France in Algeria. He also observed with some astonishment that, since 4 June 1960, the state had not been content merely to punish those who attacked its security; it now persecuted those who attacked its *authority* and that was unprecedented in a democratic country. He protested against the multiplication of parallel police forces which had never taken action against the FLN.

'Where does the truth lie?' he cried. 'Who will say? Neither we nor you. Neither M. Gerthoffer nor I. We are not here to elucidate the historical truth; that is not our business; that is the business of the historian who will write history in a hundred years' time, when it will be known what were the hidden cards, the secret protocols, the pressures exerted by Kennedy, Mr X, Mr Y, Khruschev and Nasser, by the bankers and oil magnates who pull the strings.'

And he concluded: 'Do you know what you will do if you pass three death sentences? You will produce three more corpses in the Algerian war; you will make orphans of seven children—seven—and widows of three women. Just stop and consider that.'

Maître Le Corroller, for his part, looked to history to provide justification for 'tyrannicide'. He cited Grégoire of Tours, Victor Hugo and Albert Camus. He launched into a violent tirade against the death sentence, particularly in political cases. The final plea was made by Maître Tixier-Vignancourt. The celebrated lawyer (he had not yet become a gaullist) adroitly quoted de Gaulle himself in support of the accused. He recalled an incident unique in the annals of justice: Claude Piegts' defence counsel was never granted an interview with the President of the Republic in order to present his plea for mercy on behalf of the little *pied-noir* from Castiglione who was shot at the Trou d'Enfer at 4.12 a.m. on 7 June 1962; the President who condemned him had not even thought fit to be present at the execution as the law demands. One may think what one likes, he said, about the 'crime' committed by a man, but no honest citizen can accept such summary justice.

In this connection Maître Tixier-Vignancourt referred to the astonishing statement by the Prime Minister, Michel Debré: 'We will meet illegality with illegality.' He also recalled the curious behaviour of the police officers despatched to Algeria from France under assumed names: Michel Hacq, for instance, director of the criminal police, called himself 'Professor Hermelin' in Algiers. He also attempted to prove that the shots fired by the conspirators had been intended to intimidate, not to kill; the object was to stop de Gaulle's car by shooting at the tyres, he said. He ended by telling the bench that a mass was being said every morning asking for the blessing of Heaven on the accused.

Sentence was pronounced at 11.30 p.m. on 4 March 1963 after the judges had deliberated for two hours forty minutes. 'The three minutes required to boil an egg would have been enough,' la Tocnaye remarked bitterly.

There were three death sentences—Bastien-Thiry, la Tocnaye and

Prévost, so the Public Prosecutor was satisfied, at least partially; he had demanded the death sentence for Buisines but Prévost had asked to take the place of his friend whom he had persuaded to join the commando and this request had been granted.

There were three other death sentences *in absentia*: Watin, Marton and Bernier.

Buisines was sentenced to life imprisonment, as were Louis de Condé and Naudin *in absentia*.

Bertin and Magade were given fifteen years' imprisonment, Constantin seven years and Ducasse three years.

Two events took place which have so far never been connected. At 11.30 p.m. on 4 March—in other words very nearly 5 March 1963—Bastien-Thiry was sentenced to death by the Court of Military Justice. At 10.30 a.m. next day, 6 March, M. Henri Lafond, chairman of the Banque de l'Union Parisienne, was assassinated at the corner of Avenue du Roule and Rue de Chézy in Neuilly. On the surface these two events were disconnected. In fact, the second was the direct consequence of the first.

At the time, the assassination of one of the great French bankers made a great stir. It was a real execution and all the press wondered what the motive was. At once it was thought that this was a political assassination and the OAS was accused of having done it for purposes of intimidation. In fact it was all much more simple.

At about 10.30 a.m. Henri Lafond emerged from his house, No. 102 Avenue du Roule in Neuilly, as he did every morning. He went towards his car which was a Rover, registration number 1789 KS 75, parked in front of a branch of the Banque Nationale de Commerce et Industrie. On seeing him approach as usual Roger Bouscaillou, his chauffeur, put down the newspaper he was reading, got out of the Rover and went to open the right-hand rear door.

'Good morning, sir,' the chauffeur said.

'Morning, Roger.'

Leaving the rear door open, the chauffeur got back behind his wheel and turned to pull the door to from his seat. At that moment a man seized the door, opened it wide, leant in towards the banker and asked him: 'Are you Monsieur Lafond?'

'Yes,' the banker replied in some surprise.

Thereupon the man drew a revolver and fired two shots at the banker who collapsed on the back seat. He then turned his gun on the chauffeur and fired twice. The chauffeur collapsed in his turn. The man fired a final shot at the banker and then fled.

Several witnesses saw the man running away and jumping into a black Citroën Idée with a white roof which started off with a screech of tyres and vanished into the traffic. All the witnesses agreed on one point: the killer was wearing a mackintosh, a hat and (most important) red gloves.

One witness, M. Petit, street-sweeper No. 104 in the town of Neuilly, who was only some ten yards from the scene, swore that the man was very fat and limped slightly. Every policeman immediately thought of Watin, 'Public Enemy No. 1', who still remained elusive.

In financial and political circles news of the murder spread like wildfire. The public at large did not know Henri Lafond. For some he was merely a quiet, orderly neighbour, probably well off. In Chapelle-en-Serval in the department of Oise he was known as a well-to-do Parisian who spent his weekends in his country house with his wife; on Sundays he would go to early morning mass and then to the Mortefontaine golf club where he had been a member since 1952; after playing a round of golf he would chat to others in the bar, sipping a glass of whisky. His was a calm existence without drama or love affairs—a peaceful family man.

In the world of politics and finance, however, Henri Lafond was a real power in the land. This was discovered as soon as his death became known. In the first place the bank of which he was chairman, the Banque de l'Union Parisienne, was the largest French bank after the Bank of France and the Netherlands Bank; in 1962 its profits were officially given as 9,250,000 *francs lourds*. It was in direct or indirect control of a number of companies such as the Saint-Nazaire shipyards, Petrofina and the Compagnie Française des Pétroles.

The French *Who's Who* devoted forty-six lines to Henri Lafond's career: 'Born 20 August 1894 at Thaumiers (Cher) and married to Mlle Thivet. One child, Jacqueline.' It went on to show that he was a graduate of the Ecole Polytechnique and a mining engineer. The list of companies of which he was a board member was impressive: it included Litcho Gold Mines, Shanghai Tramways, Lafarge and Pechiney Cement.

Wherever he appeared the scenario was the same: the board of a company would co-opt him as adviser and in a few years, sometimes even a few months, his financial acumen had made him an administrator, sometimes chairman. He had been in the Vichy administration as Secretary-General of the Ministry of Power from 1940 to 1942 but had managed to extract himself honourably from this hornets' nest. His death revealed the considerable influence which he exerted in the Employers' Federation of which he was the *éminence grise*. He was a close friend of Georges Villiers, chairman of the federation. Nothing of major importance in industry or finance took place without Henri Lafond knowing or being the instigator of it.

This murder in the open street produced a vast reaction on the part of the police. The inevitable Commissaire Bouvier was on the spot in ten minutes, followed shortly afterwards by the Minister of the Interior, Roger Frey himself, for whom this was a fresh headache. (He announced that he would take personal charge of the investigations and would be in touch with Bouvier twenty-four hours out of twenty-four.) Journalists and observers wondered what were the true reasons for the execution of one of the most exalted backstage personalities in the world of finance who had been invited to lunch by General de Gaulle only three days before. The general's own brother, Pierre de Gaulle, was one of Henri Lafond's immediate associates since he was on the board of the Banque de l'Union Parisienne.

Any ideas of the crime being ordinary foul play or connected with some love affair were dismissed—the banker's private life was above suspicion. The motive could therefore only be political. Some threatening letters from the OAS were found among the banker's papers. They were not very recent, however, going back to the period of André Canal's ('Le Monocle') arrest in May 1962. Commissaire Bouvier did not think them of great importance; all influential bankers had received similar letters, but only Henri Lafond had been killed.

General de Gaulle took a personal interest in the investigations which were pursued with Bouvier's customary energy, but they were a lamentable failure. A year later the file was closed, leaving the affair still open. The police thought that the OAS had something to do with the murder but they did not know why. Perhaps it was because of the help given by the banker to the Algerian economy after the Evian agreements? He had in fact been persuaded to follow de Gaulle in his policy of disengaging France from Algeria but, finance having its prerogatives, France and her bankers reckoned on keeping a financial finger in the Algerian pie. It was equally remembered that Henri Lafond had blocked one hundred million stolen from one of his banks in an OAS hold-up in Oran; but others had done likewise, both helping the Algerian economy and blocking money destined for the OAS, and none of them had been killed. Moreover, when Lafond died, the Algerian affair had been settled nine months ago and the time for revenge seemed to have passed.

The police and the observers were forced back upon another explanation. This presupposed that the underground had not yet abandoned the idea of eliminating de Gaulle and bringing about a change of power. They were still trying to kill de Gaulle at the first opportunity. Less than three weeks before Lafond's death an attempt at the Ecole Militaire had been thwarted—as we shall see. To strike a blow at the authorities, however, it was useless to shoot a minister or a police commissioner; those sort of people were expendable. On the other hand, there were men who were not expendable—the 'great stewards' of the State, men essential to the authorities who were invariably consulted when great plans were being formed. Since he was one of these great backstage personalities, it was thought, that was why Henri Lafond had been shot down. His death would have an intimidating effect upon others who would be less anxious to help the gaullist authorities. Having constructed this satisfying explanation, the minister closed the file and turned his attention to other matters.

Today, however, the dossier now filed away in a cupboard of the Ministry of the Interior can be reopened. A name can be linked with the death of Henri Lafond; it is that of Bastien-Thiry.

Today it is known that the leader of the Petit-Clamart conspirators was in direct touch with certain mysterious and extremely powerful forces, of which the 'Old General Staff' was the manifestation and the great Catholic employers the driving force. As we have seen, a considerable section of the employers was in favour of the elimination of de Gaulle who, in their eyes, was pursuing a pro-communist policy by turning his back on America and flirting with Soviet Russia—and also by promoting the establishment of communism in Algeria. Integrationist circles, supported by a not inconsiderable section of the army, had supported the OAS at its inception and had continued to provide it with money, weapons and safe houses. These were undoubtedly the men who had master-minded the Pont-sur-Seine and Petit-Clamart operations. Henri Lafond, one of the most important figures among catholic employers, had been involved in financing the OAS—as he had in financing the FLN when the wind changed.

It is the duty of a banker to foresee political developments and keep his options open in all directions; he must not be taken by surprise by any particular event, such as the success of an assassination attempt. Lafond, who was a very good banker indeed, had therefore financed the OAS through the 'Old General Staff' and, at this level, had been in contact with the conspirators. The threatening letters he had received from the OAS were clearly intended to ensure that he should not become suspect in the eyes of the other side.

It must not be forgotten that, on the financial front, Lafond was one of the advisers to whom de Gaulle listened. The general had asked him personally to help the new Algeria financially and Henri Lafond had agreed. He lunched regularly with de Gaulle and was on excellent terms with his family, Pierre de Gaulle being one of his closest associates. Pierre de Gaulle and Henri Lafond were on terms of more than mere friendship. Business had brought them together and at one time Lafond had carried out a real salvage operation for the man whom the general called 'the least of my worries'.

With Bastien-Thiry under arrest there were a number of gentlemen in Paris who spent some sleepless nights. If he were to talk, the scandal would be a big one—the sort of scandal which can topple a régime.

Bastien-Thiry did not talk. In the first place he was an upright man with a very strong character; even torture would not have loosened his tongue. Secondly the authorities were not too anxious for him to talk and when no one asks you questions, you do not have to reply.

At the top level it was all a matter of course. The idea came to be accepted that Bastien-Thiry would make an excellent martyr. At the lower levels, however, people refused to accept that he should die (from the outset there was no doubt that he would be condemned to death since the great man was insistent upon it). A single word from one man, de Gaulle, was the only way of saving Bastien-Thiry from the death penalty. Everyone knew the general's obduracy: nothing would make him change his mind. He could not forgive the fact that his wife had been shot at and he demanded rapid exemplary justice.

Only one thing could make him reverse his decision: discovery of some method of pressure. There was a financial affair closely affecting someone near and dear to de Gaulle. The only records of this affair, however, were to be found in Henri Lafond's personal safe and the archives of certain newspapers. It is difficult to conceal everything but production of actual proof is another matter. Only one man could do it: Lafond.

When the Petit-Clamart trial had just opened Henri Lafond was surprised to see in the bar of Mortefontaine golf club a man who frequently acted as liaison officer between the 'Old General Staff' and the 'outside world'; he had even been a consultant in the Petit-Clamart attempt. A banker is an orderly being and anything which upsets the even flow of his life is no good omen. The ensuing conversation went roughly as follows, the 'ambassador' plunging straight into his subject:

'I have a deal to propose to you. We want to save Bastien-Thiry.'

'I am not the court, nor am I General de Gaulle.'

'No, but you know him very well and he listens to you.'

Lafond got the point.

'I see no reason for me to talk to the general about this. If you are alluding to certain payments, you know as well as I do that there is no trace of them. Anyway it would be a waste of time; the general is immovable on this subject. No one can make him change his mind.'

'Yes, you can!'

The banker replied: 'As I have said, I have no reason to interfere in this affair. Moreover I have no method of exerting pressure.'

The 'Old General Staff's' emissary weighed his words carefully. 'Yes you have,' he said at last. 'The file buried in one of your safes.'

Lafond shook his head. 'No. I do not approve of that sort of thing. It is old history and the general would never forgive me.'

'And we shall never forgive you if you do not.'

The two men looked at each other. The 'ambassador' went on: 'A man's life is at stake, a valuable man's life. De Gaulle could spare him for France. You are the only man who could make him see that.'

'And if I refuse?'

'I am authorised to tell you that you will be shot once Bastien-Thiry has been condemned to death. I do not approve of this sort of thing either, but that's the way it is.'

Lafond remained silent for a moment or two and then suddenly burst out laughing. One or two others at the end of the bar turned round.

'You can't be serious. I've done nothing but help you all these last months. I guarantee that you could not do such a thing.'

The 'ambassador' threw a note on the counter, took up his mackintosh which he had placed on a stool and went up to the banker almost genially:

'Chairman,' he said, 'we know that you are lunching with General de Gaulle at the Elysée in two days' time—*tete-à-tete*. You can say anything you like to him. But I repeat that if Bastien-Thiry is sentenced to death, you will be shot.'

Then he went out. The banker remained lost in thought for a moment. Then he tossed his head. 'They're just overgrown children,' he murmured.

Clearly he was not taking the threat of the 'Old General Staff's' special envoy seriously. He never told anyone about it and took no special precautions.

When he heard that Bastien-Thiry had been sentenced to death, he remembered the conversation in the clubhouse. The day of 5 March passed uneventfully, however, and he dismissed the matter finally from his mind.

He had forgotten about it altogether when, at about 10.30 a.m. on the morning of Wednesday, 6 March, he came down the six flights of his apartment block and went towards his car. Ever since 9.30 a.m. Jean-Nicolas Marcetteau de Brem had been standing on the pavement at the corner of Avenue du Roule and the Rue de Chézy in Neuilly.

He knew that he had plenty of time; he had been following the banker's every movement for a week. He was sure that the chairman of Union Parisienne would take the threat seriously. He could not conceive that so intelligent a man would condemn himself to death. Watin was in no doubt that Lafond would be shot if he did not do what he had been asked.

When he heard that Bastien-Thiry had been sentenced, Watin was ready. Henri Lafond had been 'cased'; his movements were known. A planned operation could be carried out next day. The only proviso was that Jean de Brem, with whom Watin had struck up a friendship and was hiding, could steal a car before 9 a.m.; it had been decided that the best place to shoot the banker was the pavement in front of his house as he was getting into his car.

At this point Jean de Brem intervened: 'I ask you to allow me to shoot this man.'

Watin was taken aback: 'You can't be thinking of that.'

'On the contrary I think of nothing else. For me it is a matter of conscience. I beg of you.'

Watin realised that he was serious and would not give way.

De Brem was a strange being. Watin could not really understand him. He had been born in Vendée in 1935; his father was a sleeping partner in the Société Générale; he had two sisters and one brother. In 1954 he enlisted in a Colonial Parachute Regiment, returning after three years with the rank of reserve 2nd Lieutenant. He tried to enter journalism. He spent probationary periods of one month with *Combat* and six months with *Paris-Match*; then he worked for a time for *Contact*, the journal of the Electricity Authority run by Paul Auriol. Finally he decided to freelance in order to write a book, *Testament d'un Européen*, which was never finished but showed that he had promise as an author.

He was part dreamer, part realist, part poet, part man of action, haunted by what he saw, what he feared or what he hoped. He had an almost obsessional longing to be useful, and a scrupulous determination to do things well. At the time of the Petit-Clamart attempt, for instance, it had been planned that he should drive one of the vehicles but he had thought it better to refuse since he did not feel himself ready. There was no question of his courage; he sincerely believed that he would not do the job perfectly and he did not wish the operation to fail through any fault of his. Before the Petit-Clamart trial opened, Watin had been planning the attempt in the Ecole Militaire, the story of which will be told later; he had suggested that Jean de Brem join him to satisfy his thirst for action. (In fact Jean de Brem felt to some extent responsible for the failure of Petit-Clamart and kept saying: 'I ought to have been there.')

On this occasion, too, de Brem refused to accompany Watin. His mind was fixed on the execution of Lafond which was already being planned, should the banker refuse to come to the help of Bastien-Thiry. This was the operation in which he was determined to succeed in order to re-habilitate himself in his own eyes for his failure to participate in the Petit-Clamart affair.

On the morning of 6 March Jean de Brem went over in his mind what he had to do. He suddenly felt quite calm as the banker emerged from his house. It all seemed to him simple and easy. He recognised Henri Lafond from the many photographs he had seen. He wished to be sure, however, that he was making no mistake. Pulling the door towards him as the banker was just sitting down, he asked: 'Are you M. Lafond?'

'Yes,' the banker replied in some surprise.

De Brem then drew from his pocket his large-calibre revolver (11 mm 43) which he was holding gripped in his red-gloved hand and, looking at the banker, murmured: 'From Bastien-Thiry.'

At point-blank range he fired two bullets at the banker's heart. Turning round, half leaning into the car, he then fired twice at the chauffeur, who was seriously wounded but in fact survived. He fired once more at the banker who had already collapsed on the back seat; then, keeping full control of himself, he hurried across towards a black Citroën Idée parked a little further on. The man waiting for him behind the wheel started off smoothly, swept him up as he passed and then stepped on it. The Idée which, it was later discovered, had been stolen the night before in the Rue du Moulin-Vert in the XIVth *Arrondissement,* disappeared in the direction of Avenue Jean-Mermoz.

None of the witnesses could give a description of the man who had done the firing; the red gloves gambit was a well-known one: they were all that the witnesses had noticed; they had forgotten to observe other details. The spectre of Watin was everywhere and this, no doubt, influenced the street-sweeper who swore that the assassin was a fairly large man, about forty-five years of age and that he limped. Despite all Commissaire Bouvier's efforts and those of the Minister of the Interior himself, the police and the authorities never knew why M. Henri Lafond had been assassinated two hours before lunch on 6 March.

Oddly enough, the man who shot him met a very similar fate six weeks later.

Having now rehabilitated himself in his own eyes, Jean de Brem continued his career in the OAS–CNR ranks. On the evening of 18 April he was trying, with a student, to steal a car in the Rue de l'Estrapade, when he was surprised by a police car. To cover his escape he fired at the police, one of whom was mortally wounded. Jean de Brem fell in his turn, hit in the head by another policeman.

Jean-Marie Bastien-Thiry had been shot thirty-seven days earlier.

As far as Bastien-Thiry was concerned the judicial machine was allowed no time for reflection. He was sentenced on 5 March and executed at 6.42 a.m. on the 12th at the Fort d'Ivry.

In his 'statement' to his judges of the Court of Military Justice on 3 February he had written: 'The *de facto* authorities have the power to condemn us but they have not the right.' He was under no illusions: he knew that he would die. He was so certain that the *démarche* made to the Elysée by Maître Richard Dupuy, one of his defence counsel, had no prospect of success that he refused to sign a plea for mercy. In fact de Gaulle received Maître Dupuy coldly, saying: 'I am listening to you, Maître.' When the barrister had finished, he simply replied: 'I have heard you.'

At about 2 a.m. on the night of 11 March a number of men with torches were busy among the brambles and debris of Thiais cemetery; they were digging a rough grave in the area reserved for executed prisoners. At the same time an unusually large force of *gardes mobiles,* soldiers and *gendarmes* took up position round Fresnes prison and at the Fort d'Ivry.

By 4.30 a.m. the prison was completely surrounded. Radio and television vehicles were there and a crowd began to gather. One by one the cars of magistrates, lawyers and other personalities passed through the great gateway.

Bastien-Thiry was sleeping on his camp-bed in his cell which was lit night and day. He had gone to sleep peacefully. He was ready to die. He had said as much to one of his lawyers: 'I was ready from the very first day.'

At 4.45 a.m. the prison governor and the Public Prosecutor entered the cell. One of Bastien-Thiry's defence counsel went up and put a hand on his shoulder. Bastien-Thiry opened his eyes, showed no surprise, got up and said: 'Am I the only one?'

'The other two have been reprieved.'

'Thank God.'

Mass was celebrated and he asked the priest to give him only half the elements, the other half to be reserved for his wife. When mass was ended the chaplain turned to him and said: 'Christ's sacrifice is over. Yours now begins, my friend.'

He was given a bowl of coffee. Meanwhile his counsel implored him to sign a statement to be submitted immediately to the Public Prosecutor. Grudgingly he wrote:

'I ask for a stay of execution, first in view of the fact that my appeal to the Council of State has not been taken and is still a matter of enquiry, secondly in view of the arrest of President Bidault; this may be a new factor, possibly leading to a revision of my trial. [This was a reference to the arrest abroad of Georges Bidault and there was a possibility of his extradition.] I have been illegally sentenced and my execution will be murder. I protest my innocence before my children and my fellow-citizens.'

'Is it really worthwhile,' he murmured as his lawyers passed the letter to Gerthoffer, the Public Prosecutor.

The latter read it and then shook his head: 'I insist that this be disregarded.'

It was disregarded. When the Black Maria passed through the great gateway it was raining. The cortège moved off: it was an impressive sight—thirty-six outriders, twelve cars and six vans. When it arrived at Fort d'Ivry it was still raining. The prisoner was allowed his sky-blue Air Force greatcoat. The firing squad, consisting of young airmen, was in position. Bastien-Thiry had not let go of his rosary. The salvo rang out. He fell without a word. It was 6.42 a.m. At 7.30 he was laid in the prisoners' graveyard which was guarded for a week.

The next day, as it so happened, there was a great reception at the Elysée for all Attorneys-General. Everyone seemed to be very much at ease.

To the very end Bastien-Thiry had only one worry—his family. He had been extremely grieved by the fact that his father disapproved of what he had done. His only regret was that he had to leave behind him a wife and three daughters.

His daughters still bear his name today.

❧ PART III ❧

Dusk

CHAPTER 30

The Kamikaze

We now revert to 1 July 1962. From this date OAS headquarters no longer existed. All its members departed—to France, Italy, Germany, Spain, Switzerland or Belgium. Colonel Godard appeared in Belgium and met Jacques Soustelle, from whom he demanded a month's 'holiday'; this was granted and he left for Denmark. Colonel Vaudrey went to Italy and thence to Belgium. This was the break-up.

All these men were still affected by the fearful blow of total abandonment against which they had fought with every ounce of their energy. Having failed to stop it, they were suffering from a sort of post-operative shock.

Thereafter the desire for action reasserted itself in most cases. Contacts were re-established, centred on politicians who were already abroad and who still had the cause at heart, in particular Georges Bidault and Jacques Soustelle. These two men became the focus of some sort of assemblage of men and resources.

For many of the shipwrecked mariners of the OAS Bidault represented a sort of legitimate authority since he had been duly 'invested' on 13 May 1962 by General Salan before the latter's arrest.

For his part, Soustelle carried genuine prestige. Some months earlier he had agreed to form a sort of secret directorate with Bidault. When the question arose of negotiating with the FLN in an attempt to safeguard the co-existence of the French of Algeria and the new moslem authorities, it was to Bidault and Soustelle that Susini despatched his emissaries, including Maître Kalfleche and Robert Abdeslam, the Kabyle deputy, in order to obtain agreement. This had been given unequivocally: 'We agree that you should contact the Provisional Government in Algiers on condition that the final phase of negotiations takes place in Rome and in our presence.'

The failure of these negotiations merely increased the divisions among the men still fighting for French Algeria, an objective which no longer existed. The failure was laid at Susini's door, as Colonel Godard had foreseen. Accord between Soustelle and Susini was impossible from the outset; marriage between a domestic cat and a desert fox is contrary to nature.

Susini asked Colonel Broizat to talk to Soustelle who was hiding in Rome in the house of a furniture dealer whose brother, called Naim, was a representative of the Irgun and had run a photography business in Algiers. Susini laid down his terms: he demanded formation of a genuine organisation, whether legal or not, with efficient direction and a plan of action worked out in detail.

Broizat received a polite refusal from Colonel Argoud speaking in the name of Soustelle—'Susini must either agree to obey orders or stay on the touchlines.' Broizat was struck by the fact that the people he met seemed to have no political views and very few resources. Like Achilles, therefore, Susini retired to his tent for a time and began writing his memoirs while awaiting better days.

Such was the state of confusion and dispersion when the news of Petit-Clamart was broadcast by the Italian newspapers. This new set-back, for such it was, at least showed the émigrés that the underground circuits in France were still active. Their objective had changed since they were now no longer fighting for French Algeria. They were continuing the struggle for political reasons.

One thing is certain: neither Soustelle nor Susini knew of the preparations for the Petit-Clamart attempt; it was the work of another organisation generally known as the 'Old Army General Staff' and connected with the 'National Resistance Council (Home)'—as opposed to the 'National Resistance Council (Overseas)' of which Bidault was chairman. By circuitous means a report reached the exiles in Italy; it included documents confiscated on the Pyrenees frontier by the Security Service when they had arrested a doctor named Zdrujewski who had been found to be carrying nearly 500 lbs of papers. A number of highly placed personages were referred to in connection with the 'National Resistance Council (Home)'—an admiral, the brother-in-law of a catholic author, politicians, priests, men with handles to their names, generals.

Although these people were not necessarily involved in the Petit-Clamart affair, the mere list of names indicated that the thoughts of many people were turning in the same direction: what to do if an assassination attempt against de Gaulle succeeded.

Nevertheless, the failure at Petit-Clamart put a temporary stop to the plans of the 'Old General Staff' which now had to get its second wind. The scattered groups of OAS France were in the same state of mind. A focus took shape in Brussels in the person of Colonel Argoud, who had escaped from the Canaries on 22 February 1962 and taken refuge in Belgium. (His was a fantastic escape. The French prisoners were allowed a bathe in the sea every day under the supervision of their Spanish guards. Argoud liked walking very fast and the guards became used to seeing him outdistance everybody on the way back to his room. One afternoon he seized the opportunity to steal a boat and row out to sea. He was picked up by a passing ship with no questions asked thanks to false papers which he had forged himself.)

Hearing that Argoud was in Brussels, Captain Sergent, head of OAS France, decided to pay him a visit. His welcome was extremely chilly. Sergent only found out the reason next day—André Canal ('Le Monocle') was himself in Brussels and he had not forgotten his 'meeting' with Sergent's men when they had tried to do away with him. He must have told Argoud who did not appreciate such goings-on. Sergent therefore found himself up against a brick wall. Argoud listened to him politely but refused the private interview for which Sergent asked: 'If you do not want to talk in front of others, then very well, we will not talk at all.'

The colonel rubbed salt into the wound by divulging that all OAS groups in France had asked that he (Argoud) take over command— 'including Godot and Curutchet, your assistants,' he said to Sergent.

On the Canal problem Argoud refused to take sides, saying: 'It is a matter between you two.'

The meeting between the two hostile brothers-in-arms took place next day in a large dormitory which had been set up for exiles in transit. Colonel Argoud hid behind a curtain while the two men confronted each other. Without preliminary courtesies 'Le Monocle' began: 'People wanted to kill me, on your orders, so they said. I await your explanations.'

In considerable embarrassment Sergent explained that the order had not come from him but that his men had been exasperated by Canal's behaviour in refusing to obey directives from the Delegate-General. Behind his curtain Argoud listened attentively.

Canal tossed his head: 'Since it was your men's intention to kill me, I demand a public apology from Lieutenant Marbot before discussing with you further; failing that, I shall consider him an enemy, with all that that implies.'

Canal seemed deadly serious. Sergent tried to extricate himself by singing his assistant's praises but Canal left the room with no change in his aggressive attitude. His next meeting with Sergent would undoubtedly have led to shooting, had he not been arrested five days later in a street in Paris after a chase, the story of which has already been told.

Realising that for the moment he could do no good in Brussels, Sergent decided to go to Rome to meet Jacques Soustelle. Obeying the rules, he asked for and was granted permission by the 'office of the Delegate-General'.

In Rome he was surprised to find that Colonel Argoud was ahead of him, followed a little later by Georges Bidault himself. A series of high-level meetings took place, from which emerged an entirely new 'National Resistance Council' under the chairmanship of Bidault and known as the 'Overseas Council'. It had nothing to do with the other 'Resistance Council' known as 'Home' apart from a few contacts through emissaries such as Fremonville.

The last meeting of this 'Rome Conference' took place on 20 May, a month after Salan's arrest and at the moment when certain of the Delta commandos were arriving in Paris to try to liberate Degueldre and carry out 'Operation Chamois' against de Gaulle. (20 May was also the first day of the *pied-noir* exodus from Algeria in their tens of thousands.)

The reconciliation between Argoud and Sergent was officially registered in a document signed by both men: 'From 20 May 1962 Colonel Argoud has assumed command of OAS France. To assist him Captain Sergent is taking over the functions of Chief of Staff.'

This new organisation, later known as the 'National Resistance Council —OAS' (CNR–OAS) undoubtedly came too late and it encountered vigorous opposition from certain inside groups. It became notable for the futility of its actions. It produced a short recrudescence of activity in Brussels in a villa called Le Petit Manoir at Keerbergen in the forest of Malines. A considerable number of people assembled there and the 'Belgian section' of the CNR was organised under a 'delegate', Captain de Régis, known as 'François'. In any case, this activity terminated as might be expected—at the end of three weeks the headquarters in the Forest of Malines was raided by the Belgian police. Belgium, in fact, could refuse de Gaulle nothing and when the country later granted asylum to Bidault, it first secretly asked—and obtained—agreement from the French government.

That government was in fact using all its resources—and they were many—to liquidate the remnants of French Algeria. One of these resources was the diplomatic weapon and abundant use was made of it.

Nevertheless, despite the dispersion of all the debris of the OAS, two nuclei of resistance soon emerged. One was Paris where the remnants of the 'subversive elements' foregathered and took some action; the other was Rome where Susini and Soustelle formed a strange duet.

There were not many people left in Paris, however. Sergent and Curutchet had fled abroad when the members of the Intelligence and Operations Section of OAS France were arrested. A man named Aycaguer, one of the régime's informers, had contrived to infiltrate the circuit and, as a result, the principal leaders had been arrested.

It can be said that by 1 July, the day of Algerian independence, OAS France had ceased to exist. Fourteen men, including Henri d'Armaniac, had been arrested; they were sentenced on 17 March 1964 by the Court of State Security and given terms of imprisonment ranging up to twenty years.

However, there remained a hard core of militants who gradually attempted to resume action with the help of certain men who had arrived from Algeria. One of these was of some importance—Jean-Claude Perez, formerly head of the Intelligence and Operations Section in Algiers. He had escaped from Algeria by somewhat mysterious means and had a certain number of commandos under his orders.

These scattered groups of differing origins—one of the reasons why the police never contrived to uncover them all—were still looking for some opportunity to do away with de Gaulle: he still remained the man to be struck down. Some accused him of a sell-out in Algeria leading to the massacre of thousands of *pieds-noirs*. Others thought that, if he were removed, France could revert to a more Atlantic and traditionalist policy.

These men of action were also well-read. Some of them knew their French history and realised that successful assassinations are the work of *kamikazes*. The lone-wolf 'regicide' killed 'the tyrant', sacrificing his own life in the process. The list was a long one, from Jacques Clément to Gorguloff, including Ravaillac, Louvel, Casério, Matéo Morral, Godse the brahmin, and even Bastien-Thiry.

The problem, therefore, was to find a man brave enough to pay with his life for the death of de Gaulle. The general himself did not believe that there was such a man in France. 'There will never be a *kamikaze* in France,' he kept repeating, forgetting, no doubt, how Henri IV had been killed.

Nevertheless, there was a man willing to sacrifice his life to kill the general. We will not give his name since his parents are still alive and still mourn him. At the time he was aged twenty and was a member of one of those groups of students working for the 'Old General Staff'. He had been used by Bastien-Thiry, together with many of his fellow-students, to collect detailed information on the routes used by the general. His Christian name was Bernard.

One evening he had a long discussion with his group leader during which he announced his intention to assassinate de Gaulle at point blank range in the knowledge that he himself would not survive. The group leader was impressed by the young man's apparent sincerity and passed the word on to his superiors, and so Jean-Claude Perez came to know of it. The ex-head of the Intelligence and Operations Section in Algiers was in Paris, where he had regained contact with some of his old commandos and had been accepted as head of the CNR (Home). He realised at once that the student's proposition might be of importance and asked to meet him before making up his mind.

The interview took place in the autumn of 1962 in an apartment near the Parc Montsouris. Jean-Claude Perez and two other members of the

CNR listened while Bernard told them at length of his hatred for de Gaulle as a result of the death of one of his close relatives in Algeria. The Algerian drama had left a deep scar on the student, almost to the point of unbalancing him mentally.

'You are not the first who has been willing to sacrifice himself to kill the head of state,' one of Perez' friends said. 'We have had similar proposals in the past but none of them has actually come to anything.'

'I, however, have made up my mind. When you will, where you will, whatever the circumstances, whatever the resources you give me to do it with.'

'Excellent. We will give you warning.'

Months passed. CNR headquarters had almost forgotten Bernard's proposition when a favourable opportunity arose. On Saturday, 19 January 1963, de Gaulle was due to be present at the general meeting of ex-graduates of the National School of Administration which was to take place in the Hotel George V. A large number of people would be present and so it did not seem impossible to infiltrate a single armed man among the hundreds of those invited. With the assistance of certain members of the CNR who were ex-graduates of the School the necessary papers were procured to enable Bernard to attend the meeting.

When, therefore, de Gaulle entered the hotel meeting-room accompanied by his ministers—Pompidou, Joxe, Giscard d'Estaing, Frey, Peyrefitte and Debré—there was among the crowd a somewhat pale young man nervously clutching the butt of a P 38 revolver concealed in his pocket. In his other coat pocket he had two grenades.

Surrounded by a host of officials together with uniformed and plain-clothes police, de Gaulle mounted the rostrum and delivered his speech in which, among other things, he reminded the graduates of the School (who included Giscard and Peyrefitte) that the authorities did not expect them to 'proffer public advice on certain acts of State'.

Despite all his efforts, Bernard could never get near enough to de Gaulle. There were hundreds of police between the general and his audience. Bernard could only see him in the distance and could never get into a position to shoot with any chance of hitting him.

Feeling his position ridiculous, Bernard abandoned the attempt and returned to report failure to Jean-Claude Perez. Perez in no way reproached him, knowing from experience how difficult such an assignment was. 'Do not blame yourself,' he said. 'We will start again when a similar opportunity arises.'

Bernard departed sadly. Three days later he committed suicide using the revolver intended to kill de Gaulle and which he had kept. He left a letter saying: 'I had promised to kill the general. I have not done it. I had promised to sacrifice my life for the purpose. I would not like anyone to think that it was an empty promise. Here is the proof.'

Bernard was no doubt somewhat mentally unhinged. There is no doubt, however, that had he been able to get close enough to de Gaulle, he would have used his revolver on him without hesitation: his suicide constitutes the guarantee. So it is reasonable to record that yet once more de Gaulle had escaped death even if, on this occasion, his 'luck of the devil' took the form of an impenetrable wall of policemen.

CHAPTER 31

The Return of 'La Boiteuse'

The race to kill de Gaulle was therefore still open. Among the hard-core intransigents there was one in particular who had no use for high-flown sentiments. He knew that the best way to capture a fortress was to storm it after a good artillery preparation. His two weapons were surprise and force. In his eyes a man posted at the right place and pressing the trigger at the right time was worth more than all the shintoist philosophies.

This single-minded and determined man was Georges Watin, the miracle-man of Petit-Clamart, the man whom every policeman was hunting as 'Public Enemy No. 1'. Watin was certainly a miracle. Of all people he was the most easily recognisable in the street with his stocky build and his pronounced limp. Nevertheless he had slipped through every net thanks to his cunning, his caution and his knowledge of police psychology.

Ever since the Petit-Clamart failure Watin had been itching for action. He ruminated over his favourite idea—that next time he would use a telescopic rifle. In the light of experience, however, he was only willing to act if presented with an absolutely certain opportunity. He was supported in this by a man to whom little reference has so far been made but who, as we have seen, had played a major rôle in all the attempts, in particular Petit-Clamart. This was Jean Bichon, known as 'Blanche'. Oddly enough these two underground fighters had one characteristic in common: both limped.

Ever since Petit-Clamart these two fugitives had been looking for an opportunity. They lived in hiding, helped by certain firm friends who thought as they did. These friends too were on the watch for the perfect opportunity and it was one of them—a woman—who found it.

French Algeria and its fighters had their sympathisers in all ministries, all agencies, even in the Elysée itself. Some were so sympathetic that they were thirsting for action. (We have seen how a senior officer in the

Elysée kept Bastien-Thiry informed of de Gaulle's movements.) There were also very highly placed officials who were unstinting in their assistance to the OAS and the National Resistance Council. The activists never lacked accomplices, particularly in certain police and intelligence circles.

One of these sympathisers was Madame Paule Rousselet, *née* Hibon, who called herself Comtesse de Lifiac and worked as translator and teacher of English at the Ecole Militaire. She had kept in close touch with Jean Bichon ('Blanche') whom she had met some ten years earlier in a catholic group. She was therefore fully conversant with the plans of Watin and Bichon.

At the Ecole Militaire Paule Rousselet had never made any secret of her anti-gaullist sentiments, particularly in front of a sergeant-major in the administration, Marius Tho, a native of Ajaccio. She and the sergeant-major would often have a drink together after hours and Tho delighted in telling stories about his campaigns in Indo-China and Algeria, and in emphasising his nostalgia for the 'lost Algeria'.

On 30 January 1963 Paule Rousselet met the sergeant-major in the courtyard of the Ecole Militaire. The talk of the day was the opening, two days previously, of the trial of Bastien-Thiry and the Petit-Clamart conspirators. Naturally they spoke about it.

'I guarantee you,' the sergeant-major said, 'that if I had been one of the party, I would not have missed the Old Man.'

Paule Rousselet at once saw that she could turn Tho's feelings to good account. She had in fact just heard that General de Gaulle was due to visit the Ecole Militaire.

'Perhaps it's not too late,' she said. 'I know people who think that way. If you would like, I can introduce you.'

'Whenever you like,' the other replied enthusiastically.

'I must talk to them first. If you like, let us arrange to meet at the Tourville at 8 p.m. on 1 February, the day after tomorrow.'

Two days later, at precisely 8 p.m., the 'countess' collected the sergeant-major and drove him to a new apartment block in the Villa des Pyrénées. She rang at the door of a third-floor apartment. A blonde girl opened it and, with a friendly, knowing gesture, let the two in.

In the lounge a captain came up to the sergeant-major and smilingly held out his hand. The sergeant-major required no second bidding. He knew this captain; he had often seen him at the Ecole Militaire where he was a member of Madame Rousselet's class. He was Captain Robert Poinard. The sergeant-major felt full of importance: he was working on equal terms with an officer.

Then he realised that there was someone else sitting in one of the armchairs, someone powerfully built, thick-necked, square-jawed, bespectacled and with a crew cut. He recognised the man immediately

since his photograph had appeared in the press on innumerable occasions
—Georges Watin, the 'Limper'. Here was the famous Georges Watin,
the *bête noire* of every police force in France, getting up and in his turn
smilingly shaking the little sergeant-major's hand.

The sergeant-major seated himself, glass of whisky in hand, and the
conversation soon turned to serious matters.

'I intend to kill de Gaulle when he visits the Ecole Militaire,' Watin
said without beating about the bush. 'You know both the people and the
place very well and can help me a great deal. When is he due to come?'

'There are two dates planned for the visit,' the sergeant-major replied.
'The first is the day after tomorrow.'

'Well then, if it's the day after tomorrow, it's the day after tomorrow,'
Watin said.

They examined the situation. Tho explained that the Ecole Militaire
was a maze of buildings, courtyards, annexes, stairways, passages, nooks
and crannies. If a man fired from a window and knew the way to an exit,
the complexities would be of help to him. But time was required to
organise this escape. Watin very quickly abandoned any plan for rapid
action and asked Tho to give him a detailed plan of the Academy so that
he could do a professional job, working on the second date and hoping
that it would be the one chosen.

'Tomorrow,' Watin decided, 'Captain Poinard will go to the Ecole
Militaire and I ask you to give him a complete guided tour. Is that
agreed?'

The sergeant-major went home but he did not sleep that night. He
realised that he had become involved in an affair which was too big for
him.

The next day he received Captain Poinard unenthusiastically. The
captain spent a long time in the attics of the Academy and on the helicopter landing pad. Tho nevertheless promised to procure plans of the
Academy and warn the captain as soon as he had them. He also announced
that the first date for the visit had been cancelled and that the general
was due to come on 15 February.

Tho spent another sleepless night. Whether from fear or conscience he
now only had one idea in his head, to stop the assassination attempt by
warning the authorities. Now came the agonising question: which
authorities? Academy headquarters? They would undoubtedly penalise
him for his original 'thoughtlessness'. The police? But which police?

On the Saturday morning he had a sudden inspiration when he saw in
the courtyard an official car belonging to the Prime Minister's office.
He went up to the chauffeur, whom he knew, and, in some embarrassment, divulged that he had knowledge of an assassination attempt being
prepared against the head of state.

The chauffeur was dumbfounded. He too felt that this business was too big for him and said: 'I can only see one thing that you can do. Go and tell the whole story to Commissaire Comiti, who is a member of the President's security service.'

Commissaire Comiti in his turn was thunderstruck. But this was not the first time that he had been told such stories. Since some of them were mere day-dreams, he thought it best not to take action:

'Thank you for coming to me, but this is not my business; it is that of Military Security. You must go to them.'

The sergeant-major was now in an even greater state of jitters since he realised that he might expect reprisals from his new-found 'friends'; having taken the first step, however, he went to look for the Military Security officer on duty at the Academy. This officer alerted his superiors who despatched a vehicle at once to take the sergeant-major to the office of Colonel Bellec of Military Security headquarters.

The colonel listened at length to the sergeant-major's story and at once reassured him; the law prescribed that anyone giving information of a plot was guaranteed against any judicial proceedings. The gist of the colonel's remarks was: 'No harm will come to you if you carry out our orders. You are to remain in contact with your "friends" and even give them the plan they have asked for. Here is a telephone number you can call whenever something fresh occurs.'

Vastly relieved, the sergeant-major carried out his orders to the letter. He had casually told the colonel that Paule Rousselet had organised a meeting for him with a certain Jean Bichon (the first time that this name had come up officially in connection with an assassination attempt against de Gaulle) and that he was to see this man again. When the time came Tho divulged how the operation was to be carried out: on 14 February, the eve of de Gaulle's visit, Tho was to introduce Watin and his party into the Military Academy; Watin would be carrying a telescopic rifle hidden in a violin case and this would be used for the attempt. The party would be given a snack in the NCO's mess, which was more or less Tho's domain. Then they would spend the night in the veterinary lines, in the sick-box for horses.

Meanwhile, as may be imagined, Colonel Bellec had not been idle. The affair had been taken to the highest level, even to the general's office. Two ministers immediately felt that it was their business: Roger Frey, the Minister of the Interior, and Pierre Messmer, the Armed Forces Minister, who was ultimately responsible for the Ecole Militaire.

Roger Frey thought that the conspirators should be allowed to proceed but be kept under strict surveillance. He hoped in this way to uncover the entire circuit and even reach the mysterious leaders of the plot, whose names he guessed but against whom he had no proof. For him, therefore, this was a purely political affair.

For Pierre Messmer the primary consideration was the risk run by de Gaulle and he was anxious to have all of them under lock and key without losing a moment.

The argument between the two ministers was a sharp one, so sharp that Military Security found itself in an impasse, not knowing whom to obey; a decision by the Prime Minister became essential. Argument continued in Pompidou's office for several hours. Each minister pleaded his case. Frey considered that the plot was still fairly nebulous despite the confirmed presence of Watin. His point of view was summarised thus: 'All the main participants are being watched twenty-four hours out of twenty-four with the exception of Watin, whom we have not succeeded in locating despite all our efforts. If we let him into the Ecole Militaire and close the trap behind him, we shall at last lay hands on the most dangerous man in the OAS–CNR circuit. The repercussions on public opinion will be considerable.'

'You want to let the rat in among the cheese,' Messmer replied sarcastically. 'You say yourself that this man is a devil. We cannot allow the general to run such a risk.'

Pompidou let them have their say and then gave his decision:

'The risk run by the general justifies immediate police action, even if premature. We will not let the rat in among the cheese; we will arrest them all the previous evening and we will announce the fact on the day of the general's visit to the Ecole Militaire. In this way you, Messmer, need not be afraid of the risk and you, Frey, will be satisfied since public opinion will be struck by the efficiency of the police.'

Frey tried to protest: 'That means that Watin will slip through our fingers yet once more.'

'In any case,' Pompidou said finally, 'I have spoken about it to the general and he shares my view.'

Once the general had spoken no one could do other than conform—which they both did. A meeting of all those responsible for the President's security was arranged at once in order to decide on the procedure. General Feuvrier, recently nominated as head of Military Security, was commissioned to conduct the enquiry but the official Security Service (the DST) was charged with arresting the conspirators. 'D Day' was fixed for 14 February, the day before the President's visit.

The first step was a large-scale police operation with the object of arresting Watin who, according to recent 'reliable' clues, was in a building in Montparnasse. A formidable police force cordoned off the area, taking up position with their customary discretion: this was indeed a case of using a steam-hammer to crack a nut. Naturally when the police arrived 'the nut' was no longer at home; 'La Boiteuse' had decamped two hours earlier.

The rest of the operation proceeded according to plan. All those people whose names had been mentioned in Sergeant-Major Tho's hearing and who were directly or indirectly connected with the plot, were arrested without difficulty. In fact, however, the catch was a moderate one; the net only brought up Captain Poinard, the 'countess' and a veterinary surgeon.

The fact was that the Ecole Militaire operation had been cancelled at the last moment. Through his contacts in the Ministry of the Interior and Military Security Jean Bichon knew the plans of the police. He at once put the 'security' rules into force and burnt his bridges. Not knowing who had squealed, he sent an express letter to the 'countess' telling her that he was cancelling next day's operation and that it was for her to warn the sergeant-major discreetly.

The 'countess' telephoned Tho asking him to meet her that evening at a café, the Rally des Commandos. The sergeant-major of course warned his 'masters' and went to the café as arranged; there the 'countess' warned him that the police had discovered Captain Poinard and that the operation had been cancelled. As soon as the 'countess' had left, the sergeant-major telephoned Colonel Bellec who immediately passed the news higher up. It was decided to accelerate action in order not to be cheated of the official victory in the eyes of public opinion.

Despite the meagre results of the police operation, the greatest publicity was given to the discovery of the 'Ecole Militaire plot' at the moment when the general made his visit. The newspapers carried eight-column headlines: 'Assassination attempt against de Gaulle frustrated: he was to be killed this morning at the Ecole Militaire with a telescopic rifle. Six officers arrested.' They were, nevertheless, forced to add in small print: 'Watin, the leader of the commando and already involved in the Petit-Clamart affair, is on the run.'

The first to congratulate General de Gaulle on yet another escape from assassination was Léopold Senghor, President of Senegal, who was his guest at lunch. But the general showed no great joy. He was champing at the bit, furious at the publicity which Pompidou's office had given to the affair. He summoned his Prime Minister that same afternoon:

'This is intolerable. I told you to play down this uninteresting story.'

'But, General, it is good that the French, and foreigners too, should know that your life is constantly threatened. Public opinion will only be more favourable to severe sentences at the Petit-Clamart trial.'

'I'm doing my job. You do yours.'

According to his private office the general was 'extremely irritated' and administered a memorable rocket to Roger Frey, his Minister responsible for the police, and Pierre Messmer, his Armed Forces Minister, which both accepted without flinching. Paul-Marie de la Gorce, one of the observers most closely in touch with the Elysée, noted: 'This irritation had its repercussions in several ministries.'

Pompidou nevertheless gained one advantage: the general had

authorised him to put a final end to subversion. In other words at last he could neutralise all that remained of the men of French Algeria all over Europe.

In his large, neat, professorial handwriting Pompidou noted a number of names on a sheet of paper—Bidault, Soustelle, Susini, Argoud, Sergent, Curutchet, Watin. That very evening several teams of *barbouzes* set forth for Rome, Brussels and Munich supported by the entire French diplomatic machine. Several ministers of Foreign Affairs found requests for urgent audiences on their desks.

In Munich the *barbouzes* had a well-defined objective—Georges Bidault, who was still the standard-bearer of OAS–CNR and a dangerous man because of his international influence. Ever since December it had been known that Bidault had established himself in Munich. Two months previously the activists had decided to concentrate in the Bavarian capital since Brussels was no longer considered safe. A press agency called Teamstar had been set up in Munich by Paul Ribeaud with money provided by Colonel Argoud. Paul Ribeaud's brother Guy was Bidault's private secretary. Naturally, therefore, Bidault and Guy Ribeaud arrived in Munich, where they felt safer. They took an apartment but this was very soon discovered by journalists and so they had to go and live in small unknown hotels near the main railway station. Argoud and General Gardy arrived in their turn, followed by Curutchet, Sergent's assistant. Sergent himself preferred to remain in Belgium where, on 10 February, he summoned a major meeting of the remnants of OAS–CNR: some fifteen underground fighters were present.

By January the gaullist secret service was all ready to deal with their target in Munich. It used for the purpose a cleric and a man who had been a member of Bidault's office some years before and in whom Bidault had confidence. The latter announced that he had five million francs to hand to the ex-Prime Minister and by this subterfuge contrived to meet him. Thereupon the two 'emissaries' returned to Paris to report that Bidault was definitely in Munich and could easily be put out of action.

The day after the Ecole Militaire affair Paris gave the green light and a team of 'operational' *barbouzes* arrived in Munich by 20 February. They found a disappointment awaiting them. Bidault had been warned by some mysterious means and was no longer there. He had vanished. In fact he and his secretary had taken refuge in a little village some sixty miles from Munich.

The *barbouzes* had only one line to follow in order to discover Bidault —the Teamstar agency, of whose existence they were aware. They went there in force and gave Paul Ribeaud a rough handling; he denied knowledge of Bidault's whereabouts but told them that Argoud was in Munich. In fact, Ribeaud thought this information of little importance since Argoud was actually in Rome at this moment, conferring with Soustelle.

When Paris heard of this development, an order was issued to forget Bidault for the moment and deal with Argoud. The ex-colonel was soon discovered in Rome. A meeting of *barbouzes* took place in Geneva and responsibility for the 'Argoud operation' was given to Major Bonfils. Bidault had to be 'brought back alive' so that de Gaulle might have his trial but in Argoud's case no such precautions were necessary—if he resisted, he could be shot. The kidnapping was to take place in Germany.

Learning of the arrival of the *barbouzes* in Munich, Curutchet and Gardy tried in vain to warn Argoud. Then they thought it best to vanish; Curutchet rejoined Sergent in Brussels and Gardy went to Cologne with his ADC, Captain (Navy) Piquet.

Colonel Argoud's arrival in Munich by the plane from Rome on 25 February had been 'announced' by the observers on duty at Fiumicino airport, Rome. At about 8.30 p.m. he arrived at the Hotel Eden Wolff and reserved two rooms, one in the name of Cinel and the other in that of Marshal. He went to dine in a nearby restaurant. It was the carnival season in Munich. The streets were full and gay; masks were everywhere; people were running, dancing and shouting to each other. On the way back to his hotel Argoud was suddenly accosted by two extremely polite gentlemen: 'German police. Come with us.'

Next morning, 26 February, he was found, bound and gagged, in a street near Notre Dame in Paris. But he was alive—although some of his kidnappers would have dearly liked to kill him on the spot.

This incredible kidnapping was illustrative of the methods of the various parallel French police forces, all acting on orders from the authorities. It created a considerable stir. When the news reached Bidault, hiding in his little village, he realised that his own life was in danger and that the gaullists would stop at nothing to lay hands on him. As a good diplomat he knew that the only security lay in coming out into the open. Early in March he placed himself officially under the protection of the German government.

French diplomacy went into action at once, exerting considerable pressure on the Bonn government. The result was Bidault's exile to Brazil, where he was despatched on 8 March 1963. He had now been finally eliminated from the political scene and he remained in Brazil for five years.

French diplomacy, however, continued its victorious offensive against those activists who had taken refuge abroad; almost every country bowed to de Gaulle and expelled the undesirables. Jean-Claude Perez, for instance, had to embark on a series of journeys which took him from the Argentine to Chile and thence to Spain.

Things did not go so smoothly either for Soustelle, although he was extremely cautious and, even more important, had protectors in high places abroad. He was arrested for the first time at Fiumicino airport, Rome, and expelled to Switzerland, whence he returned clandestinely to Italy. A little later he was recognised at Cointrin airport in Switzerland by a Lebanese journalist and was again expelled—officially at least. The Swiss and Italian authorities thus publicly met de Gaulle's demands but unofficially they continued to help the ex-Governor-General of Algeria.

Finally, in France the victory of the gaullist authorities was complete. After the latest set-back at the Ecole Militaire even the obstinately recalcitrant Watin laid down his arms. He realised that, despite all his efforts and all his courage, he could do nothing against a man seemingly protected by the devil's own luck. He vanished. Similarly, Sergent quickly disappeared. His exit, however, took place in style. On 14 April 1963 he decided to assume leadership of a 'National Council of the Revolution'.

'It is my pride,' he said in his proclamation, 'that today I incorporate legitimate authority . . . The spirit of revolution must now take the place of the spirit of resistance . . . We desire a United States of Europe and Euro-Africa; we have our mother-country . . . Those who are leading the country to its doom, and in particular the present Head of State, are henceforth responsible before me, as they will one day be responsible before the people and before history. I have decided to assume leadership of the Secret Army and to turn the National Resistance Council into a National Council of Revolution.'

Once this had been written, signed and issued, practically nothing more was heard of Captain Sergent and he vanished from the political scene for ever.

CHAPTER 32

A Lethal Camera

So the police-state repression was apparently triumphant and silence descended on the OAS–CNR. Even the 'Old General Staff' of the Army, this 'secret technico-synarchy of the Right' submerged and drew in its periscope after the Ecole Militaire attempt.

Yet the flame flared up again in Brussels.

Among the debris of OAS France and the National Resistance Council was to be found, in a villa in Brussels, Louis de Condé, one of the survivors of Petit-Clamart. With him was Captain Jean Mémain, an ex-engineer officer from the Airborne Troops Base Training Camp in Pau; he had deserted on 27 July 1962 and two arrest warrants were out against him, one from Judge Manant in Paris and the other from the Armed Forces Standing Tribunal in Bordeaux. Apart from one or two assignments given them at this period, the two men whiled away their time primarily in reading the French press. One morning they lit upon an announcement of a forthcoming visit by de Gaulle to Greece, from 15 to 19 May 1963.

'There we are! There's the opportunity!', Condé cried.

As it so happened, for some days the two had been discussing an invention developed by Captain Mémain, who was a good technician and practical improviser. His idea was to insert a 6.35 mm barrel into a camera. To the outward eye the camera would look perfectly normal and it could even continue to take photographs. Through an aperture below the lens, however, six bullets impregnated with cyanide could be fired at any target selected. Condé had shown very great interest in this device: it could be used by a tourist without attracting attention.

De Gaulle's visit to Athens was an ideal opportunity for him to succeed where he had failed at Petit-Clamart. He immediately passed word to his superiors, who gave their agreement and Mémain started to construct the apparatus that very day. For good measure he even made two models.

235

Trials proved conclusive and so Condé disguised himself as a tourist and took an aeroplane to Athens a few days before de Gaulle's arrival in Greece. In his luggage he carried false identity papers, 250,000 old francs given him by the Brussels headquarters and two specimens of the doctored camera. He stopped off in Rome where he met Henri X, one of Soustelle's close associates, and handed him one of the two cameras.

In Athens he played the tourist, visiting the ruins by day and night-clubs by night to keep his mind off the action he was about to undertake. Two days before the general's arrival, by which time he had made a full reconnaissance of the places selected for the attack, he spent a particularly eventful evening during which he was robbed of his money, his papers and his return tickets in the slums of Athens. This was obviously catastrophic. His only hope of escape lay in rapid flight immediately after the attempt. He immediately sent a telegram to his Brussels contact asking for fresh papers and money. Communications were not easy at this period, however. Condé received no reply that day. Next day he had still heard nothing and, when he went to the avenue down which de Gaulle was to pass and where, according to plan, he would have been killed, he realised that he could not try anything without risking being caught very quickly since he had neither money nor papers.

Dejectedly he watched the triumphal arrival of the general who passed within twelve feet of him. Condé could only press the release of his camera, thus at least obtaining a historic photograph of de Gaulle offering an ideal target. Not until that afternoon did he receive his papers and money enabling him to return to Brussels where all he could provide as proof that he had carried out his abortive assignment was a reel of film which was developed. The photographs were considered excellent; they included one of de Gaulle standing in an open car saluting the crowd and presenting his august profile at a distance of twelve feet—a sitting target even for a moderate marksman.

The photographs and the doctored camera were placed in a suitcase belonging to one of the members of the Brussels Resistance Council. A few days later this man, who was getting bored like all the exiles, decided to give himself an evening out and went to a well-known night-club in the suburbs of Brussels. Music, girls and whisky quickly had their effect on him and a brawl started in the night-club. The police intervened and arrested everybody. They soon saw that this man had papers showing him to be a French citizen and, moreover, he was carrying a loaded revolver. The Belgian CID at once realised that they had laid hands on a representative of the OAS and searched his house. In the suitcase they found the photograph of de Gaulle and the doctored camera which left no doubt about the activities of this gentleman. They alerted the French police who immediately despatched a team of sleuths by special aircraft.

The Belgians, it should be noted in passing, refused to hand over their prisoner to the French, as the latter insistently demanded. Their attitude was therefore firmer than that of the Senegalese government in the subsequent case of Jean-Marie Curutchet.

Shortly afterwards, however, attention became focused on another area, shifting from north to south as de Gaulle prepared to pay a visit to southern France during the month of September.

CHAPTER 33

Cancellations

For a period of nearly three months, from 25 September to 12 December 1963, motorists using Route Nationale 550 between Orange and Carpentras never knew that they were passing close to an enormous bomb intended to blow up de Gaulle. It had been prepared and positioned by a curious network, connected with OAS France but in reality independent.

The network had been formed in 1958 when General de Gaulle came to power, by the former supporters of General Giraud who, as we know, had been one of de Gaulle's first political victims. It was headed by the former leader of an FTP *maquis* (*Francs-Tireurs Partisans*) in Ardèche who had since become a garage proprietor; it consisted of five members who did not know each other. In their turn these five members had each recruited five further members, working independently in each case—this was the famous cell system invented by the communists during the 1941–1945 resistance. In this way it was impossible for the police to penetrate the circuit, still less break it up.

Early in 1961 this organisation placed itself at the disposal of what was later to become OAS France, the south-eastern sector of which was headed by Jean Reimbold, professor of French at the *lycée* in Toulon. The object at that time was to support the April *putsch*. After the failure of the *putsch* the network remained in being and devoted itself to propaganda.

When it was announced that de Gaulle was to visit Vaucluse, 'The Hand' decided to take action against him, since the head of state was visiting *his* territory. As a matter of form OAS France was asked to give the green light but preparations were begun without waiting for a reply.

On the route due to be used by de Gaulle certain roadworks, designed to iron out a bend, were in progress some two miles from Orange, just short of Jonquières. Between the old road, which was still in use, and the new one under construction there was a small ditch. It was this ditch that 'The Hand' decided to use since the convoy would have to slow down to 25 mph to get round the bend.

In the ditch 'The Hand's' men laid a bomb consisting of 50 lbs of plastic provided by an officer of the 2nd *Cuirassiers* stationed at Orange. A wire ran to a thicket about 80 yards away, where the firing mechanism was located. Installation of the system was easy since one of the roadworks foremen was a member of the organisation.

Everything was in place by 24 September, the day before de Gaulle's arrival, when OAS France sent an order not to explode the bomb. The wisdom of such negative orders is questionable, particularly when issued by an organisation as ineffective as OAS France which was a prey to divergent tendencies. The fact remains, however, that 'The Hand' received a formal order to take no action.

Naturally it was too late to remove the bomb; *gendarmes* were patrolling the route all the time and the security services were on the alert. 'The Hand' consequently left his bomb where it was. The members of the network at least had the satisfaction of observing that the people of Orange stayed at home and gave the head of state the cold shoulder; only the forces of law and order and the useless bomb were there to greet him.

On 27 September, two days after the general had passed, the works foreman took up the wire. The bomb could not be removed until 12 December, nearly three months later, since some of the workmen were camping on the spot. Some of the innocent motorists who passed close by no doubt shivered in retrospect.

Meanwhile Jean-Marie Curutchet, operations officer of OAS France, had been arrested.

Sergent's ex-assistant had been dogged by bad luck ever since 12 April 1963, when he had first been arrested quietly by the Swiss police. Within an hour the French government had despatched a telegram asking for his extradition. The Swiss took until October to reject this request and decided to expel Curutchet to Uruguay. During the journey to Uruguay Curutchet seized the opportunity of a stop-off at Lisbon to disappear and turn up in Rome via Spain.

On 24 November 1963 Curutchet was again arrested, this time by the Italian police; through Dr d'Amato, head of *Affari riservati*, they offered him a choice: either to remain interned with his family in Italy or to be sent off once more to Uruguay. Curutchet naturally chose the latter alternative—the French government had once more issued a request for his extradition.

D'Amato announced triumphantly that his office had consulted the French government which agreed that Curutchet should be allowed to go to Uruguay and that he would not be molested during the refuelling stop at Dakar on the way from Rome to Montevideo. In any case, d'Amato added, he would be travelling under Italian diplomatic protection.

Accordingly on 28 November 1963 Curutchet and his family boarded an Alitalia Boeing 707 *en route* for Montevideo.

The previous day, as on every Wednesday, a cabinet meeting was held in the Elysée. De Gaulle had just returned from the funeral of John F. Kennedy who had been shot in Dallas. The general was in bad temper. On his return he had said to some of his closer associates: 'His story is the same as mine. What happened to Kennedy very nearly happened to me. That was like a cowboy story, but this is merely an OAS story.'

During the meeting Roger Frey reported on the general situation and said that he had just reached agreement with the Italian government that Captain Curutchet should be exiled to Uruguay. He ended by saying:

'So we are at last rid of a dangerous OAS leader.'

De Gaulle said nothing for a few moments and then spat out: 'Get him.'

Somewhat timidly one member of the cabinet tried to object—Pompidou:

'But, General, Senegal is an independent state.'

'Independent?', de Gaulle growled. 'I only know one thing—I am the one who does the paying.'

It was now for Foccart, desk officer for African affairs in the general's office, to play the hand. There was no question of taking official action nor of informing either the French diplomatic authorities in Rome or the Italian police. Curutchet was to be intercepted in Dakar in defiance of all agreements and all international protocol. Whatever one may think of what Curutchet had done in the past, this was a method which, under the circumstances, was tantamount to piracy. Curutchet was captured, while actually in the Alitalia aircraft, by the Senegalese police, taken in charge and handed over to the French authorities.

His trial was as expeditious as those of other dissidents. There was so little doubt about the outcome that M. Marty, governor of Fresnes prison, was ordered by the Chancellery to prepare a condemned cell even before the verdict had been pronounced. Thanks to the obstinacy of one of the judges, however, Curutchet was only sentenced to life imprisonment.

CHAPTER 34

Money Matters

Jean-Marie Curutchet's adventures and the episodes of Athens and Orange mark the end of a period, with the disappearance or exit from the stage of most of the main actors. All the time, however, there remained one special and exceptional actor who, from his hide-out in Rome, continued to try to checkmate the king with the few pieces left to him.

This man was the exact opposite of de Gaulle. Slim, well-built, blond, young and circumspect—such was, and still is, Jean-Jacques Susini.

On his desk in Rome he kept a bizarre present, brought him by Henri X, Soustelle's right hand man: it was the second doctored camera manufactured by Captain Mémain, an exact replica of the one which Louis de Condé had taken to Athens. Susini used it as a paper-weight.

Hated by some, admired by many more, feared by all, Susini remains one of the most characteristic figures of the Algerian adventure. He had been the last to leave Algerian territory as it was invaded by Boumedienne's brand-new tanks. He did so on 20 July 1962 and landed in Italy on the 29th, the day before his twenty-ninth birthday. From 1 July Algeria had been independent. The last *pieds-noirs* had left for Alicante on board the *El Mabrouk* on 29 June. From 1 July the OAS headquarters had ceased to exist. On 1 August Susini established himself in Ancona, with Colonel Broizat, and took stock of the position. For him there was no question of moral disarmament. His attitude to developments was that of the revolutionary—to him they were mere episodes in a continuing struggle.

He began to write his memoirs but at the same time received many visitors from France; he busied himself in settling the financial affairs of the OAS, on which much ink was expended. The funds of OAS Algeria had not been passed to the National Resistance Council.

When the OAS headquarters in Algiers disbanded, only four of the leaders remained—Colonel Godard, Colonel Gardes, Colonel Gorel and Jean-Jacques Susini. These four men, however, had in their hand a very

considerable trump card, whose existence—followed by its disappearance
—led to a vast expenditure of ink. This was the famous war treasure-
chest of the OAS: at the time it consisted of one-and-a-half milliard old
francs standing to the credit of Algiers and Constantine (Oran had one
milliard of its own). All four agreed to divide it into three parts. One part
was to go to the militants in the form of an indemnity to enable them to
return to France. A second part was to be at the disposal of the four
leaders to enable them to re-form organisations outside Algeria. Finally
a third part was to be held in the treasure-chest under the responsibility
of Colonel Gorel. During a meeting at El Biar in the hills of Algiers he
had given the Delta commandos a solemn undertaking either to pay them
an indemnity equivalent to that which they would receive if no further
organisation could be formed, or to take them on the books again if
action in France could be restarted.

The history of this third part subsequently led to heated internal
arguments. Some maintain that one quarter of it was handed out but
that the remaining three-quarters have disappeared. In any case it is a
fact that Jean-Claude Perez, the head of the Delta commandos, received
a sum of 350 million old francs under the heading 'Operation Survival';
it was to be distributed to each member of the commandos before
departure from Algiers—500,000 for a bachelor, one million for a married
man with an additional 500,000 for each dependant child. Each of the
headquarters' leaders also received thirty million in order to continue
the struggle abroad. The rest, in other words about one milliard old
francs, was to be the responsibility of Colonel Gorel.

This money had come from collections and also from hold-ups
organised over a period of a year. For instance, half of it came from one
hold-up in the Bank of Oran when $2\frac{1}{2}$ milliard had been taken in a single
night. These hold-ups had generally taken place with the tacit agreement
of the boards of the banks: in their eyes they were a way of helping the
OAS without incurring penalties.

The first of the numerous dramas to which the 'OAS treasure-chest' gave
rise, goes back as far as 28 May 1962. On that day Susini's secretary,
Jean Garcia known as Diego, handed him a message from Dr Perez,
head of the Intelligence and Operations section of the OAS. It said: 'Tunny-
fishing in Spain ends in October.' Susini went pale. This meant that
Dr Perez had decided to leave Algeria. Susini informed the other
members of the headquarters and set out to find Perez, but he could not
be discovered.

As far as the remaining leaders were concerned the most serious aspect
was that Perez had left Algeria without paying their indemnities to the
members of his commandos. When the decision to make payment had
been taken, Perez had maintained that he only had 250 million in his

possession. 'I need a further 100 million,' he explained, 'if I am to pay everybody. It is for Gorel to provide me with the money.'

Colonel Gorel handed him the 100 million. Meanwhile, however, the other members of the headquarters had begun to wonder; according to reports reaching them, 30 million of the proceeds of hold-ups were still blocked in Perez' section and must be in his possession. At no time had the head of the Intelligence and Operations section referred to these 30 million. When he himself disappeared with the entire 350 million without having paid the indemnities to his commandos, the eyes of the others were opened. They immediately arranged a meeting of all Delta commandos to examine the case of Dr Perez. All agreed that their leader had betrayed them and orders were immediately issued to everyone to keep watch on the ports and other exits. Each group leader was even given a photograph of Dr Perez who had now been condemned to death and was being hunted by the OAS, an order for 'specific action' having been signed by Colonel Godard and countersigned by Susini.

During the day of 8 June, however, it was learnt that that morning Dr Perez had succeeded in giving them the slip and in boarding the *El Mabrouk*, where another OAS militant had hidden him in his cabin. The OAS had in fact searched all the cabins with the exception of that of the militant whom they considered one of themselves.

So exit Dr Perez together with 350 million francs.

But this was not all. Before disappearing Dr Perez had ordered two break-ins, the targets being two safe-deposit boxes in a Hussein Dey bank. The order specified their numbers. On investigation it was found that they were the boxes rented for the OAS in the name of Colonel Gorel and containing about 30 million in all. Before leaving, therefore, Perez had ordered his commandos to lay hands on yet a further slice of the communal OAS treasure-chest. There was yet another blunder: the Delta commandos had not received their monthly pay. Gorel was summoned and confirmed that he had handed to one of Jean-Claude Perez' assistants eleven million francs for this purpose.

The reason for Dr Perez' extraordinary escapade was not simply a desire to decamp from Algeria taking the money with him for his personal use. He was in total disagreement with the other leaders on methods of pursuing the struggle and had decided to continue it in his own way with such capital as he could lay hands on. It was subsequently proved that Perez had distributed sums as large as 5 or 10 million to those of his men whom he considered most deserving. He had also provided subsistence in Spain for the members of his commandos until the day when he considered himself demobilised from the service of a lost cause. He returned to his medical profession, becoming medical adviser to a large pharmaceutical laboratory in Madrid. After the amnesty law of July 1968 he set up a practice in Paris.

Dr Perez was only at fault *vis-à-vis* his old friends of the headquarters in that he rendered no account of the use made of a certain sum drawn from the central funds of the clandestine organisation. It was probably well used. Objectivity requires that one should reproduce here an article published on 18 July 1962 in *Paris-Presse* and headed: 'In a letter to Godard and Susini Dr Perez "renders account" to the OAS.' The text of the article is as follows:

'Doctor Jean-Claude Perez, one of the OAS leaders who participated in the initial contacts with the provisional executive, has just sent a letter of self-justification, which is also an indictment, to Colonel Godard, Jean-Jacques Susini, Alain de Sérigny and Jacques Soustelle.

'It will be remembered that he disappeared from Algiers during the first week of June and that he has been accused of escaping to Spain, taking with him some 450 million old francs from the OAS treasure-chest.

'Here is the letter:

Gentlemen,

The various stages of our struggle developed between 26 April 1961 and 21 April 1962, on which latter date the OAS died as a potential military force.

French Algeria had become a tactical objective unattainable in the short term and a battle cry which could not be exploited by the opposition at home.

On 23 April I had a conversation with Susini during which I expressed the wish that we commit ourselves publicly to work for an independent Algerian executive in which Europeans would have not only genuine politico-juridical guarantees but also guarantees backed by armed force.

Since the weight our word carried in these discussions depended essentially in our terrorism, I had not envisaged a truce prior to the conclusion of fresh agreements. I had asked all heads of families to evacuate their wives and children so that Algiers might be placed in a state of total war. Susini refused.

Since 15 May there had been mention within the special teams, or to be more exact a mention was made by Y, Degueldre's successor, of the name of Jacques Chevalier, a man who has always contrived to move with history. In this way I learnt that the ex-mayor of Algiers was in close touch with Caruana, one of his friends who was acting as a company commander in the Delta commandos.

On the evening of 1 May Caruana issued to the special teams in my name and that of Susini an order to call off all operations. This truce was a grave error and it cost us eight days out of the thirty which remained to us to save the Algerian population.

On the morning of Saturday, 2 June, I received Caruana and six

Delta commando leaders in an apartment of the Redoute on the hills of Algiers. I expressed my anger to the Delta commando leaders. I gave them forty-eight hours to form a local European force of 12,000 men. If nothing had happened by midnight on Monday, I said, I would effect the transfer of the revolutionary potential at my disposal to another place.

Moreover, between Friday morning and Saturday evening four police operations were mounted against my various headquarters. It was not difficult to perceive that I had been denounced. Furthermore, during a meeting held by M on the Wednesday, it was stated that I had left but not before having withdrawn a very considerable sum from the till.

So Susini, who would never have had the courage to embark upon this new political course of his own volition, was now ready to offer my head on the altar of his nuptials with the Provisional Algerian Government.

My special teams advised me to go with them or alternatively to order them to kill Godard, Susini, the financier holding 1,200 million, Caruana and eight other persons. I would have had to carry out a veritable night of the long knives. But we had to keep the financier alive so that the teams might draw their money.

On Friday 8 June, therefore, I decided to leave after having ordered disengagement.

For some days now I have been hearing the anticipated rumours: Godard, who has never commanded anything, Cimeterre, who spends his time busybodying and banking money which others have collected, and Susini who will go to any lengths to be a minister of the Algerian Republic, have gone so far as to state that I left with 250 million [Editor's note: Perez only refers to 250 million old francs whereas the rumour in Algiers is that he took 450 million]; this is without foundation. Had I had such a sum, I should have taken good care not to leave it in Algiers and would have taken it with me for the revolutionary war which we are conducting.

Copies for information to: MM. Bidault, Soustelle, Argoud, Gardy, Schiaffino, Sérigny'

This was precisely the accusation made a great deal later against Colonel Gorel himself—another drama. He had been the holder of very large sums of money and, when he emerged from prison, he refused to hand over his accounts to the leaders who demanded them. Gorel no doubt considered his accounts to be in perfect order and, moreover, he maintained that the disbandment of the OAS released him from any obligation in this respect.

In the light of the facts his view seems justified. Colonel Gorel, who had spent twenty years as a military administrator in the Ministry of War in the Rue Saint-Dominique, had arrived in Algiers in 1961 in the normal course of duty. Colonel Gardes, who knew Gorel well and was at the time overloaded with innumerable financial problems, asked him to undertake the financial running of OAS. Gorel rendered very great service to the organisation, bringing into its administration his own special brand of technical competence, which Colonel Gardes admitted that he himself did not possess. The other colonels were similarly placed; they dealt meticulously with their strategic problems but financial problems were totally foreign to them.

Colonel Gorel, who took over from Colonel Gardes in November 1961 and was a highly competent technician, very soon realised that all the other colonels were not only incompetent in financial matters but also completely uninterested. At staff meetings, to ensure that all those present could understand, Gorel only produced highly simplified reports, showing merely two columns—receipts and expenditure. The OAS leaders were perfectly happy. No check was ever envisaged; they had total confidence in Gorel. General Salan himself steadfastly refused to become involved either in the detail or the generalities of OAS resources. To the very end he refused even to meet the treasurer. In short, Salan never met Gorel. As supreme commander he liked to know those responsible for intelligence, operations or political action but for him it was enough that some faceless treasurer should provide him with the means to carry out the strategy which he laid down.

The fact was that, from the financial point of view, Colonel Gorel was sole master of the financial ship. He had to submit accounts to no one and was supervised by no commission of control. Psychologically it was understandable that several years later, when he came out of prison and the Algerian upheaval was already past history, he saw no reason to provide accounts for which he had never been asked before.

In 1962, when he was travelling frequently to Italy to see the ex-OAS members present there, he adopted the same attitude to Colonel Argoud and Captain Curutchet—which they much resented. General Salan had ordered that 100 million be placed at the disposal of Bidault and his National Resistance Council. Gorel seemed in no hurry to comply. He held long conversations with Colonel Argoud, to whom he laid down *his* terms: he agreed to pay the sum over, not as a whole but in monthly contributions of 10 million, and in return demanded the right to inspect and check all the Council's expenses and plans. He had never asked for so much in Algeria. At the time Argoud made no secret of his fury, saying: 'It's crazy. A paymaster laying down his terms! A fellow who has spent his life counting greatcoat buttons! And he has the effrontery, since he is holding money which does not even belong to him, to dictate policy to us!'

For his part, Jean-Marie Curutchet said in his book (*Je veux la tourmente*, published by Laffont in 1973): 'Gorel, the paymaster, made a very unpleasing impression on me. He was an obstinate, unattractive man with a mind of below-average flexibility.'

Gorel was finally arrested as a result of one of his visits to Colonel Argoud in Milan. The Italian police discovered the false name under which he was hiding and passed it to the French police who had little difficulty in drawing their conclusions.

When he was arrested on 8 October 1962 the police discovered a list of names in the lining of his pants, names of some of his associates and contacts. A wave of arrests followed. Naturally he bravely refused to admit that he was the famous 'Cimeterre', the treasurer of OAS. As a result the police used a subtle form of blackmail on him. On his list of associates was a woman leading a double life, unknown to her husband, which had not affected their marriage relationship; she worked in the underground from political conviction. She was one of 'Cimeterre's' liaison officers and he met her from time to time in all sorts of different places such as railway station lobbies or hotel rooms (all perfectly above board).

'You refuse to admit that you are Cimeterre?' the police inspector said to Gorel. 'Very good. We know, however, that among other people the said Cimeterre meets a good-looking woman, particularly in hotels. The woman's husband does not know. This evening, therefore, we are going to arrange a little meeting at the Quai des Orfèvres to which I shall invite your wife, the other woman and her husband. I shall show them all the hotel registration cards. Since you are not Cimeterre, everything will be all right, I imagine.'

'But you know perfectly well that there is nothing between this woman and . . . Cimeterre.'

'That's correct. But it will be a long and difficult job to prove it.'

Gorel thought for a moment and then said: 'All right. I am Cimeterre.'

Next day he repeated his denial before the examining magistrate, alleging that the police had extracted an admission from him by using blackmail and that he had given way to avoid compromising an honest woman. He was nevertheless sentenced to four years' imprisonment and only emerged as a free man on 14 July 1966 when French Algeria had long since become history. The OAS was dead.

It was almost a different world that he re-entered—apart from one detail which concerned him intimately. This was the state of the OAS treasure-chest which was exactly as it had been when he was committed to prison, because he was, so to speak, the custodian of it.

In 1966 the surviving members of OAS headquarters, all of whom had received copies of its financial transactions, primarily via Switzerland, knew that the accounts had not been audited. Others were well informed;

still others doubted whether an OAS 'treasure-chest' existed at all. The latter included Colonel Gorel's cell companions; they had lived cheek by jowl with him for four years and some of them were common criminals always on the look-out for good business. Several were released a year or more after him.

Gorel himself maintains that he no longer has a penny. There are two totally contradictory theories. The mystery remains—and will remain—unsolved.

This was the situation when, on 20 December 1968, two and a half years after his release, Gorel disappeared. The field for investigation is vast, all the more so since organised flight by the man whose 'interests' were most concerned cannot be ruled out as a possible interpretation of his disappearance.

The fate of treasurers of clandestine movements seems to be a tragic one; similarly their war 'treasures' seem to have a sort of curse laid upon them. There is a striking similarity between the fate of the OAS 'treasure' and that of the FLN. The two men responsible for FLN finances are both dead: Mohammed Kidder was shot at the door of his hotel in Madrid by a man of Boumedienne's Military Security; Krim Belkacem was strangled in his hotel room in Frankfurt.

CHAPTER 35

The Cat and the Fox

One thing is certain: the arrest of Colonel Gorel in 1962, when he indubitably still had large-scale funds available, exerted a profound influence upon the last major assassination attempt against de Gaulle at Mont Faron on 15 August 1964. The fact that it failed despite its diabolically subtle organisation was largely due to lack of financial resources.

Five successive but independent attempts were planned for that day but for lack of money only one could be mounted. Strict compartmentation between the five plans would have made any police infiltration impossible and enabled at least one of them to succeed.

Jean-Jacques Susini devoted all his genius for organisation and planning to the preparation of this attempt. The starting point was Rome.

Susini's stay in the Eternal City almost began with a disaster. While still in Bologna writing his memoirs he had rented an apartment in Rome under the name of M. Agostini. Having done so, however, he was in no hurry to leave Bologna and his landlady in Rome became uneasy over his non-arrival. One morning she read in the newspapers that a certain French citizen named Agostini had just had a bad car accident. She went both to the French Embassy and the police at once to report the matter. Checks were made forthwith; the Embassy thought of the OAS, the police of some drugs business. Both organisations placed the apartment rented by Susini under strict, though unobtrusive, surveillance.

Meanwhile Susini arrived—in the best of health. After two months of observation, during which all the suspect's comings and goings were noted, the Italian police launched a large-scale operation. On 23 January 1963 sixty police surrounded the building before going in to the assault. The whole affair was so ponderous that Susini had plenty of time to evacuate his papers before being arrested without incident.

The Italian authorities offered him three alternatives: internment in a camp in Sardinia, departure for Canada with the agreement of the French government (which was prepared to pay all expenses) or expulsion across the frontier of his choice. Susini chose the third alternative and was conducted to Switzerland where he spent ten days before crossing back into Italy under the respectable name of M. Cesari. He rented a villa some thirty miles south of Rome overlooking a beach which had become famous a few years earlier owing to the Vilma Montesi affair (the death of a girl whose mysterious fate had shocked all Roman high society).

Before this escapade Susini had met a man destined to play a major rôle in the story of this new period—Henri X, Jacques Soustelle's right-hand man and confidant. Henri X was a *pied-noir* who as well as being a writer also had an international reputation as a scientist.

In April 1961, at the time of the generals' *putsch*, he had fled to Rome where his qualifications soon earned him an official post with the international organisations.

Quite naturally his ideas led him to meet Jacques Soustelle who had also taken refuge in Rome (Henri X had of course known him in Algiers in 1943 when Soustelle was in charge of the BCRA [wartime intelligence organisation]). He quickly became a close friend of the ex-Governor-General of Algeria.

With Dr Garcia, one of Susini's close associates, acting as intermediary, Henri X agreed to meet the man who carried second-top weight in the Rome organisation. The first interview took place in an empty apartment which had been occupied first by Colonel Vaudrey and then by Colonel Argoud. It was a somewhat stormy meeting. Though outwardly calm, the two men told each other certain home truths. Henri X reproached Susini for having entered into negotiation with the FLN. Susini replied that he did not intend to be lectured by someone who had not risked his life in Algeria.

As a result of this meeting Henri X gave Soustelle an adverse report on the former student leader of Algiers. Nevertheless contacts continued through Jean Garcia and one day he came back to Susini with a proposition: 'These gentlemen have suggested that I return to France to organise an assassination attempt against de Gaulle.'

Susini did not hesitate for a moment: 'Don't you go. I know that Soustelle has said that "there is no career in being a regicide". Since, however, he is extremely intelligent, he no doubt visualises making a career for himself as soon as the regicide has operated. We won't have another Bonnier de la Chapelle or another Darlan story. I advise you to go back to Switzerland and finish your studies in medicine.'

Garcia left for Switzerland but direct contacts between Susini and Henri X were nevertheless resumed. Both were university graduates, steeped in ancient history and literature, and their conversations soon became friendly. Though still committed to Soustelle, Henri X shifted his position. Out of these contacts came a programme for action, in particular regarding the possible publication in France of a weekly which did actually appear under the title of *168* (the 168 hours of the week). Only a single issue, carrying the signatures of Jacques Laurent and Raoul Girardet among others, was actually completed.

These conversations soon produced an atmosphere of confidence between the two men. Henri X, who had an official position, was struck by Susini's dedication to his cause, by the fact that he lived clandestinely and curtly refused all offers of employment, even those from the Italian secret service. The contrast with Soustelle, the other underground fighter, was striking: Soustelle had three apartments, at the Lido di Ostia, where he usually lived, in Lausanne which he visited frequently, and finally in Rome near the Piazza Colona, where was to be found his private secretary, Roger Gonzales, an ex-businessman from Aïn-Taya. Soustelle travelled a great deal and gave parties: in short, his standard of living was high. He did not draw money from the OAS. Presumably it came from his personal fortune or contributions from certain friends.

As a result of Henri X's revelations Susini became more familiar with the secretive being Soustelle had become. His clandestine existence was a strange one; he was hardly ever worried. In fact the French government found him somewhat embarrassing. He had been one of de Gaulle's senior ministers. In 1943 he had been head of the BCRA in Algiers, the French secret service which had originated in London—on liberation it became the DGER (*Direction Générale des Etats et des Recherches*—General Reporting and Investigation Agency) and then the SDECE (*Service de Documentation Extérieure et de Contre-Espionnage*—External Documentation and Counter-espionage Service). In 1958 both Frey and Debré had owed their careers to Soustelle. He was under the protection of the Italian secret service which never refused to help him. It had good reason for this—it had been approached by the British MI5 which looked upon Soustelle as a friend to be protected (he had been in close touch with the British secret services during the war and was still on very friendly terms with them).

This strange partnership between Soustelle, the domestic cat, and Susini, the desert fox, developed through intermediaries and was not unproductive. Lines were established to France and a political design took shape supported by an important personage in the Senate. Certain French intelligence officers travelled to Rome to meet the ex-head of the BCRA. Contact was also established with certain military authorities in France, who proposed to place their military areas under a state of siege should de Gaulle be removed from the public scene in one way or another. Their basic reason was to prevent any seizure of power by the communists in such a situation. The prospect was an attractive one and the surest way of arriving at this situation was to assassinate the head of state.

During a series of luncheons between Susini and Henri X an

assassination attempt was on the menu. They talked of the various attempts which had failed, particularly that of Louis de Condé in Athens. They discussed the seizure by the Belgian police of a certain quantity of equipment in a Brussels villa—weapons and 300 grams of cyanide designed to poison the bullets to be fired at de Gaulle.

They remembered a plan for an attempt during President Kennedy's funeral in Washington which de Gaulle was due to attend. The plan had never even approached the execution phase, for the FBI had been mysteriously warned and had taken extraordinary precautions for de Gaulle's security: the assassination of a head of state during the funeral of another head of state who had himself been assassinated would have been highly embarrassing to the American authorities.

From these conversations between Henri X and Susini there gradually grew the idea of organising an attempt themselves; from the political point of view this seemed to be the only way of halting de Gaulle's *rapprochement* with the East. In the view of these two humanists, however, there could be no question of reverting to Bougrenay de la Tocnaye's methods, which amounted to overturning a haywain like the bandits of old days and then firing on the convoy. Nor would they accept Watin's method—spraying a car with machinegun bullets. They visualised some far more subtle procedure, involving much more systematic engineering of the operation. They would only consider some method which was scientifically perfect and which would guarantee the security of the participants. On this point the two men were in complete agreement.

Henri X's scientific bent came into action at once. He saw as the perfect arrangement a 'television assassination' with the killer at a distance following his target on a television screen and pressing a button when the victim passed near a previously positioned bomb. In fact he proposed to position a remote-controlled bomb which would explode on a radio signal transmitted from a distance, thus ensuring the operator's escape.

Susini accepted the idea with enthusiasm. Henri X went home to study the technical arrangements, while Susini, meanwhile, examined where and when such an attempt might be made. His first idea was to find some precise spot where de Gaulle would necessarily be at a given moment; it had to be accessible beforehand to a group whose task would be to position the bomb without attracting attention.

All these factors, fed into Susini's computer-brain, produced one solitary answer—the official dais from which de Gaulle would watch the 14 July parade on the Champs-Elysées. He drew up a detailed plan for the operation at once and then plunged into the preparations.

The first essential was to find out precisely where the official dais was located. Was it always at exactly the same spot? The only way to discover was to compare a series of press photographs taken over the last four or five years. He therefore passed word to a journalist friend asking him to filch a series of press photographs from the archives of a major Paris newspaper.

The second problem was how to position the bomb without attracting attention. Susini remembered a method used by the Delta commandos in Algiers to enable them to work with impunity; they had disguised themselves as gasmen or firemen. He therefore had to know whether it would be possible for a team of gasmen to repair a gas main on the Champs-Elysées in the middle of the night and what sort of check might be made on them. He put these questions to certain friends in the offices of the Public Works department. He also asked whether it was possible to obtain the necessary permits.

Two commandos (under Jean-Pierre Ramos and Gilles Buscia) were ready for action. Adequate equipment was required, of course, together with a competent commander who could carry out the work in the most professional manner possible. The party was to consist of no more than six men with two guard vehicles. For weapons they were to carry light machine guns. The best time seemed to be 1 or 2 a.m. The bomb itself was to consist of a barrel filled with 200 lbs of plastic and located in one of the banks of flowers bordering the avenue; the barrel would be tilted towards the official dais. There was no alternative to the bank of flowers since Henri X had informed Susini that the mechanism which he proposed would include a small aerial of fine wire about eight inches high. The bomb could not, therefore, be placed underneath the cement paving.

There remained the problem of the damage which would be caused. The explosion would undoubtedly result in hundreds of casualties. This aspect of the matter made the two men stop to think. Their first thought was that only the cream of gaullism would be affected since the public at large would not be admitted to the area, and in their eyes the gaullists alone were responsible for the thousands of deaths occasioned by the abandonment of Algeria. Without even a protest de Gaulle had allowed Boumedienne's 'Army of National Liberation' to enter Algeria without striking a blow and square accounts with thousands of men of the most varied backgrounds. During the final weeks when the French had been in control in Algeria, 3,000 out of the 900,000 Europeans remaining had been kidnapped; it was comparable to the disappearance in France of 500,000 people in a single month with bodies being found in ditches, as had happened in Algeria. What would the general state of mind in France have been in that case? What if *France-Soir* had published whole pages every day headed 'News is wanted of A who has disappeared', as had happened in Algeria?

Fortunately, by the spring the Champs-Elysées plan had been abandoned. The journalist commissioned to obtain the photographs was slow in doing so. He admitted later that he was afraid of becoming involved subsequently. His excuse was that he was not a fighting man, only a simple journalist. In any case, the range of information necessary for the operation was great enough to necessitate its assembly well in advance and not in a last-minute rush.

During a walk along Lake Nemi, Susini set out the situation to Henri X. Not only was there delay in the arrival of the information but the question of financial resources was not yet settled. It was Soustelle who held the money required to maintain the commandos and buy the equipment required. But the ex-Governor-General appeared to be in no hurry to provide; the effects of Gorel's imprisonment were already making themselves felt.

'We are already in March,' Susini said, 'and I am still without too many of the components to enable me to mount the operation as I would like. I think it would be wise to cancel it and mount another safer one.'

'Have you an idea?' Henri X asked.

Susini handed him a copy of *Le Monde*. An announcement was underlined in red pencil: 'On 15 August General de Gaulle will unveil the mausoleums of the memorial to the Allied landing in Provence at Mont Faron.'

'The advantage is,' Susini added, 'that de Gaulle is to unveil a number of mausoleums in the area—five in all. We can therefore mount five successive operations.'

Henri X spoke to Soustelle and confirmation of the news was obtained. On Soustelle's desk enormous headlines announced de Gaulle's triumphal tour of Mexico. '*La mano en la mano*,' Soustelle chuckled. He knew Mexico very well indeed. He is one of the four or five world-famous experts on Aztec history.

'This reminds me of an astounding story,' Soustelle said to Henri X, 'which happened not long ago in Mexico at the time when they were having a revolution every week over there. A senior member of the legitimate government had just been assassinated. The government gave him a magnificent funeral; all the ministers accompanied the President to the cemetery to pay homage to their dead colleague. They did not know, of course, that the revolutionaries had foreseen what would happen and had crammed all the tombs around with dynamite. The entire government was removed from office in that one day.'

Was Soustelle talking in parables? In any case Henri X reported the matter to Susini.

'I will send someone to Colombey this week,' Susini said. 'He will examine all the possibilities on the spot. It is a fact that de Gaulle often goes to his daughter's grave.'

On reflection, however, Susini thought it best to abandon the idea of the booby-trapped cemetery. An operation at Mont Faron seemed to him safer. Colombey is only a small village where any stranger was immediately obvious to the considerable police force which was always there. No assistance could be expected on the spot and such an unusual operation as the opening of sealed tombs could hardly pass unnoticed.

Positioning a bomb at Mont Faron did not present comparable problems.

CHAPTER 36

An Infernal Machine

Mont Faron is a hill about 1,700 feet high, a little over a mile north of Toulon and overlooking the port. A well-kept road leads to the top where Fort de la Croix-Faron stands, occupied by the Navy.

About a mile and a half from the top is an old fortification known as the 'Beaumont tower' which was in process of reconstruction at the time; it was the site for the memorial to the Allied landing in Provence on 15 August 1944; it was to include a museum, a diorama and a cinema. De Gaulle had decided to inaugurate it in person on this same date, 15 August, twenty years later. It was an isolated spot where it would be easy for a party to bury a bomb during the night. Moreover, the general had announced his intention to unveil a number of mausoleums at various points on the coast where the troops of Generals de Lattre de Tassigny and Patch had landed.

Once the decision to organise an attempt at Mont Faron had been taken, Susini allocated the various rôles.

Certain groups on the Côte d'Azur under Soustelle's control were commissioned to make the reconnaissance. Roger Gonzales, secretary to de Gaulle's ex-minister, was responsible for contacting certain people on the spot. A series of photographs was taken of Mont Faron from all angles and these were passed to Susini a few days later. They were accurate and clear, confirming Susini in his conviction that the attempt was easy to organise. A second team, also under Soustelle's control, was made responsible for the transfer to France of the equipment prepared by Henri X.

Henri X had had to overcome enormous technical difficulties in producing his transmitter-receiver system owing to the necessity for miniaturisation. Technically his results were exceptional. Following the expert examination made after the attempt, the press reported that there were only four technicians in France capable of producing such a masterpiece of miniaturisation. Having no laboratory, he did his initial work in his own apartment looking out on to the artificial lake of a residential suburb in Rome. He worked entirely alone. When he considered that his apparatus had reached the right stage, he decided to carry out trials.

He took his family out for the day to Mont Circe, a rocky spur on the Latium coast above the Pontine marshes. At this point the rocks open out into caves washed by the sea, the best known of which, so it is said, was inhabited by Circe, Homer's enchantress who changed Ulysses' men into pigs. Mont Circe is a holiday area for the Romans who frequently spend their Sundays there.

Henri X went there on a weekday so as not to be disturbed. Leaving his family he successfully exploded a number of small charges.

Inside the receiver there was a tungsten filament which became red-hot when activated. On the transmitter was a small button which had to be pressed for fifteen seconds before being released: this caused radio waves to be transmitted. Henri X had had great difficulty in arranging the wavelength. The receiver must not be sensitive to any haphazard short-wave combination. He had therefore set up a 'wave-length key', as if the receiver had had a lock and the transmitter formed the key. The system would only function if the receiver had an aerial out in the open. The waves would carry for about 300–400 yards but Henri X considered that the transmitter should be no more than 200 yards away if one wanted to be sure that it would work.

Both transmitter and receiver were so small that they would fit into a cigarette packet. This was how they were taken across the frontier by a doctor from Mentone recruited by Gonzales (Gonzales' circuit actually smuggled across two specimens of Henri X's invention).

Towards the end of April Henri X had finished his two specimens. Susini insisted that he should make five or six so that a series of attempts could be made. Very soon, however, the question of money became acute. Five or six attempts postulated considerable sums for the movement and equipment of the various parties.

'Personally I have no more than two million,' Susini explained to Henri X. 'Ask Soustelle to provide me with a further five million.'

'I don't think that there will be any difficulty. In any case you are lunching with him in a few days' time.'

Weeks passed and the luncheon did not take place. Soustelle was travelling a great deal and was never free. Susini soon found himself facing a dilemma: either to make do with his own financial resources and mount only one attempt or to give up. In his view, success was the vital matter and so he decided to act and go ahead with the single attempt.

'I still think today,' he says now, 'that if I had had the resources to mount five or six attempts, I should have succeeded. Even if we had had a traitor amongst us, the compartmentation of the various teams would have ensured that we did not fail.' (Events subsequently showed that he was right; of the two teams which he controlled personally, only one was uncovered by the police. Not a single member of the other team was ever touched.)

The plan provided for two teams, one to position the bomb and the other to carry out the firing. Each was totally unknown to the other. The leader of Team No. 1 was in Rome—his name was Gilles Buscia.

Buscia was a Corsican and proud of the fact. He invariably wore a mackintosh with épaulettes and walked like a soldier on the march. He had hard steely eyes. His imperturbability when in a tight corner was astounding. He was a true commando leader, brave to the point of foolhardiness. He was adept at evading the police. His files showed that he had been born in Bizerta on 2 January 1938, that he had no fixed address, that he was a school-teacher and went by the names of Joseph Delaporte and Michel Abitri. He had been accused of killing Major Kubaziak in Aix-en-Provence, had been arrested and incarcerated in Fresnes prison. On 4 September 1963 he escaped with Frassati, one of his fellow-accused, helped by one of the prison warders named Ceccaldi. He had then gone to Rome where he met Susini and Henri X.

Susini naturally thought of him as leader of the team which was to lay the bomb. Buscia had many friends and would have no difficulty in recruiting men in France. Susini accordingly despatched him to Geneva where he found a 'guide' called Emmanuel waiting for him. He used one of the twenty-six secret routes into France which bypassed both customs and police posts. Buscia had learnt Susini's instructions by heart: go back to France; recruit some men; go to Mont Faron where construction work was still in progress; working by night, build in a bomb containing 66 lbs of plastic and $6\frac{1}{2}$ lbs of TNT connected to a receiver with an aerial at least eight inches high. (On one of the photographs Susini had even marked with a cross the exact spot at which the bomb should be placed—underneath the stairway leading to the platform.)

Even before he reached France Buscia, whose mind was on the recruitment of his men, asked Emmanuel to take him to Vallorbe-Saint-Ours, a small Swiss village where was a friend of his. The friend was Samuel Lehman, an ex-Foreign Legionary who had belonged to OAS France in 1962.

Lehman, who was then thirty-two years of age, had enlisted twice in the Foreign Legion and had even been sentenced in Switzerland for serving in a foreign army. On release he had met an ex-sergeant deserter who had persuaded him to join the OAS in Marseille. A little later he was arrested while trying to collect a suitcase full of arms from the left-luggage office in Saint-Charles station. He had served a year in prison under preventive detention and had been given a suspended sentence of two years' imprisonment by the Court of State Security.

Lehman agreed to join Buscia in France and Buscia went on to Marseille, crossing the frontier clandestinely. On arrival in Marseille Buscia contacted another friend, Jean-Baptiste Cianfarani, who had been arrested at Saint-Charles station at the same time as Lehman. Cianfarani had just been released after twenty-one months under detention. Buscia commissioned him to deal with the logistics of the operation, in other words lodging and transport for the party. Cianfarani immediately recruited three students who shared his political ideas: Alain, son of a surgeon in Marseille, Philippe, and Pierre, a student of political science whom he had known in college in Toul.

Pierre introduced his friends to Henri Talmant, a militant of long standing whose father had been the founder of the *Action française* movement in Algeria. Talmant kept an antique shop called Arme de France in the Boulevard Garibaldi. During the preparation of the attempt this shop served as base for the entire team.

Cianfarani's men were certainly not working for money. During the week preceding the attempt they were so short of cash that their daily fare consisted of one long loaf of bread soaked in sugared water.

Buscia kept Susini informed by telephone, using a code. He announced that he was going to Paris to contact some of Susini's friends who were to deal with the political aftermath of the attempt. Buscia returned to Marseille with one of these friends to act as guide: Yves Rossignol, a student of agronomy, who was subsequently badly hurt in a car accident while travelling in the south.

Buscia now announced to Susini that he had been to Mentone to collect the transmitter and receiver. He had also been to Aubagne to collect the 66 lbs of plastic held by a friend. Finally he announced that he was ready to proceed to the active phase of his mission: to go to Mont Faron and build in the bomb.

Now assured that his instructions were being followed, Susini left for Switzerland to recruit the team to be responsible for the firing. He went to a villa belonging to a Swiss friend who had lived in Algeria and whose two sons had had their throats cut by the FLN. There he assembled some twenty reliable militants and made a short speech to them:

'I am entirely confident of all of you here. I can therefore talk in the certainty that nothing said here will ever emerge. Our lives are at stake. On 15 August next a bomb will explode three feet from General de Gaulle. This bomb is already in position and is remote-controlled. I am here to select those who will be members of the team which will press the button. The team will consist of some ten persons since it will be necessary to ensure that the operators can escape and leave France. I know that you are all ready to serve but I would draw your attention to the gravity of the action which I am asking you to undertake. I shall therefore understand perfectly if some say No and others say Yes. But you must be as definite as the Bible: your Yea must be Yea and your Nay must be Nay. Each of you has half an hour to go out into the grounds and think. In half an hour you will give me your answers, one by one. So long!'

One by one they returned. Susini kept a tally of the answers: there were as many 'Yes' as there were 'No'. He selected ten people to form the firing party: one couple, a young man and a girl who hardly knew each other, and eight men to be responsible for their protection and escape—ten persons in all, none of whose names ever became known to the police. Of the couple the young man was a student aged twenty-eight, named Denis. The girl, whose christian name was Janine, was aged twenty-five.

At one moment Susini had thought of sending his own wife, who was pregnant. She had volunteered to go, arguing that a pregnant woman could go anywhere without being suspect. Finally, however, he refused.

Sending the others home, he remained with those selected and explained his plan to them at length:

'I intend to arrange that you escape. To do this you must follow my instructions to the letter. I look at things from the enemy's point of view and I think all the time of the investigations which will inevitably take place. Those of you who are actually going to operate will be carrying a transistor radio slung over the shoulder, in which the remote-control system will be concealed. Remember that a large number of photographs will be taken by the police, some from a helicopter, and that their first idea will be to examine closely all those carrying transistors.'

Realising that suspicion might attach to a couple of lovers who spent too much time in the restaurant on the platform of Mont Faron, he gave the young couple very precise instructions as to the moment at which they should arrive and the attitude which they should adopt. They were to appear as a couple of lovers flirting and taking photographs of de Gaulle because there was a historic figure passing. On a detailed plan of the restaurant he showed them which table to take and where they should be at the moment of the explosion; there was a hidden corner where they would have nothing to fear (splinters would be lethal within a radius of 200 yards).

The restaurant faced the monument, the entrance of which was on the opposite side. As soon as de Gaulle and his entourage reached the foot of the steps, the couple were to emerge, pass the hidden corner and press the button for fifteen seconds (the explosion would not take place until two minutes after release of the button, so accurate timing was required); they were then to take cover in their hidden corner.

Susini then explained his plan for the 'recovery' of the two operators. He repeated his formal order that under no circumstances were any of them to contact any member of the other teams, whose names they did not know in any case. Chance is unpredictable, however, and Susini knew that safety lay in keeping them in watertight compartments. The future was to show how right he was.

Susini did not know, however, that Buscia had not altogether obeyed this order and had contacted Yves Rossignol who belonged to another action group. When he heard of it, Susini was furious: he knew that this contact entailed the risk of numerous arrests—far more than there would have been had this clue not been provided.

Susini waited in Switzerland for a time since he had been warned that two of his acquaintances, the journalists Philippe Héduy and Hubert Basso, wished to meet him. The precautions taken before they met Susini were reminiscent of a spy film: they were led hither and thither through Geneva to ensure that no policeman could possibly be following them.

'They were a little surprised,' Susini says, 'but I had to take these sort of precautions if I wanted to ensure the success of the operation. Naturally I could not tell them the real reason which had brought me to Geneva.'

Héduy and Basso had in fact come to propose to Susini a meeting with Sergent, at the latter's request. At the time this seemed unimportant to Susini, although he appreciated Sergent's wish for a *rapprochement*.

Next day Susini went back to Rome where Gilles Buscia had arrived on the previous day. The two men met in a restaurant behind the Coliseum, aptly named The Gladiator.

'Mission carried out,' Buscia said by way of introduction.

Susini had not felt so satisfied for a long time. At last things seemed to be working out according to plan.

'You put it in the right place?'

'Not exactly. We worked quietly all night, for there was no one about. We went over the platform with a fine toothcomb but found nowhere where we could dig in 66 lbs of explosive. Finally I found a crack and I used that.'

Susini was pleased. He knew that he could trust Buscia.

'I brought three men back with me, including Lehman, an ex-Foreign Legion NCO who helped me position the bomb at Mont Faron.'

'You are sure of them?'

'Absolutely. I know them well.'

Susini took Buscia's men on the books, from the financial and logistic points of view increasing the size of Buscia's party which Susini was already maintaining; also on his books was the prison warder who had helped Buscia and Frascatti to escape and who was hiding with his family in northern Italy. Susini made one or two telephone calls to ensure that the new arrivals were housed and then called Geneva to give the firing party the definite green light. He could now only possess his soul in patience.

On 15 August Susini was glued to his transistor. He listened to the reports and heard de Gaulle's series of speeches at Mont Faron. Knowing the place to perfection, he imagined de Gaulle mounting the steps underneath which death was lurking. Nothing happened.

In front of the memorial de Gaulle made a further speech. Still nothing. The ceremony was at an end and nothing had occurred.

Susini was uneasy. Ten of his men were on the spot. Still without news he slept badly.

Next morning the young man who was due to have pressed the button and had driven through the night to Rome, arrived to report. The reason for the failure was a ludicrous one: de Gaulle was due to arrive at Mont Faron at 4 p.m. and the team two hours earlier, in other words at 2 p.m. But the police had barred all access to Mont Faron from midday.

'We arrived,' the young man explained, 'with the set slung over my shoulder and hidden under a coat in case of photographs taken from a helicopter. We tried everything but the route was blocked. We were exactly on time—2 p.m. as per your instructions. The girl who was with me even tried to chat up the CRS but without result. She had a perfectly valid press card on her too, but we were not allowed through. We were in despair but there was nothing we could do.'

Susini realised that the fates were not on his side. He wanted to think, to take a little time off and consider matters before continuing the struggle —he would not give up.

CHAPTER 37

The Urn that Exploded

Thirteen days later, on 28 August 1964, the Rome radio networks featured an unusual news item: flames had suddenly issued from a flower-pot on the steps of the mausoleum, indicating that an assassination attempt had been prepared at Mont Faron; the theory was supported by the fact that a 6-lb bomb had been found in the pot.

Susini immediately went to see Henri X who was then living in a villa in Toriciana, next to another villa inhabited by the Italian secret service officer who was permanently responsible for Soustelle's security in Rome. Susini and Henri X discussed the situation. They thought that Buscia had made a mistake and had not reported the precise position of the bomb—Susini had taken the word 'crack' in its literal sense. Had he said that the bomb was in the flower-pot, Susini would have arranged to recover it as soon as it had failed to explode. He had assumed, however, that the bomb had been *built in*.

Buscia was summoned and confirmed that he had indeed placed the bomb in the flower-pot. De Gaulle had passed within inches of it and so the idea was a good one. Buscia stated, however, that instead of *six pounds* of explosive, he had placed *sixty-six* pounds in the pot—sixty pounds of plastic and six of TNT. The latter gives off gas when heated by the sun and could therefore produce a flame.

Henri X and Susini immediately drew their conclusions: someone who knew what he was doing had thrown a lighted cigarette end into the flower-pot after having extracted the sixty pounds of plastic. But who? This was fairly obvious: the object was to exploit the incident politically, particularly in a year when presidential elections were due to take place and were likely to be difficult (as in fact it proved—for the first time in his life de Gaulle was taken to a ballot by Mitterrand).

Days went by without the exiles obtaining any further information: the police enquiry was being conducted with exemplary discretion.

263

Buscia's men were travelling 'somewhere in the world'. They eventually returned to Europe and Buscia with some others re-entered France secretly and passed through Marseille.

On 8 April 1965 Buscia lunched in a restaurant near the Marseille Opera with Pierre, the student, and Jean-Paul Lo Cicero, with whom he left the restaurant at about 3 p.m. He was wearing a black mackintosh which he had borrowed from Jean-Jacques Susini a few days before. The two men passed the Vieux Port and took the Rue de la République. On arrival at the corner of Rue Colbert, Lo Cicero remembered that he was out of cigarettes.

'I'll go on,' Buscia said; 'you catch up.'

Cicero bought his cigarettes and as he emerged saw Buscia surrounded by police who were taking him away. He ran back to the restaurant which they had just left but Pierre had already gone home. Cicero followed him and told him that Buscia had been arrested. Thinking that the police would keep their capture secret in order to make Buscia talk by methods never officially admitted, Pierre telephoned a newspaper, *Le Méridional*, which published the story next morning, thus disarming the police. (Buscia had in fact been arrested by the General Intelligence [*Renseignements généraux*] police and not by the branch normally in charge of such enquiries.)

Reports on this affair soon reached Rome and so Susini was able to gain some idea of what had happened at Mont Faron and what had led to Buscia's arrest. A few days earlier Lehman, the ex-Foreign Legionary in whom Buscia had such confidence, had been seen at about 11 p.m. by two informants (one of whom was the student Pierre) coming out of the Kronenbourg bar at the corner of Rue Canebière and Boulevard Garibaldi in the company of a police inspector of General Intelligence whose duty it was to keep watch on right-wing circles. Lehman was the only man who knew that Buscia had returned to Marseille.

A few days later, moreover, Lehman, who had returned scot-free to Switzerland, made a series of appalling statements to the press about the Mont Faron assassination attempt; his story was highly coloured but full of names and details. He had already told the same story to the police who had naturally followed it up at once while allowing him to escape to Switzerland with no questions asked.

The report of the enquiry was headed: 'Placing of an explosive device on a public highway with criminal intent, a crime committed in connection with an individual or collective enterprise, the purpose or tendency of which was to substitute an illegal authority for the authority of the State.' It produced a dossier of 364 pages of evidence with 22 seals and 6 folios of first-class photographs which was laid on the desk of the President of the Court of State Security.

Twelve persons were arrested; three others were indicted *in absentia* —Susini, Henri X and, ironically, Lehman. It must be admitted that the enquiry was a model of its type.

The story began at 2.45 p.m. on 28 August 1964 when workmen in the Mont Faron memorial saw a 'considerable' jet of flame issuing from the flower-pot at the foot of the steps leading to the monument. As they rushed up to put out the fire which might well spread to the neighbouring pine-woods, the flower-pot blew up, scattering earth and the remains of all sorts of unusual objects all around; among the latter were batteries, electric leads, a bulb and a miniaturised radio apparatus, badly charred. Army bomb disposal experts arrived with the police and found fragments of explosive which they immediately destroyed according to regulations.

The thoughts of the police inevitably went back to de Gaulle's visit thirteen days before and they immediately informed all 'competent' authorities from the Prefect to the Public Prosecutor of the Court of State Security. When the news arrived on the Minister of the Interior's desk, it was probably no great surprise, as we shall see.

The lay-out of the area was given in detail in the report. The steps leading to the monument were about one hundred yards in length, starting from the road below and ending on a fairly wide platform. At the foot of the steps, on the left facing the monument, was a little wall bordering the road. The flower-pot was at the junction of the wall and the steps. It was 27 inches high, 23 inches in diameter at the centre and a foot in diameter at the base. On the base was inscribed 'CPA 7'.

On 15 August de Gaulle had stood motionless at this spot for several minutes listening to an address of welcome from the Minister for Ex-Servicemen. The flower-pot was less than a yard away from him.

The technical experts from the army and police listed their treasure trove. In quick succession they had discovered: a tangle of electric leads, six metal caps forming the ends of 1-lb slabs of TNT, a coil of wire, thirteen shock-proof 1·5-volt batteries trade-marked 'Malory & Kib', a vacuum relay-valve marked 'Amperite 6 No. 120 Relay', and various splinters of iron and wood.

By 29 August the experts had recorded their initial conclusions: this was an explosive charge with a mechanism for radio-controlled ignition. They also referred, however, to the presence of 'an incendiary device obviously intended to destroy the whole arrangement'. The explosive was regulation TNT as used in the French army.

Enquiries were made in the area to find out whether six slabs of TNT were missing, particularly from Mont Faron Fort where a stock of explosives was held. Regulations and controls were strict, however, and there was no report of anything missing. The explosive had therefore come from elsewhere.

M. Henri Forestier, chief engineer of Paris Municipal Laboratory, who has been mentioned before in connection with the Pont-sur-Seine bomb, was commissioned to study the débris in order, if possible, to reconstruct the mechanism of the infernal machine. The state of the remnants was such that he could not entirely reconstruct the electrical circuit; he noted, however, that the inventor of the system was a remarkable technician.

The incendiary device intended to destroy the whole thing, on the other hand, was almost amateurish: it consisted of aluminium powder, sodium chlorate, iron oxide, black powder and mineral oil. The expert also noted that sulphates were present, intended to delay the chemical action of this mixture.

The expert did discover, however, that the bomb was intended to explode as the result of the transmission of a series of radio waves which only produced their effect at the end of two minutes—the figure '120' on the valve indicated a 120-second delay.

The police wondered why the system had not functioned at the time of de Gaulle's visit. To this question—a genuine one—they could at first find no answer. They concluded that an assassination attempt had been prepared, the system being installed some days before 15 August, that the bomb had not exploded for some reason unknown and that the perpetrators had attempted to cover their tracks by placing an incendiary device in the flower-pot.

It will be obvious at once that this theory was ridiculous; as we have seen, Susini himself had never ordered removal of the bomb. Had he in fact known that the bomb had been placed in the flower-pot, he would have ordered its removal, not the addition of some chancy system of blowing it up. Any party capable of installing an incendiary device, probably at night, could just as well have removed the bomb together with its ignition receiver.

Forestier, the expert who never for a moment considered the possibility of some machination on the part of the police, wondered why the would-be assassins had not used their own remote-controlled firing system to destroy the whole thing. 'The reason,' he wrote, 'is that they had only limited confidence in the assembly. Lack of confidence in the firing system meant that they could not simply remove the device from the flower-pot since they would be afraid of a premature explosion during this operation.'

It never entered Forestier's head that the sixty pounds of plastic placed in the flower-pot by Buscia might have been removed by another team of experts who had no fear of a 'premature explosion'. This, however, is what had happened.

The police, meanwhile, were trying to discover where the components of the machine had been bought. The batteries were of a well-known commercial make and therefore gave no clue; no recent theft of TNT from any depot had been reported. They therefore concentrated their efforts on the origin of the valve 'Amperite 6 No. 120'. This type of valve was manufactured by the Amperite Company, 600 Palisade Avenue, Union City, New Jersey, USA.

After minute research the origin of the radio receiver circuit, which was of 'Philco' type, was discovered. The receiver was a 'Controlair 3', again manufactured by an American firm which only had two representatives in Europe, a M. Garofali in Bologna and Aero-Piccola in Turin. In all probability, therefore, the device had been made in Italy since its components came from there.

Apart from the technical enquiry police investigations in the normal sense of the word were energetically pursued by Commissaire Mesini assisted by every known type of police force, official, parallel or tangential. His first move was to list the various firms which had worked on the building of the mausoleum and go through their employees. This produced nothing. The men of 29 Engineer Battalion from Avignon, who had worked on the site and had used explosives, were interrogated at length; not an ounce of explosive was missing and, moreover, they had not used TNT.

The fatal pot was the object of intense police investigation. They soon knew its history by heart. This ornamental jar had first seen the light of day in 1960 at Diemeringen in the department of Bas-Rhin, where it had been manufactured by the Grandes Poteries Alsaciennes. It had been warehoused by a firm named Guyomar in Toulon and at 11.13 a.m. on 5 August 1961 had been bought by a M. Brandy who lived in the Beaumont Tower near the end of the cable-car hoist from Toulon. M. Brandy had passed it to M. Rivetti, a gardener employed by the cable-car company, who, in 1961, had placed it at the spot where it stood at the moment of the assassination attempt.

In April 1961 this same gardener had planted in the pot a cutting from a plant known as *Griffe de Sorcière* which is well known as a slow grower. Over a period of months the plant had not grown very much—a number of witnesses were quite definite on the subject.

All the more astonishing, therefore, was a photograph taken by the security service when preparing the security arrangements; *it showed the pot capped by luxuriant vegetation. Moreover subsequently this vegetation had disappeared.* Here was another mystery.

The police came to the conclusion that the jar destroyed in the mini-explosion was the same as that which had been placed there in 1961 and that it had not been moved.

During their enquiries another small detail came to light: at the moment of the mini-explosion on 28 August, M. Drancourt, one of the keepers of the memorial, noticed a black Citroën Déesse moving slowly towards the top of the hill *immediately after the conflagration.*

The vital part of the investigations concerned the suspects. One list could be eliminated forthwith—those who had been favoured with 'preventive action' on the part of the police in preparation for the head of state's visit. Some had been 'removed' and others arrested; certain officers had even been confined to barracks on the day of de Gaulle's arrival.

The police then turned their attention to 'activists or subversive movements who, though on the wane, sometimes still show activity'. They investigated the remnants of various clandestine circuits and drew up a list of suspects: it included Château-Jobert's MCR; Sergent's CNR; circuits run by certain OAS leaders in exile such as Jean-Claude Perez and Jean-Jacques Susini; and certain dangerous individuals, among whom was listed Gilles Buscia who had escaped from Fresnes.

The police were therefore forced to embark on a full-scale historical study of all subversive movements originating from the Algerian affair. Fortunately the study could be confined to the south of France, but Toulon offered a rich field for analysis. In May 1963 the arrest of Lieutenant-Commander Roy had revealed the existence of a 'Navy' branch of the National Resistance Council. The theory was confirmed in August 1962 when Lieutenant-Commander Georges Buscia, brother of Gilles, deserted; both were arrested as deserters in February 1963. On 21 January 1964 Captain Woringer, second-in-command of the escort vessel *La Galissonnière*, was arrested in his turn on suspicion of being head of the National Resistance Council (Navy) under the cover-name of 'Gitane'. In addition, a number of attacks on policemen and a number of explosions had taken place in Toulon which thus began to look like one of the strongholds of activism.

The suspicions of the investigators naturally concentrated on the one local man who had succeeded in escaping—Gilles Buscia. Other suspects, both civil and military, were still on the run; some had been reported abroad. Mere suspicion, however, was not good enough for the police machine, which required certainty. So a process of elimination was started.

The Château-Jobert gang was quickly cleared: Pierre Mourier, the colonel's assistant, was arrested and he was clearly very taken aback. From another source the police learnt that the colonel himself had sent emissaries to try and find out who was responsible for the Mont Faron attempt.

Chance once more came to the assistance of the police in the south. They heard that on 4 December 1964 their Paris colleagues had arrested Séverin Luciani who was found to be in possession of a number of highly interesting documents, in particular false papers, letters and documents in code. Among the false papers they found photographs of Gilles Buscia. Among the letters was one signed 'Robert', a cover-name often used by Buscia. Examination of the handwriting made the police certain that it had been written by Buscia. It also included a characteristic passage: 'You are wrong to worry about the use to which the 100,000 francs which you sent me have been put. The general tone of my letters, which has been wrongly interpreted, together possibly with a misleading version of the facts spread by R, have led you to think that they were used in "the Affair". They have in fact been used to enable us to live. You say that you are *no longer* [Buscia's italics] willing to meet the expenses of my "one-way" collaboration with our compatriot. That you are *not* willing would seem closer to the truth (and I am not referring to the affair of SE which ought to have interested everybody).'

The police experts ruminated over this letter which had been written on 12 November 1964. They came to the conclusion that 'the Affair' must be that of Mont Faron and that the 'compatriot' could be none other than Jean-Jacques Susini. From being an ordinary suspect Buscia had now become suspect No. 1.

On being deciphered, the other documents proved to be a veritable mine of information for the police. They produced names, addresses, telephone numbers and notes. Among the names was found: 'Grimaldi— Mont Faron—near Prado building D.' So the words 'Mont Faron' had appeared for the first time.

Investigation of these clues, however, proved unfruitful, as did interrogation of Séverin Luciani who preserved an obstinate silence in face of all questioning. Among his papers, however, appeared a cheque for 2,500 francs signed by a certain Germain Jouffret who had an account with the Société Générale at Gap in Hautes-Alpes.

Jouffret was a watchmaker in Gap and he appeared before the police investigators in a very nervous state. He explained that in July 1962 a man calling himself Robert had asked to see his employee, Yves Lo Cicero. The interview had lasted no more than a few minutes and the watchmaker had thought no more of it until the day when he had discovered from his usual newspaper that the said Robert was none other than Gilles Buscia, wanted for the murder of Major Kubaziak. His own employee, Yves Lo Cicero, had been arrested with his brother Jean-Paul for helping Buscia to hide his men who were mostly deserters from the Foreign Legion. Germain Jouffret had been questioned at the time and had told the police all he knew.

He then recounted the sequel. Early in July 1964 he was bending over a watch which was being particularly fractious when the doorbell of his shop rang. He looked up and there was Gilles Buscia, in a tightly belted mackintosh, looking at him menacingly with his hands in his pockets. In the back of his shop he had to listen to what Buscia had to say. He did not feel very much at ease since he had talked a great deal when Lo Cicero had been arrested.

Buscia told him that he, Jouffret, had been condemned to death by the OAS for having denounced to the police a member of that organisation named Eric, an ex-Foreign Legionary. He added, however, that he had authority not to execute the sentence if the watchmaker would pay 5,000 francs to his organisation.

The watchmaker accepted at once but, not having sufficient money on hand, he proposed 1,500 francs in cash and two cheques, one for 1,000 francs dated 31 August 1964 and the other for 2,500 francs dated 31 December 1964, the name of the payee being left blank in each case. The police traced the first cheque: it had been cashed by a certain Jérôme Feliciaggi. The second was found on Séverin Luciani. The watchmaker told the police that there had been another man with Buscia but his memory of him was too vague for a description.

The police now had proof, however, that Gilles Buscia had been in France in July 1964, one month before Mont Faron. Since he was already being hunted by every police force, he had certainly not come to France simply to blackmail a watchmaker. He must have had some more serious reason—preparation of an assassination attempt, for instance.

Buscia was used to living underground and he knew how to evade the police. After Mont Faron the information provided by Lehman, who was one of Commissaire Caille's informers in General Intelligence, was enough to give the investigation a new lead. General Intelligence (which was in fact a political police force) followed Buscia for some time thanks to information provided by Lehman. They only arrested him when they considered that he could not teach them much more about his contacts.

When he was arrested Gilles Buscia had on him a revolver, a passport in the name of Michel Abitri and a driving licence in the name of Joseph Delaporte, both of which carried his own photograph. He was also carrying an identity card in the name of Pierre Vachette (born at Vallières, Creuse, on 10 October 1938) and adorned with a superb photograph at which the police turned a blind eye. The photograph, though an excellent likeness, reminded them of no one. They had never seen that face before —all of which shows that even the cleverest policemen are sometimes prey to human weaknesses such as loss of memory. The photograph was that of Lehman who had just handed Buscia to them on a plate.

During his ten days' detention without legal aid Buscia was assailed with questions (the police could not go further owing to the announcement of the arrest in Le Méridional); meanwhile multifarious checks were made to discover traces of his movements under his various identities. Gilles Buscia naturally refused to say anything but the investigators nevertheless contrived to reconstruct the timetable of his activities from the time of his escape from Fresnes on 4 September 1963.

In Buscia's pocket the police had found a copy of a letter addressed to a certain major who was quickly identified as Major Mondolini—his name appeared on Séverin Luciani's papers under the heading 'Mondol-Roquebillières'. On suspicion of having provided false papers for Buscia, Mondolini, who worked in the Nice sub-division, was arrested in his turn. His office, his apartment and his country house were searched from top to bottom, but in vain.

Another team of police had been commissioned to find a certain suit-case which Buscia had handed to a friend. He had been seen doing so while being followed prior to his arrest. Some person unknown had taken the suitcase and gone into No. 8 Rue de Montelieu in Marseille. At this address lived a certain Pierre Sinibaldi who, when arrested, denied knowledge of anyone named Buscia; all he did, he said, was to keep certain things belonging to one of his friends, Jean-Paul Lo Cicero.

The latter, who had just been released from prison, had left for Roujan in Herault where he was arrested; the sleuths of General Intelligence recognised him as the man to whom Buscia had handed the suitcase. Lo Cicero, of course, stated that he had intended to hand the suitcase to Sinibaldi but, since the latter was not at home, he had returned it to Buscia. Since his story involved him in no crime in the eyes of the law, he was released with the honours of war.

The police were furious. They knew that Buscia wrote a great deal and that he must possess records which would make absorbingly inter-esting reading. These records, of course, must be in the famous (and undiscoverable) suitcase. When they mentioned the matter to Buscia, all he did was to reply: 'Suitcase? What suitcase? I've never had a suitcase.'

Nevertheless the routine police checks gradually began to pay off. They discovered, for instance, that on 7 July 1964 a green Peugeot 404 had been hired from Hertz in Toulon by a certain Joseph Delaporte—the name used by Buscia on his driving licence. The car had not been returned and so, on 25 July, Hertz filed a complaint. The car was found in Marseille on 20 August, in other words five days after the abortive attempt at Mont Faron. This was the vehicle used by Buscia to visit the watchmaker in Gap; Jouffret definitely recognised it.

At this point comes a classic example of rivalry between different police forces.

The police in charge of the investigation did not know what General Intelligence was doing. The latter, who had interrogated Lehman at length, discovered proof that he had been in Marseille in March, in other words a few days before Buscia's arrest. A certain Pierre Vachette had hired from Hertz in Marseille a Peugeot 404 which was discovered, damaged, in a garage in Saint-Zacharie, Var. On 18 March this same Vachette had hired another Peugeot 404 from Hertz in Marignane; it was found on 31 March in Marseille, fitted with false number plates.

It must not be forgotten that at this stage Buscia was being followed by the General Intelligence sleuths and that Lehman was supposed to be living with him. It seems odd, therefore, that General Intelligence arrested Buscia but allowed Lehman to escape to Switzerland where, as we have seen, he was to make sensational disclosures considerably later.

Nevertheless, despite the definite evidence of the local constable in Saint-Zacharie, of the car-hire agency in Toulon and of the Gap watchmaker, all of whom recognised him, Buscia persisted in denying everything. When the police asked him to speak of his part in the Mont Faron attempt, Buscia, the interrogators noted, 'gave negative replies' or 'preserved total silence'. Of course he would chat with them on other matters —the weather, holiday expenses and even general French politics. Then he would be smiling, sometimes even sarcastic. As soon, however, as the police attempted to slip a catch question into the conversation, he stiffened and closed up like a clam. As a result, apart from certain rather vague evidence, the file remained empty. There was no proof that Gilles Buscia had taken part in the Mont Faron attempt.

The police redoubled their efforts. One of them produced proof that Samuel Lehman had been in Marseille; on the night of 31 March/1 April 1965 he had slept at the Hotel Unic under the name of Vachette; the hotel night-porter definitely recognised his photograph. After this he had mysteriously disappeared, under the very noses of that élite corps of policemen known as General Intelligence. Having escaped to Switzerland, he could now enjoy a well-earned rest in his chalet in Vallorbe-Saint-Ours.

But this man, who seemed proof against anything, suddenly suffered a crisis of conscience. Without any obligation to do so and with the sole purpose, one supposes, of relieving his mental torture, he presented himself of his own accord to his country's authorities (he was a Swiss national, it will be remembered) and swore to them that it was he who had constructed the bomb intended to kill General de Gaulle at Mont Faron on the previous 15 August.

The Swiss authorities took a record of his statements but kept them secret. This did not prevent (in the words of the official report) 'Lehman's revelations reaching our colleagues in headquarters in Paris through an informer and a summary of evidence was drawn up'.

Not until a few days later did Lehman sell his story to an international press agency and it appeared in a number of French, British, German and Swiss newspapers (the German weekly *Blick* even devoted a series of four articles to it). The ex-Foreign Legionary gave a complete account of the Mont Faron affair from its conception until his return to Switzerland. It is a story which deserves to be told.

CHAPTER 38

The Worm in the Apple

For Lehman the Mont Faron affair began on Palm Sunday 1964 when Buscia came to see him in Vallorbe. He accompanied Buscia to Marseille and various other destinations including Paris; finally he went with him to Rome. There he met Susini and later Henri X. As a foursome they examined the possibility of an assassination attempt against de Gaulle.

Lehman explained to Henri X (an eminent scientist) that he, Lehman, was an expert in miniaturisation; before his military service he had worked in Switzerland as a mechanic on photographic equipment, as a watch repairer and as a fitter in plastics. Henri X, dazzled by these recommendations, asked him to construct a bomb to be ignited by remote control through a radio receiver. Lehman agreed, set up shop in the house of a Roman count and spent several weeks working on the apparatus.

Continuing his 'revelations' Lehman then explained that he had finished construction of the bomb about mid-June and that conclusive trials had been carried out, to the admiration of all. He had been given a promise that the apparatus would be sent to him via a doctor in Mentone and, with a satisfying sensation of duty well done, he had returned with Buscia to the Marseille area.

A week later the device arrived via the doctor and he put the finishing touches to it; he gave an accurate description of it which tallied with the results of the investigation into the debris of the bomb. These details led the police to give credence to the rest of his report.

Using his knowledge of the affair to embellish his personal story, Lehman then explained that an OAS man had been sent to take photographs of the memorial but that the prints had been a total failure and quite useless. He and Buscia had therefore been obliged to go to the place themselves. They had both agreed to place the bomb underneath 'the access bridge of the memorial'.

They went back there again on 28 July, accompanied on this occasion by Yves Rossignol, a personal friend of Susini who acted as chauffeur and bodyguard. Shortly after midnight Rossignol and Lehman left Buscia having a good time and went back to Mont Faron yet again; more detailed examination revealed certain difficulties concerning the positioning of the bomb and, on his own initiative, Lehman decided that it would be placed in a flower-pot which was located at just the right spot. He emptied the earth from the pot and put the bomb inside; he replaced the earth removing the surplus in some sacking and scattering it some distance away. The bomb, still according to Lehman, consisted of 55 lbs of cheddite and three slabs of TNT. He had of course switched on the receiver. Rossignol, who had kept watch, grenade in hand, then took him back to Marseille and immediately left for Paris.

Lehman went back to Rome to await D Day; he had been selected to return to the spot with Buscia on 15 August and press the button of the remote-control transmitter. He then said that, in case there should be some hitch, he had constructed a second device which he had handed to a man named Gonfond living in Aubagne. Rossignol went with him on this trip.

Lehman then gave his version of the bomb's failure to explode on 15 August. He was then in Rome, he said, together with Buscia, waiting for a money order which was to be sent them by Séverin Luciani. The money order did not arrive; it was impossible to contact Susini or Henri X and so they were forced to remain in Rome for lack of money. Buscia had then alerted one of his friends by telephone—Lehman did not know the name—telling him to go to Mont Faron with the transmitter. The friend arrived too late, however, as the police had barred access to the area from midday.

Lehman then went on to say that he had subsequently constructed seven devices of the same type which Buscia wished to use for a number of attacks on the *barbouzes*. Not being in agreement with 'such an extreme measure', he had himself destroyed six of them and had handed the seventh to a school-teacher in Lançon, also named Luciani. This last bomb was to be used for an assassination attempt on the Champs-Elysées on 14 July 1965.

In the process Lehman incriminated a large number of people, mentioning the names of Susini, Henri X, Cianfarani and many others.

Some time later (at the end of June 1965) Lehman, apparently still in the mood for confidences, went to the Swiss authorities and confessed to trafficking in forged dollars. In accordance with international agreement the Swiss alerted their French colleagues. French police representatives immediately went to Lausanne to hear Lehman's new tale. On this occasion the ex-Foreign Legionary confirmed that his previous disclosures to the press were the truth, the whole truth and nothing but the truth.

In the eyes of the French police, who did not know the mechanics of Susini's operation, Lehman's disclosures were 'vital and apparently truthful'.

The first step on the part of the investigators was obviously to compare the statements from Switzerland with the facts and evidence which they already possessed. One thing leapt to th eeye: the 55 lbs of cheddite, which Lehman said he had himself placed in the flower-pot, had not been discovered. They were less inquisitive as far as other matters were concerned; everything seemed to tally with what they had already discovered.

They therefore turned their attention at once to the people denounced by Lehman. Many of them they already knew; others they unearthed by cross-checks. The Mentone doctor, for instance, was quickly identified; his name appeared on the documents seized from Buscia as 'D. 469-295. Ear—nose—throat—eyes'. Susini and Henri X were out of reach since they were abroad. Rossignol, however, was in France. Since he had never been the subject of investigation, there had been no need to check whether he had lived in the area. Since, however, Lehman had stated that he had taken part in the Mont Faron affair, a search for him was instituted and it was in fact found that he had slept at the Hotel Beaulieu several times and had hired cars on four occasions between 28 July 1964 and 3 February 1965.

Gonfond, to whom, Lehman said, he had handed the second bomb, had already been arrested by the police in January 1965 since the counterfoil of a 500-franc money order made out to him had been found among Séverin Luciani's papers. At that time Gonfond had explained that this was in repayment for food purchased for two unemployed *pieds-noirs* who had been given shelter in a hunting lodge at Ribaux, Var. The two *pieds-noirs* were in fact members of Buscia's party. Since it had not been possible to prove that Gonfond was involved, he had been released.

Armed with their list, the police launched their offensive. On 14 May 1965 they re-arrested Gonfond; at the same time they detained Dr D from Mentone and Jules-César Luciani, headmaster of the school in Lançon who, according to Lehman, possessed the 'reserve' bomb, the replica of that used at Mont Faron. Rossignol was also arrested in Paris. As might be expected, searches in the houses of all four yielded nothing.

Of all these the man who caused the greatest headaches to the police was Robert Gonfond from Aubagne, the man to whom Lehman said he had given a bomb with its accompanying apparatus. He began by swearing that he had never been asked to house any sort of package and that he had never seen Lehman, whose photograph was shown to him. He knew nothing about the Mont Faron story and had learnt about it from the newspapers like everyone else. When pressed he eventually remembered that a friend named Yves Charavel had in fact asked him to house a

suitcase one day—a green suitcase—no, a red one—or perhaps yellow—
unless it was blue. In any case someone came and collected it—a tall
man—no, a little man—and dark—or perhaps a redhead—anyway someone. Yves Charavel, the friend, had been killed in an accident on
30 August 1964 and so these statements could not be checked. His
evidence amounted to a mass of 'subterfuge, contradiction and false-
hood'.

For his part, Dr D made no secret of his sympathies. In 1960 he had
joined the Union for French Algeria formed in the Midi by Jean
Reimbold, but he had no hand in militant subversion. Early in the
summer of 1964 an acquaintance of his named Pierre Agliany, an insurance agent in Roquebrune, had asked him to take a letter addressed to
him and, in return, hand a letter to a man who would arrive in his
consulting room saying: 'I have something the matter with my nose,
throat, ears and eyes.' The man arrived some time later and the letter
was handed to him. On leaving he asked the way to Gorbio, a little village
near by. Early in 1965 another man arrived with the same password but
he had no letter to hand over and the doctor had sent him packing.

Dr D had also had certain telephone messages from a man called
Roger, who lived in Italy; he passed on to Agliany the meeting-points
fixed by this man. He had only met Roger once, at Bordighera in Italy;
this had been at Agliany's request and only for the purpose of treating
him medically. Naturally Dr D swore that he had never been asked to
house any equipment whatsoever, a statement which cast doubt on
Lehman's accusations.

When arrested in his villa at Roquebrune, Pierre Agliany admitted that
he had made the acquaintance of a member of OAS Algeria in 1962 but
had refused to help him. The man had left for Italy but had reappeared
under the name of Roger, asking Agliany to act as intermediary between
him and certain Frenchmen to whom he wished to pass leaflets and
clandestine newspapers. The two men became friendly and met on
several occasions in Italy, not far from the frontier. Agliany's rôle,
however, was no more than that of post-box and Dr D was a simple
intermediary.

Yes, Agliany said, Roger had talked of a *coup* but it had merely been
an attack on the walls of a prison where important prisoners were held—
Tulle no doubt. In order to pass the material across the frontier Agliany
proposed to enlist the help of a stock-breeder named Armand Botton
living near Mentone. He was also a teacher of ju-jitsu and as such often
had reason to go to Italy. A meeting between the three men took place in
late June 1964 at Diano-Marino on the Italian riviera. At the end of July
the material was smuggled across the border and some person unknown
collected it from Botton. After the news of the abortive attempt at Mont

Faron, Agliary had practically severed relations with Roger who had refused to give any explanation on the subject.

The police thought that they could now reconstruct the phase of the movement of the equipment via Botton. Dr D had told Buscia the way to Gorbio which was the way to Botton's house. Buscia had then collected the equipment in order (as the police still thought) to give it to Lehman so that he could 'finish' the assembly of the bomb and remote-control apparatus.

Unfortunately for the progress of the enquiry the police found Armand Botton a person on whom they could pin nothing; he simply denied everything, adding yet another headache to that created by Gonfond. The police report to Paul-Julien Doll, examining magistrate of the Court of State Security, ran: 'We have not been able to decide whether his mind is as thick as his waist or whether, on the contrary, this was a sophisticated defence designed to keep us at bay.'

To all the questions of the police Botton replied with a torrent of obscure confused explanations. The only point which he was prepared to discuss was that of the road leading to his property: it was not the Gorbio road.

So the 'sophisticated defence' still held firm.

Yves Rossignol was arrested in Paris and questioned by men of No. 4 Section of Judicial Police headquarters. The record was sent to Marseille where Commissaire Mesini added it to his file. Oddly enough, Rossignol largely corroborated Lehman's statements. Yes, he had gone to Mont Faron with Lehman alone while Buscia stayed in town. Yes, he had kept watch while Lehman, still alone, positioned the bomb. No, he had not had a grenade at that moment. No, he was sorry but he had not gone to Aubagne with Lehman to hand over the reserve transmitter to Gonfond, whom, moreover, he did not know. Yes, of course, he knew Susini: he had been a student in Algiers when Susini was President of the Students Association. No, the purpose of the attempt at Mont Faron was not to kill de Gaulle; Lehman had told him that the bomb was not lethal and was merely a sort of visiting card designed to intimidate.

In short, Rossignol did no more than confirm the police in their conviction that Lehman had told the truth and had been the master-mind of the whole affair.

Having been mentioned by Lehman, Jean-Baptiste Cianfarani, when his turn came, could not deny that he knew the Swiss well. They had been in prison together in 1962 for similar crimes but Cianfarani had been released much later.

He had been re-arrested shortly after Buscia, the police having found one of his visiting cards on Sinibaldi. The police were forced to admit, however, that this was nothing much to make a fuss about and he was released—only to be re-arrested on 1 July 1965 at Sartène in Corsica as a result of Lehman's further confession about a forged-dollar ring.

On this occasion the police did not refer much to forged notes but concentrated on Cianfarani's possible participation in the Mont Faron attempt. Naturally, Cianfarani admitted once more that he knew Lehman well. He had seen him again in Marseille, he said, in June 1964 and, since Lehman had said that he was enlisting in the Foreign Legion, he, Cianfarani, had put him up for a few days. He had also introduced him to a student friend named Alain, who had in his turn taken Lehman in. He had gone to Toulon with Lehman, but simply on a friendly basis. There they had met their mutual friend Gilles Buscia who had taken them for a drive to Roquebrune in his car. At Roquebrune Buscia had gone off for an hour. Cianfarani had left the two others on their return to Toulon.

What were the reasons for this journey? Cianfarani did not know at all—Buscia was not talkative. As for the Mont Faron affair, he had heard about it, like everyone else, over the radio and through the newspapers. He had never heard any reference to the possible assassination of General Delgado, the exiled Portuguese revolutionary. This was another affair in which Lehman had admitted participation.

Cianfarani willingly admitted that he had subsequently seen Lehman again and gone with him, Buscia and Rossignol to Gap. All four had had a really slap-up meal in an inn there and had then returned—if all those who had a good meal like that were regarded as security suspects, the whole of France would be in prison. . . .

Returning from this escapade, they had a car accident on the La Mure road and Rossignol was cut in the face. They all returned separately to Marseille under their own steam.

That was Cianfarani's story, and it was not much help to the investigators. Cianfarani added that he knew that the struggle for Algeria was at an end and that all he wanted was to continue his studies, which did not mean that he could not sometimes go out on the town with his friends.

Alain, who was also a student, confirmed Cianfarani's statements. He had given beds to Lehman and Rossignol but there was no law against helping a friend who dropped in. What could he be accused of? Nothing, apparently, since the police let him go.

Interrogation of Jules-César Luciani, the Lançon schoolmaster, was more profitable for the police. His family came from Moca-Croce in Corsica but he had been born in Saigon in 1904. He was only very distantly related to Séverin and Toussaint, the Luciani brothers.

He admitted that, on the recommendation of a friend, he had been visited one day by a man he did not know who asked him for help. He gave the man 200 francs. A month later the unknown returned and was given another 100 francs. He did not know who this man was and only found out from the newspapers when the man was arrested. He was Gilles Buscia, and Luciani was all the more distressed at having helped him since he was very friendly with the family of Major Kubaziak, in whose murder Buscia was accused of being involved.

Jules-César Luciani admitted that his friends sometimes called him Julien and the investigators recognised in this a cover-name which frequently appeared in the papers confiscated from the house of his namesake, Séverin Luciani.

The schoolmaster seemed to the investigators to be a man in a very tormented state of mind. On 21 May 1965, after a week of fruitless questioning, he asked to speak to his usual interrogator, Inspector Bouillot. He said that he wished to salve his conscience by divulging that, on his second visit, Gilles Buscia had given him a suitcase and a parcel which he had stored in a hut on the Eyguières road. Overjoyed, the police leapt into a car, taking Luciani with them, to go and collect the two packages. One of them, a cardboard box, seemed so suspect that Forestier, the expert, was asked to open it at his own risk. Inside was a glorious surprise: electric batteries, various pieces of equipment together with a transistorised radio transmitter with no trade-mark and with a fixed aerial. There was also a small box which the experts opened with maximum precautions. It contained: a Philco transistor radio receiver, the exact replica of that found (in pieces) in the Mont Faron flower-pot; an Amperite 120 relay-valve; a relay connected to a coil similar to that in the pot and six 1·5-volt Malory batteries. All this was packed tight with cotton-wool in the box and firmly clamped down; certain wires were protruding.

This was undoubtedly an exact replica of the device which had been placed in the Mont Faron flower-pot. Here at last was the missing proof.

Lehman's revelations, therefore, had resulted in the discovery of a large proportion of those who had prepared the Mont Faron attempt and had provided proof of their involvement, particularly in so far as Buscia was concerned. Interrogations had also uncovered certain other people to whom Lehman had not referred, in particular Agliany and Botton.

The investigation also produced repercussions unconnected with the assassination attempt. Paul V and Antoine B, for instance, two young men whose names also appeared in Séverin Luciani's papers, were interrogated at length. The investigators thought that they had something to do with the attempt but were soon forced to change their tune: the two were involved in no more than a simple case of cheating at the examinations for the Faculty of Science in Montpellier. Antoine B had agreed to sit the preliminary examination in place of Paul V who did not think that he could pass. B had failed, however, and so V had had to repeat the operation with the help of a certain Toussaint L, a graduate of the Ecole Polytechnique, who had succeeded in passing. B and V were arrested and charged with cheating at the examinations; Toussaint L could not be found.

Now at last, however, the investigators could take stock. Oddly enough, they were not convinced that Jean-Jacques Susini had been the organiser of the attempt. To them he remained an incomprehensible person whose feet were not always on the ground, a mysterious figure who had left his imprint on every development ever since 13 May 1958. He had been condemned to death *in absentia* on 10 December 1964; he was regarded as a 'thinker', a sort of theorist of subversion always with some plot on hand. The investigators asked themselves: 'Was he really the leader of a plot aiming at the physical elimination of the head of state or had he merely thought that such action would be a paying proposition from the political point of view?'

To tighten their net around Susini the police conducted a minute search of the house of his sister Virginie, married to a journalist named Partial Terrier. They found certain notes made by the latter in the course of business describing an interview with Susini in Rome but they produced nothing new.

Although the police had no certainty that Susini had been involved in the Mont Faron attempt, they did their best to arrange his expulsion from Italy. All they had to do was to indicate to the press that Susini was the organiser of the plot and the Italian government would be forced to react. Susini, who knew nothing of this threat to his safety, was busy organising a way of getting his wife and son out of Italy with the help of a friend who was prepared to pass the child off as her own.

On 28 May 1965 a telephone call from Paris told him that he was featured, with a great display of photographs, in the French morning newspapers. He knew that the Italian newspapers would carry his photograph next morning so as to keep in step with gaullist propaganda which was now bringing the radio and television into action.

The Italian secret service advised him to leave his apartment at once so that the official police would not find him. He decided to hide in a place where the police would not look for him—in the apartment of a cabinet minister. Susini knew the minister's daughter very well; she was a whole-hearted supporter of French Algeria, and the apartment had been the meeting point for certain Frenchmen in Rome. Soustelle was often seen there; it was frequently his rendezvous with Guilain de Bénouville who made many trips to Rome in order to see him. This minister's daughter was also responsible for the fact that certain colonels visiting

Rome, including Vaudrey and even Godard, could move about the city in an official car with an escort. So Susini, in his gilded cage, waited for the storm to blow over.

Soustelle himself was accused by the French press, particularly by *France-Soir* which referred to close cooperation between the action groups run by Soustelle and Susini respectively. The involvement of the ex-Governor-General of Algeria, however, was presented as a sort of case for the defence: Soustelle's men, it was said, had only agreed to participate in order to ensure that the attempt failed.

The police did not altogether subscribe to this theory. Their investigations had shown that a number of people, including Buscia, had had a hand in the affair. As far as Lehman was concerned the ordinary police force, who did not know everything (particularly what was going on in the networks run by parallel police forces), thought that he was the linchpin of the whole business. They never doubted for a moment that it was he who had constructed the bomb and placed it in position. They took his stories at their face value and did not become suspicious even when they discovered that in certain respects he had been lying.

Lehman had said that he had thrown the other six devices he had constructed into the sea off the Marseille corniche; a team of navy frogmen was therefore despatched to try and recover them. Naturally they found nothing except some old shoes and pots and pans.

On one other point the police were puzzled: not the non-discovery of the 55 lbs of cheddite which Lehman maintained that he had placed in the flower-pot, but the question of who had 'tried to efface all traces of the attempt by lighting a fire on 28 August 1964, the partial failure of which had led in fact to its discovery'.

Lehman maintained that he had no knowledge of an attempt to cover the tracks. He thought that the fire was a case of spontaneous combustion. This was not accepted by the experts, however, since they had discovered certain delaying substances and in particular the presence of an alumino-thermal compound designed to destroy the device.

The investigators dismissed at once the theory that the 'fire-raisers' had wished to draw attention to a non-lethal device in order to give public opinion a psychological shock. They were convinced that the purpose of the fire-raisers was to destroy all traces of the abortive attempt in order to keep their business secret. With this as their starting point, they examined the part played by each man.

As in the case of Susini, they knew little about Henri X as a personality. They thought—wrongly—that after the generals' *putsch* in April 1961 he had become the treasurer of Mission III using the cover-names of 'Grouchy', 'Rockefeller' and 'Bruno Walter'. They also pinned on him another cover-name, 'Roger', which made him the contact man on the Italian frontier with the Buscia group. (Roger was in fact Jacques

Soustelle's secretary, Roger Gonzales, who had not even taken the trouble to change his christian name.)

In the opinion of the French police Henri X would not have been capable of constructing a remote-control system and had therefore asked Lehman to do it for him; this tended to support the theory that he had acquired his doctorate of science as part of some package deal. Finally they maintained that he was 'of no fixed address' and 'on the run' when in fact he was in a public position in Rome.

On Gilles Buscia the investigators were better informed. They knew that in him they had the organiser who had gone to Switzerland to find Lehman and had been in charge of the collection of the material. He had supervised the operation throughout. He it was, so they thought, who was to press the button together with Lehman on the day of the attempt.

Buscia definitely seemed to be the leader who inspired both respect and fear. The police conceded that self-interest was not his motive—the money which he collected was used simply to ensure that his men could exist. They also conceded that he was undeniably brave. All sorts of qualities could be attributed to him, however; the police had quite enough evidence to bring him before the Court of State Security which welcomed him with open arms and sentenced him to hard labour for life. (Susini was once more sentenced to death *in absentia*, as was Henri X.)

The only case against Yves Rossignol was that he had acted as 'cover' for Buscia and Lehman; since he was on no one's books, he could pilot the two men round without the police on point duty becoming suspicious. The other two extras could only be accused of acting as 'post-boxes' or 'guides'.

The case of Séverin Luciani was more complicated. He had made the acquaintance of the Paris police when he had emptied a revolver in the direction of two senior officers, Colonels Wagner and Ordini. Together with the Buscia brothers he had then been involved in the activities of a commando which was preparing an assassination attempt on Georges Pompidou, an affair serious enough to earn him a sentence of twenty years' imprisonment at the hands of the Court of State Security—given *in absentia* of course, since he was not arrested until 4 December 1964. His arrest enabled the police to lay their hands on a certain number of documents which, as we have seen, gave a fresh impetus to their investigation into the Mont Faron affair. One policeman said of these documents: 'They are a real *Who's Who* of subversion'. Nevertheless, in so far as Mont Faron was concerned, Luciani could only be accused of having provided money, hide-outs and false papers for the conspirators.

So, as may be imagined, the dossier could now be finally closed. The police were entitled to be pleased with themselves: they had unravelled part of the mystery. But, of course, a yawning gap still remained in the Mont Faron affair: *who had removed from the flower-pot the sixty pounds of plastic which Buscia had undoubtedly placed there himself?*

CHAPTER 39

The Veil Lifts

One man, who was not in France, set out to find the answer to this question.

Jean-Jacques Susini, still living a clandestine but not cloistered existence in Rome, decided to conduct his own enquiry into the mystery of Mont Faron. He had not the resources usually available to the police but he did have an incomparable network of informants in all circles, including some in the French government.

The truth emerged quite quickly.

He first received confirmation that Lehman had been an informer for Commissaire Caille of General Intelligence. In the first place, when arrested at Saint-Charles station in Marseille for OAS activity, Lehman had been released at once, whereas Cianfarani, who had been arrested at the same time, spent over a year in prison. Secondly, and even more curiously, he had been allowed to re-enlist in the Foreign Legion despite his avowed subversive activity. Undoubtedly, he had taken advantage of Gilles Buscia's confidence and the latter had literally put his head in the lion's mouth. From a certain moment Buscia had been continuously shadowed by men of General Intelligence and in any case they had been kept abreast of developments. Inevitably, therefore, they knew of the preparation of the attempt and they had allowed it to proceed. This produced a logical explanation for the whole sequence of events.

As soon as the bomb had been positioned, a team of French secret service agents went to Mont Faron by night and proceeded to modify the system; *they disconnected the receiver and removed the sixty pounds of plastic.* They knew the exact composition of the bomb through Lehman, who was in fact a good technician and knew its secrets. There was therefore no difficulty about making the modifications. *They left in the flower-pot the six pounds of TNT and a receiver which could not be actuated.*

They made a minor error, however. Having damaged the plant which was in the pot, *they replaced it by another similar but more luxuriant plant*

283

which the investigators found surprising. The latter noted that, on a photograph taken by the Security Service, the plant was definitely more luxuriant than it should have been. As soon as this mistake came to light it was made good on the following night.

One thing was certain: *the 'bomb' which they left in the pot could not explode under any circumstances since there was no detonator inserted into the TNT.* As a precaution they demanded that the area be sealed off two hours before the time scheduled. It was in fact possible that another bomb had been concealed by another team without Lehman's knowledge. They worked out that those responsible for pressing the button would only arrive on the spot a short time before H Hour to avoid being discovered by the security service which was very much on the alert. *They were therefore sure that the head of state was running no risk.*

The result was that the ceremony proceeded normally and without the slightest incident. It only remained for them to exploit this abortive attempt psychologically—in fact the object of the whole exercise.

On 28 August, when the sun was particularly hot and there was no doubt that the TNT in the flower-pot would be giving off fumes, a 'passer-by' threw a lighted cigarette end into the pot and the conflagration occurred, triggering off an anti-subversion offensive. Buscia was ultimately arrested, having been denounced, and Susini became the main target (the publicity ballyhoo lasted a full week with headlines in all the newspapers).

Moreover, it was proved before the Court of State Security that the bomb had undoubtedly been tampered with. Maître Roger, Yves Rossignol's defence counsel, obtained a lenient sentence for his client by proving conclusively that the bomb had been modified.

The failure of this attempt sounded the death-knell of these subversive flights of fancy. Another attempt had been planned but the investigations into the Mont Faron affair doomed it to failure. The plan was to use the second bomb constructed by Henri X with the same remote-control system. This bomb, from which only the plastic was missing, had been hidden, as we have seen, in a hut belonging to Jules-César Luciani, the Lançon schoolmaster. It had been left with him by Gilles Buscia, who was to use it (in the event of failure at Mont Faron) on the occasion of a visit which de Gaulle was due to make on 13 May 1965 to Sainte-Hermine in Vendée.

On that day the general was to lay a wreath by Clemenceau's statue and then make a speech. The monument was twelve feet high and included a central figure of Clemenceau in stone, dressed as a French soldier, and another French soldier, also in stone, standing to attention, the whole against a rocky background. The bomb was to be concealed in the base of the statue, which was very large. The plan was to dislodge a fragment of rock and replace it by the bomb, the aerial being hidden among the flowers or rock plants. Ignition would take place from a distance by radio signal, exactly as planned for Mont Faron.

Once more the indefatigable Samuel Lehman told the police of the project. He assured them that his 'tip' was a good one and that once again it was Buscia who was responsible for organising the attempt. Since Buscia had been arrested on 8 April 1965 and the Vendée attempt was not due until 13 May, the police were quite clear that he could not be the operator. They were not so certain that someone else might not arrive in Sainte-Hermine. The activist leaders might have selected a man to collect the second remote-controlled bomb and place it at the base of the statue or, if he thought the area too well guarded, at some other spot which General de Gaulle would pass.

For the moment, despite their efforts and despite the willing co-operation of Lehman, the police had not managed to lay their hands on bomb No. 2. They followed up various clues but they were primarily on the look-out for a man whom Lehman had indicated as important and who might be holding the bomb. This was Séverin Luciani's brother, Toussaint.

Toussaint Luciani was a graduate of the Ecole Polytechnique and an air force officer like Bastien-Thiry; he had been on special leave from the air force since 15 March 1965 and could not be found. Traces of his movements were discovered in various places and the police thought that he had replaced his brother, now under arrest, as the logistics director of the attempt. Jules-César Luciani, who was a friend of Toussaint, admitted that the latter had been to see him a few days before he himself had been arrested and had said that he wanted to go to Corsica.

The Ajaccio police were warned and immediately began to shadow Toussaint's brother-in-law, who lived in Ajaccio. They learnt that this man, Gérard Félix, had been seen for the last few days in the company of some man unknown. On 22 May Félix was seen with him again. The police rushed up but Félix was too quick for them, jumped into his car, still with the unknown man, and took the road for the mountains. The two contrived to outdistance the police and, after a mile or so, turned down a small country lane. When the police caught up, the unknown man had disappeared into the bush. French Algeria had recruited another underground fighter.

A general alert was issued. Several companies of *gendarmes* and CRS went off in search of the unknown man but he could not be found. The brother-in-law, who was 'called on to speak', in the standard homeric phrase, stubbornly refused to answer any leading questions. The police were about to release him since they could prove nothing against him, when a search of his house revealed a Colt revolver hidden under the flooring. For this crime he was brought before the Court of State Security.

A report now arrived from Paris to the effect that Toussaint Luciani had been seen in the capital; with the prospect of an assassination attempt in Vendée the police now no longer knew which saint to invoke. They went through the Sainte-Hermine area with a fine comb during the days preceding de Gaulle's visit; the statue was thoroughly sounded and was guarded day and night right up to the ceremony.

The ceremony took place amidst much patriotic fervour. A series of speeches was made. De Gaulle paid his homage to 'The Tiger' and remained motionless for a full quarter of an hour at the foot of the statue. Any bomb laid near by would undoubtedly have put an end to his career.

This last failure brings to an end the series of major public assassination attempts from which de Gaulle escaped—and to which maximum publicity was given. Undoubtedly they fostered the legend of the man of 18 June 1940.

Nevertheless, neither Mont Faron nor the Vendée were the last attempts in point of time. One more took place, to which the newspapers did not refer. It was the work of quite young students, almost schoolboys, and, though without resources, they were within an ace of succeeding where the experienced professionals of subversion had failed.

CHAPTER 40

The Final Flicker

Early in 1964 a group of young people at the *lycée* in Salon-de-Provence formed themselves into the 'Mass Propaganda Action Section' of the National Resistance Council. For France as a whole this organisation was directed by Sergent; in the Midi its head was Jean Reimbold, a Toulon professor who had joined the underground. This branch of the National Resistance Council formed part of the 9th Military Region.

The young people concerned were aged between sixteen and twenty and it was they who took the initiative in the final attempt against de Gaulle. The group consisted of: Rémy Drelon-Mounier, aged seventeen, who acted as leader—he was the son of a soldier; next came Pierre Barrès, son of an architect, a *pied-noir* from Oran; Jean-Pierre Barré, son of a *pied-noir* employee from Algeria; Norbert Garcia, son of a taxi-driver from Oran; Louis de Gosse, son of a soldier; and Georges-Maurice Mercier, son of a magistrate. These young people had taken upon themselves certain propaganda duties, the most exciting of which was to slip OAS leaflets through the letter-boxes of well-to-do citizens while they were asleep. They corresponded with their leader, Jean Reimbold, through various intermediaries in Marseille.

For these idealist schoolboys, full of enthusiasm, these tasks soon came to be considered too humdrum. It was not long before they were dreaming of action to change the destiny of France.

Their parents, of course, knew nothing of their membership of the OAS and thought that the weary faces of their offspring were due to an overloaded programme of homework. In fact they were spending half their nights outside, producing cyclostyled leaflets and then slipping them under doors.

Gradually the idea of mounting an attack on de Gaulle took shape. Initially they had no money, no weapons and no genuine leader. They had no experience as revolutionary fighters and no training in underground work. Nevertheless they plunged into their adventure with no

287

inhibitions. Each youngster rummaged through the drawers of his father's desk to see if he could find a revolver. They collected two.

Then they began wandering round the yards and quarries bordering the Rhône and the Durance, where major work was in progress. In this way they succeeded in stealing 8–10 lbs of dynamite. In a factory in Orgon they laid their hands on 3,000 detonators, some Bickford fuse and some time pencils. A few days later, as if by intuition, they went to a quarry at Lançon and removed in a single night $1\frac{3}{4}$ tons of dynamite—one of the largest coups ever carried out in France.

The 'merchandise' was stored in a stone building with a steel door and it was this that had attracted their attention. Being unable to force it, they turned their attention to the walls, which gave way. Realising that they could not cart it all away in the Peugeot 403 van which they had stolen, they deputed one of their number to borrow a Citroën lorry from a friend who was a member of their supporting network.

At about 1 a.m. both vehicles were ready and the cases of dynamite were loaded. They hid them, some in the farm of a friend and some in the woods. Armed with this war-chest, the schoolboys felt ready for anything: they could now envisage an attack on de Gaulle using explosives. They could also get to work in the area, not only to punish certain gaullists but also to initiate their young soldiers in the art of war. A single detail is enough to illustrate the reckless happy-go-lucky attitude of these youngsters—not one of them possessed a driving licence.

Their first operation was a failure. Its target was a café in Istres which had been the venue for an FLN meeting. The next objective was the Rex cinema in Aix-en-Provence—a jerrican of petrol caught fire but the dynamite did not explode. Their third operation took place on 21 June 1964 at the labour exchange in Marseille. Technically it was a success. Moreover, in this adventure they were really on their own; some weeks previously the group had severed all contact with the National Resistance Council.

Emboldened by this success the group of schoolboys continued on their way; they had explosives but they were short of money. Meanwhile they decided to call their adventure 'Operation Oscar' in memory of the famous schoolboy in the film *Disparus de Saint-Agil*.

The best way to obtain money was by organising a hold-up. They had soon selected their target: the pay for the men of the Air Force School in Salon was taken from Marseille to Salon in a Citroën 2 CV. During the planning of this operation they decided to steal a Peugeot 403 van; three of them would be disguised as riot police and hold up the Citroën, using the 403 (the normal police vehicle).

A development now led to postponement of the hold-up: de Gaulle was shortly to pay an official visit to Cherbourg. Robert, one of the young people in the gang, had already served a two-year prison sentence for belonging to an OAS circuit and he explained that, while in jug, he had met a man from Cherbourg who had always dreamt of trying to assassinate de Gaulle.

Mounier and Robert collected all the money they could and left for Cherbourg where they were welcomed with open arms by this friend, who was an ex-member of OAS; he was also a smart businessman with plenty of money. He was fired with enthusiasm for the youngsters' scheme. De Gaulle was in fact due to come to Cherbourg during the month of July and would make a speech on the Place Charles-de-Gaulle.

The three conspirators soon fixed their plan. They would rent a maid's room on the fifth floor of a building looking out on to the Place Charles-De-Gaulle and during the speech one of them would shoot him with a Magnum rifle, generally used for deer. Ernest—the christian name of the rich businessman in Cherbourg—had bought it with the idea of going on safari, never thinking that his rifle might be used for such big game as was now planned. For good measure Ernest bought a considerable quantity of additional equipment ranging from field glasses to inflatable boats. Naturally, too, he acquired a veritable arsenal of revolvers and ammunition together with a .22 rifle.

Robert was to do the firing while Mounier, together with three or four of the other schoolboys who would come up for the occasion, was to ensure the team's escape.

They returned to Salon to resume the planning of their hold-up since they were becoming increasingly short of funds.

Just as they were about to go into action they had a serious setback: some farmhands discovered one of their caches of dynamite and alerted the police, who seized much of their stock and then launched a major offensive in the area. Two of the gang, Rémy Mounier and Pierre Barrès, who were known for their anti-gaullist views, were arrested on 25 June. It was proved that they had been involved in the attack on the Marseille labour exchange and they were sentenced to two and three years imprisonment respectively by the Court of State Security. Robert, who was on the run, was sentenced *in absentia* to imprisonment for life.

While in prison at Toul Rémy Mounier, still resolute, made the acquaintance of certain young men who were about to be discharged. He enlisted one of them for his 'Operation Oscar' and commissioned him to restart preparations pending his own release. Bernard, the 'new man's' christian name, was therefore to go and collect 1,000 lbs of explosive hidden on a farm and then contact Mounier's two friends, Daniel and Robert, both of whom were on the run in Spain.

Naturally the Cherbourg plan had to be abandoned meanwhile; it was a case of *force majeure*.

Mounier was released at Christmas 1965 at the same time as two others:

an ex-Foreign Legionary, whose christian name was Jeannot and whom Mounier recruited into his gang, and an ex-soldier from Indo-China, an experienced warrior whose christian name was Gilbert.

The party installed itself in Paris where, it was decided, Operation Oscar would be mounted. They were faced with the same problems as at Salon, however: how were they to do it, and where was the money to come from?

Mounier had studied the Mont Faron affair in detail and with admiration; he was definitely in favour of an attack using explosive, ignition being by remote-controlled radio. The party took up his idea with enthusiasm: a car was to be crammed with explosive and, when de Gaulle's Déesse passed, an operator 200 yards away would set off the explosion simply by pressing a button. No one would notice an ordinary vehicle parked by the roadside or suspect (since it was then a novel technique) that it was booby-trapped.

The party had plenty of explosive—the 1,000 lbs of dynamite were now at Cherbourg where they were being stored by Ernest. They merely had to be brought to Paris at the right moment. The car presented no problem either: all they had to do was to steal one, taking the necessary precautions.

There remained the more worrying problem of money. Armed with a list of CNR and OAS sympathisers, Mounier went on a real round tour of France to collect cash. He visited Rennes, Bordeaux, Agen, Toulouse, Marseille and Moulin but unfortunately the harvest was pitiable—barely 400,000 old francs. But why worry? The money would be devoted to the manufacture of a remote-control transmitter-receiver system which would trigger off the explosive.

Mounier then departed in search of an expert; he found one in the shape of a *pied-noir* electrical engineer, aged about sixty, whom he had known in Toul gaol where he had been known for his skill in constructing radio sets. The engineer agreed with no questions asked and, while he was at work on the firing system, the party brought the 1,000 lbs of explosive into Paris and one evening stole an Estafette in Levallois.

The engineer delivered the firing system early in March 1966. All was therefore prepared except for the place and the time. Since de Gaulle's movements were invariably announced in the press, all they had to do was to read the newspapers and await a favourable moment.

This arrived when it was announced that the general would visit the Soviet Union from 20 June to 1 July 1966. As usual he would use the normal route between Orly and the Elysée via the Avenue du Maine and the Boulevard Montparnasse.

The conspirators selected two possible points; one was the narrowest stretch of the Avenue du Maine opposite a restaurant, Au Père Tranquille; the other was opposite Le Dragon d'Argent restaurant on the Boulevard

Montparnasse. They finally decided to position the Estafette opposite No. 30 Avenue du Maine. In the Estafette would be 200 lbs of dynamite and one or two boxes of scrap-iron to produce a shrapnel effect. De Gaulle's car would inevitably have to pass within a yard of the Estafette which would blow up at that precise moment. If the general's route was changed, they would be warned by the police dispositions which would be apparent from dawn onwards. They would then merely have to move the Estafette.

Both the men and the equipment were now ready. All they had to do was to wait patiently for 1 July. One last, but important detail, however, remained to be settled. The men of the 'Oscar' commando knew that, even if their attack succeeded, they would be mercilessly hunted by every police force in France. Admittedly the political face of the country would be changed, but they would still be regicides. They would therefore have to disappear abroad for a time as soon as they had made their attack. For this, as always, money was required. To obtain this quickly and in quantity they could think of nothing other than to organise a hold-up.

Mounier selected three men to go with him. They set off in a Simca 1000 stolen in Neuilly during the night (from a *pied-noir*, they found out later) and drove towards the warehouse area in Bercy. Their information was that the pay—a very large sum—for the workers in a large wine concern would be counted out that morning by five or six men only. It was the entire pay packet for the month of June.

Each of the four men had an automatic pistol on him. The Simca 1000 drove into the vast depot. Mounier immediately realised that the information given him had been wrong—there were some thirty men present at the counting and it would undoubtedly be necessary to shoot. Moreover, escape would be extremely difficult through the congested warehouse area. They had prepared their attack on de Gaulle with extreme care but in the case of this hold-up they had acted like amateurs. Mounier accordingly decided to abandon the operation and ordered the driver, Gilbert the ex-soldier from Indo-China, to retrace his steps.

They managed to leave without being noticed but Gilbert, who knew very little of Paris, inadvertently drove the wrong way up a one-way street near the Champs de Mars. A black Peugeot 403 which had been following them—quite by chance—overtook them and flagged them down. Gilbert's reaction was instantaneous: he trod on the gas and a chase worthy of the best gangster films began through the streets of Paris.

Again owing to his ignorance of the Paris traffic Gilbert achieved the feat of going up the Boulevard Latour-Maubourg in the wrong direction and more or less at rush hour. Seeing an enormous bus bearing down on them, he wrenched his wheel round and took to the pavement. The four men jumped out, pistols in hand, and began to run with passers-by shouting and police sirens wailing in all directions.

Gilbert was lucky enough to grab a passing taxi, the driver of which, who was probably deaf, drove him well away from the turmoil. Mounier, Daniel and Jeannot, the ex-Foreign Legionary, ran off towards Rue Saint-Dominique, terrifying the passers-by with their pistols and followed by a chorus of police whistles and sirens. Rémy Mounier, realising that salvation lay in dispersion, put away his gun and went into the first building he saw. He climbed to the top floor, where he got rid of his pistol, his mackintosh and his muffler, and then, after waiting ten minutes, emerged from the building quite casually and went into a bar.

The whole area was alive with police. A few minutes later they came into the café. Mounier thought that he had been followed and this was the end of his adventure; the police, however, did no more than check customers' papers, including his, and then left after asking both the proprietor and the customers whether they had noticed anything suspicious. No one said anything about the latest arrival who in any case had come in quite naturally.

Hundreds of police searched all the buildings in the neighbourhood and discovered the objects discarded by Rémy Mounier. To be more precise, they found only the mackintosh and muffler, the pistol probably having been surreptitiously removed by an inmate of the building.

Meanwhile Daniel and Jeannot continued their mad chase through the area. In the Rue de Grenelle they were cornered by a plain-clothes policeman who tried to tackle Daniel. They got away fairly quickly but Daniel's coat remained in the hands of the policeman; with a professional air he went through the pockets and found the identity papers which Daniel had been carrying despite Mounier's strict instructions to the contrary (Mounier himself had disobeyed his own orders, a fact which actually saved him).

Daniel and Jeannot continued their marathon, evading several other policemen but, in the Place des Invalides, they literally fell into an auxiliary police car.

Two hours later Mounier was back in his apartment on the Avenue du Maine—quite close to the spot chosen for the attack. There he found Gilbert who had been there for some time. Of the four musketeers they were the only two to escape.

They had not a penny. They had lost their guns. They were discouraged. 'Operation Oscar' definitely vanished into thin air. Next day, however, de Gaulle's Déesse passed within inches of an Estafette crammed with dynamite but which did not blow up because there were no operators. The transmitter had in fact been carefully concealed by Daniel who was now under arrest.

Daniel and Jeannot adroitly extracted themselves from their predicament. They told a melancholy story of a drinking session and of meeting a bizarre character who took them for a drive in a car which he admitted had been stolen as soon as the police appeared. This was the reason for their headlong flight. As regards the gun with which they had threatened the plain-clothes policeman, this, they said, was merely a toy pistol and they had thrown it down a drain.

In fact, before being arrested, they had succeeded in hiding their two guns in the gas meter of No. 4 Avenue de Lowendal. The pistols were recovered later by some friends. The two were sentenced to six months in prison for assaulting the police and stealing a car. Naturally they never breathed a word of Operation Oscar. Half the party having been put out of action on the eve of the attack, the operation was postponed *sine die*.

The height of irony was reached when, a few days later, the Estafette was stolen by persons unknown. There is presumably half a ton of dynamite moving around somewhere in France.

So the schoolboys' odyssey ended in farce. It should nevertheless be taken seriously since it very nearly succeeded in putting an end to de Gaulle's career on 1 July 1966 in the Boulevard Montparnasse.

De Gaulle survived some thirty attempted criminal assaults on his person; he had been closer to death than most other heads of state in the course of his career. Finally, however, he died at 7.25 p.m. on Monday, 9 November 1970, sitting in his armchair like any ordinary person and watching a sentimental television serial called 'Nanou'.

From the time of the Mont Faron affair the opposition to de Gaulle used political methods rather than guns. The psychological offensive against Soustelle and Susini launched by the authorities bore fruit. Soustelle suddenly disappeared from the international scene. Only Jean-Jacques Susini was left in Rome; once the turmoil caused by the Mont Faron cigarette-end had died down, he again began to receive visits from 'gentlemen from Paris'.

During the next two years—say until mid-1968—certain highly-placed people proposed yet another enterprise to this indefatigable campaigner: it would be supported, they said, by the same men who had directed Bastien-Thiry (and who still had their hands on the levers of power). Ever true to himself, Susini laid down political, financial and logistic terms which they could not meet. So he turned down the offer, saying simply: 'No more hack-work.'

In fact Susini considered that assassination attempts against de Gaulle were now outdated politically. So, fully realising the implications, at Christmas 1967 he made a vital telephone call to Paris asking his men to lay down their arms and try to re-integrate themselves professionally.

'I am by no means giving up,' he told them. 'But the sacrifices you have made are not matched by the results obtained. We will resume the struggle if circumstances so necessitate.'

People will always wonder what the consequences for the country would have been had an attack on de Gaulle succeeded.

Politically they would undoubtedly have been considerable. From the point of view of personalities they would certainly have been spectacular. The undercover police forces themselves had passed to the OAS–CNR activists a list of two hundred persons active in French politics who would be executed immediately if General de Gaulle were killed (a simple and well-known method of intimidation). The list included the names of Gaston Monnerville, Gaston Defferre, Guy Mollet and even Antoine Pinay, who was interviewed on the subject by *Paris-Match* on the eve of the presidential elections in December 1965.

These undercover forces had given proof of their capacity and their qualities, particularly at the time of the anti-OAS repression in Algiers. Leaving aside all the vast and futile historical hypotheses, therefore, it is reasonable to suppose that the assassination of de Gaulle would have led to quite unimaginable chaos.